Modern Theatres
1950–2020

Modern Theatres 1950–2020 is an investigation of theatres, concert halls and opera houses in Asia, Europe, the Middle East and North and South America.

The book explores in detail 30 of the most significant theatres, concert halls, opera houses and dance spaces that opened between 1950 and 2010. Each theatre is reviewed and assessed by experts in theatre buildings, such as architects, acousticians, consultants and theatre practitioners, and illustrated with full-colour photographs and comparative plans and sections. A further 20 theatres that have opened from 2009 to 2020 are concisely reviewed and illustrated.

An excellent resource for students of theatre planning, theatre architecture and architectural design, *Modern Theatres 1950–2020* discusses the role of performing arts buildings in cities, explores their public and performance spaces and examines the acoustics and technologies needed in a great building.

David Staples has been a theatre consultant for over 40 years, working on opera houses, concert halls and theatres in 67 countries. His projects include the Oslo Opera in Norway, Esplanade in Singapore, Lowry in England and Portland Center for Performing Arts in Oregon, USA. He has lectured on every continent except Antarctica and is a former chair of the Society of Theatre Consultants, a member of the International Society of Performing Arts, of Opera Europa, a Fellow of the Association of British Theatre Technicians and a Chartered Fellow of the Chartered Management Institute.

Modern Theatres
1950–2020

EDITED BY DAVID STAPLES

DRAWINGS BY DAVID HAMER

Routledge
Taylor & Francis Group

NEW YORK AND LONDON

First published 2021
by Routledge
605 Third Avenue, New York, NY 10158

and by Routledge
2 Park Square, Milton Park, Abingdon, Oxon, OX14 4RN

Routledge is an imprint of the Taylor & Francis Group, an informa business

Library of Congress Cataloging-in-Publication Data
Names: Staples, David, editor. | Hamer, David (Architect), illustrator.
Title: Modern theatres 1950–2020 / edited by David Staples; drawings by David Hamer.
Description: New York: Routledge, 2021. | Includes index.
Identifiers: LCCN 2020045635 (print) | LCCN 2020045636 (ebook) |
   ISBN 9781138484368 (hardback) | ISBN 9781138484382 (paperback) |
   ISBN 9781351052184 (ebook)
Subjects: LCSH: Theaters. | Music-halls. | Theater architecture. | Theaters—Stage-
   setting and scenery.
Classification: LCC NA6821 .M56 2021 (print) | LCC NA6821 (ebook) | DDC 725/.822—dc23

LC record available at https://lccn.loc.gov/2020045635
LC ebook record available at https://lccn.loc.gov/2020045636

www.routledge.com/9781138484382

ISBN: 978-1-138-48436-8 (hbk)
ISBN: 978-1-138-48438-2 (pbk)
ISBN: 978-1-351-05218-4 (ebk)

Typeset in Serifa Std
by Apex CoVantage, LLC

To John and Catherine

Contents

The Eighties

The Nineties

The New Millennium

Foreword

Let me confess, I have often found myself standing at the front of the stage in a new opera house saying, "Who the hell designed this?". From Paris to St Petersburg, from Athens to Tokyo, from Valencia to Houston, Texas I have been lucky enough to direct in more than 20 new opera houses in as many countries. Yet in general "new" refers only to the standard age-old template being given a new costume, either on the outside in a dazzling exhibitionism that has no bearing on the place where work is to be made, or on the inside where it is so often forgotten that an auditorium's primary function begins only when the lights go down.

But, of course, work is made… and whatever physical characteristics a theatre possesses inevitably contribute to that work. Paris's Opéra Bastille is a cavernous, cold space where passion is hard to communicate – unless, as in Verdi's *Don Carlo*, it can underline the desolate loneliness of human beings lost in their failure to find intimacy. There are new opera houses seeking out this intimacy, this human connection. Glyndebourne's wooden O, for example, enables its audience to be embraced by both the epic and the domestic… Assuming, that is, they are willing to be embraced. Unfortunately, this vital symbiosis is also one of the casualties of the prevailing industry architecture of coproduction for which opera houses sacrifice their own individual personality for the expediency of one-size-fits-all.

My own search for vital engagement, for bolder encounter, has taken my work beyond the stage, harnessing the auditorium and even the foyer to offer a richer, what is now called immersive experience. I have experimented with moving the audience onto the stage and eventually away from theatres altogether, searching for a genuinely new shared experience between performance and audience: found spaces, urban disused buildings with history, character, life where the audience and performance can be indivisible.

My hope is for a future which fearlessly examines the very way we can present opera, dares to throw out the age-old template to focus on new encounters; on how the audience is led from the street into an experience both familiar and mysterious: surprising every time, making old stories new, hearing familiar music through new ears; flexible, agile, disruptive, unique…

Sir Graham Vick

Acknowledgements

This book is the result of an enormous collaborative effort involving many expert and knowledgeable contributors, three leading theatre journals, the International Theatre Engineering and Architecture Conference (ITEAC), the Association of British Theatre Technicians (ABTT) and several other organisations and individuals.

Some 40 people from 14 countries have contributed essays or chapters to *Modern Theatres*. They are theatre people and from the worlds of music and opera. They are talented architects, engineers, technicians, managers and leaders involved in the planning, design, equipping and building of theatres, concert halls and opera houses. Photographs and brief CVs of all the contributors can be found at page 553.

The idea for *Modern Theatres* emerged in 2015 from several informal discussions. The concept was developed and explored with people I respected around the world. I asked people if they would become involved with the research and writing. Without exception they expressed their willingness to be involved.

This book would not have been possible without their support, expertise, enthusiasm and hard work. It is much appreciated, thank you.

Richard Brett was one of the most forward-thinking and inspirational people in the theatre engineering fraternity. A successful engineer, Richard believed there was scope to improve the quality of theatre buildings and their technologies. He conceived of a conference to bring together those involved for intensive discussion and debate. With the support of the Association of British Theatre Technicians, this grew to become the *International Theatre Engineering and Architecture Conference* (ITEAC) with participants from across the globe.

Richard Brett was conference director for three ITEAC conferences, in 2004, 2008 and 2012. Unfortunately, ill health and his untimely death necessitated changes in the process of planning subsequent conferences. An Editorial Board was introduced to bring together a pool of knowledgeable people with good address books who could curate an exciting, informative and thought-provoking conference. Richard Brett and the ABTT asked David to chair the Editorial Board of ITEAC 2014. The editorial board for ITEAC 2018 was again chaired by David Staples with Mark Ager, Josh Dachs, Paddy Dillon, Tim Foster, Ric Green, Louis Janssen, Lucy Osbourne, Robin Townley and Karin Winkelsesser as members.

Each of the five ITEAC conferences has moved forward the body of knowledge and shared that knowledge between practitioners and clients.

The Association of British Theatre Technicians (ABTT), its Council and especially Robin Townley, its chief executive, have played a significant role in the development of *Modern Theatres*. The five International Theatre Engineering and Architecture Conferences have been produced under the auspices of the ABTT, who have also generously contributed to securing the rights for some of the photographs reproduced in the book.

When planning commenced in 2015 for the 2018 conference, David Staples and Robin Townley discussed how we might initiate a research project that could inform and feed into ITEAC 2018. This grew to become the *Modern Theatres* initiative.

Three magazines were supportive and agreed to publish articles as they became available – over 30 articles have appeared in English, German and American.

- *Bühnentechnische Rundschau* (BTR) is the journal of Deutsche Theatertechnische Gesellschaft e.v. (DTHG), the German association devoted to theatre, its technicians and technologies. DTHG was founded in 1907. Karin Winkelsesser, its former editor, has given immense support to the *Modern Theatres* initiative.
- *Sightline* is the journal of the Association of British Theatre Technicians and carries articles about theatre technologies, theatre buildings, safety and other significant issues. Paul Connolly, the editor, agreed to carry the *Modern Theatres* articles and his successor Rebecca Moreland has enthusiastically supported *Modern Theatres*.
- *Theatre Design and Technology Journal* (TD&T) has been published quarterly for more than 50 years by the United States Institute of Theatre Technology (USITT), an organization to promote dialogue, research and learning among practitioners of theatre design and technology. Eileen Curlew, the editor of TD&T, has been a valuable ally to *Modern Theatres*.

Several of Charles Dickens novels were originally published in parts. *Pickwick Papers* appeared in 19 parts while *The Old Curiosity Shop* was first published in 88 weekly parts. These partworks were eventually assembled into full novels. Modern Theatres has in some ways emulated such partworks with individual essays and articles appearing in one or more of the three magazines.

Three people have worked on specific aspects of this book and I need to acknowledge their expertise, diligence and contribution:

- David Hamer was a professional colleague at Theatre Projects Consultants. David is a talented theatre designer and a skilled draftsman. This book is illustrated with a series of comparative drawings. In times past the preceding sentence might have continued … *from the pen of David Hamer*. This would be an anachronism today as David's drawings have emanated from sophisticated computers and software.
- This book has nearly 400 photographs, each of which needed to be sourced and appropriate reproduction rights secured. Sarah Wells, our picture researcher, has been handed manuscripts from innumerable authors sometimes with very specific photo requirements and sometimes with vague requests for a photo of the auditorium with people in it. She has diligently tracked down the right photos.
- Sandy Beaunay is a virtual PA who has worked with the team to transform contributors' articles into the very specific format required by the publisher. She has cheerfully chased authors for CVs and photos.

The performing arts world is full of creative, talented and amusing people – it is a pleasure to call my friends. There are a number of organisations that exist to provide forums for discussion, deliberation and exchange. I am proud to have been a member of the

- International Society of Performing Arts (ISPA) which exists to strengthen the performing arts globally through the advancement of leadership, the exchange of ideas, and by fostering a diverse and engaged membership. Thirteen members of ISPA have contributed to Modern Theatres. I have been a member of ISPA for over 40 years and am honoured to have been given the Patrick Hayes Award and the International Citation of Merit for a lifetime's achievements.
- Association of British Theatre Technicians (ABTT) is a charity and membership organisation that campaigns on behalf of the theatre industry to ensure legislation is appropriate to the industry's needs. It provides technical advice, consultation, training and is a vital resource to those working in the technical theatre industry. The ABTT has kindly given me Honorary Membership and Fellowship of the Association.
- Opera Europa is a very congenial group of opera directors, managers and technicians who collectively run most of the opera houses in Europe. We have shared many nights at the opera.

- Institute of Theatres Consultants is the smallest and most specialised of these groups. Its members advise clients and architects on all aspects of theatre – the buildings, technologies and operations.

Many architects, technicians and consultants have contributed to this book. I wanted the Foreword to be written by someone who actually works in the buildings the rest of us plan and design. Ideally a performer, designer or director. Graham Vick is such a person. One of the world's leading opera directors known for his experimental and revisionist staging's. Graham has worked in many of the world's leading opera houses. He knows their strengths and foibles. He is the founder and artistic director of Birmingham Opera Company which specialises in innovative and avant-garde productions often presented in unusual and unconventional venues. Graham has worked in many theatre buildings but also shows it is possible to produce truly innovative work in found spaces. I am grateful for his provocative foreword.

For over 44 years I worked as a theatre consultant with colleagues at Theatre Projects Consultants. We worked together on new and refurbished theatres ranging from National Theatres, opera houses and concert halls to many smaller scale community and educational projects. We worked with clients, architects and design teams in over 75 countries.

I am indebted especially to Richard Pilbrow, the inspirational and creative founder of Theatre Projects who has been my colleague, mentor and friend through some wonderful adventures.

I need to conclude by extending special thanks to one person who while mentioned above has made an extraordinary contribution to *Modern Theatres*. Karin Winkelsesser started her career in 1984 as coordinator and translator at the German theatre consultants: Biste and Gerling in Berlin. In this function she acquired a wide knowledge in the field of stage technology and architecture and established an international network. She became editor of *Bühnentechnische Rundschau*, was chair of DTHG and an active member of OISTAT.

Karin has been closely involved with the Modern Theatres initiative. She served on the editorial board of ITEAC 2018 and has been an enthusiastic collaborator, critic and generator of ideas. She authored one of the first chapters on the Philharmonie Berlin. Karin retired in 2019 from her position as Editor of BTR.

Finally, I must acknowledge the help, guidance and assistance of all at my publisher Routledge.

David Staples

London 2020

Introduction

This book is the fruit of many people's labours over five years from 2016 to 2021.

Its inspiration, however, derives from a much earlier time, specifically from the work of the remarkable Edwin Sachs. This eminent Victorian, who at various times in his career performed the roles of architect, stagehand, engineer and fireman, wrote the classic work *Modern Theatres and Opera Houses,* completed in 1898 when he was just 28 years old. Published in three volumes in the earliest days of photography, the book contains a few black-and-white photographs; its strength is the detailed drawings of European opera houses and theatres. It also reproduces many of the European fire codes that then applied to theatres while a fascinating section lists all the theatres damaged or destroyed by fire in the 19th century. During this period of gas and candle lighting the average theatre was destroyed by fire every 12 years.

Dr Dave Willmore, biographer of Edwin Sachs, has contributed a chapter to this book which explores the work of Sachs while pointing out some of the anomalies therein.

Many other books have been published on the historic opera houses and theatres of Europe and the world, but remarkably few deal with theatres from the second half of the 20th century.

A more recent influence on me and my collaborators has been the work of Richard Brett, the consultant who in 2002 initiated a series of conferences about theatre buildings, their engineering and technologies. That first International Theatre Engineering and Architecture Conference (ITEAC) was repeated in 2006 and 2010, with Richard at the helm as Director. Following his untimely death, two further conferences were held in 2014 and 2018.

Planning for the 2018 event began in 2015, when we discussed how the conference might benefit from speakers who had undertaken research and analysis on specific topics and theatres. Two ideas emerged:

1. To ask leading thinkers and experts in their fields to write essays on specific topics – with a view to using these to inform conference sessions
2. To ask architects, theatre people, consultants, etc. to re-appraise 30 "significant" theatres that had opened between 1950 and 2010.

This book is a development of those ideas, and it needed the recruitment of experienced men and women as collaborators. This could have been a complex, lengthy task with many rejections, but amazingly, the process was surprisingly smooth. A mock-up was prepared and almost all those approached were enthusiastic and willing to be involved.

Three magazines were especially supportive and agreed to publish articles as they became available from 2015 to 2020. They were:

- ***Bühnentechnische Rundschau*** (BTR), the journal of Deutsche Theatertechnische Gesellschaft e.v. (DTHG), the German Association devoted to theatre, its technicians and technologies.
- ***Sightline***, the journal of the Association of British Theatre Technicians (ABTT). This carries articles about theatre technologies, theatre building safety and other significant issues.
- ***Theatre Design and Technology Journal*** (TD&T) has been published quarterly for more than 50 years by the United States Institute of Theatre Technology (USITT), an organization that promotes dialogue, research, and learning among practitioners of theatre design and technology.

More than 30 articles have appeared in these journals, in either English, German or American English leading up to the publication of this book. It has reassured me to think that many of the classic novels of Charles Dickens and other great writers first appeared, in similar fashion, as partworks.

Just as the world of publishing has changed out of all recognition since Dickens' day, so change has come to the performing arts. Orchestras may continue to perform Bach, Brahms and Beethoven but they also embrace new music that challenges traditional forms. Performing arts spaces have been transformed. Thousands of found spaces have been pressed into performance use. Concert halls in 2020 are radically different from those constructed in the 1950s, although opera houses have seen rather less change.

My personal involvement dates back to 1975 when Richard Brett recruited me to Theatre Projects Consultants. I was subsequently mentored and inspired by Richard Pilbrow, one of the luminaries of our industry. When I joined Theatre Projects in my early twenties, I thought it might keep me busy for four or five years, before I moved onto something else. Forty-four years on, I can think of no job that could have been more varied and rewarding.

Over that time, I've worked with some of the most creative people in the performing arts world. I have also worked on some of the most interesting theatres, concert halls and opera houses, each of them planned, designed and constructed by talented teams of architects, consultants, engineers, project managers, contractors and the myriad others who make up a modern design team.

Almost every project has been brought to fruition by a project champion, be that person a citizen, community leader, government minister, president, sheikh, sultan, emir or communist party secretary. Some have been effective dictators, others more subtle motivators, and it has been fascinating to see how many different ways there are to get such things done.

Of course, I have also been lucky enough to see thousands of performances of drama, music (of all types) opera, comedy and dance, in a total of 67 countries – with each one evoking special memories of what it took to make those performances possible.

This book is entitled *Modern Theatres*. By 'modern' we mean theatres that opened between 1950 and 2020, and we have used the word 'theatre' to embrace all types of performing arts building – playhouses or drama theatres, opera houses, concert halls and recital rooms, dance theatres, studios, educational and community performing arts spaces. A more comprehensive but ungainly title would have been *Modern Theatres, Opera Houses, Concert Halls, Playhouses, Dance Venues and Other Spaces for Live Performance*.

The book is in three sections:

1. **Essays**. Several people have written essays on topics relating to the cities, buildings, architecture and technologies associated with theatre buildings. The essays are introduced in Chapter 1.

2. **Thirty significant theatres 1950 to 2010**. The original intention was to review 30 significant theatres that opened between 1950 and 2010. We wanted to allow sufficient time after opening for a fair evaluation and appreciation of each building to be made. So, the list was cut at 2010. On the companion website at www.routledge.com/9781138484382 you will also find a 'bonus' 31st theatre, the DR Koncerthuset in Copenhagen. This essay, written by Allan Xenius Grige, explains how the project was planned, designed and constructed.

3. **Snapshots of twenty recent theatres 2009 to 2020**. The subsequent years proved a rich period for new theatres of all scales and types, so it was decided to add snapshots of 20 further buildings – a selection of those completed or due to complete up until 2020.

David Staples

PART 1.00

ASPECTS OF MODERN THEATRES

1.00

Introduction
David Staples

A number of experts were invited to contribute essays covering many aspects of theatre buildings and their technologies. The essays commence with some thoughts on changes in society and cities. They go on to discuss types of theatre – opera houses, concert halls and playhouses and conclude with comments on acoustics and theatre technologies.

Authors were asked to focus their thoughts on the period 1950 to 2020 but the essays start with one by Dr David Wilmore on Edwin Sachs, a Victorian architect, stagehand, engineer and fireman. He pioneered a scientific approach to the examination and prevention of fires. But perhaps Sachs' greatest legacy are the three volumes entitled *Modern Opera Houses and Theatres* he published in 1896, 1897 and 1898 – almost exactly 120 years ago. This extraordinary work documented in immaculate detail many of the most important theatres of that period. Sachs was an inspiration to those involved in this volume and we stand in awe of his achievement, which we cannot hope to repeat in this work but acknowledge wholeheartedly.

The period 1950 to 2020 has seen profound change in society, technologies, politics and the world. Those changes have affected and influenced the performing arts and performing arts buildings. In 1950 the old world order and hierarchy of cities had been disrupted by the Second World War. The iron curtain divided Europe while the 1970's oil price boom brought the Middle East to prominence. The 20th century was described as America's century. After only two decades the 21st century is already being labelled China's century.

A recent study offers a classification of cities, with only New York and London described as Alpha++. The next tier, Alpha+, embraces Beijing, Dubai, Hong Kong, Paris, Shanghai, Singapore, Sydney and Tokyo, several of which were insignificant in 1950 but have grown to prominence in a short period. The editor offers a chapter on cities and the changes not only in successful, growing cities but the role of performing arts buildings in urban renewal and regeneration.

Theatres are public buildings; they must attract the public and audiences if they are to be successful. They also have an important role to play in their community, town or city. Two authors have explored aspects of this public face. Boštjan Vuga, a Slovenian architect, has contributed an essay on publicness and place making. Moving inside the building, theatre consultant Robert Shook has written about the public – front of house – spaces.

Alistair Fair is an academic and writer about theatre spaces while Josh Dachs is one of the world's leading theatre consultants. From opposite sides of the Atlantic their essays comment on changes in theatre architecture. Alistair's "Towards a New Theatre Architecture" is informed by the UK experience while Josh's "Prevailing Themes in 20th-Century Theatre Architecture" brings a North American perspective.

Three people have discussed 'types' of theatres. Nicholas Payne, having headed several major opera companies, is Executive Director of Opera Europa and has written on 'The Modern Opera House'. Chris Blair is a leading acoustic consultant (and conductor) who discusses the evolution of the concert hall. Concert halls have seen possibly the most profound change of any type of performing arts building. Playhouses and the rediscovery of the 3D nature of rooms is explored in an essay by theatre architect Tim Foster.

The essays conclude with some examinations of acoustics and the technologies that are essential to make sure a building works. Acoustician Sébastien Jouan discusses acoustics and the acoustic techniques used in the design of modern theatres.

Mark Arger, stage engineer, has been at the forefront of design and innovation in stage equipment. He offers an informed perspective on stage engineering innovation.

The biggest innovation in stage lighting was the discovery of electricity; the move from gas to electricity stopped the devastating theatre fires of the 19th century. The Savoy Theatre in London was not only the first theatre to be lit by electricity but also the first public building in the world to be entirely lit by electricity. No such radical innovation has taken place in stage lighting between 1950 and 2020, but lighting technology has undergone important developments. Mark White of Electronic Theatre Controls (ETC) is a former chair of the ABTT and explores the changes that have taken place in stage lighting.

In 1950 amplification and sound systems were crude and of poor (or very poor) quality. Today they are incredibly sophisticated, not only used to amplify or play an effect but increasingly being used as an integral part of performances and compositions. All musicals are amplified, and actors are increasingly amplified – seamlessly. Most contemporary dance is performed to a recorded soundtrack. Even opera houses and concert halls are embracing sound systems. Chris Full explores some of the innovations and changes.

The final essay by Raj Patel is possibly the most speculative. The last ten years have seen growing interest and use of new media and technologies like virtual and augmented reality. Theatres are increasingly using spectacular projections and video mapping. What are the impacts and opportunities in 2020?

Edwin Sachs

1.01

Edwin O. Sachs
A British Theatrical Enigma
David Wilmore

Born on the 5th April 1870 in St. John's Wood, London, Edwin Sachs was trained as an architect in Berlin, and after a period as a government pupil he studied at the famous Königliche Technische Hochshule in Charlottenburg and worked as an architectural assistant to Böckmann & Ende, who specialised in public buildings rather than theatres. In 1890 he became an ensign in the Berlin Royal Fire Brigade and then went on to gain a supernumerary commission in the Vienna Metropolitan Fire Brigade. This was followed by service in the Paris Fire Brigade before he returned to London to take part in more fire-fighting. He qualified as an architect at the age of 22 in 1892 and appears to have set up his own architectural practice almost immediately.

The next four years were spent writing his magnum opus, *Modern Opera Houses and Theatres* – a three-volume elephant folio treatise published consecutively in 1896,1897 and 1898 – the first volume being co-authored by Ernest A.E. Woodrow, a fellow architect who was also fascinated by theatre architecture. However, in a prefatory note to the second volume Sachs stated that Woodrow had much to his regret been unable to continue with the project.

The concept of a parallèle – a publication which presents architectural drawings in a consistent manner and at a constant scale was not a new idea even in 1896 – but it was largely something that had been published within mainland Europe. Sachs seized upon the idea as a marvellous way in which to compare and contrast both the advantages and disadvantages associated with theatre design and construction.

It is clear that Sachs had had a wonderful opportunity to examine and record many of the splendid theatres and opera houses of Europe whilst completing his architectural education – theatres and opera houses that were wholly funded, both in capital and revenue terms, by the state. Returning to Britain Sachs was faced with the realisation that theatre design and construction in this country was wholly in the realm of the commercial theatrical impresario. In consequence the theatres of Great Britain, unlike so many of its other public buildings, did not, certainly from the outside, reflect the artistic or the architectural ambition of the British Empire. This seems to be something which Sachs could neither accept nor even forgive in architectural terms – and something for which, even with the perspective of over 120 years, it is difficult to reconcile. One cannot even begin to imagine the morning in 1898 when Volume III of *Modern Opera Houses and Theatres* was delivered to 9, Warwick Court, London – the registered office of the most prolific British theatre architect of the late nineteenth century, Frank Matcham. Unsurprisingly Matcham, like many other well-known theatre people including W.S. Gilbert, C.J. Phipps, Augustus Harris, Alfred Darbyshire and Henry Irving, had supported Sachs in his endeavours and was a

MODERN
OPERA HOUSES
AND THEATRES

BY

EDWIN O. SACHS
ARCHITECT,

AND

ERNEST A. E. WOODROW,
A.R.I.B.A.

Title page from Edwin Sachs' *Modern Opera Houses and Theatres*

named subscriber in the preface to all three volumes. Sachs' analysis of his subscriber's work comes from a wholly European perspective, it provides little national context and is . . . well, quite frankly jaw dropping!

In the work of Frank Matcham, I need hardly say that there has never been any pretence of architectural rendering, and that his reputation for successful construction of playhouses is based entirely on his economic planning. That this is the case there can be little doubt, and that in construction it is less 'tricky' than the work of the specialist previously named [C.J.

Phipps], goes without saying. There is no doubt, too, that his plans have a certain individuality, and that his scheme generally serves the unambitious purpose of the occupiers in a satisfactory manner. However, to fully illustrate such theatres in a volume dealing with theatre architecture in its best sense would be as anomalous as to include the ordinary 'jerry-builder's' cottages in a volume on domestic architecture. It has been my purpose to select typical and interesting examples of theatre architecture in all parts of Europe, and if I did not include such work as that of C.J. Phipps and Frank Matcham in these volumes, I am afraid England would have to stand almost entirely unrepresented. That such work is typical cannot be denied, and I am sure it is interesting in comparison with the other examples which predominate in these volumes.

Matcham's response to this unrestrained criticism has, perhaps fortunately, not survived but we can only begin to imagine what he might have thought about it. Sachs' criticism is wholly predicated on his idealist ambition for architectural statement rather than on the realities of commercial theatre design in Great Britain at the end of the 19th century. In mitigation we may put this criticism down in part to the exuberance of youth for Sachs was still only 28 years old. Moreover his critique is perhaps worth considering within the context of his relationships, Matcham and to a lesser extent Phipps are chastised for their economy of design whereas Ernest Runtz, Alfred Darbyshire and Oswald Wylson (of Wylson and Long) both receive high praise for their theatre designs – but then they would – both being members of the British Fire Prevention Committee Executive chaired and founded by none other than Edwin O. Sachs. To accuse him of cronyism would be unfair, for friendship and respect is often established and earned through work. It is however inconceivable to imagine Matcham wanting to sit on that committee after such a written public condemnation of his work. Furthermore, the irony of it is now plain for all to see, for 120 years later Matcham's work is respected and understood within the politico-social climate of theatre building in Great Britain during the late nineteenth century. Matcham's designs were produced in response to the needs of his clients, and it should perhaps be said that Sachs was for whatever reason a 19th-century theatric tourist

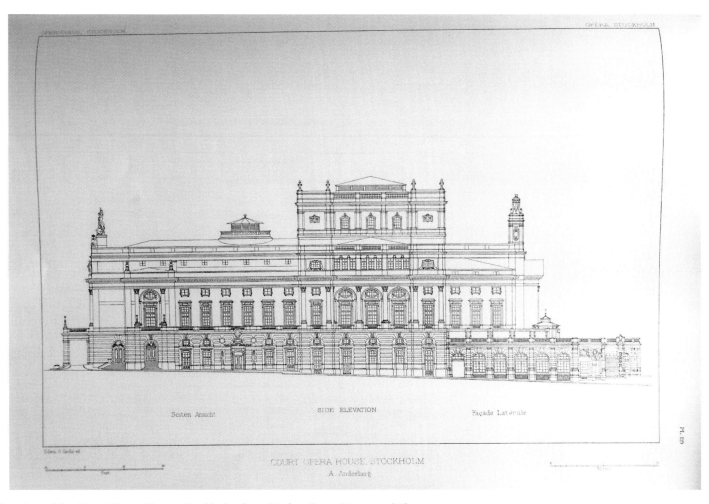

Side elevation of the Court Opera House, Stockholm from *Modern Opera Houses and Theatres*

and certainly not a commercial architect. The list of Sachs' known architectural outputs throughout his career is somewhat thin:

1897: An additional top-storey on his residence 5, Ulster Terrace, Regent's Park, London.

1896–1898: Reconstruction of the stage at the Theatre Royal, Drury Lane, London.

1899: Theatre Consultant for the Grand Theatre, Llandudno designed by George Alfred Humphreys for the Mostyn Estate.

1900: Honorary architect for the "Building Trades Gift to the Nation", Homes for Discharged Soldiers, Bisley, Surrey.

1901: Designs for an unidentified theatre stage in India.

1901: Designs for the Uralite Factory, Higham, Kent.

1901: Designs for the reconstruction of the stage house, Royal Opera House, London.

1902: Designs for the Shannon Factory in Dalston, London.

1902: Designs for Mr. Albert Ochs of Walmer Lodge, Kent.

1907: Designs for the reconstruction of the Khedival Opera House in Cairo (not executed).

1910: Designs for the reconstruction of the interior of his offices in 3–7 Waterloo Place, London.

Instead of focusing his career on commercial architectural work, Sachs became an organiser, a catalyst and a stimulator of thought, work

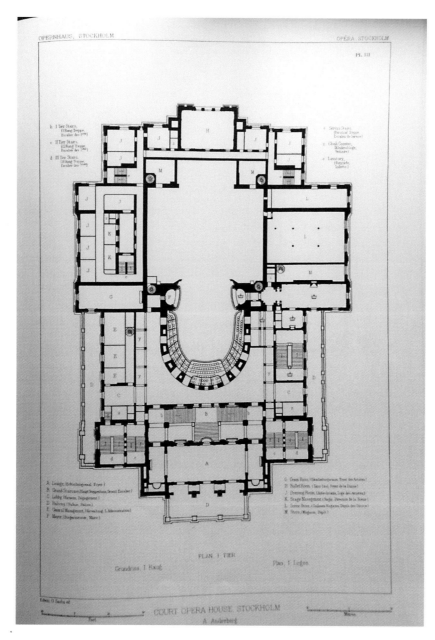

Plan of the Court Opera House, Stockholm from *Modern Opera Houses and Theatres*

and deed. His understanding of purist theatre planning was perhaps unprecedented, whilst his experience of practical commercial theatre planning, encumbered with all the constraints, limitations and reality that came with just such a commission was almost non-existent.

Whilst his extensive experience of European travel is well recorded, particularly through his work with the British Fire Prevention Committee, his visits to provincial theatres are unrecorded and the way in which he assembled all the information for his treatise is therefore worthy of further examination. A work of this kind demands a Herculean effort in a non-electronic age when even European postal communication was sometimes challenging. Sachs' love of European mainland theatre architecture is evident from the treatise and, in consequence, his analysis

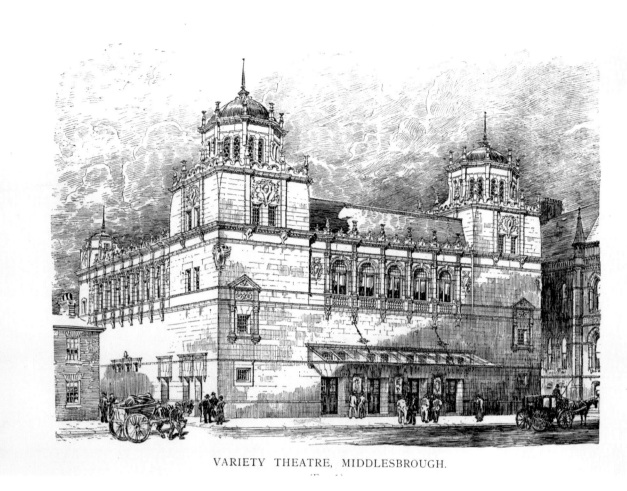

VARIETY THEATRE, MIDDLESBROUGH.

Empire Theatre of Varieties, Middlesbrough – Architect: Ernest Runtz, built 1899 (extant)

and as we have seen in certain instances disdain for British theatres creates, perhaps unintentionally, a skewed picture especially within the provinces. Precisely how Sachs created his short-list of British examples is unknown, but from the evidence he provides relating to the Grand Theatre & Opera House in Leeds, we can only conclude that he never actually visited the building and was working from information supplied by a third party.

His concluding description of the building is as follows;

The plans are sufficiently clear to explain themselves, and I need only add that the general lines of the auditorium are very effective. There are few features that call for special comment, but for the staircase accommodation must be said to insufficient.

The façade gives the structure the character of a public building, but scarcely explains its purpose as a place of entertainment. As I have already indicated, the early date of the erection must not be overlooked if we would form a true estimate of the value of the playhouse.[1]

By the time that Sachs came to publish this, both George Corson, the architect who "fronted" the project, and the real architectural designer James Robison Watson had died and in consequence Sachs must have had to rely on second-hand information from a local Leeds correspondent. We can categorically state that Sachs can never have visited the building for if he had, his entry would have been dramatically different. J.R. Watson, a now long forgotten provincial architect was, it would seem, the Edwin Sachs of the 1870s – he was possessed with the desire to improve theatre design and construction and spent several years travelling Europe with the likely intention of publishing a treatise on the subject. Sadly, this never came to fruition but his contribution to theatre design and construction survives to this very day, still in many ways unrecognised for its revolutionary step-changes in theatre design. Completed as early as 1878, the theatre was designed to incorporate the best of modern technology, funded largely by the burgeoning industrialists of a rapidly expanding city swept up in the whirlwind of the industrial revolution. The board consisted of iron-founders, merchants and businessmen who recognised the direct correlation between a city's architectural complexion as a reflection of its sophistication and ambition. Watson grasped this opportunity, rejecting all that had gone before in preference to everything that was happening around him. He rejected the extensive use of timber, introducing concrete floors throughout the building some 20 years before the formation of the British Fire Prevention Committee and almost 30 years before the formation of the Concrete Institute (later the Institution of Structural Engineers), founded and chaired in its early years by none other than Edwin Sachs.

However, the stage machinery of the Leeds Grand Theatre & Opera House was even more revolutionary and – unlike many other disastrous attempts to change the English Wood Stage e.g. Rowland Macdonald Stephenson's 1840 stage machinery for the Royalty Theatre in Soho Square – this actually worked. Whilst Watson based his ideas on the principles of the British Theatre and embraced the techniques of the English Wood Stage, it was constructed almost wholly from wrought iron. Yet Sachs ignored, or more likely was oblivious to the fact, failing to mention it in the treatise and commenting in his Stage Construction supplement that,

The curious feature, however, of the [stage reform] movement in England, is not so much the absence of extreme changes in the scenery of our stages, as the almost entire absence of the application of modern science and modern methods in the interest of stage management. Even the few exceptions which do exist generally concern only the substitution of electricity for gas in stage lighting, or some minor or mechanical appliances to facilitate what is termed a 'quick change'. We are for once untrue to our national reputation for practical adaptations; and this, moreover, in a case where there is unlimited scope for energetic young engineers.[2]

Had Sachs been in full possession of the facts about the Grand Theatre & Opera House in Leeds, history might have been different. The importance of the theatre would have been raised in perpetuity and the machinery might have survived the onslaught of English National Opera North (as it then was), who removed it in 1980 to create a rehearsal room in the substage void.

The criticism of Sachs is of course in today's high-tech world a soft target. Who would have thought 20 years ago that it might be possible to go online, search "Edwin O. Sachs" on the British Library Newspaper website and instantly resource several hundred references? Sachs was working almost in isolation with extraordinarily limited resources. His monumental treatise has served and will continue to serve future generations of theatre and architectural historians. It is for the researcher to provide and articulate the context of the work, to examine the content for what it is and to make value judgements accordingly.

Notes

1   Sachs, Edwin O., *Modern Opera Houses and Theatres*, B.T. Batsford, London, 1897, Vol. II, p. 44.
2   Sachs, Edwin O., *Modern Opera Houses and Theatres*, B.T. Batsford, London, 1898, Vol. III, p. 2.

Further Reading

Wilmore, David (ed.), *Edwin O. Sachs: Architect, Stagehand, Engineer & Fireman*, Theatreshire Books Ltd., Braisty Woods, 1998.

Cities, Global and Regenerating

David Staples

This chapter looks at two radically different types of city and the effects performing, and arts buildings can have on those cities.

The world has always had large and hugely influential cities in terms of politics, trade, etc. The post-war years have seen the emergence of 'world' or 'global' cities that have grown rapidly in recent decades and in many situations have emerged from obscurity to become important cities in a relatively short period.

At the opposite extreme decaying or declining cities have used new cultural buildings as part of strategies to renew and regenerate the city. In between are the thousands of cities that are neither growing towards world city status or declining.

The previous paragraphs talk of cities, but what is the difference between a town and a city, for both may have a theatre, gallery, museum or performance space? There is no single definition of a city and some fairly unusual criteria that justify city status in different countries. However, a city is generally a substantial settlement providing services and amenities to a larger urban area.

World or Global Cities

In May 1886 *The Illustrated London News* described Liverpool as a 'world city', implying a city with major international trade and commerce. In the second half of the 19th century the wealth of Liverpool rivalled that of London. Liverpool was described as a world city largely because of its huge port and the flow of goods through that port. It also dominated the transatlantic slave trade. For centuries cities and countries prospered and grew on the basis of manufacture and trade in physical things – agricultural produce, raw materials, goods, etc. The 20th century saw a shift towards finance as the main business of leading cities and countries which gradually usurped trade in products. World cities tend to also be world centres for banking and finance.

Today, many different names and terms have emerged to describe and classify large, successful cities. Global city is perhaps the most common. Lists and indices have been compiled under names like Global Power City Index, Global Economic Power Index, the Global Cities Index and

Shanghai skyline at night

the Global City Competitiveness Index. A think-tank, the Globalisation and World Cities Research Network has categorised cities as Alpha, Beta and Gamma based on their international connectedness. It is perhaps not surprising that the highest tier, Alpha ++, has only two cities: New York and London. The second tier, Alpha +, has eight cities and some surprises: Beijing, Dubai, Hong Kong, Paris, Shanghai, Singapore, Sydney and Tokyo. Six are in Asia and Australia while one, Dubai, barely existed in 1960.

These league tables of global or world cities initially focussed on economic, trade or financial criteria – a metric that is easy to measure. However, they also consider other less tangible factors – human capital, high quality education and research, innovation, technological factors, infrastructure, medical, culture, etc. It is increasingly understood that 'quality of life' is of fundamental importance alongside financial success.

Singapore is a good example; it was a British Crown Colony until 1963 when, with Malaysia, it gained independence. In 1965 Singapore separated from Malaysia and became a Sovereign Nation. It is not self-sufficient in water and over 90 per cent of its food is imported. As a newly independent country the initial focus was on building a successful, small, independent country with a focus on education and economic development. Singapore rapidly moved from a low wage assembly economy to an intellect-based society. After a very focussed period building an economically viable country, the political leadership realised that quality of life and cultural issues had been ignored. The government put in place initiatives to develop the arts and culture including institutions and new buildings.

Global or world cities are large (Shanghai's population effectively doubled between 1990 and 2014, when it exceeded 24 million). This has led to a massive growth in demand for entertainment and culture. The performing arts have boomed. New performing arts buildings have been constructed alongside museums and visual arts spaces. Cities (and their mayors) often want signature pieces of architecture for their universities, airports, concert halls and opera houses. Good business for 'starchitects'.

How does the cultural infrastructure develop in large, rapidly growing 'global' cities? There is no one model or route. Each city differs but it is possible to discern some common characteristics. City and central governments are often involved in the initial development and growth of cities' cultural facilities and offering. Many cities have started cultural festivals or planned and constructed museums, galleries and performing arts buildings. Up and down the Gulf there is virtually a cultural arms race underway. With governments involved there is often a desire to create a signature or iconic building designed by a "Starchitect". The cultural project stands alongside the new airport as a sign of growth, success and ambition.

As the city grows, a second level of development can be seen, with the commercial development community becoming involved. As public demand for entertainment increases there will be increasing pressure for theatres to house such entertainment. Developers will partner or collaborate with entertainment companies to establish new venues. Frequently the new theatre will be planned as part of a mixed-use development integrated with retail, hospitality, hotel and residential elements.

Occasionally the public and private sectors may come together. The government or a cultural agency may indicate to developers the need or aspiration for a new cultural facility and encourage the development community to incorporate the needed facility into a new development.

Smaller cities will have a handful of performing arts spaces. As communities grow, more specialised facilities will be provided. A large, mature city will have a concert hall for classical (and other) music, an opera house for opera, ballet and possibly musicals, playhouses or drama theatres accommodate plays, and recital rooms will develop along with more commercial ventures for entertainment offerings. In an ideal world the provision of a diverse range of performing arts spaces would be carefully planned and coordinated. This rarely happens and development is generally more haphazard.

Growing cities know there are a series of first level (or hard) attractors for business and commerce – a trained workforce; land; financial incentives; etc. But there is a growing recognition that broader, quality of life (soft) issues including arts and cultural offerings are important in building successful cities.

Regenerating Cities, Creative Clusters, Cultural Quarters

The previous paragraphs have discussed world, global or alpha cities. The majority of cities are not successful and rapidly growing; indeed there are many less successful, struggling or failing cities. Many cities are attempting to reverse a decline, whether economic or in terms of population. The arts have been

Guggenheim Museum, Bilbao

identified as a way of revitalising such cities. It you Google "arts-led regeneration" you will be offered nearly 9,000,000 results. There is a wealth of material exploring ways in which investment in culture and especially building projects can benefit cities and play a part in urban renewal. There are equally many articles questioning the role the arts can realistically play in urban renewal.

"Bilbao Bounce" or "The Guggenheim Effect" are terms used to describe the transformation of Bilbao, a northern Spanish city. Its traditional industries, port, steel and ship building were in decline, but the city decided to invest in regeneration and renewal. Many attribute the success of this urban renewal to Frank Gehry's Guggenheim Museum which opened in 1997, and it is certainly the most visible of the new projects in the city.

The New York-based Solomon R. Guggenheim Foundation led by Director Thomas Krens held discussions with the Basque government about creating a branch of the famed museum in Bilbao. The government made a substantial financial commitment to the construction of the museum, to acquire art and to support the operating costs of the new museum. In exchange the Foundation agreed to manage the museum, loan artworks from their collection and arrange exhibitions. The museum has been a success since its opening in October 1997, creating jobs, bringing tourists to the city and generating economic benefits. It is proclaimed a huge accomplishment by many and has spurred other cities and institutions to try and emulate its success in regenerating a city.

The Guggenheim, while important, was one of a number of parallel initiatives, including a new metro system with stations designed by British architect Norman Foster. Spanish architect Santiago Calatrava designed the Zubizuri footbridge across the Nervion River and a new airport terminal. There were also other significant infrastructure projects. The success of the urban renewal did not rest solely on the museum. Some commentators, while acknowledging the iconic and image building effect of the Museum have attacked it as a franchise of a large American institution and have queried the long-term benefits, beyond tourism, it will bring to the city.

There have been many studies that aim to evaluate the economic impact of new arts buildings. America led the charge in such studies during the 1970s and 1980s, with many studies commissioned. Other countries and communities followed and used similar methodologies to assess the economic benefits that flowed from cultural initiatives, including festivals and new buildings. Economic impact studies became an advocacy tool. Today, their importance and validity have been questioned and although still a useful instrument they carry less credibility.

Cities, their political leadership and planners are constantly looking for ways to develop their communities. Much has been informed by the work and thinking of Richard Florida, whose work and books have advanced the idea of a "creative class", the presence of which attracts other creative people, business and prosperity to a city. Recent years have seen increased interest in the concept of cultural quarters, cultural districts or creative hubs. This concept often flows from a belief that a city is more vibrant if it is successful in attracting and retaining a creative population. Cultural quarters have been through a period of growth and have become fashionable among city planners. Some cultural quarters/creative hubs will be hugely successful. Others will struggle. A cultural district is an element in city development that must stand alongside other development strategies.

Synopsis

The previous paragraphs have commented on global cities and by contrast those needing or seeking regeneration. Between those extremes lie many towns and cities that will never become world cities and equally do not need radical urban renewal. Recent decades have shown an increased acknowledgement that a vibrant cultural element is important in a city's growth and development.

Global cities, by definition, are huge, they are large and wealthy enough to develop not one but many cultural districts and facilities. As their population grows and they prosper economically, improvements in quality of life including cultural offerings need to keep pace with their population growth and expansion.

Regenerating or renewing cities can use the performing and visual arts as one part of a strategy for development. Culture alone will not regenerate a city. Cities that ignore the arts and culture are at risk of losing out to more nimble and better planned communities offering better facilities for their populations.

Theatres and Publicness

Boštjan Vuga

Opera houses, concert halls, theatres and other performance venues are generally characterized as introverted buildings in the framework of their urban context – in cities. The main activities for which these buildings were built – the performance of a play, concert or other event – take place in the core of the building, in the dark, in the auditorium, on the stage, far from the perimeter and the outer walls of the building. The core of the building demands a specific treatment as regards technical, acoustic, accessibility and visibility concerns. In so doing it tends to seclude the building from the outside. The theatre building therefore acts as a "machine", with the core of the building "wrapped" by its backstage areas, service and dressing rooms, and the front spaces (or public side) with foyers and facilities for audience and spectators. The core of the building, apart from the stage tower, doesn't actually constitute a feature of the urban theatre building; the core is not a visually compelling or attractive element in the larger cityscape beyond. The core is, owing to its standardized technical requirements, safely hidden from the urban life outside. The theatre building communicates with the outdoors, with its urban surroundings through the foyers and foyer walls, which when seen from the outside define the main entrance facade of the building. The foyers serve as one of the transition zones from outdoor street life to indoor performance life, from a driveway, a plaza or garden outside the building to the walls that separate the foyer of the front building from the auditorium at the core. The spatial character of the foyer and the type of activity that takes place there generates the level or degree of publicness of the "machine", and the public character of the theatre building.

The added value an architectural object brings consists in its public space and in the integration of the public space into its physical space. The public character, the publicness of an architectural object, defines an object's catalytic potential to impact its physical and social urban context, to attract people and become a destination in the city.

Publicness is not only the result of a project brief requiring the implementation of a certain proportion of public functions in the domain of an architectural object. It is the result of an architectural approach that integrates spaces for the general public into the building, spaces that don't necessarily suggest predetermined uses, linked and bound to the building's primary purpose and intended use. Publicness is the result of an architect's ability to envision the wider architectural, spatial and social effects of the theatre within the micro and macro contexts of its surroundings.

Publicness is grafted in/onto the building. The graft is first accommodated in the structure, then starts impacting the building's operations and functioning. Eventually, the theatre building could be visited

Elbphilharmonie Plaza, Hamburg

and experienced owing more to its publicness than to its primary intended use.

Publicness encourages more extensive use of a theatre building by individuals and social groups throughout the day and year-round. It gives rise to increased usage and thereby avoids the creation of new urban grey zones in cities or towns. Publicness makes the place! Publicness makes the place sustainable because it prolongs the building's use!

The character of the front building, its foyer spaces and the walls fronting the exterior, together with the urban surroundings define the

publicness of a theatre building. The more porous the foyer's walls, the smoother the outdoor and indoor transition zones between the city's urban space and the core of the building, the greater the theatre's publicness. These transition zones – outdoor plazas, atriums, esplanades, galleries, foyer gardens – act as hardware that stimulates informal and unplanned events, as well as simple gatherings, relaxation and active wandering throughout the day, long before and after the scheduled performances in the core of the building. The publicness of a theatre building is therefore defined by the spatial character of the transition zones, their atmosphere and the activities that unfold therein. One goes to the theatre building to relax, read, eat, shop, attend a workshop or an informal performance. One goes there during the day when there are no performances on the program. The theatre building becomes, as the result of its publicness, a place for meetings, a free-time destination, a community meeting point. Its publicness has the potential to exert a larger impact and constitute an engaging urban development in the immediate surroundings.

It was actually the changes in the character of the front building – the foyer in the 20th century, the shift from a relatively narrow concourse with staircases around the auditorium to a large, multi-level space with various micro-environments between the main entrance facade of the building and the wall of the auditorium – that contributed to the increased publicness of theatre buildings. It was these changes in the character of the foyer that made theatres more accessible and more attractive to a wider audience. These changes represent an attempt to turn the introverted character of the theatre building inside-out, into an extroverted building with porous boundaries, into a lively, dynamic and rich indoor space together with its adjacent outdoor spaces, into urban living rooms where one also goes, whether attending a performance or simply using the space as it allows. And it is precisely this change in the character of the foyer that communicates a less elitist and more democratic, socially inclusive theatre building and experience.

Garnier Opera, Paris, front facade

Garnier Opera, Paris, Grand Staircase

We can stand in front of a great and respected theatre building from the late 19th century, built to represent and reinforce the institution, as well as represent both the city, town and state. The Palais Garnier Opera, Paris, Staatsoper in Vienna or La Scala in Milan are all formidable, civic and important, but all are also essentially quite uninviting buildings, with limited access and all of them closed when there are no performances running. These buildings are monuments in the cities in which they are located, they contribute to building the institutions they represent and which, together with the buildings themselves, contribute to the city's recognition and visibility factors. We see hordes of visitors and tourists admiring the exterior grandeur of the (neo)classical facades, which communicate the power and stability of the state. The facade, the outer wall is a heavy boundary, a barrier. One has to be privileged to get inside, behind the wall, into the foyer. Here, sets of staircases lead to various entrances to the auditorium. The two-dimensional grandeur of the entrance facade translates into the three-dimensional grandeur of the staircases, concourses, entryways, smoking-rooms and champagne rooms. We have but a 30-minute slot to see and be seen before the performance and a mere 15 minutes during the intervals. There is no connection to the outside, to the urban context, apart from a narrow space of loggia above the entrance, or the balcony where those attending a performance may appear during the break and make their presence known to the city. The publicness factor of these imposing structures is very low. They are massive structures in the urban context, with their main doors closed most of the day. As such, they have never been meant to generate any kind of public urban life in their immediate vicinity.

A great leap towards opening up theatre buildings and toward the democratization of their respective institutions started with the Malmö Stadsteater in Sweden, which opened in 1944 and continued during the heroic years of modernization following the Second World War. The Musiktheater im Revier in Gelsenkirchen is a second, good example. They communicate and project the various activities in their foyers through entirely glazed entrance walls. Instead of the hard border, the massive facade of the classical theatre buildings that serves to create a sense of suspense, an effect of expectation or even desire as we enter,

here the foyer space is unveiled and opened up entirely to and towards the urban environs of the city. Visitors, those there to see and be seen, can feel something like a fish in a giant golden bowl when viewed from the outside. During the day these foyers are semi-dark, dimmed spaces, unattractive and usually closed. Come evening they are lit up, and passers-by can gaze in and through the building, almost into the very core of the institution. But still, why would anyone want to go there without a ticket to a performance or even properly dressed for an event? Modernist theatres are civic buildings and are supposedly less monumental and more approachable than their classical ancestors. The glass facades and a pedestrian-friendly outdoor plaza generate a feeling of openness about the buildings, but the doors still remain closed until 60 minutes before the show. Substituting a massive neoclassical facade-wall with a glass

Malmö Stadsteater, Sweden

Musiktheater im Revier (MiR), Gelsenkirchen

membrane is not enough. The publicness of these buildings is still very minimal – and could be even lower than back at the classical theatre buildings we've discussed previously due to their siting/placement in the urban context. They are detached, free-standing buildings where an entrance plaza at the front and manipulated surfaces at the back separate them from the urban context. These buildings rarely generate any urban or social effect that would define or mark them as urban attractors or catalysts. They represent the power of the city and the state in an analogical way, as did the classical theatres.

What then should be done to increase the publicness of theatre buildings? What are the main reasons we should try and conceive new and renovated theatre buildings that exhibit a high level of publicness? Why is publicness so important as a strategy in contemporary urban planning and development?

Theatre buildings are civic buildings. Cities only construct a new theatre building every 30 years or more, and many modernist theatres are 50–70 years old. They need be renovated and adapted to the kinds of performances we see today, as well as to the different lifestyles of their audiences and visitors. A high level of publicness of new or renovated theatre buildings would help accelerate urban development in their micro and macro contexts and make them more inclusive, would stimulate greater participation and engagement. Theatre buildings could position themselves as hubs, centres of urban life, day and night, for various interest groups and essentially everyone, young and old. The boundaries between these buildings and their surroundings are becoming increasingly porous, the distinction between outdoor and indoor transition zones is becoming blurred, and the array of free and easily accessible activities in their foyer areas is on the rise. The publicness

of the theatre building itself can exert real influence on the institutions' own musical program or dramatic productions and on the very nature of their performances. Many also find their place in the informal spaces of foyers and outdoor plazas.

The Royal National Theatre and the Royal Festival Hall in London are modernist theatres that exhibit an exceptional level of publicness, which has substantially contributed to the creation of the South Bank as an attractive and popular public space in the centre of London. Both buildings have become hybrids, combining their primary function/use – a theatre and a concert hall – with a wide range of other events and

Royal Festival Hall, London, animated external areas

activities staged over various floors of the foyers and extended outwards on layered horizontal terraces. The "open foyer policy" opened the foyers to the public all day, seven days a week, with free exhibitions, lunchtime concerts, education programmes, evening jazz performances, shops, bars and buffets. The hybridization of the theatre buildings with typical urban leisure activities in and in front of their foyers serves to attract the public, which turns a place into a destination. There we experience a lively urban mix of formal and casual, of spontaneity and well-planned events and performances staged in the theatre or the auditoriums. The boundaries between inside and outside, between the urban public space and the foyer space are less fixed and defined and we can transit smoothly from one to another.

How do theatre buildings with open public foyers communicate within the context of their urban surroundings? How does their publicness influence their physical appearance, their architecture? Would blurred boundaries and smooth transition zones in the foyers and the ambiences we experience in them render them indistinct from commercial shopping malls, sports arenas or Cineplexes with similar retail facilities? What creates a theatre building's architectural and spatial character – as the foyers become filled with an array of booths and bars, and restaurants increasingly spread their seats wider and further into the depths of the building? What is their added architectural value in the city context that goes beyond the attractive yet mere consumerist facilities of the open foyers? What makes them specific, recognizable and important civic buildings?

Winspear Opera House, Dallas, Texas, outdoor space

The Winspear Opera Building in Dallas has a large solar canopy that extends from the building out towards the park around it. The canopy is a response to the hot Dallas climate and creates a pleasant, cool, shaded outdoor public space. Vertical sliding glass panels moving the full length and height of the structure establish a fluid indoor–outdoor connection, and the entry lobby, a restaurant and a bar extend far outward towards the pools, lawns and outdoor seating areas. People come here to relax in their free time, attend an outdoor event, as well as to see and be seen on the grand foyer's multi-level staircase before attending the performance.

The Winspear Opera acts as a catalyst for urban life in the larger urban context of Dallas, with its public space under the canopy far more than a mere space for yet more consumption.

The Oslo Opera is a brilliant theatre building in that it creates a public space or plaza on its roof, which is tilted and rises up and over the building, connecting the land with the very proximate fjord below. The sculpted roof landscape constitutes a real added value component for the building and is a destination entirely in itself. It is a place for strolling, skating, for observing the city. It is a commonly owned public surface,

Oslo Opera, publicly accessible roof

a place of anti-consumption, a social monument, and accessible to all. The building's roof, more than anything else, more than its foyer or the auditorium below, has grown into a new landmark for Oslo.

Is the public plaza on the top of the existing building structure at the new Elbphilharmonie in Hamburg a proper example of the public character of a theatre building? The plaza, as an observation deck with magnificent views to the city, the port and the river, is reached via a long escalator from the ground floor. From here, the foyer of the concert halls placed *above* the plaza, can be accessed. Moving through the plaza with its cavernous sequences of ever-changing views and glimpses of the city is a very strong experience, and one to remember.

These are three examples of recent theatre buildings that embody a high level of publicness. These three buildings in particular have impacted the larger urban area around them and serve to make them destinations in the cities that host them. Whether above, under or around the core of the building, the auditorium and the stage, the all-access public areas of these buildings are primarily places to stroll, to relax and enjoy, to observe, to experience the architectural and urban spatial qualities of the surroundings. These are connected with commercial spaces in the form of foyer shops, bars and restaurants. And in the end, these areas also serve as places for free performances, concerts and events that extend the activity of these institutions outward and beyond the core of the building. These foyer performances could contribute to a shift in the perception of a theatre's production. Free for all, accessible to all . Shop, eat and attend the impromptu concert. Listen to a reading as an introduction to the main event in the theatre hall proper. Or just stroll past a dance rehearsal on the lawn outside the foyer.

Step outside! Break the barrier of the auditorium wall and foyer, between the core and the front building. Generate publicness with production, not (only) with consumption.

Which tendencies will, in the end, generate the public component of future theatre buildings in today's post-digital age? What will provide some specific character, appearance, operativity and atmosphere for theatre buildings, elements that will turn them into an urban hub, a cultural and leisure centre in the city? Pro-sumption? Some combination of production and consumption, where there is no clear boundary between work time and free time, where roles are exchanged and everyone can be both a performer and a spectator, where everyone can produce and consume. Are the new theatre buildings erasing the ultimate barrier between the front and the core of the building? Imagine these two mixed and hybridized.

A foyer becomes a stage and the audience changes its position in the auditorium. A multi-use space offers a strong, new and unique spatial experience; and a recognisable and moving architecture appears to create a new destination.

This is the ultimate publicness of theatres.

Prevailing Themes in 20th-Century Theatre Architecture

Joshua Dachs

Theatre architecture, to state the obvious, is a product of its times. Everything about buildings designed for performance is the result of a confluence of social, economic, artistic, political and aesthetic forces specific to the time and place of its conception, and that's what makes them some of the most interesting buildings there are to look at or work on.

Books have been written about the semiotics of Architecture – the idea that the overall spatial conception and aesthetic expression of a work of architecture can be read as a text describing the specific social order and value system of the culture in which it was created, and the same is obviously true of Theatre Architecture and always has been. Just think of the *meaning* of the form of the Greek Amphitheatre, developed simultaneously with democracy itself, and the social stratification enshrined in Shakespeare's Globe or any Italian opera house. Theatre holds the mirror up to life both on and off the stage.

Theatre architecture in the second half of the 20th century, upon which this book is reflecting, was arguably subject to more change, and faster, than was experienced in many preceding centuries. Some of the reasons for this are obvious; technological advances in steel construction, electric lighting, a concerted effort to develop building safety standards, and so forth. But the 20th century was also turbulent. There were two World Wars, a crushing depression, and massive social upheaval, with a reordering of borders, economies, lifestyles, and governments. This can't have helped but be reflected in the choices that were made in cultural projects over the course of that century, and most of all in the work of the theatre artists themselves who are the true innovators of theatre architecture, and always have been.

But theatres are more than just signifiers – they are designed to structure activity. David Wiles, in his wonderful books on theatre, reminds us that the theatre is fundamentally a spatial practice – a theatre artist devises ways to occupy space, and devises movement and actions within it to convey meaning, provoke thought, and elicit emotion. In this way the theatre space itself is both the artist's container and text.

This is why theatre architecture is so fundamental to the ongoing development of the art forms these buildings contain. Theatre buildings enable or eventually constrain the development of art forms, and new developments in the art forms may require new kinds of buildings – or none at all.

Century demarcations themselves are arbitrary. Some 20th-century phenomena have their roots in the 18th century and will persist into the early decades of the 21st century. Other trends will arise with great energy, then disappear in a handful of years. Still, one can speak in terms of some general themes that drove and shaped theatre architecture in the 20th century and continue to shape it today. They fall into some broad categories:

Greek Amphitheatre, Epidaurus

Artist-Driven Initiatives

1. **A Profusion of Alternative Forms** – Theatre Artists are the principal drivers of innovation and change in theater architecture, and the 20th century experienced a sort of Cambrian Explosion of theater forms. At the beginning of the century the proscenium theatre was effectively the only form of theatre in the West. Itself an innovation of artists dating to the late 16th century, the formal, frontal form had propagated all over the Western world and its colonies and emulators, even while diversifying in scale, decor, and stage capability for various performance types and commercial settings. Whenever there is a rigid straitjacket of this sort artists seek to escape it – it's a natural law of some kind – and the 20th century saw a parade of intriguing artists seeking alternative ways of working. Their motivations were as varied as the artists themselves, and most focused on new ways of writing, acting and producing

Shakespeare's Globe, London

that would transform what we saw on our stages. But others felt compelled to struggle with how to use space itself. They explored forgotten old forms or improvised entirely new ones. Arena staging, open staging, thrust staging, and their many hybrids and variations were rediscovered, explored, and adopted. In many ways, it was a century of experimentation. Some experiments proved fruitful, others less so.

2. **The Search for a Truly Flexible Theatre** – This explosion of theatre forms came along just at the time that Jerzy Grotowski was devising environments specifically tailored for his performances,

and Peter Brook's book *The Empty Space* popularized the phrase "any space can be a theatre".

These ideas inspired artists all over the world. If we can make theatre frontally, in the round, in a thrust, in a devised environment, or in ANY space at all, what's an earnest young theatre artist to do? One obvious response was to attempt to make an EVERY-theatre; a space that was flexible enough to become anything you needed it to be. Many have struggled with the seeming paradoxes: permanent yet flexible; easy to rearrange but without a constraining system; a blank slate that must be imbued with meaning;

institutionalized yet experimental. It has been a great source of exploration and produced some interesting – and many depressing – results. There were some unique projects along the way, like the Modular Theatre at Cal Arts, a great book by Per Erdstrom and Pentti Piha called *Rum Och Teater* (*Rooms and Theatres*) with their fabulous cartoons and diagrams, and many amazing experiments in geometry, platform systems, and mechanization peaking perhaps in the 1970s.

It turns out that any system is inherently constraining, and total flexibility is labour intensive and defies simple mechanization. Many theatres have been created that provide a limited range of reconfiguration, hoping to trade breadth of flexibility for actual utility. Some believe a completely flexible theatre is like a unicorn – you may believe they exist, but you are unlikely to see one in your lifetime.

3.   **A Migration to Found Spaces** – As I mentioned at the outset, theatre artists are the real theatre architects, and the way they choose to select and occupy space for performance is what sets the course of new waves of development. Many theatre artists have rejected purpose-built theatre spaces, preferring to work in spaces like the Jahrhunderthalle in Bochum, Germany, or the Park Avenue Armory in New York that were built for other uses.

Bochum Jahrhunderthalle Hall 1, built as an exhibition hall in 1902, but used for sixty years as a gas-fired power plant before conversion to a festival venue in 2003

Park Avenue Armory, New York

In these spaces they find a freedom from convention that dedicated spaces lack. Additionally, in a particular building's history or the way it has been scarred by time they may find a special emotional resonance that enriches their work. This trend is a clear demonstration of the power of semiotics in theatre architecture, and the special way that *place* conveys meaning.

Economic and Political and Social Pressures

4. **Bigger is Better!** – Another course of development that arguably began in the era of Edwin O. Sachs's great three-volume tome *Modern European Opera Houses* in 1890 is the way advances in engineering, amplification, and lighting made larger and larger halls possible. Encouraged by commercial interests, philanthropic organizations like the Ford Foundation, and governments (and abetted by George Izenour of *Theatre Architecture and Engineering* fame, who treated theatre architecture as an engineering problem, rather than as an experiential one), the post-WWII West embraced Culture and its values in a big way.

    Shining white marble theatres, concert halls, and opera houses were built throughout the West with larger and larger capacities, especially in the US. It was an era of big cars, big hair, and big

theatres. Even concert halls were routinely sized between 2500 and 3000 seats. In 1966 the Metropolitan Opera House was built, with 3800 seats, and commercial producers insisted that it didn't make sense to build touring venues for Broadway shows with fewer than 3000 seats. Oversized venues proliferated.

It wasn't long before it became clear that this produced awful experiences. Scale, it turns out, is perhaps the greatest determinant of a theatre space's success in supporting powerful, meaningful, impactful performances.

In the last two decades of the century theatre capacities finally started to drop, and this trend has continued to the present day.

5. **The Evolution of the Multi-Use Hall** – A related 20th-century theme, particularly as the post-war wave of cultural development reached cities too small to warrant multi-venue complexes, was the significant advance of our ability to produce halls that were actually very good for a wide range of art forms. In place of some of the overlarge mid-century barns which targeted an acoustical environment that split the difference between what was needed for symphony and amplified programs like musicals (thereby pleasing no one), we learned to make smaller rooms with extra volume for reverberation and clever systems of variable absorption that could be deployed or retracted to tailor the acoustic to the art form on stage. And we

Metropolitan Opera auditorium, New York, 3,800 seats

learned to make concert shells that can easily be moved out of the way so as not to interfere with incoming theatre, musicals, ballet or opera. This has produced a number of fine halls in the US that are very effective for the local symphony, opera, ballet, and Broadway touring presenters.

The Impact of the Architectural Profession

6. **Modernism** – During its heroic early days after the First World War, modern architects were afire with revolutionary fervor. They set about rejecting the stylistic trappings and organizing principals of

architecture made for 19th-century Imperial societies. Instead they strove to develop a new vocabulary based on contemporary materials and technologies, reflecting the new age of flight, of power stations, and a romantic view of industry.

They also had a great passion for turning traditional spatial ideas on their head, inverting *figure* and *ground*. No more would buildings be made of discrete rooms strung together like jewels, with large important ones connected to each other by smaller more intimate chains of connective tissue. Instead space would flow continuously – through the landscape, through cities, from outside to inside and back again, directed and punctuated by planes and objects implying spaces, view lines, and patterns of movement along the way. Instead of shapely, figural rooms in a solid matrix we now have figural objects in free and open space, with fewer opaque walls and much more glass. *Transparency* became a call to arms.

Eventually auditoriums were treated as solid objects floating in open voids, encased in glass. For better or worse, public spaces were transformed from hierarchically conceived suites of specialized rooms into monolithic, amorphous open spaces filling the gap between object-halls and the glass wrapper.

Sadly, for theatre practitioners, auditoriums fared much worse when subjected to the rigours of modernism. Architects eliminated overtly hierarchical seating plans and their compact footprints, side walls lined with viewers, and vertical organization in favour of large "democratic" fan-shaped rooms. They rejected decoration and other measures that could help modulate the visual scale of over-large rooms and surfaces and allowed enormous blank walls to surround the stage and the poor little actor. Modernism produced some of the worst theatres seen in centuries – perhaps ever.

Advancements in the Theatre Planning and Design Professions

7. **Remembering What We Value** – "*Back to the Future*", as Richard Pilbrow dubbed it long ago, was the thoughtful study by theatre consultants of pre-modern theatre spaces and applying key learnings from the past to contemporary projects. It emerged in reaction to mid-century misdeeds in order to re-learn what was once common knowledge but now was lost, and to remember what it was that we valued in theatre spaces in the first place. The entirely healthy idea of looking to the past for inspiration has led to a variety of good to great projects and raised the bar generally, and together with acoustics, is one of the factors in successfully driving seating capacities down. For me, the frequently seen Courtyard Theatre typology (such as the Dorfman née Cottesloe at the NT) is a pure expression of this desire; dust off an old model to recapture what

has been lost – in that case a typology that sat at a unique historical juncture between the Elizabethan courtyard "amphitheatres" and the Italianate proscenium theatre, so a kind of 'Roots' thing for the English proscenium theatre folks. In my own practice, we've enjoyed learning from old opera houses and Broadway theatres and applying those lessons to our contemporary venues. While this has led to some wonderful 20th-century buildings executed in a proudly 19th-century architectural idiom, it has also led to wonderful buildings in which the best-practices from historical theatres with respect to geometry, seating envelopment, scale modulation, and their capacity to instill a sense of visceral connection and intimacy among people are applied and expressed in a completely contemporary language by architects willing to engage with this central challenge.

8. **The Rise of Acoustics** – This profession didn't really exist until the 20th century, and its rise has had a deep impact on performance spaces in profound ways; some good, some bad. Figuring out a successful approach to multi-purpose halls in the last decades of the century is one of its great accomplishments. As acousticians have come to wield enormous power on design teams, a sad tension can develop between being close/seeing well and absolutist pure physics-experiment acoustic "requirements", which can result in distant balconies and blank surfaces where people should be. Some of you have heard me rant on that theme before. I will spare you. But acoustics has unquestionably played an enormous role in shaping the architecture of the 20th century's spaces for live performance, and hearing well is actually a good thing.

The wheel of time keeps turning, and culture keeps evolving. New building types emerge in response to the interests of a new century's artists. Older traditional art forms evolve too, in response to new economic and social pressures, and the differing social habits and expectations of new generations of cultural consumers. Architecture has become more fashion-conscious than ever, and designers who are uninterested in engaging with the real core issues of theatre architecture are producing some unfortunate fashion victims. But other architects are still intrigued and inspired by the

Tobin Center, San Antonio, Texas. A 19th-century opera house form expressed in a contemporary architectural idiom, with colour-changing LED balcony-fronts.

challenge of making an exciting space for social engagement while being true to their own architectural principals. As always, it will be interesting to see where theatre artists, economic and social changes, and evolving architectural fashions will lead us in this new century.

Towards a New Theatre Architecture
Developments in Britain after 1950
Alistair Fair

In 1960, the management of Birmingham Repertory Theatre outlined their intention to construct a new theatre to replace their early 20th-century building. They had in mind the competition that theatre faced from cinema and television, as well as new ideas of staging and the actor/audience relationship. They were also interested in the place of theatre within a modernising cityscape, and the role of culture in everyday life. As a result, they proposed a fundamental re-thinking of the theatre building: 'The live theatre, if it is to stay live, must in future think along entirely different lines from hitherto.'[1] Birmingham Rep's search for a new kind of theatre, designed from first principles, evoked the central premise of 20th-century modern architecture. Modernists typically argued that the architectural styles and strategies of the past were no longer adequate in the face of the century's apparently unique challenges and opportunities.

Some of the themes evident in the buildings that resulted are the subjects of this brief essay, which, within the limited space available, offers an architectural-historical perspective on British theatres of the second half of the 20th century.[2] The examples considered here are principally drawn from the United Kingdom, but many of the themes have international parallels.

One starting point might be the sheer diversity of post-1950 theatre architecture. With reference to post-war theatre design in the United States, the historian Arnold Aronson has suggested that:

If there was a general consensus that a new form of theatre was indeed needed, there was most assuredly no single answer to the question, "What form should the new theatre take?" And that multiplicity of answers, in fact, became the answer: there was no longer a uniform style of theatre and thus there could not be a standard model of theatre architecture.[3]

In these circumstances, theatre design was shaped by the ideas of a varied cast – actors, directors, architects, engineers, and, increasingly, theatre consultants – and in an increasingly international context. The results were bespoke expressions of those ideas. Thus, for example, the new Birmingham Rep of 1971 contrasted with the new Crucible Theatre in Sheffield of the same year.[4] Both were 'producing' theatres originating their own shows with public subsidy. However, directorial preferences meant that the Rep features a single straight rake of seating facing a proscenium-arch stage, whereas the Crucible has a 'thrust' stage. Externally, the Rep's concrete arches and expansive glazing (by the architect Graham Winteringham) recall contemporaneous developments in Brasilia.[5] Meanwhile the Crucible's solidity and angled geometries embody a broader strain of polygonal monumentality advocated by certain 1960s architects.[6]

The modern architecture of Britain's post-war theatres was sometimes understood to connote the progressive intentions of those who

Birmingham Repertory Theatre, exterior

commissioned, worked in, and funded these new buildings.[7] In the late 1940s and 1950s, Scandinavian examples such as the Gothenburg Concert Hall (1938–1940) and Malmö City Theatre (1940–1944) offered particular inspiration; both were visited in the late 1940s by the designers of London's Royal Festival Hall (1951).[8] These Scandinavian buildings clearly expressed their constituent parts – stage, auditorium, and so on – as distinct masses. They also revealed an emerging design tendency in which the solid wedge of the auditorium was juxtaposed with a more open, glazed front elevation. This balance of mass and transparency inspired the design of the Festival Hall, where the foyers flow around and below the auditorium. It is also found in such West German examples as the new theatres at Münster (1956) and Gelsenkirchen (1958).[9] These theatres were among the first new professional theatres in post-war western Europe and were viewed with considerable interest by British designers even if, as British visitors often concluded, their vast scale and complex stage technologies seemed unrepeatable in less well-funded contexts.[10]

Birmingham Repertory Theatre, auditorium

Like their West German counterparts, many of the new British theatres that sprang up from the late 1950s represented a distinctly 'civic' conception of the type. From the end of the 1940s, small but growing amounts of public subsidy were routinely made available to British theatre – and especially to the country's Repertory companies – as a result of the formation in 1945 of the Arts Council of Great Britain and the passage in 1948 of the Local Government Act (which permitted local authorities to devote a small proportion of their 'rates' (tax) income to culture and the arts).

The country's first purpose-built civic theatre was Coventry's Belgrade Theatre of 1958, which was also the first all-new permanent professional theatre built in Britain since 1939. Looking not unlike a mini-Festival Hall, it was designed to be the focal point of a new public square. A wave of new theatres followed, all around Britain. Although the largest example of the theatre-building boom of the 1960s and 1970s was the National Theatre in London (Denys Lasdun, 1964–1976), the story is dominated by developments outside London. Theatres such as Nottingham Playhouse (Peter Moro, 1963), Sheffield's Crucible Theatre (Renton Howard Wood, 1971), Colchester Mercury (Norman Downie, 1972), and Eden Court, Inverness (Law and Dunbar-Nasmith, 1976) were accomplished in their design; many contributed to a 'renaissance' in non-London theatre and achieved notable artistic reputations.

British theatres were frequently invoked in debates about civic pride. For example, Henry Wrong, the first administrator of the Barbican Arts Centre in London, argued in the early 1980s that just as railway stations had during the 19th century replaced cathedrals as symbols of a town's status, so had arts centres taken the place of stations in recent years.[11] At the same time, a 'civic' approach could prompt critical comment. In some cases (e.g. Leicester and Derby), new theatres were deliberately constructed in shopping centres, rather than among municipal buildings. The idea was in part to embed theatre in everyday life.[12] By the end of the 1970s, more 'vernacular', less monumental approaches to theatre architecture were also evident. A 'domesticisation' of the theatre is evident in such examples as the Wolsey, Ipswich (1979), by Roderick Ham, who was, like Moro, one of the leading designers of theatres in 1960s and 1970s Britain. The Wolsey consciously evoked the East Anglian vernacular; with its tiled roofs and projecting windows, it suggested a house scaled up to the size of a public building.

Another approach embraced impermanency. During the 1960s, the architect Cedric Price and the director Joan Littlewood explored the idea of a 'Fun Palace', a centre conceived not as a static monument but rather as something more flexible and responsive to the changing needs of its users. A framework into which structures could be inserted to accommodate a diverse range of activities, the unbuilt Fun Palace was to be a key influence on Renzo Piano and Richard Rogers' Pompidou Centre in Paris

Crucible Theatre, Sheffield, exterior

of 1971–1977. Similarly representative of a search for the impermanent was the Royal Exchange Theatre, Manchester (1976), whose metal and glass theatre 'module' was inserted into a vast redundant Victorian hall. Meanwhile architectural polish could be abandoned completely in the form of the 'found space'. Advocated by prominent directors including Peter Brook and Ariane Mnouchkine, this kind of venue was typically created within historic, often decaying buildings, the imperfections of which were left on show to create an evocative dialogue between architecture and performance.

If the location and architectural language of a theatre could, therefore, make some deliberate statement, so too could a theatre's interior spaces. Typical of the period is the provision of increasingly expansive foyers with room for refreshment, display, and socialising, and the opening of these spaces all day, not only at performance times. Similarly typical was the abandonment of the older tendency to segregate patrons' access to a theatre's front-of-house areas by ticket price. Key examples include the accomplished Thorndike Theatre, Leatherhead (1969), where Roderick Ham arranged the public spaces as a series of spatially exciting

Crucible Theatre, Sheffield, auditorium

balconies and galleries, connected physically by stairs and visually by open views.

Yet more significant was the rethinking of the auditorium. The early 20th century saw a growing number of attempts to re-imagine the actor/audience relationship without the perceived separation of the proscenium arch. The intensity of the discussions increased during the 1950s. Re-thinking the actor/audience relationship could be a thorny subject in

which individuals had often-conflicting views, as the protracted discussions which took place between 1964 and 1966 among members of the National Theatre's Building Committee reveal.[13]

Various arguments were advanced in support of change, including the potential to distinguish theatre from cinema and television by emphasising its three-dimensional, live nature. Such qualities were implicit in the kind of 'in-the-round' staging favoured by the director Stephen Joseph during the 1950s and 1960s, and they also informed the 'thrust' staging preferred by Tyrone Guthrie. Guthrie was inspired in part by his experience at the end of the 1920s of Terence Gray's Cambridge Festival Theatre, where the audience and actor inhabited a single space with no proscenium arch, the auditorium being connected to the stage by a flight of steps.[14]

There were nonetheless many who remained convinced of the value of the basic principles of the proscenium-arch stage.[15] One solution to the debate was to embrace flexibility, i.e., to create a space which could be rearranged to accommodate a number of different actor–audience relationships. Such spaces could seem to be especially modern, particularly if the changes were carried out by mechanical means (as they would have been in Walter Gropius' unbuilt but oft-cited *Totaltheater* project of 1928). Yet while flexible studios were from the 1960s onwards increasingly built on university campuses and as adjuncts to conventional theatres, flexibility at a larger scale has proved more difficult to achieve. As a result, 'formed' auditoria have remained more typical among larger theatres, perhaps with a degree of flexibility in the forestage area. The Derngate in Northampton (1983) is one of the few successful examples to attempt greater flexibility. Its design reprised the idea of movable galleried 'towers' previously explored by the theatre consultant, Theatre Projects, in a successful theatre at Christ's Hospital school (1974); the towers at Derngate were to be moved with air-cushion technology. The result is that the auditorium perimeter can be rearranged to allow theatre, music, arena events such as boxing, and banquets.

The way in which Derngate's galleries and walls are 'papered with people' locates its auditorium within a line of development that begins in the mid-1960s with the Forum at Billingham and continues in the 1970s with Eden Court Theatre in Inverness and the National Theatre's

Musiktheater im Revier (MiR), Gelsenkirchen, Germany, exterior

Cottesloe (Dorfman) auditorium. In 1984, speaking of the smaller but similar Wilde Theatre opened at Bracknell, the designer Francis Reid concluded that this kind of auditorium – by now dubbed the 'courtyard' – was 'the form that seems likely to characterise late twentieth-century theatre building',[16] and indeed examples continue to be constructed internationally. A key figure in the evolution of this type was Iain Mackintosh of Theatre Projects Consultants, a fan of the galleried theatres of the 18th and 19th centuries. At Eden Court and the Cottesloe, Mackintosh advocated a densely packed and tiered arrangement of the audience as a counterbalance to the single-tier straight rakes that had been common in the 1960s, Birmingham Rep included.

Mackintosh's work demonstrates the growing significance in British theatre design of the theatre consultant, a role which emerged in West

Belgrade Theatre, Coventry, exterior

Germany during the 1950s with largely technical responsibilities but which often in Britain also encompassed conceptual matters, especially where architects had little theatre experience. In Britain, Theatre Projects Consultants was founded in 1957. Around the same time, the historian Richard Southern was increasingly finding work as a consultant, his projects including Nottingham Playhouse and, in London, the Barbican Arts Centre. By the 1960s the profession was increasingly organised. For example, the Association of British Theatre Technicians was founded in 1961 as a British chapter of the International Association of Theatre Technicians (AITT). Its Theatre Architecture and Planning committee

Wolsey Theatre, Ipswich, exterior

Thorndike Theatre, Leatherhead, foyers

played a key role in reviewing design proposals to highlight potential functional problems.

How should we conclude this very brief account? One theme which emerges is the growing number of figures involved in conceiving and designing (and operating) theatres. The process often takes in those who may make decisions about funding, actors and directors whose ideas may inform the design itself, as well as architects, theatre consultants, engineers and, increasingly, project managers and 'cost consultants'. This proliferation of professional roles is not unique to theatre, but it does pose challenges for a type of building where subjective and intangible factors are often accorded as much significance as more measurable kinds of function. A second theme in post-1945 British theatre architecture is that of diversity – that a theatre might equally be a purpose-designed, multi-auditorium complex or an ad hoc conversion. Continuity, too, is important, whether that be understood in terms of the continuity of history in a 'found space', the preference of the Arts Council of Great Britain during the 1960s for traditional high-cultural practices, or the extent to which the tiered 'courtyard' auditorium revives something of the Elizabethan inn yard. The survival of the proscenium arch is also notable. Ultimately, however, our conclusion has to relate to the very architecture of theatre. Britain's modern theatres not only played (and continue to play) a significant role in accommodating and framing performances, but also reflect broader debates – about the actor/audience relationship, the design of the modern city, and the place of culture in contemporary society. By looking at the buildings designed for theatre we can therefore start better to understand modern architectural, urban, and social history.

Cottesloe Theatre, National Theatre, London, auditorium

Notes

1 Library of Birmingham, MS 978/1/6/1/1, 'The Birmingham Repertory Theatre: Its Present and Future', November 1960, p. 3.
2 For a full discussion, see Alistair Fair, *Modern Playhouses: An Architectural History of Britain's New Theatres, 1945–1985* (Oxford, 2018).
3 Arnold Aronson, 'Ideal Theatres: One Roof or Two?', in *Setting the Scene: Perspectives on Twentieth-Century Theatre Architecture*, ed. Alistair Fair (Farnham, 2015), pp. 179–199 (p. 180).
4 Elain Harwood, *Space Hope and Brutalism: English Architecture 1945–1975* (New Haven and London, 2015), p. 419.
5 'Repertory Theatre, Birmingham', *Architects' Journal* 154/51 (22 December 1971), pp. 1431–1437.
6 Philip Goad, 'Post-war and Polygonal: Special Plans for Australian Architecture, 1950–70', *Architectural Theory Review* 15/2 (2010), pp. 166–186.
7 E.g. Alistair Fair, '"A new image of the living theatre": the genesis and design of the Belgrade Theatre, Coventry', *Architectural History* 54 (2011), pp. 347–382.
8 Miles Glendinning, *Modern Architect: The Life and Times of Robert Matthew* (London, 2008), p. 91.
9 For West Germany, see Elain Harwood, 'Theatres in West Germany, 1945–70', in *Setting the Scene: Perspectives on Twentieth-Century Theatre Architecture*, ed. Alistair Fair (Farnham, 2015), pp. 103–132.
10 Ibid., p. 126.
11 Bristol, Richard Southern Archive, 79/1/8–0015/2, undated *Sunday Times* clipping of c. 1981.
12 Library of Birmingham, MS 2339/3/4/4, minutes of a City/Repertory/Arts Council subcommittee, 24 November 1960.
13 Daniel Rosenthal, *The National Theatre Story* (London, 2013), pp. 92–94; 107–109.
14 Iain Mackintosh, *Architecture, Actor and Audience* (London, 1993), pp. 48–50.
15 Fair, '"A new image"', pp. 369–372.
16 Francis Reid, 'Theatre of Change', *Architects' Journal* 179 (6 June 1984), pp. 24–27.

Front of House Moves to the Forefront

Robert Shook

Many of the iconic theatre buildings that serve as architectural benchmarks are grand, imposing structures that are cultural epicenters in their communities. Palais Garnier, Royal Opera House Covent Garden, Vienna Staatsoper, and Carnegie Hall are all examples of high- minded architecture in the service of artistic performance.

Such institutions historically provided spectacular spaces to welcome the public, but at no small expense, and rarely open to the public for any reason, and at any other time, than immediately before and during a performance. Perhaps because of this, and perhaps because adequate funding has more recently become less available, many theatres built in the last century have provided a minimal amount of audience space; nowhere was this more true than in West End and Broadway commercial theatres.

Throughout most of the 20th century, theatre builders rarely regarded the audience lobby much above a sort of support space for patrons to stretch their legs during intermissions. All pertinent lobby planning revolved around intermission occupancy, attempting to provide barely sufficient floor space for standing and socializing plus circulation to and from restrooms and food and beverage stands. Only rarely did these lobbies survive the planning process to truly be of adequate size. Theatre planning experts frequently and dutifully manned the barricades during

value management exercises in often vain attempts to protect the lobby from the ravages of inadequate budgets. We were told, "Look at Broadway theatres, they have almost no lobby space at all," and "The audience doesn't decide which theatre to attend based on lobby size." So we frequently built modest lobbies, and those spaces continued to be unlit and unoccupied for most of the day, providing no clues to the passers-by as to the potential excitement beyond.

In the 21st century, however, theatre lobbies have come to occupy a new place of importance in the planning of a performing arts building (and frequently in their community). The industry has awoken to the possibilities – indeed, the joys! – of the lobby-as-attractor, as well as lobby-as-profit-center. This new way of viewing all aspects of the front of house parallels a radical change in audience attendance trends.

The old model of audience attendance was based on the public considering a theatre as a destination. Plans were made days or weeks in advance – actually, *months* in advance for subscribers – and the paying guests showed up at the theatre's doorstep shortly before the opening curtain, coming from a restaurant meal that was also considered and booked in advance. Coats were checked, auditorium entry doors located, and the audience was seated for performance with barely any acknowledgement of the transitional chamber through which they had just passed.

Garnier Opera, Paris, Grand Staircase

The new attendance model involves much less advance planning. Modern audiences have so many quality entertainment options, literally at their fingertips, that little thought is given to anything beyond, "What shall we do tonight?". These short planning horizons demand options that fulfill a wide gamut of needs: parking, eating, socializing, participating, and more socializing. This is not an evening built around a specific event. In fact, where a theatre performance is part of the evening, the theatre experience can often be the most restrictive – no phones, no texting, no talking, and please stay put – and for many the least attractive.

This new model suggests that many phases of a night's entertainment be captured within a single building. A theatre lobby might now include lounge and gathering space, event space, bar, coffee shop, fast food (i.e., grab-and-go), and potentially several types of retail – general, theatrical, and show-related. Some or all of these enterprises might be tenants leasing space from the theatre operator, and some might be operator owned.

The lobby of the Boston Opera House

In either case, all of this related activity need not restrict its operating hours to nights of performance only. The theatres will certainly benefit from these various enterprises being open all day, particularly in locations with healthy foot traffic during the day.

The American sociologist Ray Oldenburg has for decades chronicled the modern human desire for a Third Place. In *The Great Good Place*, he writes,

. . . daily life, in order to be relaxed and fulfilling, must find its balance in three realms of experience. One is domestic, a second is gainful or productive, and the third is inclusively sociable, offering both the basis of community and the celebration of it.

Historic examples of Third Places include the UK's pubs and France's cafes. More recently in the US and Australia, coffee shops are now successfully catering to this need. The attributes that Oldenburg assigns to the Third Place include:

- On neutral ground
- Inclusive
- Supportive of conversation
- Accessible and accommodating
- Playful
- A home away from home

One need only look at some existing examples to realize how theatre lobbies can be successful Third Places when they are open all day. Both the Royal National Theatre and the Southbank Centre in London, attract a lively and sizeable crowd at all hours of the day and night.

Not only do theatres realize some profits from their retail operations, but more importantly the very existence of these semi-related retail activities goes a long way toward removing barricades that often restrict the first timer from entering into an artistic endeavor. Both the

The ground floor bar at the Royal Festival Hall, the Southbank, London

Royal National Theatre, London, foyers

National and the Southbank Centre are readily permeable, inviting visitors in without a thought toward crossing a threshold toward a higher level. With less reliance on the old subscription model, performing arts institutions must become more reliant on attracting passers-by and on word-of-mouth and social media connections. Super-fast internet connections, lots of power points, a variety of lounging and grouping spaces, access to coffee and snacks, and a supportive, informal atmosphere all have great potential for keeping theatre lobbies animated throughout the day. And when more guests are visiting the lobby, more event tickets are sold.

Having said that, the operation of selling of admission to events is transitioning as well. Though the term "ticket" may remain in use for the foreseeable future, the actual piece of card stock is quickly disappearing. Guests are more likely to obtain admission via an app and carry the evidence on a personal electronic device, or print it out at home. We no longer need elaborate facilities for vending tickets as part of our front of house facilities, and once we acknowledge the lack of need for a box office, we can begin to re-think the visitor experience completely.

Theatres are now moving toward a concierge style system, which might typically involve a Guest Services counter, where patrons can purchase admission, check parcels, and procure assistive listening devices and child booster seats, all at a single location.

At Hamer Hall in Melbourne, Australia, each of the main lobby levels includes a long counter with changeable signage indicating which portion of the counter is in use for which activity on different days, and at different parts of the day. During non-performance times, portions of these counters might be used for selling coffee and snacks as well as disseminating information and admissions for future performances. Prior to a performance, a large portion of the counter is dedicated to Guest Services, with the balance remaining as coffee shop, food, and bar. During an intermission, the entire counter length becomes bar and snacks, and the counters are long enough to accommodate a sufficient number of bartenders to ensure short queues, which translates into more sales. The flexibility afforded by this "long counter" concept is also useful for supporting future operations as well; we can't pretend to know what kinds of activities might need support 30 years from now, but the long, open counters should be able to adapt without requiring major re-construction.

The planning and design of the front of house spaces are critical to their success, and there are several aspects of the planning to be considered:

Transparency and Permeability. The primary lobby space should be inviting and conducive to anticipation. It should be tall and open and transparent to the exterior. The walls should be brightly lit to make the lobby a welcoming beacon from without. Primary public entries should be clearly obvious and thoughtfully located. For many theatre buildings, completely separate entries are required from pedestrian/drop-off and from adjacent parking and/or mass transportation.

Size and Scalability. For lobbies with multiple levels, upper floors with view-out and view-down opportunities will help enliven and unify the audience. The majority of the lobby space should be open and unobstructed so as to more easily accommodate special events such as banquets and exhibitions. At the same time, it can often be helpful to provide opportunities for smaller areas to be temporarily cordoned off to accommodate groups who may be attending a performance and desire their own gathering space before, during, and after the show.

Flexibility and Support. Patrons appreciate generous amounts of seating along with drink tables, all of which should be transportable to allow event set-ups with banquet tables and the like (and requiring adequate storage space as well). Lobbies that will accommodate special events should include well-integrated technical infrastructures to allow rapid and efficient deployment of theatrical lighting and audio systems, including a flexible arrangement of "strong points" in the ceiling to allow theatrical equipment, banners, and the like to be temporarily suspended. Catering support facilities in close proximity are also extremely important, even if they are no more than a room with running water and lots of power points.

Hamer Hall, Melbourne, long counter

Way-finding. Architectural graphics for way-finding are generally required but often result in a high degree of visual clutter. A well-designed lobby will instinctively guide patrons to the critical destinations with a minimum of signage required.

Public Restrooms. One consistent – and well-founded – complaint of older theatre buildings is the lack of sufficient restroom facilities, particularly for women. Almost all theatre buildings designed prior to 1980 installed only the quantity of toilet fixtures minimally required by local building codes. However, building codes have never taken into account the special circumstances of live theatre, where restroom use is concentrated in intermissions of 15 minutes duration, or less. Theatres with code-minimum toilet provisions invariably find themselves with very long lines – particularly for the women's restrooms. Long lines at the restrooms result in (a) frustrated patrons, and (b) decreased food and beverage sales. Most professional theatre consultants apply specific time-tested formulas to determine the quantity of toilets required to keep the intermissions lines as short as possible.

Interior view of elevated restaurant in spectacular new Tokyo National Art Center in Tokyo, 2007

Many of the above planning issues specifically relate to uses of the lobby space for events other than pre-performance and intermission. Most theatres can realize the full potential of their front of house spaces by making their lobbies available for banquets, receptions, exhibitions, and even small-scale performances. In order to make this arrangement work well, it is sometimes necessary to build more area and support it with more staff than would be required otherwise, but in most cases these additional costs can be more than offset by the many inherent advantages. In addition to the generated income, and perhaps more importantly, the open-all-day lobby, combined with special event uses, serves to support one of the key missions of most theatres: audience development. They attract potential patrons who might not otherwise have ever entered the front door. If theatre buildings are to retain their status as the cultural epicentres of their communities, they must do more than present formal performances within a restrictive calendar. The public must come to view the theatres as places where exciting and enriching things happen at any time, without advertisement, and with the potential to exceed expectations.

Concert Halls, Music, and Audiences

Christopher Blair

The earliest music was played outdoors against the competing noises of nature and village. When music moved indoors it was not into purpose-designed rooms but into the dining rooms, banquet spaces, and larger rooms in homes, court buildings, etc. These were designed for other uses and music adapted to these found spaces.

For much of music history, up until the early 20th century, the available spaces strongly shaped the work of composers and performers. Basic conceptions of dissonance and harmony were influenced by whether music was to be performed outdoors or in enclosed spaces. The nature and size of the space would have an impact on compositional choices. Various styles of music were generally presented in the type of spaces for which they were intended. Indeed, music was composed and performed to suit the spaces in which it was to be presented: churches, ballrooms and banquet halls – all typically rectangular, high ceilinged rooms, the original shoebox shape. This natural match of concert music to appropriate acoustics began to be challenged with growing popularity requiring ever larger rooms, and the advent of faster and more convenient transportation opportunities, both for performers and audiences.

Historical Underpinnings – Shoeboxes, Theatres, and Growing Audiences

The "shoebox" as a form derives from 18th- and early 19th-century aristocratic ballrooms and spaces similar to London's famed Hanover Square Rooms, where much of early orchestral repertoire was first performed and achieved popularity with the public (The Hanover Square Rooms or the Queen's Concert Rooms were assembly rooms established, principally for musical performances, on the corner of Hanover Square, London, by Sir John Gallini in partnership with Johann Christian Bach and Carl Friedrich Abel in 1774. For a century this was the principal concert venue in London. The premises were demolished in 1900). Their typical characteristics were long rooms with flat floors, 7 to 12 m tall, with parallel side walls of comparatively narrow separation to accommodate the wood truss limitations of the day. This configuration provides plenty of impact, envelopment, and pleasing reverberation and blend of ensemble

Haydnsaal, Castle Esterhazy, Eisenstadt, Austria

components throughout the room. Much of the music we appreciate from the Classical and Early Romantic periods was created with this acoustic in mind.

Nevertheless, commercial popularity often outstripped the audience capacity of rooms of this form, particularly outside of the major cities in Central Europe. Theatres, with their closely spaced vertical stacking of audiences close to the stage, responded to the resultant economic opportunities from concert promoters. With this arrangement came visual intimacy and increased acoustical clarity, but usually at the sacrifice of reverberance and envelopment.

Acoustical design of concert spaces led by specialists began with Wallace Clement Sabine's work on Boston's Symphony Hall, which opened in 1900. The original concept by the architectural firm of McKim, Mead, and White called for an amphitheater geometry,

A concert by the Philharmonic Society at the Hanover Square Concert Rooms, London

ultimately abandoned upon Sabine's advice in favor of the traditional "shoebox" approach, modeled upon the highly regarded 1500-seat Neue Gewandhaus in Leipzig, built in 1884, and Boston's old (and drafty) Music Hall.

Unlike elsewhere in the world where orchestras enjoyed state patronage and could successfully appear in rooms of under 1600 seats, Boston Symphony Orchestra's deficits were underwritten by the pocketbook of a single person, Henry Lee Higginson. Consequently, audience capacity and potential income was a major consideration in the final design which, like the earlier Carnegie Hall in New York City, contains approximately 2700 seats. While not a critical success with Boston audiences in its first few years, the room has come to be regarded as among the best in the world for orchestral sound. However, this "ideal" capacity target of 2700 was to have unfortunate ramifications in the future, as we shall see.

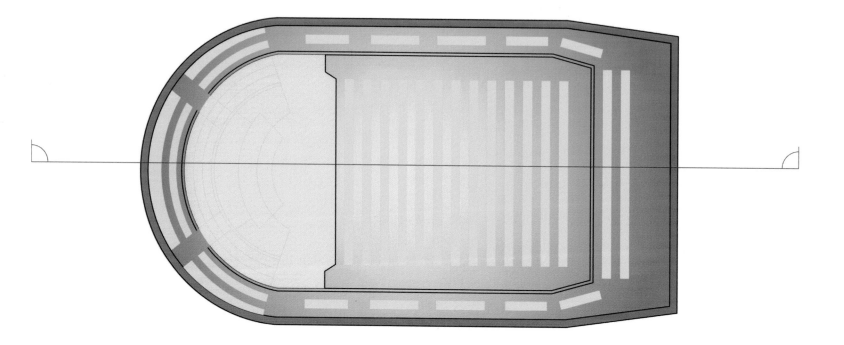

Generic plan of a Shoebox concert hall

1:500

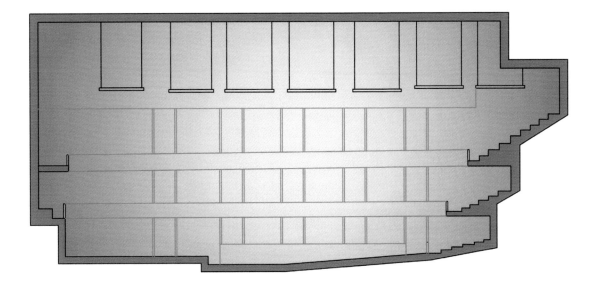

Generic section of a Shoebox concert hall

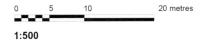

1:500

Shoebox vs. Vineyard

The modern era of acoustical design could be said to be ushered in through one spectacular failure and one surprising success from the early 1960s: Lincoln Center's Philharmonic Hall, which opened in 1962, and Berlin's Philharmonie, which opened in the following year.

One of the most thorough examinations of concert hall acoustics ever performed, and first documented in Leo Beranek's *Music, Acoustics, and Architecture* (1962), provided the underpinning of the design for Philharmonic Hall. Architectural details and acoustic measurements were collected from 53 well-known concert halls and correlated with interviews with prominent musicians and music critics to create a ranking system for these existing halls and a numerical template to predict the ranking of future designs.

As Boston Symphony Hall was always mentioned as being among the top three most admired halls for orchestral music in this study, the design concept of the new Philharmonic Hall was to follow that venerable shoebox example, with two important deviations: to accommodate 1960s standards of audience comfort and safety within similar seating area, the audience capacity was to be reduced to 2400 seats, and an

Auditorium and platform of Symphony Hall, Boston, home of the Boston Symphony Orchestra

adjustable acoustical canopy system, similar in concept to that successfully employed in the Tanglewood Music Shed, was to be provided for fine tuning.

And it probably would have worked, except for politics, poor communication, and mistakes during construction.

While the Lincoln Center project was moving forward, plans were underway to demolish Carnegie Hall. When it was learned that the new home of the New York Philharmonic was to have 300 fewer seats than Carnegie, claims of artistic elitism were put forward in the press. Leading the charge, the *New York Herald Tribune* began a campaign to increase the seating capacity of the new hall and late in the design stage it was reshaped and expanded to accommodate the critics' desires, invalidating much of the room's previous acoustical design. The acoustical consultants at Bolt, Beranek, and Newman were not informed of these basic design alterations made by the architect until it was too late to comment or suggest corrections.

Auditorium of Philharmonic Hall at Lincoln Center for the Performing Arts in New York City on opening night, 23 September 1962

Auditorium and platform of Philharmonie Berlin

Compounding these fatal decisions was the canopy installation. This element was to be adjustable in height, however, the contractor decided it would be best to weld a section of it into a fixed position, eliminating the possibility of fine tuning during listening sessions with the orchestra.

The opening was not a success. Many attempts at correction were made over the following two seasons. A major renovation, considered by many at the time to be acoustically successful, was completed in 1969, but by this time the hall had acquired a dubious acoustical reputation, the admired Carnegie Hall was saved, and visiting international orchestras chose to go there, bypassing Lincoln Center. Another major renovation under a new name, Avery Fisher Hall, led by Columbia University professor, Cyril Harris, was completed in 1976. A design by Russell Johnson's Artec Consultants to address onstage hearing issues in the orchestra was installed in the 1990s, and, as this chapter is being written in 2020, another major intervention is being planned to what is now called David Geffen Hall.

Exterior of Philharmonie Berlin

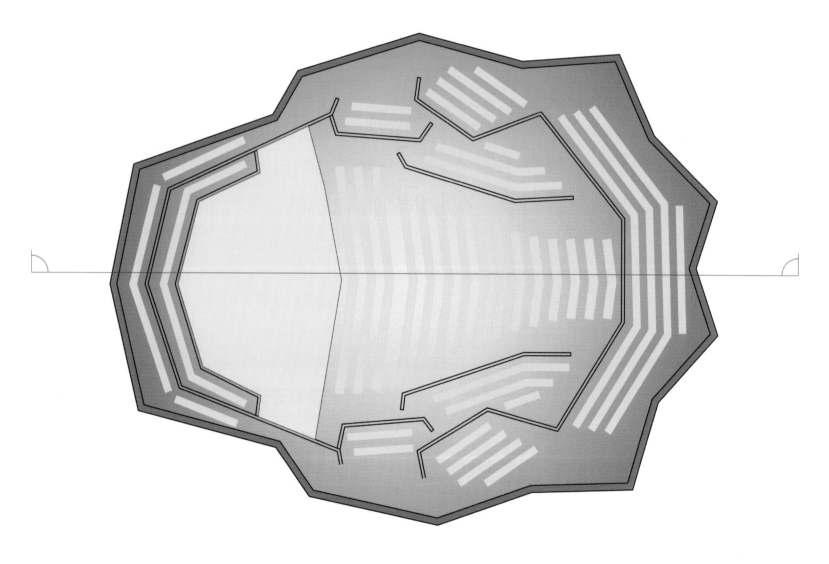

Generic plan of a vineyard concert hall

0   5   10   20 metres

1:500

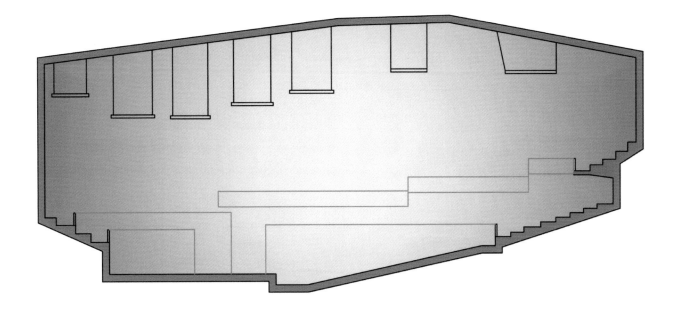

Generic section of a vineyard concert hall

1:500

The contrasts to the opening of the Philharmonie Berlin the following year could not be more vivid. First, the tried and (sometimes) true acoustic model of the shoebox was completely discarded by the architect Hans Scharoun and his acoustical consultant Lothar Cremer, in favour of an approach that wrapped the audience of 2400 completely around the orchestra platform in vineyard-like terraces. While not all seats in Berlin can claim equal acoustical merit, the visual proximity to the performer and the immediacy and clarity of musical detail provide an exciting experience. Because of the unique architectural approach and the acoustic importance of the terrace wall surfaces in providing early lateral reflections to the audience, an arms-length collaboration between acoustician and architect, exhibited in the previous example, was never an option.

This notion of pushing the orchestra platform from its traditional "sending end" location out into the room and surrounding it at sides and back with a significant percentage of audience seating fired the imaginations of orchestras, architects, clients, and acousticians over succeeding decades. It also created some rather wide room configurations, requiring geometric insertions of shaped surfaces to provide early reflection support to the centre of the audience seating; reflections that would usually arrive as a matter of course in traditional shoebox forms. These insertions pose an "enormously complicated geometrical challenge to acousticians to ensure an even distribution of reflected sound energy" and might take the form of parapet walls, as seen in Yasuhisa Toyota's Disney Hall in Los Angeles, aggressive shaping of the seating pod fascia at Ted Schultz's Roy Thomson Hall in Toronto, or the steeply angled diffusive "wings" of Harold Marshall's Christchurch Town Hall.

Because of the effort required to provide an even distribution of sound energy across the seating planes, this author sometimes refers to these as "directed energy" rooms, where a certain number of early reflections to each seating zone are sought. The result, when successful, is often a room that provides a great deal of impact and clarity, but which may be deficient in the blending of orchestral sections and in the related strength and duration of reverberant decay. Less successful experiments in this format have resulted in wide swings in the acoustical condition, even from one seat to the next.

Acoustic Design: From Numbers Driven to Listening Driven

Competing forces in the design of concert halls include client stipulations for seat count and acousticians' design focus on achieving "appropriate" numerical values of reverberation time, clarity, etc. Up until the late 1980s, particularly in the United States, with its limited governmental financial support for ensembles and venues, we see a steady increase in the number of seats provided in new concert venues, with the average approaching 2600 seats.

To provide the "ideal" mid-frequency reverberation time of approximately 2.0 seconds in these high capacity rooms, acousticians recommended ever larger cubic volumes. While reverberation durations were achieved, what was forgotten in the process was the strength of that reverberation. Larger volumes generally mean less sonic intensity per unit of time. In rooms like Davies Hall in San Francisco and Roy Thomson Hall in Toronto the reverberant loudness was weak, and disassociated from the direct ensemble sound, increasing clarity but negatively affecting the blend of the various orchestral sections. In both halls, major interventions have recently been implemented to reduce the cubic volume high in the room to increase the strength of reverberation.

Another example of data-driven design involves early energy and its relationship to clarity. While clarity metrics that parse energy in time were developed in the 1950s, Beranek's identification of the early time delay gap's (time between direct sound and the first reflection) relationship to "intimacy" sparked a generation of halls where this early energy idea became an important driver of hall design, and the more early energy the better. Lost in this discussion was the issue of temporal masking, where high early reflection levels can cover later important information. The problem is most clearly demonstrated in concert shells with low ceilings. The sound onstage becomes very loud, making it harder to hear distant players across the platform, and the ability to hear the hall's late response (carrying information on ensemble timbre, intonation, and balance) becomes impossible.

Auditorium, platform, and pipe organ in the Disney Concert Hall, Los Angeles, California

Both these deficiencies can be tied back to the origin of the measurement metrics themselves, based more upon what parameters are easy to measure rather than any relationship to how we hear and process sound. In the 1990s acousticians and musicians realized that psychoacoustics was an important informer of hall design. And the implementation of these concepts largely came from acousticians who began to rely more upon their ears, informed by historical precedence, than their measurement devices.

Suddenly, what was considered a simple matter of achieving an array of arcane measurement results (in empty rooms, no less) became much more complicated.

The concept of auralization, the process of presenting synthesized sound to replicate the reflections in as yet unbuilt rooms, became an important, if still imperfect, design (and client marketing) tool.

Audience Size: From Bigger to Smaller

Beginning in the late 1980s, particularly in the USA, came an abrupt move toward smaller concert halls of 2000 seats or fewer. This change was driven not only through a declining

Auditorium and platform of the Elbphilharmonie, Hamburg

audience base for concert music, but also factors such as space consuming accommodations for the disabled, and the realization of orchestras, theatre consultants, and acousticians that a more impactful audience experience was needed to compete with other art forms, not to mention the steadily improving quality of home audio systems.

As rooms become smaller, the arrival of reinforcing energy becomes earlier and more densely packed, increasing loudness and aural impact.

By the mid-1990s acoustician Russell Johnson postulated that the future of concert music lay in development of concert halls of about 1500 seats.

Many still conceive a concert hall as a fixed space tailored only to the presentation of "classical music". The reality today is concert halls must present every type of music – jazz, world, and frequently amplified music. New concert halls need acoustic and physical flexibility.

Acoustic Flexibility: The Challenge of the "Hard Cap"

If one examines the most successful examples of traditional shoebox halls, certain commonalities become apparent. Except for the rear of the hall, all the audience is contained in the lower half of the room. There are side tiers that bounce early lateral energy back to the listeners on the floor for clarity and envelopment. The upper side walls are largely vertical and parallel, creating a "Hard Cap" reservoir for slow decaying sound energy, resulting in an even listening environment in the seating below and a pleasant blending of orchestral sections. It is a terrific environment for unamplified orchestras and instrumentalists but a potential disaster for amplified events.

In vineyard-style halls, some examples such as Suntory Hall in Tokyo, Japan and the recently completed Sala Minas Gerais in Belo Horizonte, Brazil retain the basic concept of an upper wall hard cap, resulting in a more spatially uniform and blended response than in other examples. The hard-cap effect is functionally eliminated by adding down kicking reflective elements and/or absorptive seating areas high in the room to enhance visual intimacy. Examples of this acoustical approach include Copenhagen's Koncerthuset and the new Elbphilharmonie in Hamburg.

In both basic hall forms acoustic adjustability is commonly implemented through the addition of absorptive surfaces or, more rarely, by manipulating the cubic volume of the hall, or some combination of both approaches. Successful rooms that utilize volume manipulation to adjust acoustic response include Sala São Paulo, the Meyerson Symphony Center in Dallas, Texas, Switzerland's Lucerne Culture and Congress Center, and the multipurpose Teatro Bicentenario in León, Mexico, among others.

Physical Flexibility: The Power of the Social Experience

Today there are two main models for the planning and design of new concert halls.

The traditional shoebox hall has evolved and provides a more predictable acoustic for a full range of music genres and physical flexibility for other types of activity.

The newer vineyard form provides a more dynamic visual experience that appeals to architects and many clients. The nature of a vineyard hall places a significant number of audience either behind or at the side of the platform, giving audiences a different acoustic experience and some complain of a lack of acoustic envelopment. As performances incorporate more projection and technology the vineyard struggles to cope with more directional performances.

People talk of a hybrid form of room incorporating the best aspects of both. Time will tell.

The Modern Opera House

Nicholas Payne

The juxtaposition of the words 'modern' and 'opera house' is an oxymoron.

The earliest public opera house, opened in Venice in 1637, was built with multiple levels of seating in a roughly horseshoe shape, with space for an orchestra between the stage and the audience, and a proscenium arch framing the action on stage. The best part of 400 years later, most modern opera houses adopt the same template. Was the little Teatro Tron in the parish of San Cassiano so perfect that it cannot be improved; only expanded in scale? Unfortunately, there is no extant image of Teatro San Cassiano.

It took almost 240 years before the composer Richard Wagner banished the visible orchestra to his hidden, sunken pit at Bayreuth, and raised the proscenium so high that it is scarcely discernible in the darkened auditorium. Yet his architectural revolution has not been copied elsewhere. Was it really so unsuccessful; or have others lacked Wagner's courage?

During the last 50 years, some of the greatest architects have designed opera houses which have iconic exteriors but traditional interiors. It is as if their invention meets a brick wall when confronted with the demands of musicians for acoustic perfection. Is this physical barrier a paradigm for opera's failure to re-invent itself, for its ultimate irrelevance in today's society?

Opera is no more and no less than theatre. Or rather, it is theatre plus, the added ingredient being music. The composer is the dramatist, and, like a playwright, seeks to engage with an audience drawn from contemporary society. A public theatre or opera house is designed with that in mind. Let us examine the examples which have changed history: the ancient theatre of Epidavros; Shakespeare's Globe; the Festspielhaus in Bayreuth; the Stratford Festival Theatre in Ontario; Peter Brook's Empty Space.

Epidavros is enormous, capable of holding up to 14,000 spectators. It was designed by Polykleitos the Younger for occasional use, for short festivals which would envelop the whole populace in a cathartic experience. It was the Glastonbury Festival of the ancient world. Its triumph is that its acoustic and sightlines enable a large audience to be involved in the action. Its fan-shaped, steeply raked amphitheatre has been the model for the auditoria at Bayreuth and the Olivier at London's National Theatre.

In contrast to the court or inner city theatres where many of Shakespeare's plays were first performed, the Globe was built south of the river to produce 'rough' popular theatre. Its semi-circular galleries enclosed a pit area where poorer people might stand in close proximity to the performers. The open stage literally 'thrust' the action into the laps of the audience.

Wagner sought to re-imagine the ancient Greek experience as a total work of art or *Gesamtkunstwerk* and place of pilgrimage for modern times. His tetralogy *The Ring of the Nibelung* was composed on the model of Aeschylus's linked tragedies. The Bayreuth design, which houses 1,700 people, was replicated on a smaller scale at the Prinzregententheater in Munich at the beginning of the 20'th century.

Richard Wagner Festspielhaus, Bayreuth, Germany, musicians in the orchestra pit

The Festival Theatre in Canada's Stratford was designed in the 1950s by Tanya Moiseiwitsch to a brief by the director Tyrone Guthrie. It combined elements of Greek amphitheatre and Shakespearean thrust stage, and resembled a huge tent able to accommodate 1,800 spectators, all within 65 feet of the stage, and has been a model for other theatres in America and Britain, notably the Chichester Festival and Sheffield Crucible.

Each of these examples was designed to bring the actor into close contact with the audience, to strengthen the bond of communication. Peter Brook's concept in his book *The Empty Space* takes the idea a step further. It explores four aspects of theatre: Deadly, Holy, Rough and Immediate. Brook abjures a theatre building and declares: 'I can take any empty space and call it a bare stage. A man walks across this empty space whilst someone else is watching him, and this is all that is needed for an act of theatre to be engaged.'

By contrast, much that happens within an opera house appears to erect barriers to engagement. The most visible is the orchestra pit, which has grown in size to accommodate the extravagant demands of composers and the health-and-safety requirements of musicians. Beyond the proscenium, increasingly complex technical effects have necessitated expensive machinery and multi-level excavation below stage and ugly fly-towers above it. Tiered auditoria, distant balconies and restricted-view positions have exacerbated class divisions among an audience whom it was intended to bring together for a common experience. What are the architects and perpetrators of modern opera houses doing, at least to mitigate these divisions, at best to resolve them?

The most famous opera house of the 20th century is the Sydney Opera House. Finally inaugurated in 1973 after protracted struggles which led to the resignation of the Danish architect Jørn Utzon and the switch of halls for opera and concerts, its interiors must be judged a failure from both acoustic and spatial perspectives, though recent work has done something to improve them. Yet, the exterior design remains a miracle. Its huge shells or sails overlooking the harbour have become the symbol of the city and of Australia itself. Near the end of the 23-hour flight from London, I remember being elated when the pilot announced: 'Welcome to Australia and to the Sydney Opera House'. The Opera House represents the aspirations of the country. Sydney stands as the image for opera in the world. There can be no higher accolade.

When President Mitterrand opened the Opéra Bastille in 1989, prematurely, but the anniversary of the storming of the Bastille in 1789 was unmissable, it was designated as an 'opera of the people' in contrast to the ornate grandeur of the Palais Garnier. Accordingly, its main auditorium held 2,745 people, an unprecedentedly large number for a European opera house. Carlos Ott's design is imposing as befits its site, but the

Stratford Festival Theatre, Ontario, Canada

distance of many of the spectators from the stage discourages intimacy. Perhaps the most interesting element of the project, the *salle modulable,* inspired by the composer Pierre Boulez's concept of a flexible space to encourage new forms of opera, remained unrealised at the time. The idea has been revived 30 years later and is destined for completion in 2023 with space for 800 spectators.

The 21st century has already seen significant investment in new buildings for opera, belying the accusation that it is a dying art. Scandinavia has been at the forefront, with Copenhagen opening in 2005 and Oslo in 2008. The former was the initiative of nonagenarian shipping magnate Maersk McKinney Møller, who insisted on hands-on supervision of architect Henning Larsen's design, in order to ensure its practicality and durability. The Norwegians applied a more democratic process

in seeking consensus support for Snøhetta's design, which emphasises public ownership with a sloping roof that enables people to walk over it, and a location on the harbour area which it has helped to regenerate.

Spain has experienced a renaissance in opera appreciation during the past quarter-century. The pioneer was Teatro de la Maestranza, seating 1,800, which was conceived for Seville's hosting of Expo 1992, designed by Aurelio del Pozo and Luis Marín. In the late 1990s, both Barcelona's Liceu and Madrid's Teatro Real were extensively renovated and modernised, the former after a fire, the latter after lying dormant for fifty years. But the most dazzling building is Valencia's Palau de les Arts, which opened in 2005 as part of the huge City of Arts and Sciences dug out of the diverted Turia riverbed. The main auditorium seats 1,800 but together three performance spaces can accommodate 4,000

Sydney Opera House

simultaneously. This masterpiece of Valencia-born architect Santiago Calatrava has transformed the city with a bold vision reminiscent of Sydney.

The impact which an opera house may deliver in terms of international attraction has been recognised in hitherto untilled lands. Sultan Qaboos of Oman commissioned the spacious Royal Opera House Muscat in a mixture of Islamic and Italian influences with a magnificent German pipe organ, which opened in 2011. Two years later came the similarly hybrid Astana Opera House, initiated by President Nursultan Nazarbayev in his designated capital of Kazakhstan. Both buildings boast superb technical facilities, welcome foreign as well as native artists, and fly the flag for their emerging economies.

Despite its proud imperial and soviet history, Russia has been busy creating new facilities. Conductor Valery Gergiev has added to the historic Mariinsky Theatre an acoustically superb Theatre Concert Hall in 2007 and its Second Stage, designed by Canadian architects Diamond Schmitt and seating 2,000, which opened in 2013. In Moscow, both Bolshoi Theatre and Stanislavsky Music Theatre have been rebuilt. The latest addition is Dmitry Bertman's new Helikon Opera on Bolshaya

Nikitskaya, a wholly individual and intimate theatre seating 250 within a former 18th-century nobleman's house, which was inaugurated in 2015.

The evidence of this survey, which excludes examples such as Dallas in America and multiple new buildings in China, is that the appetite for opera is by no means dead. On the contrary, governments and philanthropists are willing to invest substantial sums to ensure its legacy. But the modern opera house is a hybrid beast. It is a secular cathedral, whose spires and domes dominate the landscape, but within the body of the church it performs familiar rituals. Few want it to abandon the true faith or repudiate the masterpieces of its heritage. Yet, there is a yearning to harness technological invention and to reach out to unconverted audiences.

Can that be achieved? How might a building contribute to the educative process? Is a building even necessary? Is an empty 'found' space enough? Graham Vick was inspired by ancient Greece to create an inclusive Birmingham Opera Company, which is deliberately homeless and performs in warehouses, clubs, tents and station concourses.

An opera house building has two primary functions. It provides an acoustic. Not for nothing is hiring an acoustician nowadays regarded

Palau de les Arts Reina Sofía, Valencia, Spain, exterior

as equally important to engaging an architect. This presupposes that opera involves the natural transmission of unamplified sound, as it has in the past. On the other hand, contemporary composers are increasingly using sophisticated means to doctor sound. Performing in large arenas in the open air demands amplification but compromises sound quality. How long before that problem is solved? Likewise, opera has traditionally involved most of the performers inhabiting the same room to homogenise the ensemble. What if it became possible to remove the orchestra to another space without affecting quality? That would abolish the Grand Union Canal between performer and audience!

Such a solution might even benefit the second function, which is the union of performer and spectator in a mutual exchange in a common space. If that was the aim of giants like Aeschylus and Shakespeare and Wagner, of Tyrone Guthrie and Peter Brook, should we not be striving to exploit every modern means at our disposal towards the same end?

During this first quarter of the 21st century we have been tinkering with available technology, rather than inventing the breakthrough discoveries. Projecting video presents another option to painted flats, but it neither saves money nor transforms visual perception. Surtitles have much improved since their introduction in 1983 and have become a convenient crutch for those too busy to read the text in advance, or a substitute for the largely discarded practice of performing opera in the language of the audience, as you would expect in a play. Sound engineers are able to mix the balance of what you hear in the theatre. Live relays, or on-demand catch-ups, can bring close-up performances to a cinema near you or the convenience of your computer at home. Undoubtedly, these devices are to be welcomed as benefits to accessibility, but they do not transform the essential experience.

That is the challenge to the next wave of architects and builders. Utzon, Calatrava, Snøhetta, Piano have designed dazzling cathedrals which have the power to inspire the imagination of a wider constituency than merely opera-goers. Now we look to those who will animate the interiors and create music drama in the empty void.

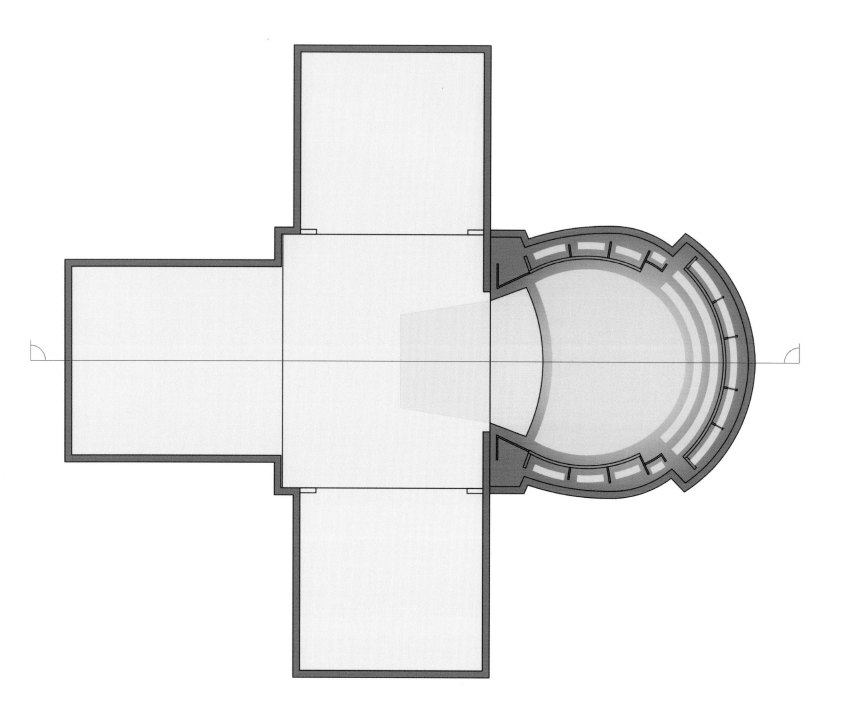

Plan of a "generic" opera house auditorium and stage

1:500

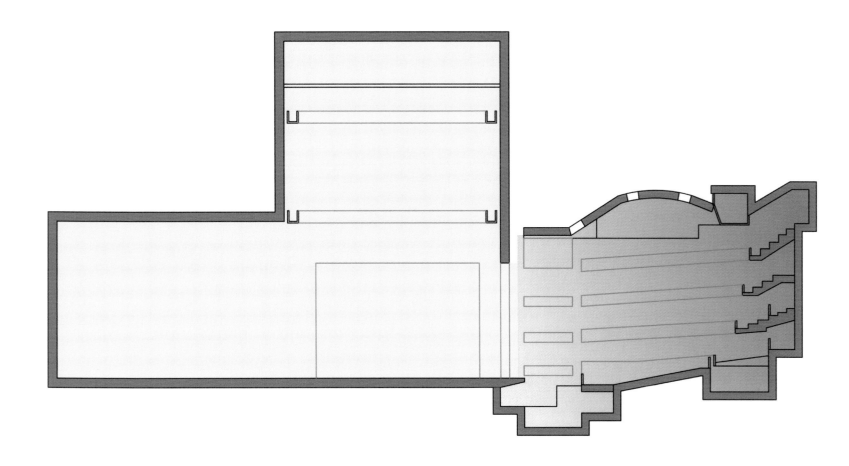

Section of a "generic" opera house auditorium and stage

0   5   10   20 metres

1:500

The Young Vic, designed by Bill Howell of HKPA, initiated the development of galleried single space theatres in the UK in 1970

Playhouses and Spaces for Drama

Tim Foster

Introduction

The purpose of this essay is to examine the development of a uniquely British phenomenon, the open stage drama theatre, a form which emerged in the decade from 1970 to 1980, has developed and flourished in the years since and has found its way to many other parts of the world. It is a typology firmly rooted in the British tradition and I will concentrate on the first ten years of its development in the UK.

The main characteristics of the type are:

- An open stage with actor and audience in the same room
- A modest size, usually in the 200–400 seat range
- Seating galleries on 3 or 4 sides and at 2 or more levels
- Flexibility of layout

Historical Origins

A brief historical detour is needed to understand the origin of this form. There are of course clear precedents in the historic English tradition, most notably the Shakespearean theatre, with its multi-faceted encircling galleries and the playhouses of the 18th century, which were also on multiple levels and were typically rectangular or semi-circular in plan. Whereas the Shakespearean stage is open-sided and located within the circular form of the galleries, the 18th-century theatre usually had a generous open forestage within the room, where the majority of the acting took place, and a proscenium stage behind, which was predominantly scenic. In both cases the actors were located in the same space as the audience, who surrounded them on three sides and in three dimensions. With a theatrical tradition which was more about text than spectacle, these forms provided a powerful sense of community and connection between the actor and the audience, as well as excellent acoustics because they were both in the same space and very close to one another.

In the 19th century the development of iron and steel structures, combined with the growing popularity of theatre as commercial entertainment, led to a gradual increase in the size of the auditorium and the stage, with the action increasingly retreating into the scenic world of the proscenium stage. The rapid growth of cinemas and cine-variety theatres in the first half of the 20th century further accelerated the move towards ever-larger spaces with a geometry that was dictated by sightlines to the proscenium or screen. Many

Garrick Theatre, London

of these theatres are still in use today and are often much loved and well suited to music and big shows that require larger seating capacities to be financially viable, but intimate they certainly are not. So it was against this background that in the second half of the 20th century a new generation of theatre practitioners sought to break out from the confines of the proscenium stage to engage more directly with the audience, leading to a rediscovery of earlier historic forms.

The Guthrie Thrust Stage

In the UK this was first manifested in the work of theatre director Tyrone Guthrie and his development of the thrust stage form. This first appeared in his production of *The Thrie Estaites* in 1948 at the second Edinburgh International Festival, which was staged in the General Assembly Hall of the Church of Scotland, a rectangular galleried hall, in which he constructed the first thrust stage. This was an open platform which projected into the centre of the space, was deeper than it was wide and was surrounded by audience on three sides. There was little scope for scenery and the audience was made more aware of itself as they viewed each other across the stage. This was a joyous rediscovery of the Shakespearean tradition where, in the words of Iain Mackintosh, "Every spectator participated in the ritual of high drama. The Assembly Hall became the focus of drama at the Edinburgh Festival for the next thirty years and theatre architecture was transformed."[1]

Having failed to persuade Stratford-upon-Avon to build a new theatre in this form, Guthrie was invited in 1952 to direct a festival season of Shakespeare in Stratford, Ontario in Canada, which led to the construction of the first purpose-built Guthrie theatre, first as a temporary tent structure in 1953 and then as a permanent building in 1956, which are dealt with in more detail in Gary McCluskie's essay elsewhere in this book. The Guthrie theatre form was widely adopted in North America, where significant thrust and arena stages (see Josh Dachs' essay) were built in the 1960s and 70s. It first found its way back to the UK in 1962 with the construction of the Chichester Festival Theatre. This was

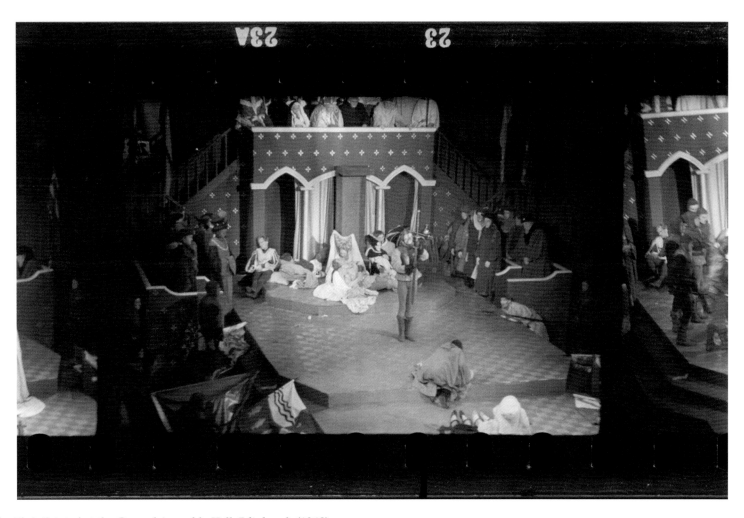

'The Thrie Estates' at the General Assembly Hall, Edinburgh (1948)

The Crucible Theatre, Sheffield (1971)

designed on a tight budget without the involvement of Guthrie or his designer Tanya Moiseiwitsch and its hexagonal stage failed to capture the essence of the Guthrie thrust, but was nevertheless important for reintroducing the idea of the single space auditorium for the first time in the post-war era. It would not be until 1971, shortly after Guthrie's death, that a true Guthrie theatre was completed in the UK at the Crucible Theatre in Sheffield.

However, the Guthrie thrust theatre, typically with well over 1,000 seats in a single tier, was of a scale which although well-suited to epic productions, particularly the plays of Shakespeare and his contemporaries, was too large for more intimate writing. It was out of this legacy that one of the most important small theatres of the mid-20th century was created at the Young Vic in London in 1970.

The Young Vic

The Young Vic was commissioned by the National Theatre when they were based at the Old Vic theatre and their new building on the South Bank was under construction. They required a second auditorium for new writing and work aimed at a young audience, but it was envisaged as a temporary building to last for

The Young Vic Theatre (1970)

only six years, until the new building was ready. The director, Frank Dunlop, had worked at the Edinburgh Festival and knew Guthrie. He has said that he asked his architect, Bill Howell of HKPA, "for a cross between the Elizabethan Fortune Theatre, Guthrie's Assembly Hall, and a circus".[2] The temporary nature of the building, the low budget and Howell's modernist background led to a building of remarkable simplicity and focus and a new kind of theatre space. The structure was an externally expressed steel frame, the walls were low cost concrete blocks, both inside and out, and the single gallery on four sides of the auditorium was in heavy bolted timber.

An existing Victorian butcher's shop on the site was retained and re-purposed to provide an entrance foyer. The 420-seat auditorium was square in plan, with chamfered corners, with a simple thrust stage surrounded by wooden benches on three sides. This was a rugged space of great simplicity, which stood in stark contrast to most of the other playhouses in London at the time, which were mostly highly decorated Victorian and Edwardian proscenium houses. Distressed and industrial finishes have now become part of the vernacular, but this was a 'rough' theatre, which was years ahead of its time and seminal in its importance. A single space with great focus and of a size which could be both intimate and epic. The 'temporary' building survived for 35 years in its original form before being remodelled and extended with great sensitivity by architects Haworth Tompkins in 2006.

The Cottesloe

The next highly significant small theatre was the Cottesloe, the smallest of the three theatres in the new National Theatre complex, designed by Denys Lasdun and completed in 1976. Originally the third auditorium had been abandoned for cost reasons, but a space had been preserved for it under the stage of the Olivier. When Peter Hall accepted the job as the first director of the new building, he did so on condition that the third auditorium would be completed. It was at this point that Iain Mackintosh of Theatre Projects Consultants was invited to propose a low-cost design which could be fitted within the vacant space. His solution was both simple and radical and heavily influenced by his knowledge of the theatres of the 18th century. This was the birth of the modern 'courtyard' theatre as we know it today. Three levels of shallow audience galleries were arranged on three sides of the room, while the central space remained flexible and could be reconfigured to create different seating layouts or as a flat floor. Elevators to facilitate these changes were not affordable but fortunately the National Theatre had the resources to make

regular changes of layout manually. It would be another 38 years before mechanisation arrived, when the theatre was refurbished by Haworth Tompkins and renamed the Dorfman in 2014.

The success of the Cottesloe lay in its flexibility and intimacy, which Iain Mackintosh described as "a framework for freedom".[3] What set it apart from a typical black box studio was its architectural character, determined by the fixed galleries. Whatever stage form is utilised in the central space the galleries provide a permanent container, the walls of which are 'papered with people'. To quote Michael Billington,

> A shrewd architectural decision was to combine classical principles with contemporary intimacy. The Cottesloe clearly has echoes of the Elizabethan courtyard and the rectangular Georgian auditorium of the Richmond Theatre, Yorkshire, but is wholly modern in its emphasis on the spectators' closeness to the action . . . the supreme virtue of the Cottesloe is that it locks you into the action in a way which the Victorian-age Royal Court doesn't .[4]

The Cottesloe had created a template for small-scale drama theatres for a generation.

The Royal Exchange, Manchester

In the same year that the National Theatre was completed in London (1976) another even more remarkable theatrical experiment opened at the Royal Exchange in Manchester. This was an in-the-round theatre module created within the enormous space of the Victorian Cotton Exchange, which is dealt with in more detail in Andy Hayles's essay (Chapter 5.05) in this book. While it sits outside the rectangular 'courtyard' typology, it was remarkable in its innovation. The form comprised two levels of galleries encircling a central flexible space and was the result of a collaboration between artistic director Michael Elliot, designer Richard Negri and the architects Levitt Bernstein. Michael Elliot had delivered an influential talk on BBC Radio in 1973 'On Not Building for Posterity', in which

The Cottesloe Theatre (1976)

The Royal Exchange Theatre, Manchester (1976)

he lamented how uninspiring the new steel and concrete theatres springing up around the country were and how quickly they would be out of date. "Tents, halls, gardens, rooms, warehouses – why have so many of one's most vital (theatrical) experiences been in them, on both sides of the absent foot-lights?" he asked.[5]

In Manchester they built a temporary prototype of their theatre, as Guthrie had done in Ontario, designed in scaffolding by Richard Negri. Only when they were satisfied with the form did they employ architects to create a more permanent version. The resulting structure was as hi-tech in its architectural expression (the Pompidou Centre in Paris was under construction and nearing completion) as it was low tech in its theatrical expression. In the words of Braham Murray, Elliot's co-director, "The effect it has on plays, especially classics, is to strip them of all unnecessary disguise/dust, and because its emphasis is on an actor in the right clothes in a light, sharing an emotional experience directly with the audience."[6]

The Tricycle Theatre

My own part in this story began in 1978, two years after the completion of the Cottesloe and the Royal Exchange, when I was asked by the then Wakefield Tricycle Company to design a theatre which could be inserted into a 1920s dance hall they had found in Kilburn, north London. They were a start-up company who had previously played in small spaces over pubs and their budget was extremely limited. I had already been captivated by the magic of the Georgian Theatre in Richmond Yorkshire (1788) as much as I was by the creative use of standard industrial products that could be bought from catalogues. I had also admired the simplicity of the Public Theater in Pittsburgh, designed by Peter Wexler, a low-cost theatre space built in scaffolding, which opened in 1975. Against this background, I came up with the idea of constructing a theatre of similar form and dimensions to Richmond out of a contractor's scaffolding system. It could be built by theatre carpenters, would be very quick to build and very cheap. Working with Iain Mackintosh we devised a rectangular courtyard form with two levels of galleries around a flexible pit. The structure was free-standing within the room and carried all its own staircases and lighting trusses, taking only lateral support from the existing walls. Balcony fronts were laced-in canvas panels, borrowed from the boating world, and seating was on upholstered benches with no arms (as at the Young Vic and Cottesloe before). We firmly believed that physical contact between audience members and not too much comfort contributed to the sense of a shared experience. The 220 seat Tricycle Theatre opened in 1980, was rebuilt after a major fire in 1987, and remained almost unaltered for 37 years until 2017, when it was sadly removed and replaced with a more comfortable but less compelling structure.

Legacy

The legacy of the courtyard form as it was rediscovered in the 1970s has continued to exert a powerful influence on the design of small and medium scale drama spaces in the last 40 years, and has also awakened an interest in a more three-dimensional design approach to larger theatres and concert halls, which are too numerous to mention here. Most notable of the theatres in the UK are the Swan at Stratford-upon-Avon (1986) which led to the much larger Courtyard and RST theatres, which are less successful due to their larger size, regional theatres in Bracknell, Leeds, the Lowry Quays and the Liverpool Everyman, the recently opened Bridge Theatre in London, and school theatres at Dulwich College, Winchester, Gresham's, Alleyn's, Cheltenham Ladies' College, Bedford and many more. In North America the form appeared in Calgary, Portland, New York and Chicago and at the

The Tricycle Theatre (1980)

The Dee and Charles Wyly Theater, Dallas (2009)

all-singing, all-dancing Dee and Charles Wyly Theater in Dallas. It is a form which can be as simple or sophisticated as clients and their budgets determine, which engages audiences like no other and remains 'a framework for freedom'.

Notes

1   'The Guthrie Thrust Stage and his Living Legacy' by Iain Mackintosh from the catalogue for the British entry to the Prague Quadrennial 2011. Association of British Theatre Technicians
2   *Making Space for Theatre* by Ronnie Mulryne and Margaret Shewring. Mulryne and Shewring 1995
3   Iain Mackintosh. *The Cottesloe at the National Theatre*, edited by Ronnie Mulryne and Margaret Shewring and Technical Editor Jason Barnes. Mulryne and Shewring 1999
4   Michael Billington. *The Cottesloe at the National Theatre*, edited by Ronnie Mulryne and Margaret Shewring and Technical Editor Jason Barnes. Mulryne and Shewring 1999
5   Michael Elliot. *Making Space for Theatre* by Ronnie Mulryne and Margaret Shewring. Mulryne and Shewring 1995
6   *Making Space for Theatre* by Ronnie Mulryne and Margaret Shewring. Mulryne and Shewring 1995

1.10

Stage Engineering Systems

Mark Ager

Stage engineering systems – the equipment and systems used to move scenery, people or other objects – have been part of theatres and opera houses for many centuries. Roman amphitheatres had complex lift systems to raise gladiators to their fates. The earliest Italian opera houses in 1630 had manually driven systems to move scenery both up and down using a flying or suspension system and horizontally around the stage. Increasingly complex stage transformations were achieved with these basic tools, using manual labour.

The discovery of electricity in the late 19th century gave rise to the powerful electric motor. At around the same time hydraulic systems (powered by the water main) came into use. These new power sources took on the role of driving the heaviest pieces of stage machinery but there was little change beyond that – positioning of the scenery was performed by human hand/eye coordination.

This age-old system has, in the last 70 years, fundamentally changed due to a single invention, and the consequences of and developments from that invention.

In December 1947 John Bardeen, Walter Brattain and William Shockley demonstrated the first working transistor at Bell Laboratories. This invention heralded the beginning of the age of computing. There had been previous computing technologies developed – Charles Babbage

conceived but never completely realised a 'mechanical difference engine' and various ingenious analogue computers had been constructed using mechanical, and subsequently electrical valve technology. However, it was the transistor which provided the key to unlocking an age of compact and affordable computing power that has hugely influenced and changed the theatre engineering industry, much as it has in many other walks of life, to a point that the technology used on stage today is unrecognisable to that which existed at the beginning of the 1950s.

What the computer allowed was the ability to automate movements, enabling scenery battens or lifts to be moved into position without human intervention. Prior to the invention of the transistor the position of each moving element (or axis) needed to be observed by an operator which severely limited the movements that could be achieved. There were some examples of linking mechanisms together (by mechanical or simple electrical means), but mostly this consisted of power amplification rather than allowing autonomous movement.

The computer provided the ability to control the axis (or multiple axes) and run to a pre-programmed position, without the need for human intervention during the motion. This gave a single operator the ability to move multiple axes to different positions and use different speeds. Further it enabled automated control of the relative positions

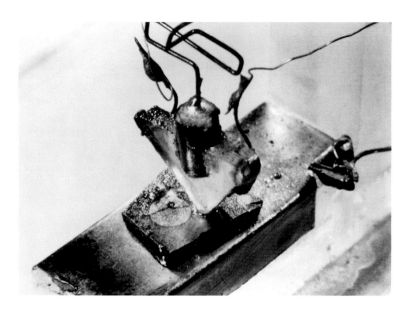

The first working transistor

between several axes whilst they moved. In today's modern theatre, multiple axes move together in intricate and complex motions and can also be linked to lighting, video, and sound systems, to create a wealth of possibilities that would have been unthinkable under purely human control. Further the ability of the computer to 'think' faster has led to a significant increase in both the loads and speeds that can be moved in live performance.

Pre-1950 the flyman could move a manual counterweight flying set of 3 to 500kg at speeds of up to 1.5m/s. Modern control systems can move multiple tonnes, safely with speeds of up to 4 or 6 m/s with pinpoint positioning accuracy – a feat that simply could not have been achieved using manual positioning systems. The computer has led to a large increase in the scale and complexity of mechanical engines used in the theatre.

Grid and manual flying at the Academy of Music, Philadelphia, USA

Met Opera (Built 1963–1966)

The first truly automated power flying system was designed and installed by the Peter Albrecht Company at the then new Metropolitan Opera House in 1965. In contrast to the purely manual (by eye) positioning that had gone before, position is achieved through an electronic system.

Multi-turn analogue potentiometers indicate the current position of the fly bar. The required position for the fly bar was then dialled in on a second multi-turn potentiometer mounted at the control desk. An electronic analogue comparator within the control system compared the required and actual position and then slowed and stopped the bar as it approached the correct position. This allowed for a number of bars to be run at the same time by a single operator. A further intelligent mechanism "The Master System" allowed two or more bars to be run in synchronisation so that they could be used together to lift larger pieces of scenery. This electro-mechanical system provided for multiple modes of linking and synchronising axes together.

At the time, the cost of drives was such that purchasing one per motor was unaffordable because each drive was assembled out of

Metropolitan Opera, NY, flying control desk

Metropolitan Opera, NY, flying patch system

individual components. Consequently, a manual patch system was installed between drives and motors which allowed the user to select which motors (around 160) to move from which drive (around 32).

The Met Opera power flying system represented the state of the art at the time. It was apparently developed in conjunction with the US military which meant the site was in lock-down during the installation. It is incredible, and a tribute to those that operate it, that the system is still in use to this day, more than half a century after it was designed.

Whilst the Metropolitan Opera House Power flying system represented a huge advance from the manual systems that had gone before, it was not a truly computerised system; it used custom electronic and electromechanical systems to provide the required functionality. The first truly computerised system was installed in the UK in the late 1970s.

National Theatre UK (1976) – (Olivier Stage) Power Flying System

The National Theatre in London was the first to use a true computer (in this case a Digital Equipment Corporation PDP11–35 computer) to control the stage systems. The PDP11–35 computer (with two parallel disk stores each with 1 Megabyte of storage), originally developed as a 'general purpose computing engine' (considered a mini computer) was used in multiple applications, and at the time was as ubiquitous as the IBM PC some 20 years later.

The design of the Olivier Theatre suggested the need for a three-dimensional flying system, based on point hoists, rather than the traditional cross stage bar. This in turn produced a requirement for a hoist control system that would allow multiple hoists to be run together in synchronisation. Clever rigging allows the hoists to be positioned at any point along a track system, by adjusting the hook clamp on stage.

Both the Metropolitan Opera and the National Theatre systems were custom built for specific theatres, with all the research and development costs taken within the project. The dream was for standardised systems (much like lighting and sound control desks) that would be replicated in multiple theatres, thereby reducing costs by spreading the research and development investment over multiple implementations.

The first generation of companies with that goal in mind began to appear in the 1980s with Hoffend in the USA, Bytecraft in Australia, and shortly after Nobel electronics in Norway. The first systems were based around a single computer, much as the National Theatre's had been. However, the challenge of controlling multiple motors at the same time is that each hoist needs a lot of monitoring/processing power to ensure that it moves and positions accurately. Some early systems struggled with the computational requirements of controlling multiple hoist movements.

An alternative that started to appear in the 1980s was to use a small computer or microprocessor for each individual motor. The challenge then was to network these multiple processors in a suitable manner such that they could all work collaboratively and respond to user commands in 'real' time.

In many parts of the world these microprocessor systems were borrowed from industrial control systems which were themselves taking on microprocessor technology. Such systems had mixed success, dependent both upon whether the underlying hardware/processing technology was able to provide the flexible control required within a theatre environment (very different to industrial control) and also whether the user interface was programmed to provide the flexibility required to meet the unique demands of working in a theatre environment rather than those of traditional industry.

Most of the first-generation systems were installed in large opera houses and national venues – created by a demand primarily from governments to have the newest and the best. However, through the 1990s other drivers for automation take-up began to appear.

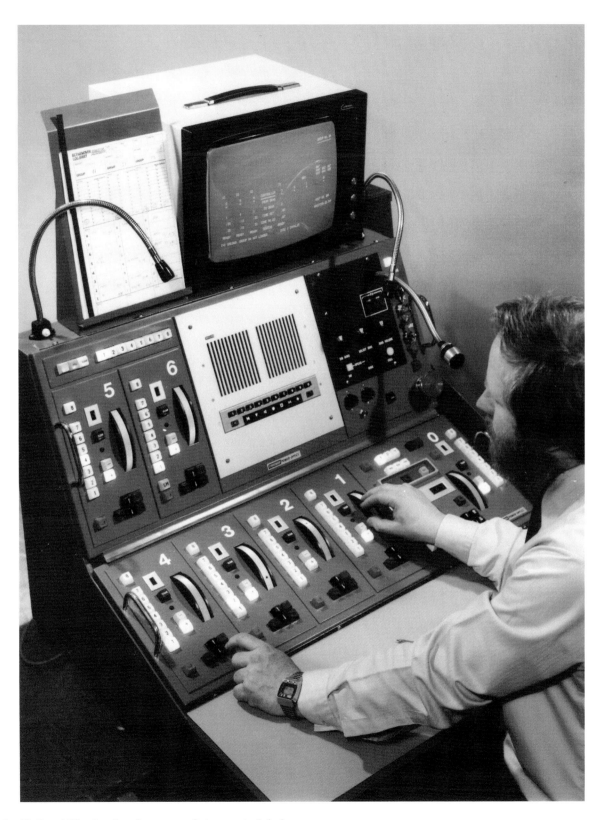

Richard Brett at the National Theatre, London power flying control desk

West End and Broadway Musicals

In the UK and the USA, the commercial demands of the West End and Broadway musicals to produce ever more spectacular shows and to keep staffing costs down led to a rapid growth in the use of standard automation systems and a raft of innovations such as multi-dimensional movements. The fast turnaround nature of these shows helped with the rapid development in the technology; whilst opera houses took years in the planning, most musicals are staged within a few months.

Automation moves until this time had largely been one-dimensional – up and down (with the exception of a few revolve/wagon drive solutions). However, the desire for ever more spectacle resulted in increasingly complex move sequences.

Martin Guerre (1996) saw the first use of two-dimensional trucks on stage. The first 3D performer flying system was used on *The Witches of Eastwick* in London (2000) followed by an even more complex six degrees of freedom motion system developed for *Chitty Chitty Bang Bang* two years later.

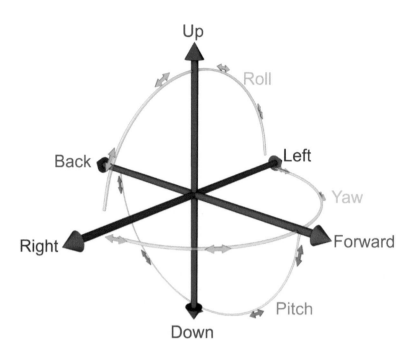

Diagram showing the six degrees of freedom

Flying car in *Chitty Chitty Bang Bang* demonstrated six degrees of freedom

Acrobat Automation Control Desk

Dutch Experience

In 1999 the Dutch government determined that the traditional counterweight system was a big health risk for stage staff; a law banning such systems became effective in January 2004. This was particularly an issue in a country which had a typically one/two-day touring structure, hence shows being loaded in/out of venues three to four times a week. The stress on the fly crew resulted in back injuries way above the average for the population. As a result, over a ten-year period virtually all the flying systems in theatres in Holland (over 100) were automated, a huge boost to the growth and acceptance of automation of power flying systems.

Germany

In the 1950s, Prof. Walter Unruh effectively defined the perfect form for an opera house stage and fly tower. Unruh designed the MET and Sydney Opera Houses, having developed and applied the principles for the perfect stage as defined by Friedrich Kranich in his ground-breaking work *Das The-atertechnik der Gegenwart* from 1929. This included a cruciform stage, with side stages, wagons, lifts etc, which by its nature demanded stage engineering and automation. This linked with the desire for opera in Germany and the engineering prow-ess of the country led to a big take-up of engineering systems within the theatre.

However, the innovation was hampered by safety standards that for some time forbade the use of cross flying (i.e. scenery bars flying up and down at the same time) and speeds above 1.2 metres/second. Further, there was a desire to ensure the absolute safety of the con-trol system – which could not be guaranteed by a single processor. For this reason, custom control systems with two processors were developed to control and monitor each motor, with internal voting to ensure that each came up with the same solution for the control. Any error between the two processors would shut down the system. This limitation resulted in custom systems being designed that were lim-ited in capability. Complex movements and links with other systems were not explored.

Modern Circus

Cirque du Soleil started as a touring troupe of circus performers in 1984 using minimal technology. However, beginning with *Mystère* in 1993 they started putting on increasingly lavish pro-ductions in custom-built theatres in Las Vegas. The commercial nature and success of the operation meant that they had increas-ingly large budgets to realise their vision, which reached a pin-nacle with KÀ in 2003.

KÀ – *Cirque du Soleil (2003–present)*

This show encompassed engineering on a huge scale, enabled by stage automation. The main stage – the Sand Cliff deck comprises a 60'x40' platform that has the ability to both raise and lower with a travel of 60', tilt

between horizontal and vertical and continuously rotate. The automation system controls over 200 axes, which, unlike in more traditional venues, move multiple times every night, often in complex cueing sequences, controlled by multiple (4) operators. The whole impetus and reason for the installation was to produce the spectacular. There is a separate chap-ter (Chapter 8.04) on this show and theatre.

Concert Touring

More recently (from around 2007) the concert touring (or rock and roll) industry has been a big driver for innova-tion, with numerous advances in automation, the demand being driven by the concert touring industry's desire to produce ever more spectacular performances for touring shows. Not only do these tours demand complex moves, but also to link seamlessly with other media (lighting, sound, and increasingly video) used within the show.

Taylor Swift's *1989 World Tour* actually took place in 2015. This showed how commonplace and complex these movement sequences and links have become, with a profiled bridge moving in three dimen-sions, linked to a 3D flying camera, the camera position being kept in the correct relative position to the performer, whist the singer moves in complex 3D profile around the venue. Distance and location information is fed from the automation system to the video system to allow the singer to be kept in shot and focus.

Innovation in Stage Engineering

The first ten years of the 21st century have seen the automa-tion of stage systems become standardised and mainstream, with many of those ground-breaking effects (often created out-side the traditional theatre industry) becoming commonplace, and an increased take-up both in fixed venues and touring.

KÀ, KÀ Theater, Las Vegas, the Sand Cliff Deck

Despite this huge change in automation control systems there has been little change in the engineering systems that they control. These systems have remained largely as they were 60 years ago – at least in the traditional theatre environment.

Over-stage Systems

There has been little change in the format of over-stage systems in the last 150 years. True, far more systems have been automated and motorised since the 1950s, and the loading capacity and speed of these systems have increased enormously (from 200kg to 1000kg and more, with speeds of 2m/s), but most theatre flying systems still consist of a series of bars or battens that extend back across the stage, spaced at 4–8" centres. This is despite the fact that this layout could be considered more appropriate to the cloths and painted back-drops that were in fashion a century ago, rather than the solid angled sets that populate today's stages. Though these battens might now be supplemented with a dozen or more point hoists, there has been little in the way of radical redesign of an age-old system.

There have been a few notable exceptions. The Olivier stage, in addition to its ground-breaking automation system, also employed a system of 170 point hoists rather than battens, which could be positioned easily anywhere around the stage. The Théâtre Royal de la Monnaie in Belgium mixes point hoists and battens (both powered and counterweight). At the same time, the increasing use of three-dimensional sets, and the desire by designers to break the two-dimensional format of the current systems suggests that there could be intelligent alternatives.

The challenge for innovation in this area comes down to the problem of touring. Even in houses built specifically for resident companies, there is always the potential for visiting companies to perform, and for the resident company to tour to other venues. Whilst 99 per cent of all theatres have the traditional batten system installed, it is difficult to see how this system might change – though it is arguable that it is no longer appropriate in an age when technology offers multiple opportunities.

The exception is in houses specifically built for shows, mainly by the likes of Cirque du Soleil and Franco Dragone. Here the rigging plots have become freeform, with an eclectic mix of point hoists and bars at all curves and angles – specific to the needs of a particular performance. They have also introduced the idea of winches on trollies, travelling on both straight and curved tracks to provide an alternative way to deliver both performers and scenery into the stage space. This idea has recently started to be taken up in more traditional theatre forms.

Under-stage Systems

The challenge of touring has also meant that there has been little innovation in the under-stage systems. Unlike the system of battens that span over the stage, there is no lift system that is standard enough to ensure that touring productions can rely on a lift (or even the means to install a lift) in each venue on the route. True there is the conventional German opera wagon/lift system much replicated in larger venues around the world, but as each venue has different dimensions of lifts and wagons, there is very little chance of the system being used in a touring environment. Often these grand and expensive systems lie idle and unused.

Horizontal moves on stage, first provided by manual, and then motorised tracking/winching systems have become prevalent in many larger musical productions starting in the 1980s. These systems employ a guide track with a skate that can be used to pull multiple scenic elements on and off stage and they have become a standard method of delivering scene changes in modern shows. The desire to tour these productions has led to the rise of the 'Show Deck', a 150–200mm high deck that contains the tracks and other automation elements for the production. Unfortunately, the majority of theatres (even those built since the 1980s) do not allow for easy integration of show decks. Raising the stage floor by 200mm adversely affects the sightlines from the stalls seating. This has resulted in productions re-raking the auditorium to accommodate the production, when a lower stage with a simple lift would have allowed simple transfers.

The Future

The last 70 years have produced a revolution in the control of stage engineering systems – enabling them to move with a degree of complexity, speed, and with loads never previously imagined. At the start of the period the new technology was used to drive traditional venue formats; however, we are beginning to see new forms of venue that are built around and are reliant on these new engineering technologies. The increasing use of video – both in projection, and fixed and moving LED screens – has further changed and merged the real and the virtual worlds into a single entertainment environment on a different scale, and in changing formats to those imagined previously, where closeups of an individual performer are merged with vast scenic panoramas within the stage space.

When factories first started using electric motors to replace the steam engines and water mills of previous eras, they were used in a very similar manner to the previous power systems. It took 50 years for the real benefits of the electric motor, with its ability to power individual items of machinery, to revolutionise factory layout and working practices. In the same way, despite the great advances in stage automation, it is still generally used to move traditional bars, stage lifts, etc. It has the possibility to provide a much larger palette of movement. This exploration has only just begun.

Taylor Swift tour

Bibliography

Richard Brett, 'The Olivier Flying System', ABTT *Sightline* magazine, Vol. 13, No. 1 (Spring 1979).

Royal Albert Hall, London, Classical Spectacular – lighting
by Durham Marenghi

1.11

Stage Lighting
Mark White

There have been radical changes in stage lighting over the last 70 years. This has included changes in the source of the light, how the lighting has been controlled from one 'cue' to another to easily reproduce the required lighting. There are now myriads of remotely controlled moving lights capable of changing colours, changing beam shape, focus, etc. developed from the rock music industry in search of visual effects, into theatres, opera houses and concert halls. The final area of change is in the art of stage lighting.

Seventy years ago, technology was rudimentary, the profession of lighting designer was unknown, and lighting was effectively pragmatic – making sure there was adequate light to see the performers. Today, the lighting designer has an array of tools and techniques, allowing truly creative and imaginative lighting of shows that existed only in the imagination of the lighting person of the 1950s. In 1950, the occupation of Lighting Designer did not exist; the task fell to in-house electricians who had learned their craft on the job using technologies developed in the late 19th and the first 20 years of the 20th century.

Lighting styles varied around the world, as did the locally available equipment. Two main streams had developed as parallel universes, one in the United States and the other in the United Kingdom and its former colonies. There were other technically advanced developments in European countries, particularly sophisticated luminaires in Germany in the 1920s and 30s, but these tended to be confined to their own countries, with limited spheres of influence. Part of the reason for the differing mainstreams was of course the mains voltage of 110/120 volts in the US and 230/240 volts in the UK and mainland Europe.

In 1950, the almost universal light source for theatre lighting was the incandescent lamp with a tungsten filament. These were essentially giant high-powered domestic light 'bulbs'. They were inefficient, meaning there was not a lot of light output for the large electrical input, most of which came out as heat. The white light was very warm, meaning only small amounts of blue light came out of the front. Due to the low levels of light output, saturated or concentrated colours remained the dream of lighting technicians. Coloured light was produced by the introduction of coloured glass or coloured gelatine filters ('gels') into the light beam, generally at the front of the lighting instrument. These tended to be of the tint variety as opposed to deep colours. The currently longest running theatrical production in London's West End, *The Mousetrap*, opened in November 1952. Using the lighting designer Michael Northen's plans, it has been estimated that it was only one third as bright as the current version using modern stage lighting instruments.

Look Back in Anger. Royal Court Theatre, 1950s

In 1950, a 'typical' UK theatre lighting installation comprised rows of incandescent bulbs mounted on battens (lengths) of wood hung from flying bars above the stage. These bulbs were often naked and dipped in translucent French varnish to give red, green and blue lighting, plus a fourth circuit of uncoloured white known as a four-colour batten. Sometimes they were fitted with white enamelled metal or porcelain reflectors shaped like a 'Chinaman's hat' to marginally increase the light output on the stage. Later, these lights were enclosed in metal containers with inbuilt mirrors and a frame in which to mount coloured glass or gel. There was very little lighting 'out front' in the auditorium and footlights were commonplace to remove the shadows under eyes and noses caused by the main light coming from overhead and not from out front. Follow spots were generally carbon arc machines and therefore presented a variety of hazards and health risks to the operators as well as a fire risk to the theatre.

Strand Electric Pattern 23 spotlights, introduced in 1953 and one of the most ubiquitous spotlights of this period. Over 500,000 units were manufactured

In 1950 there was essentially only one source of light, the tungsten lamp. 70 years later the predominant light source is the completely different Light Emitting Diode (LED). There are still other light sources in use but their time illuminating the stage is waning and a generation from now they will all but have disappeared.

There are two main types of light fixture, the flood and the spot. Flood lights, as the name suggests, spread light over a wide area and these will be very familiar to users of car parks and attendees at sports grounds. These lights have 'soft' edges, meaning the brightness tapers off to give an indistinct edge to the beam, whereas a spot light indeed directs light only to one spot and not anywhere else and generally has a hard edge. A 'follow spot' in a theatre will be a very familiar example. There are also examples of hybrid fixtures that fall somewhere in between and have adjustable beams or focus capabilities such as the essentially ubiquitous standard workhorse 'Fresnel' fixtures found in European theatres. But as an example of the differing trans-Atlantic entertainment lighting styles, Fresnel fixtures are almost completely unknown in American theatres.

All basic electric light sources have one thing in common. The raw emitter of light throws light in all directions like a sphere and the light needs to be harnessed to point it in a given direction. This harnessing or gathering of the initial photons is achieved by optical elements such as mirrors and lenses. The mirrors are rarely flat (because they do not concentrate light but merely bend it in a different direction) and are often 'conic sections' such as ellipsoids and parabolas (a PAR lamp). These mirrors focus the light beams into a concentrated parallel beam and the most familiar of these is to be found in a hand-held torch.

But in order to produce a hard-edged beam or indeed an image, lenses must be introduced into the path of the light beam. These lenses can be simple, similar to a magnifying glass, or can be very complex, like a camera lens.

The first significant change came with the invention of a much-improved tungsten light source, the tungsten halogen lamp, first commercially available in 1958. Developed by the General Electric Corporation (GEC) for other purposes such as car headlamps, the forerunner of the PAR lamp, this very bright but also very hot light source was eagerly adopted by the theatre industry. Long throw spot lights with much 'whiter' light became possible along with stronger blue coloured light and saturated or strong colours in general. The brighter light meant spotlights started being installed within the auditorium and the face and nature of theatre lighting was changed forever.

Other light sources were developed, again for other industries but enthusiastically adopted by the theatre industry. These included arc lamps without a filament which were incredibly bright, but had varying colour performance, giving a generally very cold white light but requiring bulky and expensive electronics to strike and maintain the miniature electrical arc in a small quartz tube. However, unlike tungsten lamps, they could not be dimmed. This brings us neatly into the other part of stage lighting, the ability to remotely control the lights from a distance and in large numbers.

Resistance dimmers could be installed and were generally controlled by large mechanical switchboards that in the UK were often located on a 'perch' above the prompt corner and were part of the

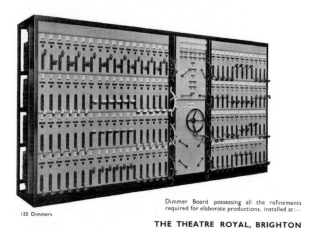

STAGE SWITCHBOARDS

Dimmer Board possessing all the refinements required for elaborate productions, installed at:—

120 Dimmers

THE THEATRE ROYAL, BRIGHTON

SPECIAL FEATURES

● Four-colour master contactors.
● Two independent contactors controlling two-way-and-off switches on 60 individual circuits.
● Slipping clutch, self-release dimmer controls.
● Ballast facilities for all stage and fly dips.
● Eight cross-control colour masters.
● Slow-motion grand master.

MAJOR EQUIPMENT CO. LTD
GORST ROAD LONDON N.W.10
ELGar 8041 (5 Lines)   MAJORLON, HARLES, LONDON
Showroom: 40, PARKER ST., KINGSWAY, W.C.1.   CHAncery 9170

GLASGOW N.W.   EDINBURGH 3   NORTH SHIELDS   MANCHESTER   BIRMINGHAM 12   COVENTRY
93 Garriochmill Rd.   18a Dundas St.   14 Back Albion St.   255 Cheetham Hill Rd.   218 Highgate Rd., Sparkbrook   Faraday Works, Stoney Stanton Rd.
Kelvin 1266   Waverley 3846   North Shields 335   Collyhurst 2078   Victoria 0509 & 1689   Coventry 2970

Major lighting control system in use in the 1950s

fixed equipment of the building. US theatres on the other hand often operated as bare 'four walls theatres' meaning that all the stage lighting electrics were hired in for each production. US theatres tended to use individual 6–12 channel resistance dimmer 'Piano Boards', each requiring an individual operator. The UK large mechanical dimmer boards operated the resistance dimmers in their separate rooms by means of a series of very thin 'tracker' wires via series of pullies. Again, the theatre industry used technologies developed for another industry or craft, that of the centuries-old playing of pipe organs from consoles with their multiple keyboards and foot pedals remotely located from the organ pipes.

Alternative electronic means of dimming tungsten lighting had been available since the late 1920s in the United States; one of the earliest was by GEC in 1928–1929 for the Chicago Lyric Theater. This method involved high-current vacuum tubes (valves in UK English) called Thyratrons which acted as a controlled rectifier using two per dimmer, one for each half of the AC cycle. These dimmers were noisy, unreliable, had a service life measured in tens of hours and were very expensive to purchase and maintain. In the 1960s, solid state versions incorporating Thyristors or SCRs (Silicon Controlled Rectifiers) became commercially available and affordable (once they were manufactured in bulk) and replaced most resistor dimmers within a decade. This heralded the age of true remote control for stage lighting, with each lighting dimmer channel now controlled by small electric voltages (0–10 volts) carried along small electric wires, one for each channel instead of the mechanical collection of wire ropes, pullies and levers. At this point the lighting control could be brought into the auditorium, albeit by a large electrical umbilical cord, giving much greater freedom to the newly emerging occupation of lighting designer.

As computer technology developed in the 1960s and 70s, the theatre industry again adapted another industry's technology and the age of the multi-channel 'memory' desk (console) came about, thus reducing the number of lighting operators required for each performance from anything up to eight to just one person. However, the development of computer-controlled lighting desks using the expensive but highly unreliable computer memory systems of the time proved to be the demise of a number of well-known lighting manufacturers. Notable steps along the way usually involved lengthy discussions with lighting designers such as Richard Pilbrow, who conceived the Strand Lightboard. The engineers were working out how to make the technology work night after night (often it did not) and the lighting designers knew how to present the many functions necessary in a useable way on the computer screen.

However, in a further complication, the various lighting equipment manufacturers had their own control protocols, usually developed at huge expense from limited resources, meaning that one manufacturer's lighting desk could not control most other manufacturers' dimmers, to the extreme annoyance (particularly in the US) of lighting rental companies that could not combine multiple manufacturers in their rental packages. The United States Institute of Theatre Technology (USITT), in a project led by Steve Terry, established a common interface protocol of digital communication between control consoles and dimmers known as *USITT DMX512-A—Asynchronous Serial Digital Data Transmission Standard for Controlling Lighting Equipment and Accessories* in 1986. Universally adopted, 512 dimmers could be controlled via one cable which was similar to those used by microphones.

The theatre lights of the 1970s had one thing in common: they were focussed on one part of the stage for the duration of the performance and they remained in the colour determined by the addition of the colour medium (gel) at the start of the performance. Edward Gordon Craig's dreams remained unrealised. Like lighting consoles, many lighting instruments that could move the beams of light from one part of the stage to another and change colour were developed mainly by individuals around the world using existing lighting instruments, but few if any were commercially successful. What was needed was a product designed from the ground up, which was a very expensive process, not adaptions of existing products. Two products that changed the world of stage lighting are described below.

In 1980, an engineer, Jim Bornhorst, working for a sound company Showco in the US state of Texas discovered that inserting and twisting 'dichroic' filters could alter the colour of the light beam. Using a high-powered but very small overhead projector lamp, the light intensity and colour density from a light that could move very quickly attracted the attention of the British rock band Genesis, who provided the capital of US$1 million to develop the technology. Thus in 1981 the Vari-Lite® brand was born, arguably the first commercially successful moving (and in their case, the first '*intelligent*') light that changed the face of the entertainment lighting industry. These moving lights were very compact, very bright and were developed for the live music industry. They generated a lot of audible noise as they generated a lot of heat internally which had to be removed by a number of high-speed electric fans before the instrument self-destructed. In the music industry the noise did not matter; in a theatre it was and still is very distracting to performers and audience.

There was a second product also developed from scratch. In the late 1980s, inventor and entrepreneur David Cunningham was prompted by Wally Russell to revisit the Kliegel Brothers' invention of the 1930s, the ellipsoidal spotlight. Cunningham recognised the need to develop a mass-produced, low-cost unit and set about designing a new tungsten halogen lamp with four filaments which he would match to a new ellipsoidal reflector, also of his design, using dichroic technology. This relatively new reflector technology meant that a lot of the infra-red heat from the tungsten light source could pass through the back of the instrument instead of down the path of the light beam. The innovation that set this apart from other theatrical lights was that for the first time an ellipsoidal mirror was designed in conjunction with a new lamp, in order to produce a far more efficient and brighter theatre spotlight. However, Cunningham was unable to interest existing lighting equipment manufacturers in developing his ideas. It was not until 1990, when he approached Fred Foster from Electronic Theatre Controls, that he found a company willing to share the development costs.

Lighting fixtures using Light Emitting Diodes (LEDs) first appeared in the early 2000s. As before, many companies and individual inventors produced the original units. As usual, the pioneers and indeed the

Rank Strand Lightboard, lighting control desk. 1976

latter-day manufacturers were/are completely dependent upon light sources developed for other uses such as traffic lights. LED light sources tend to be very bright but generally 'monochromatic', meaning that there is a very limited range of highly saturated colours that can be incorporated into theatre luminaires. This limited range means that all police cars have the same colour (blue) flashing lights and the green colour of the 'go' traffic lights is extremely similar. Many colours, such as the yellow green of a tennis ball, cannot be produced by raw LEDs and have to incorporate older 'fluorescent' technology, meaning they are not as bright or efficient as the raw LED emitters. All 'white' LEDs use fluorescent technology. In the same way that there were many versions of white in fluorescent tubes, there are many versions of white in LEDs. The lack of a full continuous spectrum of colours that merge together to make tungsten or sun light, is why many fabrics appear to be differently coloured under different light sources.

Making white light via a combination of different coloured LED emitters is known as additive mixing and provides output of theoretically thousands of colours, ranging from very deep saturated hues to white with a tint of colour, such as 'apple green white'. The ability to change colour quickly with subtle hints and tints is what truly sets lighting equipment of the 2020s apart from the lighting equipment of the 1950s.

Another prime difference is the smaller amount of electrical energy consumed, resulting in the heat output being much less (exaggerated claims of only one-tenth of the electricity consumed for the same light output have never been realised- currently at best

Vari-Lite VL1 1981, one of the earliest effective moving lights. Only 40 were ever built

around one-quarter). This has led to energy costs for theatres that have adopted LED technology being less for the lighting but also less for the removal of the heat created by tungsten lighting via air-conditioners and the like.

LEDs proved to be very disruptive technology to manufacturers of lighting equipment. They held great promise in terms of much greater efficiency, namely the unbelievably long life of the instruments, which was expected to be in the order of 50,000 hours (and is at best around 20,000 hours) and the instant control of colour. The last part is true. The trouble was, and to an extent still is, that the colour is not a 'pure' white light, that is to say, a perfect replacement for tungsten lamped fixtures. LEDs require very sophisticated electronics to make them dim (fade) as well as tungsten fixtures and require complex computer software to control the sophisticated electronics.

The foregoing is all to do with the tools available to enhance the artistic skills of the lighting designers and the console programmers. The question which arises is whether they have made lighting for entertainment better for the audience than in previous decades. Probably yes, but the look on the stage is still thoroughly dependent on the lighting designer's application of Stanley McCandless' principals of visibility, location, composition and mood, also known as brightness, position, focus and colour. Certain colours do not sit well with each other; no amount of sophisticated technology or knowledge will change that.

What of the future? Control systems will become more complex as computer technology evolves. LED emitters will continue to be developed in order to become brighter and more pleasing to the eye and use less energy. There is one essential difference, however, between lighting for the stage in 1950 compared to 2020. In 1950 there were standard light sources (tungsten) and standard coloured filters ('gels' from the gelatine filters of the 1920s) that gave easily reproducible colours by *subtractive* mixing (taking away most of the white light to leave only some of the component colours), which were more or less exactly the same all over the world. The language of colour was simple: "Rosco 22" (Flame red), "Strand 19" (Deep blue) meant that colour was going to appear on the stage from that light. 70 years later that reproducibility has disappeared due to the wide variations in colour emanating from LED emitters now producing colours by *additive* mixing. The sophistication of LED fixtures means that colours are now available that were not available before. A new language will have to be evolved to describe colour: "I want Lee 136 (Surprise Pink) but with a tiny hint of green to bring out the highlights in the leading lady's costume." Will the language of stage lighting colour be comprised of three- or four- word descriptors with one word conveying emotional meaning? When asked about this, lighting designer George Tarbuck said that his favourite colour is "Deep Despair Pink".

War Horse. Royal National Theatre London. Lighting Designer Paule Constable

Revox B77 reel to reel tape recorder

Sound, and Opera's Dirty Little Secret

Chris Full

In 2001, the magazine *Live Design* published an article entitled 'Opera's Dirty Little Secret' which speculated that opera and opera houses were increasingly using amplification. That was 20 years ago, and the debate has continued. Before diving into the jucy details, some background.

How Did It All Start?

The evolutionary progress of Theatre Sound over the last 70 years has been astonishing and exciting. It's a world where the embrace of cutting-edge technologies, re-purposing of equipment and creative skill come together to create the sound worlds that inhabit modern theatre. Today, we live in a time where possibilities are limited by our own imagination (oh, and possibly the budget)!

Backing up to the 1930s, lighting control systems were beginning to evolve but theatre sound was very much in an analogue world of 'real time' effects: thunder sheets and cannonball runs, mechanical wind and wave machines, crash boxes, were all operated in carefully choreographed sequences by stage hands to create sound effects to support the story. By the mid-1950s the turntable and sound effects records had augmented and in some cases supplanted mechanical effects, still operated by the stage management team.

In the 1960s things for theatre lighting (and scenery) were beginning to move on – with the advent of the transistor (and the thyristor), remote control with multiple preset systems became commonplace. In the world of sound an even greater transition was taking place: the humble use of turntables had given way to the new kid on the block, the Magnetic Tape Recorder.

The Pivotal Moment

A combination of choreographed stagehands and turntables could be very creative (especially for the dexterous) but this was nothing when compared to the seemingly endless creative possibilities offered by the first replay medium that offered what is arguably the greatest creative leap for sound in theatre: compositing and editing. Suddenly raw sound effects could be built into cue-able sequences, combined to create new textures and creatively manipulated. Tape echo and looping were born and your imagination was the only limit of what could be created with a razor blade and Jam Jars! The iconic Revox A77 epitomised this revolution, bringing two tracks of playback with the ability to 'bounce tracks across the tape' and 'over-dub' on top of an existing recording and all within the reach of modest theatre budgets.

The tape era also brought with it the concept of recording bespoke content. Can't find an effect? No problem, record it! Want a Sci-fi atmosphere? Create it on a synthesiser and record it! Perhaps the BBC Radiophonic workshop led the charge to use (and abuse) the latest technology to create, but theatre wasn't far behind.

Creativity Unleashed – Digital Hacking

The tape machine and its possibilities ensured the longevity of its life in theatre. However, by the early 1980s the digital sampler had progressed from the astronomically priced Fairlight CMI, one of the first Digital Audio Workstations (DAWs), to the completely accessible Akai S-900 series samplers, bringing digital technology into mainstream use. Despite current trends to embrace analogue technologies of yesteryear, it can't be overstated how important the sampler is to the world of sound: almost all of our current technologies for sound and music use sampling in some form or another.

The CD provided a way to playback the fruits of your labours. The Internet and streaming allow you to collaborate and share. All because of digital sampling. The Digital Audio Workstation provided for the first time a platform for non-destructible (reversible) audio editing and processing, quickly evolving from basic sample manipulation to full-blown production systems including incredible DSP mixing abilities.

Now that we've arrived in a time where we are no longer worried about the 'flaws' of the 1970s analogue technology, we're going to need some better reproduction systems for our spangly digital world. Thankfully, collaborations between theatre sound designers and equipment manufacturers over the last 20 years have produced huge advances to support the digital era: speaker systems have become smaller, more powerful and flexible so that they can reproduce the quietest moment to the loudest with the highest fidelity without requiring different systems; mixing consoles have specific features for theatre applications; radio microphones are both miniaturised and ruggedised to survive gruelling performance environments. All at the highest quality, allowing the creation of a world where the sound system is so integrated in a performance to be 'invisible' (if required) from the audience's perspective.

As if the excitement of sample manipulation and sound reproduction improvements weren't enough, MIDI (Musical Instrument Digital

Sound mixing console

MIDI logo

Interface) arrived on the scene in 1983, with its offer of interconnected systems with real-time control, which inspired the invention of new technologies. Midi Show Control, an extension to Midi created for and by the entertainment world, allows programmatic control of a show's content across its varied control equipment. This paved the way for the integration of playback with programmable mixers and matrices. Exciting devices like the Richmond Sound Audiobox and Level Control Systems' Super Nova platform, which was the predecessor of Meyer's D'Mitri and Constellation systems, were born, starting the journey towards a more immersive world of sound.

But What About Opera?

So, how was all this technology actually used? From the 1980s through to today, theatre sound system design takes disparate technologies (quite often from other disciplines), interconnecting them to create a sonic environment to support the narrative of the show. At one end of the scale this could mean reinforcing a show in such a natural way as to make the sound system invisible and at the other end, the sound system is proud to add its presence to the show. In all cases the technology enables the sound designer to build the show's sonic world.

Traditionally opera is firmly rooted in a live performance delivered by wonderful artists, in a naturally supportive acoustic environment accompanied by (often) large orchestras. Not much room for technology here you'd think, but even in these traditionally 'acoustic' environments, modern sound system technology adds a richness, be it with sound effects or subtle voice enhancement. It is said that several renowned world opera houses even use sophisticated acoustic enhancement systems to adjust the environment for the style of the show. But what would happen if we weren't restricted by tradition and could freely explore how technology can play not just a supporting role but represent a lead character?

Deep inside Massachusetts Institute of Technology (MIT) in Boston, USA, not unlike Skunk Works, there lies a team led by Tod Machover, with a mission to explore the 'Future of Opera', providing an exciting opportunity to explore what the next era in theatre audio may bring.

Death and the Powers

Set in the near future (a good place to explore the next generation of technology), the opera 'Death and the Powers' has a cast of humans, a chorus of robots and a story line that explores how the knowledge we collect over a lifetime, if you like, our essence, could be preserved forever in a digital form, much like sampling has done for audio. The lead character only appears on stage in physical form for the opening scenes before dying and 'uploading' himself into the 'system'. For the remainder of the show he sings off stage, as a virtual (dis-embodied) performer whose expressive performance is fed into the lighting, sound and visual effects on stage. Once this transition has happened, the show co-exists in two worlds: the 'analogue' human world (subtle reinforced audio with chamber orchestration) and the 'digital' (bold and immersive audio with more synthesised orchestration) world of the system.

One of the main design challenges for the creative team was how to create a credible manifestation of this 'dis-embodied' performance which the cast could interact with for the remainder of the show. If we analyse what truly makes a live performance unique, it is the very nuance that an artist brings to each show to create a character: the mannerisms, the vocal traits and the expressive interpretation of the music and lyrics.

Once our lead character inhabits the virtual world, he is represented by harmonious integration between lighting elements, video content and the sound system. With an actor playing the role offstage, it would be possible to capture the essence of his performance and by interconnecting

Death and the Powers, opera

the show's systems in real-time, generate a virtual character. Wearing a harness of sensors and looking a bit like an automaton, our star provided us rich expressive data on his physical and emotional performance. The supporting cast of robots and humans also contribute to the available performance data.

With all this rich data what can we do? The visual element of our virtual performer was achieved by using the data to generate and render video content (and lighting elements) on the fly. From the audio perspective, the robot voices, the voice of the lead character and the immersive world of the 'system' he inhabits also needed to be created and rendered in 3D thorough an immersive sound system stretching from the stage into and surrounding the auditorium.

Our immersive sound system would integrate Wave Field Synthesis (WFS) with high resolution Ambisonic reproduction. WFS is a technology that uses a large array of densely packed and individually controlled speakers to synthesise an audio wavefront that represents a source and its position as though the source were present. Any listener within the field of the array will perceive the source at the correct location creating the Sound Designer's nirvana of no sweet spot! This would give the perfect solution to localise the voices (human, virtual star and robots) on stage using tracking data from the performance data network. When integrated with a high resolution Ambisonics system of circa 120 speakers, it already feels like we're making progress.

But such an audacious system didn't exist and certainly not with the additional requirement of real-time rendering of audio sources. So, following in the rich tradition of audio hacking, we developed the entire audio rendering system for the show, adding cue-able control and source metadata management applications and purpose-built innovative

Death and the Powers, performer in harness for disembodied performance

bespoke audio effects suite. Armed with a suite of fully loaded Mac Pros for the audio processing, the support of leading audio manufacturers and technology minds of MIT, we were able to create the incredibly low latency real-time 3D audio platform required for the show. Apple iPad applications provided additional data input sources and the DSP capability of a Studer Vista console allowed us to manage the 380 inputs and 260 outputs.

Orchestral and performer (radio) mics allowed the mix to transition homogeneously between the two worlds of the show as well as allowing the elements to exist in one or the other, and this could be viewed as a metaphor for the future. We won't leave tradition behind but will build upon it as we always have.

So, from a world steeped in tradition, it seems that opera using multidimensional audio controlled by real-time data layered with traditional theatre underpinnings shows a possible future for theatre sound and I can't wait to explore more.

Death and the Powers was an experiment, perhaps an extreme (but exciting!) example of the use of technologies in a performance. The quality, capabilities and flexibility of sound systems have been transformed over the last 50 years. They offer the opportunity to add any sound effect or environment to any performance. Sound systems have been the norm for decades in musical theatre. The increasing use of radio mics for actors in plays is becoming common. Enhancement of singers in opera can be hidden and imperceptible – it can remain opera's dirty little secret.

The Hubble Cantata – World premiere at BRIC's Celebrate
Brooklyn Festival, August 2016

1.13

New Technologies and Performance

Raj Patel

Dance, music, singing and theatre are fundamental to human communication, exploration, cohesion, storytelling, and history. Technology, in one form or another, has been used in performance from the beginning. Our earliest ancestors' paintings in the famous caves in Lascaux are bought to life by firelight and rhythmic clapping in the reverberant caves – with locations carefully selected for acoustics that mimic the animals depicted. Theatres of Greek antiquity introduced the *deus ex machina* ("god from the machine") hand-cranked cranes of wood, pulleys and ropes – to lower actors or scenery from above to create more impactful stories. It was received with both excitement and criticism. Storytellers argued it provided audiences an immediate emotional response of awe and wonder. Critics argued it was a lazy way to deal with over-complicated plot resolution. The technology remained and is a mainstay of performance spaces today – because it enabled excitement in audiences. The challenge remains today – the appropriate use of technology is generally assessed based on whether it enriches or enhances the production.

Today performance can encapsulate the widest spectrum of experience from real to virtual, live to pre-recorded or digital, or any combination thereof. It becomes a challenge in modern performances to view technology use impartially: for digital natives (born after 1980) "technology" is almost an irrelevant term – there is little or no separation between the digital and physical worlds – while for other generations, the distinction is clearer. As the years pass, will the boundary between physical and digital blur to the point of irrelevance?

In his book *The Secret Knowledge* (2001), David Hockney explores the use of technology in painting beginning in the fifteenth century, identifying the use of the camera obscura and lenses as crucial in major breakthroughs of masterworks in fine art. Technology has been integral to the working practices of fine artists and visual artists for centuries. Without modern technology or industrial practice, many works conceived by artists today could simply not be realized.

Audiences and critics are generally less compelled to focus on the technology when reviewing these works than they are on the meaning or impact the works have. Perhaps this is simply a result of the technology being seamlessly embedded in the creation of the artwork, rather than in the experience of it. Yet in performance it is less commonly viewed the same way.

The symbiotic relationship between the arts and technology has existed through the ages. Creators have for centuries been at the forefront of technology adoption. Quick to appropriate, adapt, develop and push technology in pursuit of artistic goals, the role of the artist has been to say "How can I use this to tell my story better, or with more impact? How far can I push it before it breaks?" These experiments cause technology to adapt, in response to how it is used.

Integration of New Technology in Performance

In the context of the design of modern performance spaces, the period from 1950 to 1980 was one of relative technological calm. Technology improved, became seamlessly integrated into performances, used with more complexity, and became an accepted part of the art.

From the early 1980s to the early 2000s, developments in home and office computing, and personal digital devices accelerated and developed to a point where the impact on design of venues and performances will be felt for years to come. 3D visualization software is increasingly prevalent and sophisticated and deployed for the design of buildings, sets, and lighting. For sound and acoustics, a shift change in computer modeling allowed the design of a new venue to be "auralized" to hear a building before it was built. Processes and environments previously reserved for research institutions found their way into the design world.

Some of the key spatial sound recording and capture techniques, underpinning the auralization process, were developed in the 1960s and 1970s and became enabled by computers, high quality audio cards, and high capacity portable hard drives. These have been used to great theatrical effect: Ambisonics in 2013's *To Sleep To Dream* by Earfilms; the binaural

Arup SoundLab – a place to view and listen to buildings, performance environments, and performance sets before they are built physically, or from measurements of real spaces

dummy head in 2015's *The Encounter* by Simon McBurney. In both performances the audience were blindfolded. Performances focused on hearing alone (*The Encounter* also required the audience to wear headphones) and in both cases the imagination created a visual environment. A few years later Dolby would launch their full 3D spatial audio system as Atmos. Performance sound systems manufacturers also began creating proprietary spatial audio systems for deployment in venues and outdoor performances.

Increased projection image brightness and quality (LED and LCD projection), coupled with real time "projection mapping" by digitally altering an image to map to any surface, has radically changed how projection can be used. Significant examples of the power of such dynamic scenery was seen in the Olympics openings in Beijing, London and Rio (2008, 2012, 2016) and the staging of *The Curious Incident of the Dog in the Night-time* (2012).

There are many fascinating examples where a range of technologies have been combined to create productions that would otherwise not have been possible, or conceived around the technologies themselves that have received critical acclaim, including:

- Robots, AI and spatial audio – *Death and the Powers*
- Video, animation, projection – 1927 company *Magic Flute*
- Sets, video, film – 59 Productions *Forbidden Zone*
- AI in composition – *Beyond the Fence*

Institutions specializing in the use of technology in performance, as well as investigating the integration, overlap, and collaboration between physical and digital have existed since the 1970s but continue to expand. Ars Electronic (Linz), ZKM (Karlsruhe), IRCAM (Paris), Sonic Arts Center (Belfast), Create Cube (Virginia) all have hybrid programs and spaces for

To Sleep To Dream, Ear Films

The Curious Incident of the Dog in the Night-time

exploration. Performance spaces that put the audience in the centre of fully enveloping experiences both audio and visual have already been realized (The Sage Gateshead Hall 2) and are increasingly being planned (Salle Modulable, Lucerne).

Emerging Technology and the Digital Future

Perhaps the technologies received with the greatest suspicion or fear amongst venue designers and content creators for performing arts spaces are Virtual Reality (VR) and Augmented Reality (AR). This is not a surprise in the context of the images they stir in the imagination. For VR, a room full of people in a theatre, watching a live performance, with a device strapped to their heads and covering their eyes. With AR, the idea of a sea of people holding up their phones, with bright screens, either looking at a stage through it, or trying to look at both screen and stage at the same time. But these mental images fail to tell the whole story.

VR has in a few short years proven itself an incredibly useful tool in the design process. Communicating the complexities of the design of a venue performance space, or the experience through a building by either an audience member or the performer, is hard to capture in renderings or walk-throughs presented on a flat screen. But in VR these come to life, and the ability to discuss design nuances and develop design consensus is quickly realised. It is a powerful engagement tool. Many are still concerned about its use within a performance itself, yet there are good examples that indicate that there are hybrid engaging opportunities to be explored. *The Hubble Cantata*, a work by Paola Prestini, is ostensibly

The Cube, Moss Arts Center, Virginia Tech, Virginia, USA

a traditional opera, with live orchestra, singers and a projected set of visual images on a screen. The hybrid element is that the final act also has an immersive component using both VR and spatial audio. Its full-scale premier at Prospect Park in Brooklyn New York in August 2016 was the largest immersive VR experience conducted anywhere in the world with 6000 attendees. Cardboard VR headsets were handed to visitors when they arrived, and an app was downloadable on the site. Your phone was placed into the cardboard and a seamless introduction as part of the performance told you when to put it on. As 6000 people all took a sharp intake of breath at the first images, while the soloist sang her aria and the musicians played, there was a palpable sense that something special was happening. As the performance continued, the audience stood up, moved around, and were engaged with VR as part of the story – and that was felt equally by the performers on stage.

The National Theatre in London, recognizing the importance of VR as an impactful medium, formally created its Immersive Storytelling Studio in July 2016

> . . . to examine how virtual reality, 360 degree film, augmented reality, and other emerging technologies can widen and enhance the NT's remit to be a pioneer of dramatic storytelling and enable audiences to stand in other people's shoes . . . to allow creative teams to do things that otherwise might be difficult or impossible.
>
> (National Theatre press release, 9 June 2016)

Earlier that year, in conjunction with Play Nicely and 59 Productions, the National Theatre staged "wonder.land" a new performance of "Alice in Wonderland", using digital media extensively and VR in the pre-theatre and lobby experience.

This raises the next potential challenge for the modern performance space, the accommodation of the staff with the skills, and the associated spaces, for the creation and development of these new media into productions. The creative process itself has already changed to accommodate technology, and that will continue and include evolving production dynamics, timelines and budgets along with it.

We are still only seeing the tip of the iceberg. VR is largely used as a visual experience, and in a live setting usually incorporating other things happening in real-time around it. The promise of full VR is the ability to control the entire sensory experience. Environments and technologies to activate those senses are still in their nascent stages, but they are developing rapidly. Will we see performance spaces that incorporate the full sensory experience? We have already seen these sensory activities added in more "traditional" contexts, e.g. gaming environments, theme parks, science and history museums, 4D movie theatres, etc., so one can expect it will happen in time. Will that stop people coming to the auditorium to experience it collectively? To gather together, talk about it on the way there, experience it side by side, and then talk about it afterwards? Whether full VR will allow effective group storytelling, especially when non-linear, or user determined, with live audience, remains in question. What is clear, is the ability to deliver highly emotional storytelling from the viewpoint of a particular character. To date perhaps most poignantly in Milica Zec's *Giant* (2016) where the audience experience being a member of a family hiding in a basement in an active war zone during a bombing.

AR presents major possibilities inside and outside the performance space. The technology offers real-world interactions that VR struggles to provide: in the most basic form, the ability to deliver translations of speech to the ears of an audience member, text for the hearing-impaired, to improve the ability to understand what you are seeing and hearing through additional support material, close-up visuals, provides myriad possibilities (and a natural next step to seat-back surtitle systems). Enhancing performances by creating additional virtual characters accessible via your own device provides expanded possibilities for young audience engagement. The development and integration of technology in performance contexts not only enhances the content but can broaden audience demographics and expand access to these art forms. Extending the performance space out to the immediate environments, the street, the city, transportation system, and in the home, offers the ability to extend storytelling and engagement to outside the performance space alone, expanding the opportunities for engagement of audiences who want it. This can be discreet and easily delivered to the audience, as no special hardware is required except the ubiquitous device that most people are carrying in their pockets. Couple this with emerging hybrid spatial sound technologies that allow you to mix the sound you hear from the device over headphones with the real space, increasing engagement between one world and the other.

As these technologies continue to develop and be refined, and more importantly audio, visual, VR and AR, vibration, movement and touch come together, the possibilities for artistic use are many. These tools, or the next generation of them, will continue to find a place in performance, because artists will want to continue to experiment with them if users are engaged. This latter point is an important distinction, as artists are no longer just producing work to wow audiences with the technology that is there; they must engage with the technologies their audiences have or expect, in order to continue to develop those audiences over the long term. Likewise, given that technology is now so embedded in our culture, performance without technology in, or without technology as part of or central to stories, may soon be difficult to imagine. This too will have a knock-on effect on the design of spaces. Should technology become increasingly prevalent, further hybrid spaces will be developed to respond to it. However, this will not replace "low-tech" storytelling, in fact it will likely take it to new heights. Immersive theatre such as Punch Drunk's *Sleep No More*, dynamic performances such as Park Avenue Armory's production of *Die Soldaten* (2008), *Everything That Happened Would Happen* (Manchester International Festival 2018), dynamic use of theatre and adjacent buildings, e.g. Constantin Chiriac's *Faust* (Sibiu Festival 2018), all show there is still much to be discovered, explored, created, in delivering highly emotionally engaging theatre, with limited or no significant technology, or strategic use of limited well-known technology.

The creators' artistic imperative will remain as it has always been — how do I best tell my story? How do I want people to feel? How do I get them to feel it? If the answer is effective, strategic, intentional deployment of technology, then it will be used. Artists will continue to seize the opportunity to take technology and use it to serve their needs, in turn forcing technology, our culture, and our stories to new places.

1.14

Acoustics and the Modern Theatre

Sébastien Jouan

Long before the launch of modern acoustic design, audiences enjoyed music or drama unaware of how the space they were in impacted on the quality of the sound or how sound reflections enhanced the enjoyment of a performance.

Indeed, architectural design (forms, volumes and shapes) significantly affects the acoustics of any space and especially an auditorium. Inversely, the sensation of space is partly defined by its sound environment:

> Can architecture be heard? Most people would probably say that architecture does not produce sound, it cannot be heard. But neither does it radiate light and yet it can be seen. We see the light it reflects and thereby gain an impression of form and material. In the same way we hear the sounds it reflects and they, too, give us an impression of form and materials.[1]

Steen Eiler Rasmussen (1898–1990) was a Danish architect and urban planner. He was a writer of many books, notably *Experiencing Architecture*, and professor at the Royal Danish Academy of Fine Arts.

Acoustic design of performing art centres and auditoria has radically changed since the end of World War II. Once a black art, or with limited scientific techniques, room acoustics as a science was initiated by Wallace Clement Sabine in the early 20th century. His work on room acoustic absorption is often regarded as ground-breaking in the field of architectural acoustics. New methods were later developed by Hope Bagenal and Alex Wood in the 'new' science of room acoustics with their *Planning for Good Acoustics* in 1931 or by Vern Knudsen in his book *Architectural Acoustics* in 1932. These books were, however, work in progress and applying their recommendations, mostly based on reverberation time, gave results which were a long way from excellence (see the essay on London's Royal Festival Hall – Chapter 3.01).

Other acoustic characteristics were therefore considered, such as the sensation of envelopment, orchestral spaciousness, warmth, intimacy, definition, liveliness, brilliance, musical clarity, loudness, etc. The search for such new parameters started around 1950 and also took into consideration how the human ear processed audio information. Subjective acoustic tests with consideration of human psychology were therefore conducted. The most significant work was carried out by Lothar Cremer and Helmut Mueller in *Principles and Applications of Room Acoustics* (1982). Cremer had advised on the acoustics of many projects, including the Sydney Opera House and Philharmonie Berlin, which are discussed in later chapters.

Gathering information about concert halls and opera houses became the obvious next step. Leo Beranek started to gather acoustic data from concert halls around the world as early as 1949 for his first publication *Acoustic Measurements* and continued his work with minutia for many years. He

Audience

produced what can be considered the Bible of acousticians with *Concert Halls and Opera Houses*, which gathers acoustic data from the most prestigious performing art centres around the world up to the late 1990s.

Meanwhile, modelling techniques started to emerge as early as 1913, with Sabine using Schlieren ultrasonic photography or ripple tanks. With Schlieren photography, the idea was to study wave propagations from the ceiling and walls in 2D-sections of a scale model; the model was filled up with smoke and wave fronts made visible using strong light from behind which were registered on a photographic plate. With ripple tanks, very similar pictures can be made by sending light through a water tank with shallow waves that are created by a mechanical vibrator.

Whilst early physical models were focusing on the geometry of the space, the technique evolved. The utilisation of physical acoustic scale models mostly at 1/50 scale but also at 1/20 became common practice. The principle of an acoustic scale model is to reproduce an auditorium geometry and introduce materials mimicking those of an audience or a reflector with absorption matching those which may exist in the hall, further refining the reverberation time predictions. A sound source (a spark – located on stage) and a sound receiver (microphone in the audience) are introduced to replicate at a scale the sound reflection

sequence and produce an impulse response from which acoustic data can be extrapolated. For a 1/50 scale model, this means that the actual frequencies used for the measurements need to be 50 times the normal full-scale frequencies. These physical models also used mirrors and small laser-based light to visually mimic sound bouncing against a surface.

However, physical scale models are costly and take time and precision to construct. From the 1970s, computers were progressively used to model spaces and predict somewhat the acoustic characteristics of space. Nowadays, room acoustic computer modelling software such as CATT-Acoustics or Odeon is advanced enough to give good and reliable acoustic results. This is achieved using ray-tracing methods assuming that sound travels as a ray. This assumption is in itself a limitation and most room acoustic modelling focuses on the development of wave-based prediction, which has the beneficial advantage of considering low frequencies and the bending of sound at those frequencies. However, the predicted room acoustic results are not reliable yet and ray-tracing remains the main tool used since the 1990s.

Room acoustic computer modelling software is able to predict different acoustic parameters such as Reverberation Time and Early Decay Time (EDT), timbre with the Bass Ratio (BR), objective measures for vocal and musical clarity (D_{50} and C_{80}), Strength (G), Early Lateral Energy Fraction (LF_{80}) or the Speech Transmission Index (STI). All these important acoustic parameters are required in concert halls, opera and theatre acoustic design.

This software is also able to predict the impulse responses of a space. An impulse response is the response of a hall for a given sound source (say a singer on stage) and a given receiver (say a member of the audience seated in the first tier). This impulse response gathers all the acoustic characteristics for these specific locations in the hall as well as the directional acoustic properties of the source and receiver. In fact, a single hall has an infinite number of possible impulse responses. This explains why a symphony orchestra may sound different in the stalls, in the first tiers or even behind the orchestra in the case of a vineyard concert hall.

These impulse responses are measured in a real space or predicted by a room acoustic computer modelling software as a mono signal, binaural or even 3D sound with Ambisonic B-Format output. Ambisonics is

Acoustic model being used to test the acoustics of La Philharmonie de Paris

a method invented in the 1970s for recording, mixing and playing back 3D 360-degree audio. The technique, whilst very innovative, was not commercially adopted until recently, with the development of the VR industry, or by acousticians wanting to listen to their design using 3D 360° audio recreations.

The basic approach of Ambisonics is to consider a sound event as a full 360° sphere of sound coming from different directions around a centre point. The centre point is where the microphone is placed while recording, or where the listener's 'sweet spot' is located while playing back.

The most popular Ambisonics format today is a four-channel format called Ambisonics B-format, which uses as few as four channels to reproduce a complete sphere of sound.

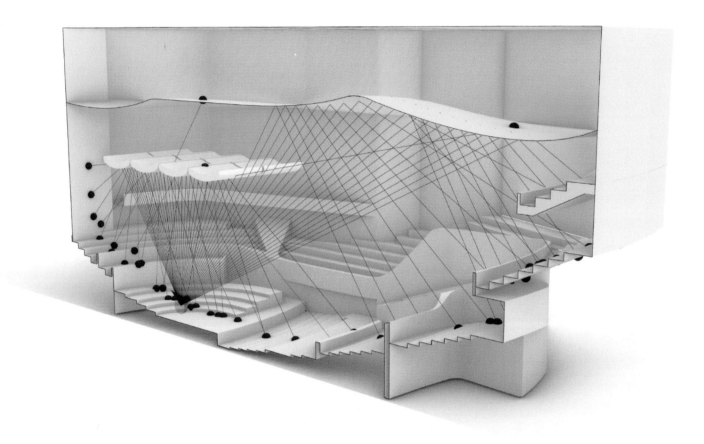

Odeon acoustic model showing the spherical propagation of sound from a source on stage

Birth of Auralisation

The latter possibility gave birth to a new technique: the auralisation of a space. Auralisation is to sound what visualisation is to sight. The concept behind auralisation is therefore to use these impulse responses and add anechoic sound to them, to hear what the space would sound like for that specific music in a space which doesn't exist yet.

Anechoic music is music recorded in a room without echo (anechoic), which results in music recorded without any room presence.

The addition of the impulse responses is in fact achieved by doing a fast-Fourier transform of the two signals (i.e. a multiplication of the two signals in the frequency domain). The result is the sound of that anechoically recorded orchestra heard in a new concert hall which is only at design stage. The technique also allows one to replicate the sound of existing halls, thus allowing listeners to compare the sound of a piece of music in several known, existing halls and a proposed new space (the idea of benchmarking).

Of course, auralisation techniques are not perfect and one cannot certify that a computer-based auralisation will correspond to the final finished concert hall as there are still some assumptions on the technique (ray-tracing instead of wave propagation, assumption on coupled volume, sound diffraction, etc.) which means that auralisation technique is somewhat equivalent to a computer visualisation of the early 2000s. It is, however, undeniably a very good technique to better understand the acoustics of a space at design stage, and to benchmark and communicate to clients acoustic differences between the hall at design stage compared to other concert halls for instance.

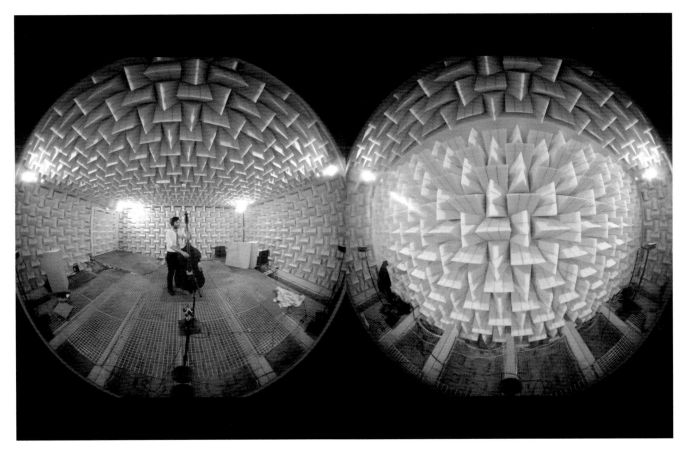

Double bass being played in an anechoic chamber

Auralisation in the early 2000s was focused on 3D sound based on Ambisonic set-up (i.e. a sphere of loudspeakers) where the listener was seated in a sweet spot at the centre of the sphere. Ambisonic first-order speaker rendering allowed for listener movement, at the cost of spatial precision so the technique was further improved thanks to the utilisation of higher order Ambisonics refining the precision of the localisation of the virtual sound source. These set-ups are installed in small studio-like spaces, with very controlled acoustics. They require very low background noise and are expensive to build. They also require no external noise penetrating the space and no ventilation noise. This often requires these spaces to be built as a box-in-box construction, which is expensive. It also means that people wanting to experience these spaces are required to travel to these studios.

Since the 2010s, auralisation has reached a new phase, with the development of 3D head-tracked binaural headphones combined with immersive goggles such as Google Oculus. These small devices can be carried in a small bag and allow acousticians to travel and meet with clients. The recent development of 3D binaural headphones is possible with two recent innovations:

First, the use of HRTFs (head-related transfer functions) which gives the sensation that sound comes from outside the headphone, giving an incredible sensation of sound realism and second, the use of a head-tracking device which fixes the sound in a given position. The latter means that when someone moves their head, the sound remains at the same position. When the 3D binaural sound is combined with visual immersive devices, the immersive experience allows users to appreciate the visual and acoustic qualities of a space.

Auralisation suite

The possibility of hearing in real time different acoustic treatments, different dimensions and volumes of a space is also starting to be used. Some researchers at Paris Sorbonne University for example are part of a wider group working on an open source framework for real-time auralisation in architectural acoustics and virtual reality. The idea is to provide real-time audio feed-back on the acoustics of any given room during its design.

The Future of Acoustic Design and Auralisation

It is difficult and risky to predict what the future of acoustic design will be and which techniques will be used to predict the acoustics of new performing arts centres. It seems though, at the time of writing that research focuses on the integration of different disciplines and skills in an ever more holistic manner required for the design of such spaces. One can see that, with the development of BIM techniques, the integration of different models from different disciplines (acoustics, lighting, fire, ventilation, etc.) will become increasingly useful. From one single graphic 3D model, it will become possible to model different aspects. We can therefore foresee that acoustic design and auralisation will be embedded in those models.

Acknowledgement

The author of this chapter collaborates with Sorbonne University for the provision of auralisation/immersion on his projects. We are grateful to Brian Katz at Sorbonne University for his assistance with this text and provision of some images.

Note

1   *Experiencing Architecture*, MIT Press, 1964, page 224.

PART 2.00

THIRTY SIGNIFICANT THEATRES
1950–2010

2.00

Introduction
David Staples

This section reviews 30 of the most significant theatres to open between 1950 and 2010. The preceding sentence immediately raises four questions:

"Why is a theatre significant?"
"Why start in 1950?"
"Why finish in 2010?"
"Why thirty theatres?"

Four questions and four answers.

"Why is a Theatre Significant?"

"Significant" was the word that emerged after considering and rejecting many other words like great, good, successful, innovative, inspirational, groundbreaking, etc., the deliberate ambiguity of the word giving considerable flexibility.

Good/Great – Initial discussions suggested we should find and use examples of "good or great" theatres from this period. But what aspect of "good" or "great"? No one would argue against the Sydney Opera House being one of the most outstanding pieces of architecture of the 20th century. However, most theatre practitioners know that it is one of the most compromised opera houses and concert halls in terms of acoustics, functionality, theatricality, etc. It would be perverse for a book on modern theatres to exclude Sydney on grounds of acoustics or practicality. It is the most recognisable opera house in the world.

Successful – A second word considered was "successful". Fortunately, most new theatres and concert halls are successful. Groups, communities, and governments invest huge sums of money to create new theatres. New buildings almost always experience a honeymoon period in the two or three years after opening. But success is not just commercial. New buildings provide performing arts groups with new facilities allowing improved standards of performance, the ability to do more innovative and successful work, etc. As almost all new theatre buildings are successful, we need to find a better qualifier.

Innovative – Some theatre buildings in the period we are examining have been truly innovative. Before architect Hans Scharoun's Philharmonie Berlin opened in 1963 the world had seen and heard classical music performed in traditional, shoe-box shaped rooms like the Musikverein in Vienna or the Concertgebouw in Amsterdam. Scharoun completely reinvented rooms for music. He rejected the shoebox, clustered the audience around the platform and was the first person to use the expression "vineyard" to describe this new form. The Philharmonie Berlin is probably the most innovative and inspirational room of this period. Concert hall design was transformed.

Significant in Community/Country – It was suggested we should examine theatres that have been significant in their community or country. Sydney Opera House is briefly mentioned above and discussed in a subsequent chapter. It transformed people's perceptions of Sydney and Australia. By contrast Salford was a declining city in the North West of England contiguous with the much larger city of Manchester. The Lowry has transformed and been significant in the regeneration of Salford.

Influencer – Some projects are 'significant' because of their influence on succeeding buildings. The Arena Stage in Washington, DC was one of the first arena stages (theatres in the round) in the United States. It inspired and influenced many theatres across America especially on university and college campuses. Similarly, the Festival Theatre, Stratford, Ontario was one of the first and most successful thrust stage theatres which also inspired the design concept for many subsequent buildings.

Role in the Performing Arts World – Some theatres are important due to their role in the performing arts world. Few theatres are built specifically for dance and this book discusses three – the Joyce Theater in New York, Sadler's Wells in London and the Lucent Danstheater in The Hague, Netherlands. The first two are houses that have brought world class performers, companies and programming to New York and London. The third has been home to Nederlands Dans Theater, one of the most innovative dance companies in the world. They have all played a significant role in the development of dance as a performing art.

"Why Start in 1950?"

The Second World War brought a halt to theatre building and the destruction of literally hundreds of theatres, concert halls and opera houses.

Only one significant theatre opened during the 1940s – the Malmö Stadsteater in neutral Sweden. Somewhat improbably the theatre opened on 23 September 1944 with a prologue by the Malmö-born poet and dramatist Hjalmar Gullberg, and a production of Shakespeare's *A Midsummer Night's Dream* on the main stage. Only 28 kilometres away across the Øresund the Danish capital Copenhagen was still an occupied city. The theatre was visited by many post-war theatre architects and its influence can be seen in subsequent buildings.

Britain's Royal Society of Arts suggested in 1943 that an international exhibition should be held to commemorate the centenary of the 1851 Great Exhibition. The post-war government decided to proceed with the Festival of Britain. The Festival had events in cities across Britain but was centred on London's South Bank. The Royal Festival Hall was a key building on the Festival of Britain site and opened on 3rd May 1951.

While our notional starting date was 1950, the Festival Hall is the first building to be reviewed in this section.

"Why Finish in 2010?"

The intention was to allow some time to have elapsed after the project opened to allow a fair and reasonably objective review of the building.

Russell Johnson was one of the world's most successful and eminent acoustic consultants. He advanced a 'six-year theory' about new theatre buildings:

- Years one and two, the building has finally opened, the pain is over, the money has stopped flowing out. Everything is good.
- Years three and four, everything goes wrong – the artistic director leaves, the roof leaks and the operating deficit is much bigger than anyone anticipated.
- Years five and six, the building has settled down and sufficient knowledgeable people have visited and seen performances to allow a fair assessment to be made.

Following this logic, it was decided to cut the list at theatres that had opened by 2010.

"Why Thirty Theatres?"

Thirty is a quite arbitrary number. It had to include sufficient projects to allow a geographic spread and also a mix of concert halls, opera houses, drama spaces, etc. It had to be an achievable number – contributors had to be found for each chapter.

As research proceeded it became apparent that many of the photographs of theatres had been shot on Kodachrome film. Kodachrome had been developed in the 1930s as 8, 16 and 35mm movie film. Its use in still cameras took off in the 1950s (our starting point) with the availability of affordable cameras. It fell out of favour as digital photography grew and the last roll of Kodachrome was processed in 2010 (the endpoint for this section). We started to think of the projects as the "Kodachrome Theatres". Kodachrome 35mm film was available with either 24 or 36 exposures. Thirty sits in the middle.

The Thirty Theatres

Any listing like this will be contentious and debated. Some of your favourite theatres will be missing, you will hopefully be surprised by the inclusion of others. There is scope to add your opinions online at www.moderntheatres.org.

There was a conscious effort to have a geographically diverse collection of theatres. Given the nationalities and heritage of the editor and collaborators it would have been all too easy to produce a list focused on the English-speaking world or Europe. Theatres have been intentionally included from many countries and every continent is included, except, sadly Africa. The editor would be keen to hear of any African projects from 1950 to 2010 thought worthy of addition to such a list.

Looking at the chosen theatres geographically. There is one theatre in Latin America – Auditório Ibirapuera 'Oscar Niemeyer' in São Paulo, Brazil.

Seven projects are in Asia and Australia – Bunka Kaikan in Tokyo and the Matsumoto Performing Arts Centre are both in Japan. The Sydney Opera House and Melbourne Arts Centre (formerly the Victorian Arts Centre) are in Australia. The Esplanade: Theatres on the Bay is Singapore's national performing arts centre. Two projects in China include the Guangzhou Opera House and the National Centre for the Performing Arts in Beijing.

The six projects in North America start in Canada with the Festival Theatre in Stratford, Ontario. Projects in the USA include the Kalita Humphreys Theater in Dallas, Texas, Arena Stage in Washington, DC, the Joyce Theater in New York City, the Walt Disney Concert Hall in Los Angeles, and the KÀ Theatre in Las Vegas.

After Brexit, there is considerable debate as to whether the United Kingdom should be considered part of Europe. Historically theatres and the performing arts have developed very differently in the UK and continental Europe, so it seems logical to list the projects separately – without offering a political view on the merits or otherwise of Brexit.

Europe has projects in Germany – Musiktheater im Revier (MiR) in Gelsenkirchen, the Philharmonie Berlin and the Schaubühne, also in Berlin. Finlandia Hall is the sole project from Finland while Norway has a new opera house in Oslo and Copenhagen has the DR Koncerthuset. Teatro Regio is in Torino (Turin), Italy. In the Netherlands, the Lucent Danstheater in The Hague is featured. Opéra Bastille is in Paris. Casa da Música is in Portugal's second city Porto and the final European project is the National Opera House (formerly the Wexford Festival Opera House) in the small town of Wexford, Ireland.

The United Kingdom has the 1951 Royal Festival Hall and further along the South Bank the Royal National Theatre. London is also home to the Sadler's Wells Theatre. In Manchester, the Royal Exchange Theatre is featured together with The Lowry in neighbouring Salford. The Derngate, Northampton is the only multi form theatre discussed in this book.

The theatres are set out on subsequent pages in chronological order. There is an essay on each building. These have been written by collaborators who have generously given their time and expertise to review the buildings. To retain some independence the theatres have been reviewed by people independent of their original design and operational teams.

The authors include architects, theatre people, academics, theatre and acoustic consultants, journalists, and historians. Authors were given a broad template to assist and guide the structure of their essays. However, authors were free to follow, adapt or ignore the template. The authors are from diverse backgrounds and come with differing expertise. The reviews of the theatres therefore reflect the authors' knowledge and interests.

Several photographs illustrate each theatre including in some cases photographs from the construction or opening. For some projects, the photographs illustrate changes that have happened to the building since opening.

Finally, for each theatre there is a comparative plan and section drawn by architect and theatre consultant David Hamer. These are to a common scale of 1:200 allowing ready comparisons between the buildings.

In writing this introduction there was an initial attempt to categorise the 30 theatres by type – opera house, concert hall, dance space, drama theatre, etc. This rapidly became a frustrating exercise, for while some projects are readily defined, others are less readily categorised. The Royal Festival Hall and Walt Disney Concert Hall are concert halls; the Royal Exchange Theatre and Arena Stage are categorically drama spaces. Others have a less clear identity – Bunka Kaikan in Tokyo and Auditório Ibirapuera in São Paulo are both used for many different types of performance and events. To add to the confusion some of the 30 projects include two or more auditoriums – The National Centre for the Performing Arts in Beijing and the Sydney Opera House have both an opera auditorium and a concert hall.

The following paragraphs start with introductions to the opera houses, concert halls, drama theatres and dance auditoriums. As the paragraphs proceed the projects become less delineated, before ending with the spectacular KÀ Theatre, designed and constructed simply to house one long-running show – Cirque du Soleil's KÀ.

Opera Houses

The listings include seven opera houses ranging from the small festival opera house in Wexford, Ireland through the splendidly Scandinavian project in Oslo, Norway to the inimitable Sydney Opera House. The reasons for their inclusion are complex. All are significant, several are great late 20th-century opera houses. Some are flawed buildings.

Before proceeding a clarification is necessary. Some of the following projects are opera houses in the traditional (European) sense of being a home for and presenting an opera and ballet company. Some whilst named as opera house (especially in the Middle East and China) are in reality large theatres presenting mixed programmes that includes some opera but also embrace large events including musicals and popular entertainment.

Musiktheater im Revier (MiR), Gelsenkirchen, Germany

The Musiktheater im Revier (MiR) in Gelsenkirchen in the North Rhine-Westphalia state of Germany is in a city of 260,000 thousand people. An industrial town built on heavy engineering and coal mining; it was extensively damaged during the Second World War including the entire destruction of its former opera house. As in many German cities there was a resolution to rebuild. MiR opened in December 1959. This was one of the first major performing arts buildings to move from the forbidding, austere facades of previous generations to an open glazed façade expressing transparency and inviting the public into the building. At the beginning of the 21st century almost all public buildings are open, inviting and transparent. MiR was to serve as a model for this type of architecture. It is a typical German driesparten theatre presenting opera, dance and drama, with a main theatre and smaller second space.

Sydney Opera House, Australia

The Sydney Opera House is certainly the most recognisable performing arts building of the 20th century and possibly one of the most recognisable buildings from that century. The Sydney Opera House resulted from an architectural competition. Such competitions allow architects to explore radical and innovative ideas for a project and site and are also often seen as presenting opportunities to new, young, and emerging architects. Sydney certainly gave opportunity to the then unknown Danish architect Jørn Utzon.

Before Utzon and the Sydney Opera House major public buildings tended to the formal, rectangular and classical forms of design. Utzon's opera house introduced curves, flowing lines and shapes that had never been seen before. The shapes proposed by Utzon were almost unbuildable. Utzon's structural engineer Ove Arup and team pioneered the use of computers in structural engineering and the creative use of materials to calculate how such shapes could be created and made to stand up.

The Sydney Opera House is flawed as a performing arts building but its architecture provided a pointer to the works of Frank Gehry, Zaha Hadid, and many others.

Teatro Regio Torino, Italy

Opera spread across Europe, but it still thought of as the Italian performing art. Virtually every city or large town in Italy had its own opera house following the form of the earliest rooms. Torino (Turin), Italy's fourth biggest city had such an opera house, the Teatro Regio, inaugurated in 1740 but unfortunately destroyed by fire in 1936. The city and people resolved to create a new opera house, an architectural competition was launched but politics and the Second World War intervened. The rebuilding was delayed into the 1960s.

Architect Carlo Mollino was eventually appointed to design a new opera house for Turin. The client and architect sought to create a new form of opera house departing from the traditional form to be found in every other city. Opera is a matter for civic pride in Italy with cities wanting their opera company and opera house to be better than their neighbours!

Molino conducted extensive research while designing the new house including travelling to visit many theatres being constructed around the world. After three hundred years of Italians building great opera houses the city of Turin got a new Teatro Regio, an innovative and radically different opera house.

Opéra Bastille, Paris, France

Paris has one of the world's great opera houses – the Palais Garnier, named after its architect Charles Garnier. Standing at the head of one of Baron Haussmann's grand boulevards the Palais Garnier is impressive in every respect – façades, foyers, auditorium, stage and supporting areas.

In 1981 the newly elected President Francois Mitterrand took up an old idea and included a new opera house "For the people" in his list of "Grands Travaux" or "Grands Projets Culturels".

The brief was published for an opera house of 2,700 seats – from originally 4,000 – and a smaller second space on a site adjacent to Place de la Bastille. Architectural competitions are a popular route to choose an architect and was the option pursued in Paris. The brief for the competition was written by experts and was incredibly detailed and prescriptive about the layout of spaces. Architects entering this competition had virtually no freedom except to choose the materials and external cladding.

Seven hundred and fifty-six entries were received for the Opéra Bastille competition, which was won by Carlos Ott, a young Uruguayan architect living in Canada. A further example of a competition providing opportunity to a new or emerging architect. After completion, the building with its gigantic stages and spaces became a mecca for opera builders.

Operahuset, Oslo, Norway

The Operahuset in Oslo (Oslo Opera House) is possibly one of the most iconic performing arts buildings since the Sydney Opera House. Designed by architects Snøhetta is rises like an iceberg from Oslofjord. The project also creates a major public square, albeit a steeply sloped space, that rises over the foyers and auditorium.

Den Norske Opera and Ballet, founded in 1958, had been housed for many years in a converted cinema. The company led the campaign for a new house and eventually persuaded the Government of Norway to get behind this initiative. This was a project led by the users and financed by government. A clear brief for the project was developed setting out exactly what the opera and ballet needed in a new building – not only great stages and technology but a specific rich acoustic in the auditorium. The brief also identified the need for a good backstage environment and community for the workers.

An international architectural competition attracted 238 entries and was won by Norwegian team Snøhetta whose building created the auditorium, stages and back of house the companies desired, all within an extraordinary envelope. This project creates a significant resource not only for the city of Oslo but for the entire population of Norway,

National Opera House, Wexford, Ireland

Wexford is a small city in Ireland (20,000 population) that has a world-renowned but small opera festival founded in 1951. For many years, the festival's operas were presented in the Theatre Royal, which dated from 1832, until it was demolished to make way for the new Wexford Opera House designed by Keith Williams Architects with 771 seats. This has subsequently been renamed The National Opera House.

Guangzhou Opera House, China

By contrast Guangzhou Opera House was built in one of the fastest growing cities and economies in the world in the first decade of the 21st entury.

The design of the Guangzhou Opera House flowed from an international architectural competition, won by Zaha Hadid Architects. Her team had grown to become one of the most renowned architectural practices at the end of the 20th century achieving fame and acclaim unimaginable to previous generations of architects and spurring the development of the moniker "Starchitect" for the most acclaimed. Guangzhou Opera House opened in 2010 after a short design and construction period.

Concert Halls

Royal Festival Hall, London, UK

The Royal Festival Hall was built in the immediate aftermath of the Second World War when Britain and Europe faced massive economic difficulties and the challenge of post-war reconstruction. It was part of the Festival of Britain, a yearlong and country wide festival intended to lift the spirits of British people in the immediate aftermath of war.

The design team for the Royal Festival Hall was rapidly assembled from some of the most talented architects and engineers of that time. In the immediate post-war period, there was little in-depth knowledge of acoustics with the result that the auditorium has significant acoustic shortcomings.

Despite these shortcomings the Festival Hall has played a hugely important role in classical and other music genres not only in London but world-wide. London's reputation as a great music city attracts every leading music group or ensemble.

Philharmonie Berlin, Germany

The Philharmonie Berlin is possibly the most transformative of all the projects in this book. Before the Philharmonie, concert halls all followed the same basic plan and section – a rectangular box with the platform at one end (sometimes with choir stalls behind the musicians), the room would have high parallel side walls, one or perhaps two shallow galleries at the rear of the auditorium and shallow seating galleries along the side walls.

Hans Scharoun was appointed architect for the Philharmonie Berlin and decided to pursue a radically different form that moved the orchestra platform more towards the centre of the room. Placing the audience in relatively small seating blocks (Scharoun's aim was seating blocks that matched the seat count of a typical orchestra), the orchestra was surrounded with audience as close as possible to intensify the experience. The result was an extraordinary new shape for a concert hall. Scharoun was the first to use the term "vineyard" to describe this new form. Architects in particular love the dynamism of the vineyard hall. For audiences it can give a better emotional and visual connection with the musicians. However, some argue that the acoustics are better in an equivalent shoebox room. Whatever, the vineyard or its' derivatives with a more open shape have become the most popular form for new concert halls around the world.

Walt Disney Concert Hall, Los Angeles, California, USA

The Walt Disney Concert Hall in Los Angeles is a direct descendant of the Philharmonie Berlin, with an auditorium that combines aspects of the surround seating found in vineyard halls together with the more classic shoebox form. This form of concert hall has come to be known as 'hybrid'. Designed by architect Frank Gehry it has both a dramatic interior and an extraordinary exterior of curving stainless steel sheets. A significant gift from the Disney family financed a large part of the construction costs of this hall

Casa de la Musica, Porto, Portugal

Casa de la Música in Porto, Portugal returns to the rectangular shoe-box form but interpreted by architect R.E.M. Koolhaas of OMA with some distinctive and unusual features. The exterior won almost universal praise for its simplicity and clean shape being a nine-floor high asymmetric polyhedron constructed in white concrete with large distinctive windows.

In the 1,238-seat shoebox auditorium (Sala Suggia) the wall behind the concert platform and the opposing wall at the rear of the room are of gently undulating glass, admitting light, connecting the interior to the exterior and giving views to the exterior. An organ is split between the left and right walls of the auditorium which are decorated with a gold motif resembling wood grain. Over the platform a light acoustic reflector appears to float.

Playhouses

Festival Theatre, Stratford, Ontario, Canada

Stratford, Ontario in Canada is a rural community of 19,000. It shares its name with Stratford-upon-Avon in England the birthplace of William Shakespeare. Based on this somewhat tenuous connection a group of local people decided in the 1950's to create a Shakespeare Festival. The project rapidly involved renowned British theatre director Tyrone Guthrie who had been experimenting with "thrust staging". The Stratford Festival was incorporated, grew and in 1957 a purpose-built theatre for it opened, one of the world's first dedicated theatres of its type. Although seating over 1,800 no seat is more than 65 feet from the stage.

The thrust stage pioneered in Stratford (designed by British designer Tanya Moiseiwitsch) has gone on to inspire theatres in many other towns and cities – Minneapolis and New York in America, Chichester and Sheffield in England and, coming full circle, the Swan Theatre in Stratford-upon-Avon.

Kalita Humphreys Theater, Dallas, Texas, USA

Frank Lloyd Wright was possibly the most famous architect of the 20th century. He was certainly one of the most renowned American architects producing many striking and successful buildings. Unfortunately, his theatre building was not among his greatest achievements. The Kalita Humphreys Theatre in Dallas, Texas is a 497-seat theatre designed to become home to the Dallas Theatre Center (DTC) one of America's major reginal theatre companies. Completed about nine months after the architect's death the Kalita Humphreys was based on schemes Lloyd Wright had prepared for other cities and was a challenging building for its users from day one.

Arena Stage, Washington, DC, USA

Arena Stage in Washington DC, which opened in 1961, was designed by architect Harry Weese and built at almost the same time as the Kalita Humphreys (1959). It is a much more successful theatre devoted to drama presented in an arena (theatre in the round) format. Arena Stage was one of the first not-for-profit theatres in the United States and an important part of the regional theatre movement. Like the Festival Theatre in Stratford, the Arena was designed from the outset to reject the traditional proscenium arch form of staging and presented plays with the audience on all four sides of the open stage. It was a forerunner for many arena stages and black box theatres, especially at universities and colleges across America.

National Theatre, London, UK

Great Britain has a rich heritage based on plays and the spoken word – many acclaim William Shakespeare as the world's greatest playwright.

Despite this heritage the country lacked a national Theatre. The concept of a National Theatre was first espoused 72 years before the National Theatre eventually opened, designed by Denys Lasdun, on London's South Bank. The intervening years saw consideration of five sites, four architects, innumerable briefs and two World Wars.

The National Theatre had a mixed response when it opened attracting significant architectural criticism. It is possibly the most influential performing arts building constructed in the United Kingdom. It is the centre of excellence and aspiration for much of Britain's dramatic theatre activity.

Royal Exchange Theatre, Manchester, UK

The Royal Exchange Theatre in Manchester grew out of two previous theatre companies – Theatre 59 and Theatre 69. They were given the Royal Exchange Hall as a possible site for a new theatre. The Hall was a massive Victorian trading hall at one time proclaimed to be the biggest room in the world.

The theatre company had an almost unique opportunity to experiment with scaffolding structures covered by a tent in the vast exchange hall. The experiments led to a decision to create and perform theatre in the round. Architects Levitt Bernstein working with theatre designer Richard Negri created a glass enclosed module with three levels of seating in a seven-sided structure surrounding a central stage.

The Royal Exchange was acclaimed when it opened and was selected by the Theatres Trust as the most important and influential theatre building of the 20th century. So, it is perhaps surprising that it has not been copied, emulated or developed even though it is a unique space.

Schaubühne am Lehniner Platz, Berlin, Germany

The Schaubühne am Lehniner Platz in Berlin is another unique performance space created within the shell of an older building. Eric Mendelsohn, one of Germany's most eminent pre-war architects created the Universum Cinema in 1928 which, with its clean lines, was influenced by the Streamline Moderne style of Art Deco architecture. Heavily damaged in the Second World War, it operated as cinema and dance hall. The Schaubühne ensemble was founded in 1968 and grew around Peter Stein the theatre and opera director. In the late 1970's they were searching for a new venue and the Berlin Senate offered the Mendelsohn building. The Schaubühne's concept was of a laboratory to develop a new theatre language, they wanted a very flexible space that could be used as one large room or subdivided to allow simultaneous performances in separate rooms.

The company was at the forefront of theatrical innovation and within the old cinema they created a supposedly flexible space with 67 elevators each 7 by 3 metres in size. While in theory this would provide the flexibility they sought, in reality changing formats takes too long and is expensive. The large dimensions of the elevators impose further constraints.

The Schaubühne is a good example of the need to experiment in theatre spaces. Experiment can move the industry forward. The Schaubühne is however a project of its time, location, and circumstances.

Dance Spaces

While many theatres accommodate ballet and dance performances, few are specifically constructed for dance as an art form.

Joyce Theater, New York, USA

The Joyce Theatre in Manhattan was created in the shell of the 1941 Elgin Theater. The renovation was designed by renowned theatre architect Hugh Hardy and reopened as the Joyce in 1981 seating 472. Although a small theatre it has a disproportionate place in the dance world because of its creative and varied dance programming in the City of New York.

Sadler's Wells Theatre, London, UK

The current Sadler's Wells Theatre in London is the sixth on the site since 1683. It is renowned as one of the most important dance-presenting theatres in the world. Fulfilling a similar role in London to the Joyce by presenting diverse dance programs. The theatre also has commissioning and artist in residence programmes. The current theatre opened in October 1998 and seats 1,500 funded in part by the UK's National Lottery.

Lucent Danstheater, The Hague, Netherlands

The Lucent Danstheater was designed to be home to one company, Nederlands Dans Theater (NDT); the previous two in this list house many visiting and touring companies. The theatre was designed as a limited-life building by Office for Metropolitan Architecture, the practice of Rem Koolhaas. It opened in 1987 initially as the Danstheater aan 't Spui in The Hague. The theatre's significance comes from NDT, the company, occupying the building with its high-quality innovative work. The theatre was demolished in 2015 and will be replaced with a new theatre in 2021.

Other Performance Spaces

Several theatres are not easily classified as they often present wide-ranging programmes or in some instances the project includes multiple auditoriums.

Bunka Kaikan, Tokyo, Japan

The Tokyo Bunka Kaikan (TBK) is a multi-purpose hall in Ueno Park, Tokyo. Opened in 1961 it has been one of the most important and influential music and cultural venues in the reconstruction period after the Second World War. TBK was commissioned by the Tokyo Metropolitan Government in response to public demand for a venue to enjoy opera and ballet in Tokyo, and to commemorate the 500th anniversary of the city.

The architect of TBK, Kunio Maekawa, apprenticed for several years with Le Corbusier's studio in Paris. TBK is a multi-purpose hall housing fully staged productions like opera and ballet alongside classical music, orchestras and smaller ensembles. At the time it was designed and constructed there was limited experience or knowledge of such buildings

and the architect and design team had to pursue innovative ideas to achieve a successful building. There are inevitably compromises, but TBK remains a significant performing arts building for Tokyo and has influenced many subsequent buildings in Japan.

Matsumoto Performing Arts Centre, Japan

Matsumoto is a mid-sized Japanese city of around 240,000 people located in Nagano Prefecture East of Tokyo. The Saito Kinen Festival Masumoto was started in 1992 by renowned conductor Seiji Ozawa. Operas and various concerts are performed at facilities throughout the city during this festival.

The Prefecture decided to construct a new building and an architectural competition was planned. A complex site was identified, it is over 200m long and around 30m wide. Toyo Ito won with a bold plan that reconciled both the brief and the site by adopting a highly creative approach.

Theatres and opera houses have traditionally been symmetrical, axial buildings. The site in Matsumoto precluded such a rigid axial arrangement and Toyo Ito created a unique route into and through the building. A staircase with imaginative glazing follows the curving wall of the building and brings audiences up to the two auditoriums and a roof top terrace.

Finlandia Hall, Helsinki, Finland

The Finlandia Hall was originally designed as a concert hall and conference centre. In the centre of Helsinki on the Töölönlahti Bay, designed by Finnish architect Alvar Aalto, it opened in December 1971. The unusual design of the main hall led to significant acoustic deficiencies and eventually a new concert hall was constructed – the Helsinki Music Centre designed by LPR Architects and acoustic consultant Yasu Toyota of Nagata Acoustics. With the opening of the new hall Finlandia Hall became a dedicated conference centre.

Arts Centre Melbourne, Australia

In Australia a rivalry exists between Sydney and Melbourne. It was therefore almost inevitable that once Sydney acquired their new Opera House Melbourne should plan and construct a similar building. Originally called the Victorian Arts Centre after the State of Victoria it was subsequently renamed Arts Centre Melbourne. Following on from the Sydney Opera House the planners and architects avoided some of the problems in the earlier building and the auditorium and stages are considerably better and more usable. The spaces are largely underground with a tall spire as the external manifestation of the building. Australians have been known to claim they have the best performing arts centre in the world; the exterior is in Sydney and the interior in Melbourne.

Derngate, Northampton, UK

Northampton is an English town located about 70 miles north of London which grew and prospered in the late 19th century with the shoe making industry. It declined as that industry faded but had a resurgence as a commuter town for London with the arrival of the M1 (Britain's first motorway). The city grew and a need was discerned for a performing arts facility to serve many needs. The wanted a concert hall and a theatre for musicals and a place for comedy and entertainment and a flat floor venue. The solution was to creatively use simple technology to create a multi-form space. There have been many attempts to create multi-purpose spaces, most have failed as the rooms do not adequately change to suit the event being presented. Derngate adopts an approach where the shape and form of the room is changed using seating towers and wagons moved on air castors.

A test of flexible theatres is to visit five or ten years after the building opens to see if the flexibility is still being used. Thirty-five years after its creation Derngate regularly changes its format from a successful concert hall to a theatre with full stage facilities for a touring musical to a venue for comedy or entertainment to a flat floor space for a banquet or sporting event. Derngate is possibly the most successful, flexible venue in this book.

The Lowry, Salford, UK

The major industry in Salford were the docks at the eastern end of the Manchester Ship canal but post-war growth in the size of merchant ships and the development of containerised shipping caused the docks

to decline and eventually close in 1982. Salford became one of the most disadvantaged cities in the United Kingdom. On almost any measure – poverty, health, education, employment – this was a deprived community.

Salford City Council developed a bold regeneration plan for the disused and demolished dockland area. From the beginning the plans featured a flagship cultural development of theatres and galleries. The architectural team of James Stirling Michael Wilford Architects were selected. In 1994 Britain established a National Lottery to raise funds for "good causes" and this provided a significant opportunity for Salford to develop. The Lowry became one of the Heritage Lottery Fund's Landmark Millennium Projects for the arts.

The Lowry opened in April 2000 and has a Lyric Theatre seating 1,730 and the smaller flexible Quays theatre seating 466. Some 2,000 square metres of gallery space displays works from the L. S. Lowry (a renowned 20th-century British painter who lived and worked in Salford) collection along with other works. The centre includes restaurants, bars, retail and generous public areas.

The area around The Lowry and the later Imperial War Museum has seen a massive injection of capital and growth of jobs following the opening of The Lowry. The BBC decided to relocate jobs from London to Manchester. MediaCityUK is a 200-acre mixed use development housing the BBC, ITV Granada and other media companies. Thus, the Lowry is at the heart of one of the most successful arts led regeneration projects in the world.

Esplanade– Theatres on the Bay, Singapore

Singapore is an island city-state of around 5.6 million people in South East Asia. It became a sovereign nation in 1965. After early years of turbulence and lacking natural resources and a hinterland the countries focus was on economic development and education.

Gradually, the Government realised that economic development alone was not sufficient to build a successful country. A number of initiatives aimed to develop culture, sports and the quality of life. The Esplanade –

Theatres on the Bay is Singapore's national performing arts centre. Planned, constructed, and paid for by the Government of Singapore it has grown to be one of the most influential facilities in Asia.

Initial planning led to an interesting architect selections process where an initial long list was winnowed down to four teams. All were invited to Singapore for a five-day workshop or charrette where each team was given time with client, users, and other groups. For the client this was effectively an extended interview process. Michael Wilford and Partners in partnership with DP Architects from Singapore were appointed architects.

The Esplanade is located near the mouth of the Singapore River on the Waterfront. The Lyric Theatre seats about 2,000 and is based on a traditional European horse-shoe shaped auditorium modified to take account of the Asian performing arts (Chinese opera, Indian dance, Malaysian and Indonesian dance) which typically have the musicians on stage alongside the performers rather than in a Western orchestra pit. The shoebox concert hall was designed my Russell Johnson and seats 1,600 on four levels. There are smaller performances spaces, a library, meeting, and gallery facilities. It also has significant food and beverage operations.

Auditório Ibirapuera 'Oscar Niemeyer', São Paulo, Brazil

São Paulo, Brazil is the largest city in the Americas and in the southern hemisphere. The city was to celebrate its 450th anniversary in 1954 and the authorities planned to create a public park and new theatre with Oscar Niemeyer as architect. The park was completed for the anniversary, but it took another 51 years before Auditório Ibirapuera finally opened in 2005.

Niemeyer was born in 1907 and was allegedly still practising architecture shortly before his death at the age of 104. His largest and most famous work was the new city of Brasilia which became the country's capital in 1960.

Auditório Ibirapuera went through 12 different versions from 1951 to its construction in the 21st century each designed by Niemeyer. The projects varied in size, ranging from 3,000 to its eventual 804 seats. Dedicated to music, the space sporadically hosts dance and theater performances. It was built of reinforced concrete and it is entirely white. The marquee that gives it access was named 'Labareda' (meaning "flame"). Painted red, it marks the Auditório and distinguishes it from the other buildings in the Park.

National Centre for the Performing Arts, Beijing, China

As China's top performing arts centre, the philosophy of the National Centre for the Performing Arts adheres to the guiding principle of 'for the people, for art and for the world' and strives for the objectives of being: a key member of prestigious international theatres; the supreme palace of performing arts in China.

The Centre was planned by the Government and after a contentious and disputed competition French architect Paul Andreu was appointed. The site adjacent to the Great Hall of the People, near the Forbidden City, and Tiananmen Square is one of the most prominent not only in Beijing but in the entire country.

The theatres are covered by a huge titanium and glass dome surrounded by a man-made lake. It has been likened to an egg dropped into a lake. The design and positioning caused considerable controversy. Audiences descend and enter through a tunnel that passes under the lake.

Inside are three theatres. The Opera Hall seats 2,426 for opera, ballet and other staged events. The Music Hall seats 2,017 for concerts while the Theatre Hall has 1,040 seats for Chinese opera and drama.

KÀ Theatre, MGM Grand Hotel, Las Vegas, Arizona, USA

The KÀ Theatre is located on the casino floor of the huge MGM Grand Hotel in Las Vegas and is possibly the most unusual theatre featured in this book. The existing theatre was gutted and rebuilt to house the show KÀ originated by Cirque du Soleil. There is no stage floor simply a large void and complex decks – the Sand Cliff Deck and Tatami Deck that can rotate, rise and fall to create complex walls and floors as needed. The *Los Angeles Times* stated it "may well be the most lavish production in the history of Western theater. It is surely the most technologically advanced." The show opened in February 2005 and is performed twice a night, five nights a week in the 1,950-seat theatre and in 13 years has been seen by over one million people.

DR Koncerthuset, Copenhagen, Denmark

In Denmark, the state broadcaster DR (originally Danmarks Radio) as in many other countries operates its own orchestra, the Danish National Symphony Orchestra. Controversially DR moved its activities to a new headquarters and broadcast campus in the Ørestad area of Copenhagen. DR Byen (DR city), covers a large area of approximately 133,000 m2 (13 hectares). The site was always conceived as including a major new concert hall for use by DR but also as a major public amenity for the residents of Copenhagen and the surrounding area, as it has proved to be. Designed by architect Jean Nouvel the building was inaugurated in 2009.

Please visit www.routledge.com/9781138484382 to see the full chapter on DR Koncerthuset.

1950s
The Fifties

Royal Festival Hall, 1951, showing shot tower to the left and Skylon to the right

Royal Festival Hall, 1951

London, UK
Architect, London County Council Architects Department – Robert Matthew, Leslie Martin

Miles Glendinning and Sébastien Jouan

The Queen's Hall, in London, opened in 1893, seating 2,500. It became London's principal concert venue and was home to the Promenade Concerts. The hall allegedly had drab décor and cramped seating but superb acoustics and became known as "the musical centre of the British Empire". On the night of 10 May 1941, however, just after the London Philharmonic Orchestra and the Royal Choral Society had given a concert, there was a heavy air raid, in which the chamber of the House of Commons and many other buildings were destroyed. An incendiary bomb hit the Queen's Hall, and the auditorium was completely gutted by fire.

Its successor, the Royal Festival Hall, opened on 3rd May 1951, and can indirectly trace its inspiration to the 1851 Great Exhibition or Crystal Palace Exhibition. The Great Exhibition held in London's South Kensington was effectively the first World's Fair.

In 1943, at the height of the Second World War, Britain's Royal Society of Arts suggested that an international exhibition be held in 1951 to celebrate the Centenary of the 1851 Great Exhibition. The post-war Labour government decided to organise an event "as a tonic to the nation" and the event became known as the Festival of Britain. Festival projects took place throughout the United Kingdom, but the central focus was London's South Bank Exhibition near Waterloo. Several buildings and structures were constructed including the Dome of Discovery, the futuristic Skylon – and the Royal Festival Hall.

The Festival was regarded as a symbol of the Labour government and the succeeding Conservative government ordered the demolition and scrapping of the structures and displays, all except the Royal Festival Hall itself.

The Royal Festival Hall was built between 1949 and 1951 by the London County Council and designed by the LCC Architects' Department, headed since 1946 by the progressive young Scottish architect-planner Robert Matthew, who assembled a talented team of young architects including Leslie Martin. The hall comprised a reinforced concrete frame structure containing a concert hall with over 2,900 seats, raised above the ground, with an open foyer and stairs flowing around and below. In its conception and reception, it was widely hailed as a standard-bearer for the new, collective, social Modern architecture. Yet as first completed in 1951, it was a somewhat hybrid creation, as its near-symmetrical massiveness and stand-alone situation linked it still to the 19th-century tradition of the grand public building, unlike the frothy exhibition pavilions around it.

1947–1951: Robert Matthew and the LCC's Original Project

In mid-1947, following a decision that the LCC should build a new cultural centre on the South Bank, LCC architect Robert Matthew moved quickly to make sure his staff would design this grand, new, democratic hub. From the start, he was determined this must be not an old-style concert hall but "a centre for musical activities of all kinds with ample space round the Hall for walking and talking, eating and drinking, and sitting about quietly", offering plenty of opportunity to look outwards across the Thames while doing all those things. But by then the proposal had already started to move rapidly from debate towards realisation, as the government decided to proceed with the Festival of Britain in the same area. He was told by the council leadership that it should contain a large concert hall of 3,500–5,000 seats, a small theatre, and a restaurant overlooking the river, an exhibition gallery, and meeting rooms.

Matthew identified a double acoustical problem as the core of the design challenge: how to insulate the concert hall from the deafening rumble of trains on a railway bridge right next door; and how to arrive at an optimum shape for the auditorium itself. The first obvious response was survey and scientific data-gathering. During the summer 1947 council recess Matthew threw himself into a crash tour of European concert halls. Scandinavia, especially Sweden, seemed to be the prime influence. Matthew was particularly impressed by Nils Einar Eriksson's Göteborgs Konserthus. It contained a main hall with 1,400 seats, and a small 450-seat hall behind. The main hall was entirely ringed by sweeping public 'promenades' and refreshment areas, including a huge, fully glazed front foyer facing Götaplatsen, and was raised up above a lower floor. With these Scandinavian precedents, the second of the two main conceptual elements of the eventual Festival Hall began to fall into place. Matthew had already ensured that it would be a 'Cultural Centre' and social focus. Now it was becoming clear that this aim could be partly secured by linking the large and small halls and the catering space through an enveloping 'social' foyer.

In July 1948, the Government 'upped the pace' by asking the LCC if the Cultural Centre could be completed in time for the opening of the festival in May 1951. Matthew agreed on condition it be overseen by a special subcommittee, chaired by the council leader himself. During July Matthew was already busy producing initial drawings, under rather unusual conditions, as he had been confined to bed for two months by a long-standing problem of lumbago.

The main design decision about the large hall was its planform, which was an acoustic-driven choice between rectangular and fan-shapes. As Matthew worked on his initial sketches, he debated this issue with advisers from Denmark, the USA and the Building Research Station. At first, his drawings favoured a fan-shaped solution.

But it emerged that, as part of the Festival planning, the building's 'footprint' in Holden's masterplan would now have to be so strictly enforced that the main and small halls, with surrounding foyers, could not both fit on the site at the same level. And the demands of science came suddenly to the fore again, when the newly-appointed acoustic consultants, Peter Parkin and Hope Bagenal of the Building Research Station (BRS), objected to the fan-shaped auditorium, believing it risked echoes, and insisted on the substitution of a rectangular shape. The obvious response to the site restriction, following the Göteborg and Stockholm precedent, was to lift the main auditorium up above the small hall, extending the foyer space below as well as around the main hall: what became known as the 'egg in a box' concept. This decision, it seems likely, was taken jointly by Matthew and the newly appointed Leslie Martin, along with Parkin and Bagenal.

By the end of November 1948, a revised scheme was ready for approval. The 3,100-seat auditorium, with its 'acoustic box' of double-thickness concrete walls, was surrounded by an envelope of access stairs, galleries and foyers, with the fan-shaped small theatre hall below and behind. The entire structure around the auditorium was to be of steel framing. The drawings showed the small hall squeezed in partly beneath the main auditorium, with an ungainly

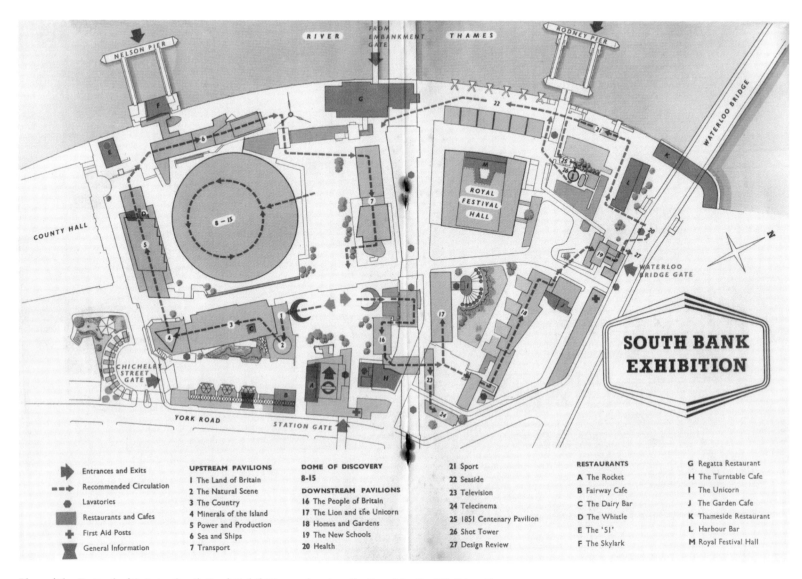

Plan of the Festival of Britain, South Bank Exhibition – showing the Royal Festival Hall location

block still projecting from the rear. All this would have been rather different from the more unified building we know today, but even this version was not destined to be built, as a sudden shortage of steel in January 1949 meant it would have to be totally redesigned almost overnight in reinforced concrete, costing 50 per cent more and potentially taking far longer. This was a strategic crisis tailor-made for the unflappable Matthew. Rather than put the completion date at risk, he decided to cut down the size of the building by simply chopping off the rear third, including the small hall and the stage and administrative areas, which would be built at some future date. The rear wall would be finished with temporary cladding. The foyer, no longer linking two halls, now took on an autonomous importance – which would later encourage architectural critics to hail it in its own right. The project had assumed its final conceptual form – not through one masterly design decision, but through a series of acci-dental, reactive developments.

May 12, 1951 Royal opening of Royal Festival Hall

Opening and Reception

This somewhat hybrid, individual-collective process would be obscured by the triumphal, propagandist presentation of the building, orchestrated largely by Matthew in the press over the following two years. The conductor Malcolm Sargent hailed it as "the temple of those spiritual joys which are so mystic but so very real".

Visiting the hall after its opening in 1951, the renowned Swiss modernist architect, Le Corbusier, declared: "In America, I battle with the superficial, here things are done seriously." He added that the building had been designed by youngsters and handed over to greybeards.

Its architecture, back in the heyday of the Festival of Britain, was received as a triumph. A building that was both modernist and monumental, with large volumes and plenty of spaces for people to discuss, drink, see people and be seen. Its acoustics however did not match the architectural acclaim it received.

Room Acoustics of the Original Concert Hall

The 2,901-seat auditorium at the core of the Royal Festival Hall had been conceived as an egg in a box by the architect and acoustician. The hall could also accommodate a 120- strong orchestra, a choir of 250 singers as well as an organ. Its prime purpose was for symphony concerts, which is to say that other uses such as speech or amplified music were subordinate to the acoustic requirements for symphonic music.

Unfortunately, the hall became known from its very opening as generally too dry and lacking warmth of sound, with a weak bass tone. In retrospect, it seems that the original acoustic designer, Hope Bagenal, had not adequately considered several crucial acoustic design parameters such as an appropriate volume per seat (V/N) required for a modern concert hall and underestimated the absorption factor provided by an audience. Musicians on the platform also had difficulty hearing themselves and others.

Initial discussions envisaged a reverberation time target of 2.2 seconds, matching that of other contemporary successful concert halls, and recommended back in 1931 by Bagenal and Wood, who were then the established authorities in acoustic design of concert halls.

Hope Bagenal's main challenge therefore started with the very large audience capacity, at almost 3,000 seats. Today, it is generally agreed that an appropriate volume per seat V/N for a modern concert hall is around 10–12m^3/seat to obtain a reverberation time in the region of 2 to 2.2 seconds. By contrast, Hope Bagenal, in an apparent effort to contain the size and volume of the hall (and above all its budget!) tried to work on a lower volume per seat V/N of 7.56m^3/seat. He reduced the reverberation time target down to 1.7 seconds.

After the rejection of the fan-shaped option, which would have provided more intimacy and proximity but no blend or fullness of sound, it was decided that the hall shape would be hybrid, with a fan-shaped platform, choir area and stalls continued by a rectangular shaped rear auditorium section. The rectangular and deep shape of the hall probably contributed to the sense of distance from the musical action and a lack of acoustic intimacy. Bagenal also famously underestimated the absorption indicator provided by an audience, with 0.33 instead of the generally accepted 0.57 per person. The single largest area of acoustic absorption in a concert hall is the audience, and any miscalculation in this area will set the acoustic design on a wrong trajectory from the start.

The hall also suffered mistakes during the construction phase. The original ceiling, which followed a line designed to reflect sound toward the rear of the audience, was initially intended to be of solid plaster 50mm thick, which would have provided a considerable mass for the low frequency reverberance, hence giving good bass tone and warmth to the sound. Unfortunately, this thickness was reduced by mistake to 10 to 20mm thickness of plaster. This mistake made the ceiling more absorbent at low frequency than originally intended. Acoustic absorption was scattered across the hall. There was a risk of echoes

Royal Festival Hall, platform

from the back walls and, consequently, the rear walls of the auditorium also included additional mid-to-high frequency acoustic treatment in the form of cushions stuffed with glass wool on 100mm battens with rockwool in the cavity. On stage, the side wooden screens separating the orchestra from the choir consisted of 10mm thick wooden panels on 100mm battens with acoustic absorption in the air space, making this surface a very good low frequency absorber. All these factors resulted in the notoriously dry acoustic conditions, with a reverberation time with an audience down to 1.5 seconds at mid-frequencies and lacking bass tone and warmth.

Reverberation is only one aspect of acoustics: other factors need be considered, such as clarity of sound, loudness and self-hearing for the orchestra. These factors were also not resolved satisfactorily, further contributing to the poor acoustics of the hall.

The other important acoustic design consideration in a concert hall is the sound insulation from external noise and vibration. The proximity of two major sources of noise, with above-ground trains on the Hungerford Bridge and underground trains running directly under the building, posed a challenge. The noise from the above-ground trains was measured, resulting in the conclusion that a double leaf concrete envelope construction would be necessary.

Royal Festival Hall, boxes

From the 1960s Alterations to the 2005–2007 Refurbishment

The Hall was substantially altered in 1964 with major changes to the river façade, entrance and foyers. This renovation also introduced an 'assisted resonance' system to try and improve the acoustics. Additional foyers and terraces were added to the building, which effectively extended it by 9 m towards the river. An entirely new façade and main entrance were created facing the river.

At that time, Leo Beranek, an acclaimed American acoustic consultant, researcher and writer, advised that the interior surfaces and treatments were absorbing too much sound. The Building Research Station developed an electronic system to increase the reverberation time, called 'assisted resonance'. This comprised strategically positioned microphones in the hall, each located in a Helmholtz Resonator and designed to limit the microphone to one specific frequency. The sound from each microphone was amplified and fed back into the hall by a loudspeaker. The system had 172 channels covering the lower frequencies of 58 Hz to 700 Hz. It was claimed to have increased the reverberation time from 1.4 to 2.5 seconds in the 125-octave band. While the assisted resonance system gave some improvement, it never fully solved the problem and, as it aged, became increasingly unreliable, leading to its use being discontinued in 1998. Around that time, the conductor Simon Rattle declared that performers "lose the will to live" when confronted with such poor acoustics.

Front facade

During the first 30 years of its existence, the Royal Festival Hall operated in a very traditional manner, with the upper level of the foyers opening shortly before the evening performance and closing immediately after the audience departed. In 1983 the Greater London Council (the successor organisation to the London County Council) introduced a radical 'open foyer' policy where the foyers were opened to the public all day, every day with exhibitions, lunchtime concerts, informal evening concerts, bars, shops and buffets. Shortly after that, in 1988 the Festival Hall was designated as a Grade 1 listed building by English Heritage – one of the first 'post-war modern listings' in England – in a recognition of its 'exceptional' architectural and historic interest.

The building closed in 2005 for another major (£91 million) refurbishment under architects Allies and Morrison. The river side of the building was changed again with a series of restaurants and cafes being created at low level. For this 2007 refurbishment, the American acousticians, Kirkegaard Associates, were selected to provide the acoustic design input. The ambition was to improve the acoustic conditions of the Royal Festival Hall whilst not altering the architectural effect of the original building. Even so, there were protests, led by the Twentieth Century Society, which objected to the removal of the original canopy, claiming that the "the architectural consequences of this will be disastrous".

Kirkegaard's work focused therefore on what was possible, namely to remove the low frequency absorption provided by the lightweight ceiling, strip off any surfaces susceptible to absorption of sound (i.e. absorption on the rear walls, carpet in some areas) and replace it with sound diffusing finishes while redesigning the platform and the canopy.

A new auditorium ceiling, heavier and denser than the original ceiling, was installed. The ceiling consists of an internal wave form consisting of lightweight glass-reinforced gypsum shells with a 250mm thick layer of plaster and bricks above. Warm wood panelling was also installed across the hall, rejuvenating the feel of the auditorium and providing the hard surfaces required to increase the reverberance. The original teak floor was reinstated, and any carpet replaced by hard floor. The stage was remodelled with a slightly less fan-shaped design and the original canopy was replaced by a small wing-shaped canopy made of modern Nomex material stretched over a frame. This contributed greatly to the improvement of the acoustic conditions for the musicians on stage, providing them with self-hearing but also reopening the available volume above the old canopy and hence improving the reverberance thanks to extra volume. The organ itself was also refurbished by its original maker, Harrison & Harrison, its depth reduced by 1.1 m to satisfy architectural and acoustic requirements. A variable acoustic system was also introduced which reduced the reverberance for amplified music events.

Despite all these efforts, however, the reverberance was merely increased to 1.65 seconds, still below the 1.7 originally intended by Hope Bagenal and far from the 2.2 seconds that a modern symphonic concert hall requires. The hall also presents balance problems in some parts while crispness is at more of a premium than warmth. But there was nevertheless a discernible improvement, and the press and musicians hailed the new acoustics, acclaiming the clear amelioration of the sound quality of the hall.

Conclusion

Over 65 years the Royal Festival Hall has grown to be one of the world's most significant concert halls, largely thanks to its geographical location in London. As a hall it has hosted most of the world's leading orchestras and music ensembles. Musicians and orchestras need to be seen and heard in London; it is important for their reputation to be reviewed by the London critics (alongside those in New York and some other cities).

But the Festival Hall has always been an acoustically flawed hall, with too dry an acoustic caused by too short a reverberation time; and even now, despite the many attempts to improve its acoustic performance, it will never be an acoustically great concert hall. Accordingly, today, in 2020, plans are afoot to create a new Centre for Music for the capital, under the co-sponsorship of the Barbican Centre, the London Symphony Orchestra and the Guildhall School of Music. The site would be at London Wall – the Barbican site which currently houses the Museum of London – and at the heart of the new Centre would be an acoustically perfect concert hall, rectifying at last a deficiency that has weighed on London concert-goers since the loss of the Queen's Hall in 1941.

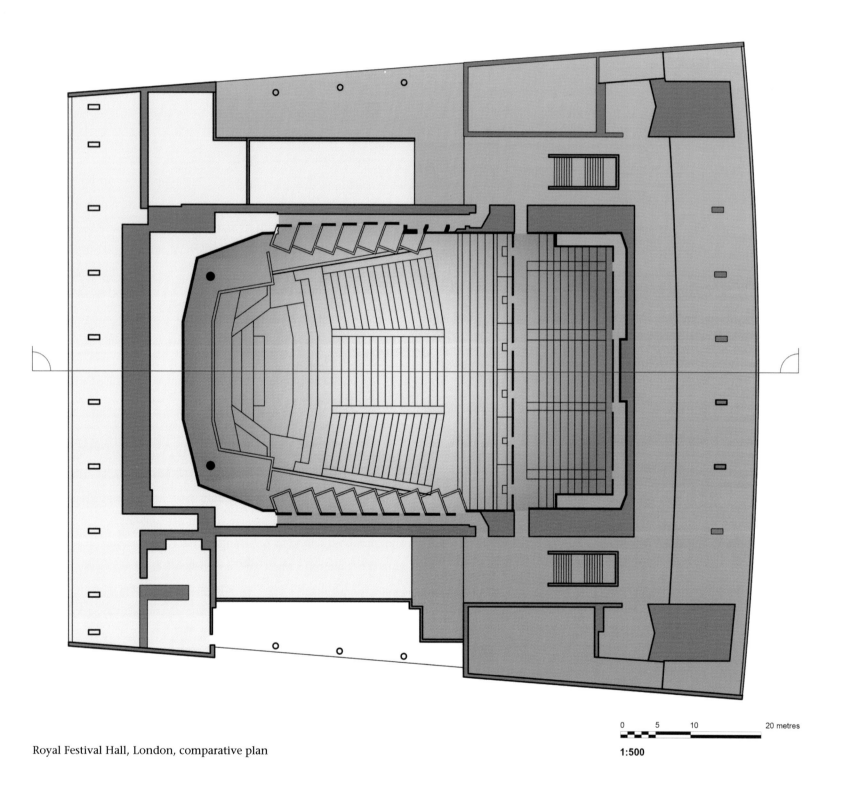

Royal Festival Hall, London, comparative plan

0   5   10   20 metres

1:500

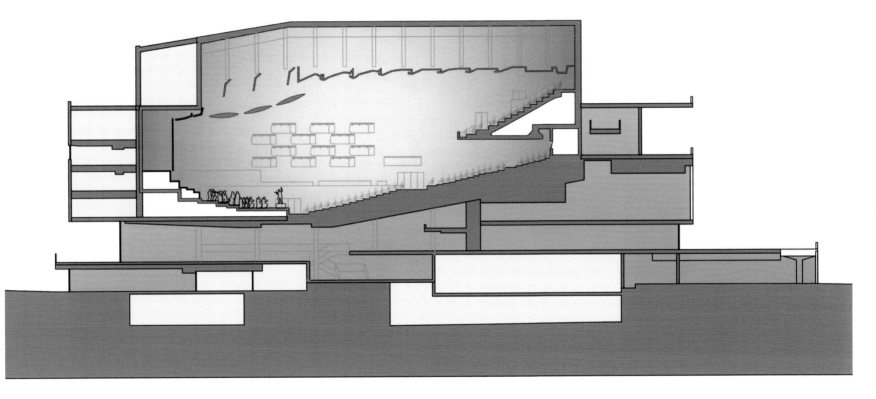

Royal Festival Hall, London, comparative section

1:500

Festival Theatre, Stratford, Ontario

Festival Theatre, 1957
Stratford, Ontario, Canada
Architect, Robert Fairfield with Tanya Moiseiwitsch
Gary McCluskie

The only thing a rural Canadian community of 19,000 had in connection with William Shakespeare in the early 1950s was the name of his hometown. Stratford, Ontario, 90 miles west of Toronto, seemed an unlikely place to become a major force in staging the Bard's plays. But when a railroad company closed up shop, local journalist Tom Patterson took on the task to reinvent Stratford as a celebrated centre for seasonal theatre. It not only became that, but also, with its innovative thrust stage design, set new standards for staging all kinds of plays with an influence that continues to resonate 65 years later.

Stratford has become one of the most significant performing arts organisations in Canada. The innovative concept and design of the Festival Theatre has been developed and replicated in many cities around the world. Wikipedia notes: "Since that time (the opening of the Stratford Festival theatre) dozens of other thrust stage venues have been built using this concept."

The zeitgeist was with this bold post-war vision. The legendary British theatre director Tyrone Guthrie, intrigued by the idea, became more so when Patterson told him there was no venue as yet to launch the festival. "Guthrie had been experimenting with thrust-like staging and saw the opportunity to custom build the kind of theatre he wanted," said David Prosser, current Communications Director at the Stratford Festival. Guthrie

had staged a landmark production of a medieval comedy in 1948 at the second Edinburgh International Festival. The venue was essentially found space – Edinburgh's General Assembly Hall of the Church of Scotland on the Mound – where a version of the thrust stage was used to great effect.

In October 1952, the Stratford Festival was incorporated, and Guthrie became its first Artistic Director, recruiting stars Alex Guinness and Irene Worth as well as actors from across Canada for the first season the following summer. The venue would consist of a concrete amphitheatre beneath a large canvas tent, a design solution of an architect recommended by an acquaintance of Guthrie's who had no theatre design experience and only six months to realize the structure. But it was the stage, designed by Tanya Moiseiwitsch, whom Guthrie recruited from the UK, that would revolutionize the production and theatrical experience of Shakespeare's plays along with many other dramatic forms in the decades that followed. Moiseiwitsch's pioneering role in 20th-century theatre included hundreds of set and costume designs for acclaimed productions in addition to subsequent thrust stage designs after Stratford, among them the Crucible Theatre, in Sheffield, UK.

"This was an original invention, not a reproduction of an Elizabethan stage," said Prosser. "It had influences of Greek and Roman theatres. The thrust was hexagonal, not a projecting square that we often associate with Shakespeare and as reproduced at Shakespeare's Globe Theatre in

Festival Theatre, the original tent

London." Stratford's protruding stage consisted of nine acting levels and eight major entrances in addition to a balcony, trapdoors and two vomitoria. Steps lead to the audience level on all sides of the thrust. The tent theatre's original configuration accommodated 1,800 seats with none more than 65 feet from the stage.

But it wasn't this radical shift from a proscenium stage that almost ended Stratford's dream before it began: like so many artistic endeavours, a lack of funding nearly bankrupted the idea. With construction underway, the debts were mounting. The Stratford community had been divided about any public investment in the enterprise, including the initial $125 commitment by the local council to send Patterson to New York to research how to launch a theatre festival. He returned unsuccessful in his attempt to meet with Laurence Olivier.

In that spring of 1953, the buzz began to grow in Stratford and grass roots support turned in the festival's favour, women's auxiliary clubs and local business groups got behind it, spurred by the sight of the tall wooden masts that would hold up the tent canopy in the park next to the Avon River. When told the Festival Foundation was having cash flow problems, the contractor building the stage instructed his staff to keep working. The Governor General Vincent Massey and a local insurance company both came forward with donations that ensured the festival would make it to opening night on July 13.

Festival Theatre, sketch

Besides the benefits of tourism to the local economy and Stratford becoming a destination in its own right, the initiative to launch the festival was seen to embody the objectives of the Massey Commission, which laid out priorities for a nascent country in search of a modern cultural identity (the Royal Commission on National Development in the Arts, Letters and Sciences; 1949–1951). One of the report's major conclusions was "... it is in the national interest to give encouragement to institutions which express national feeling, promote common understanding and add to the variety and richness of Canadian life, rural as well as urban". The Stratford Festival fit the bill.

That first season the festival mounted 22 performances of *Richard III* and 21 performances of *All's Well that Ends Well*, both starring Alex Guinness and Irene Worth. But it could be said Moiseiwitsch's stage was also a star attraction. In its July 1, 1953 review, the *Montreal Star* wrote:

The first big surprise was the amazing flexibility and the deceiving latitude of the comparatively small stage and Mr. Guthrie's three-dimensional use of it. Characters erupt out of nowhere and converged on its several platforms from all directions and just as quickly melted away into the obscurity from which they had appeared.

The newspaper's review continued to focus on the stage:

One thing certain is that they were never visually bored by Miss Moiseiwitsch's permanent set. Its inner stage and balcony are formal and solid with graceful, slender columns, but its complementary doors and stairways on either side are not symmetrically balanced. This variety of line is carried out elsewhere in various ways. The garden seat set just off the main platform, which can be built up to form an elevated throne, is not balanced on the other side and the main platform with its surrounding steps has its corners cut off. The many levels in such a small space gave Mr. Guthrie some wonderful opportunities for literally building up pyramids of figures and it was interesting to note how he varied his approach in the two plays.

For the actors, the Stratford Festival stage presented an entirely new dynamic in which to perform. In an interview with the *Brooklyn Eagle*, Guinness stated:

Twenty years of looking out straight is hard to forget. At first when we started rehearsing, we were all in a panic because Guthrie said you must show yourselves. We were like spinning tops, we couldn't relax, but as we went along we found we could settle down and relax.

To the *Herald Tribune*, Guinness described this new performance space. The stage was "...on absolutely the right lines. It is not any academic replica for professors to play about with, not highbrow or strange but vital." The actor also offered some suggestions for amending the stage design, stating in the first season the front row of seats was too close to the stage and the sweep of the auditorium's circle, at 220 degrees, was too wide and should be narrowed. For the following season, the front row was moved back. In later renovations, the arc of the auditorium was reduced to 175 degrees.

For the audience, the proximity and intimacy of the experience introduced the notion that they, too, are participants in the spectacle before them. This idea was later interpreted in other performing arts venues, including the vineyard configuration for orchestra, notably the Philharmonie Berlin, which opened in 1963, and continues to be reinterpreted and refined in many other ways.

Stratford's first Artistic Director was well aware many audience members would see spectators on the other side of the stage from them and how this changes the nature of the theatrical "illusion" and the relationship between audience and the stage. In an article in *Shakespeare Survey* No 8, Guthrie noted,

I suggest that theatrical performance is a form of ritual, that the audience is not asked to subscribe to an illusion, but to participate in the ritual. [. . .] The attraction for me of the "open" stage as opposed to the proscenium, is primarily this: that it stressed the ritual as opposed to the illusory quality of performance.

(pp. 130–131)

Michael Langham, the Stratford Festival's second Artistic Director, described the impact on acting styles as follows: [on the proscenium stage]

the actors must play to the audience and only pretend to play to each other, while on the open stage their bond of relationship is direct, true and complete, and serves to pull the audience deeply into the experience of the play. The audience is physically closer to the actors than in any but the smallest proscenium theatre at the same time as being seen from three sides, putting onto the

actor a duty towards naturalism at the same time as requiring the best technique – the blend of which is uniquely 'Stratford'.

From the perspective of staging, the bare thrust stage allows the director and designer to move away from the old pictorial realism of the proscenium stage's illusionistic scenery – which took time to move from scene to scene and held up the story. Instead, the setting on a thrust stage can be suggested through design elements, principally furniture and costuming – leaving the actors to move from scene to scene with a

Festival Theatre, the permanent theatre

new fluidity. The *Boston Herald* (August 2, 1953) noted how the Stratford stage accomplished this.

> It is particularly interesting to observe how this multi-level, multi exit permanent setting not only does away with the need for formal scenery but makes possible a continuous flow of action and movement when the text of a play, as in so much of *Richard III*, calls for the rapid manoeuvring of large crowds of people, either in procession or in violent action. That it also lends flavour and variety in the far more intimate story of *All's Well That Ends Well*, is also very encouraging for it indicates that even Shakespeare's closet dramas gain by this liberation of action.

This heightened level of engagement among actors Prosser likens to "the three-dimensional, cross-cutting cinematic quality of the thrust stage."

The success of the first season was unequivocal – the initial four-week run was extended to six – and the festival was keen to expand its repertoire for its second year. In addition to two Shakespeare works, *Measure for Measure* and *The Taming of the Shrew*, Guthrie wanted to venture beyond Elizabethan drama, for which the stage seemed particularly well suited, and added the ancient Greek play *Oedipus Rex* by Sophocles. In spite of the versatility of the thrust stage to different styles of drama, performers and audience were nonetheless reminded that this magical world created in Stratford was only a canvas flap away from the outdoors. Spectators noted the sound of rain hitting the tarp drowned out the voices on stage and the proximity of a railroad level crossing meant the shrill whistle of steam locomotives frequently unsuspended the disbelief the performers worked hard to instil in their rapt audience.

Guthrie remained as Artistic Director for the first three seasons at Stratford, leaving in 1956, before a permanent home for Moiseiwitsch's stage was built. Robert Fairfield was given the assignment to design the Festival Theatre on the strength of his initial tent solution and was indeed an evocation of the canvas with an upturned "pie-crust" perimeter and a single peaked top in the centre. It was dedicated on June 30, 1957 and opened with Christopher Plummer in *Hamlet* to a full house of 2,192 spectators. Refinements to the hall made over the years included a greatly expanded rear façade, moving the side doors outwards opposite the 'voms' or stage entrances from the tunnels beneath the auditorium seating; the stage balcony was raised by eight inches and the number of supporting pillars reduced from nine to five. In 1975, a rearrangement of the performance levels changed the acting area with a rarely done treatment and made the balcony removable.

By 1997, the then 40-year-old theatre needed refurbishment. This included renovating the lobby and adding new administrative offices, and even a greenhouse. In the auditorium, the previously mentioned arc was reduced to 175 degrees; 450 seats were removed, and the 20-inch-wide seats replaced with 22-inch seats, bringing the total to 1,742. Zig-zag sidewalls were installed to improve acoustics, an acoustical canopy was suspended above the stage and a tunnel linked the two 'voms'.

The enduring stage created by Guthrie and Moiseiwitsch has had a profound influence on the development of Canadian theatre. The ongoing success of Stratford has fostered generations of actors and brought leading international stars to the rural countryside of southwestern Ontario. As the festival's Prosser explained:

> The combination of the technique and naturalism required for Stratford's Festival Stage and its sister thrust stage, the Studio Theatre (2002, 260 seats) has arguably had a huge impact on the Canadian theatre profession as a whole, with actors from our stages taking the lessons learned there across the country – and beyond – in their other work.

Shortly after departing Stratford, Guthrie solicited interest through a newspaper ad to develop a resident theatre company in the US. Minneapolis proved most willing to support the project and the Guthrie Theatre, with a thrust stage designed by Moiseiwitsch, opened in 1963. The theatre by Ralph Rapson seated 1,441 and the seven-sided stage took up 1120 square feet (104 m²). In 1980, modifications allowed the size, shape and height of the stage to be adjusted and the back wall opened up to create more depth. In 2006, the theatre's location was slated for other purposes and was demolished, the same year a new Guthrie Theatre designed by Jean Nouvel opened as part of a three-theatre complex

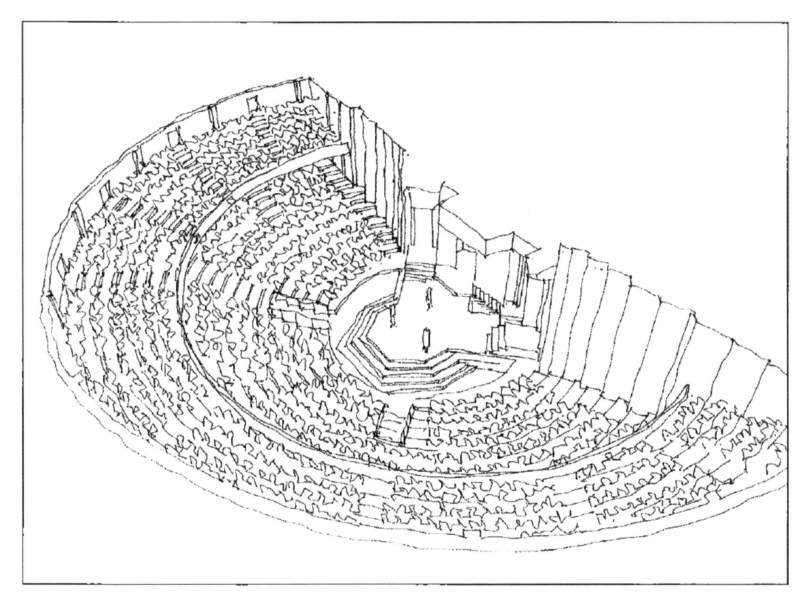

Festival Theatre, sketch by Gavin Green

that preserved the signature thrust configuration for the 1,100-seat main auditorium.

Other notable influences of the Guthrie-Moiseiwitsch thrust stage include the Vivian Beaumont Theatre at Lincoln Centre and, in the UK, the Swan Theatre in Stratford-Upon-Avon, the Chichester Festival Theatre, the Olivier Theatre at the Royal National Theatre in London, and most directly the Crucible Theatre in Sheffield. Moiseiwitsch designed the stage for the Crucible with input from its founding director Colin George, who took inspiration from her previous work. From his obituary in the fall of 2016, he was quoted as saying "... he decided the length of the thrust stage by declaiming speeches from Henry V from different parts of the theater." One terse critique of the seating on three sides of the performers came from a local councillor who stated he wouldn't "pay to look at Hamlet's backside."

Crucible Theatre, Sheffield

Is the thrust stage an almost entirely Anglo-Saxon phenomenon unique to the English-speaking world? Greece has many ancient amphitheatres, but the thrust stage has never become mainstream in German, Austrian and European theatre.

In Canada, the Festival Stage influenced the Atlantic Festival Theatre in Wolfville, Nova Scotia and the theatre at the National Arts Centre in Ottawa.

Meanwhile, the thrust stage at Stratford continues to encourage experimentation in the 21st century. In a January 2017 article, *Lighting & Sound America* magazine examines how the classic proscenium musical *A Chorus Line* was adapted at Stratford the previous season for its first ever non-proscenium staging. "A thrust space is built for the actor and soliloquy in Shakespeare. What musical has more monologues and soliloquies than *A Chorus Line*?" said the show's director, Donna Feore. The signature white line in the set design was moved from the edge of the apron to the back of the stage, freeing up emotional space down stage for when the characters go back in time in their memories.

Augmenting that shift in time was LED lighting technology never before used at the Festival Theatre that served to dramatically delineate the storytelling. A cluster of loudspeakers was hung that remained in full view as an element of the set design. Directors of concurrent productions of *Macbeth, As You Like It* and Molière's farce, *The Hypochondriac*, all chose to use the technology in their shows, taking the experimentation and adaptability of the thrust ever onward in new directions.

Footnote

The genesis of the Stratford Festival and its daring, rocky start is the subject of a 40-minute, Oscar-nominated National Film Board of Canada documentary called *The Stratford Adventure* (1954). It is available online at nfb.ca

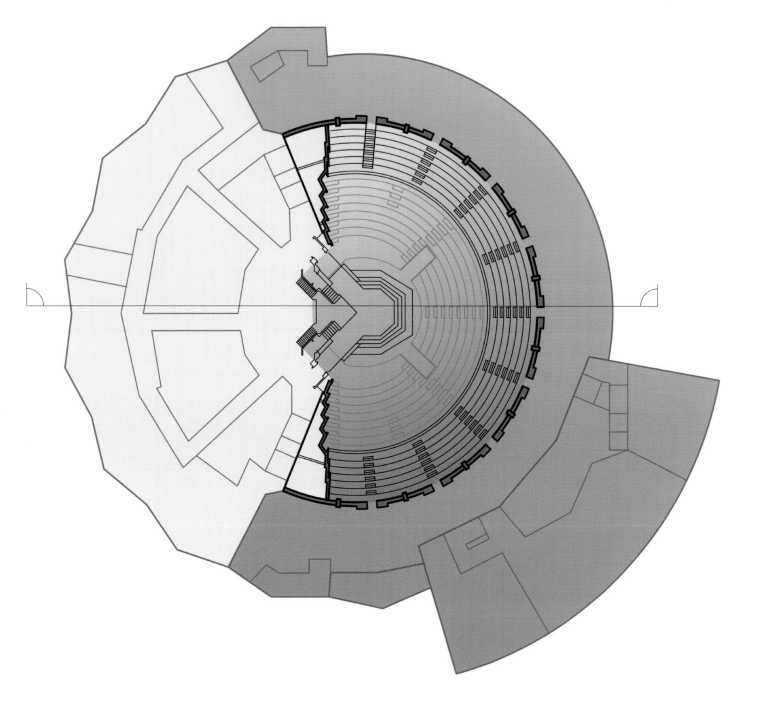

Festival Theatre, Stratford, comparative plan

1:500

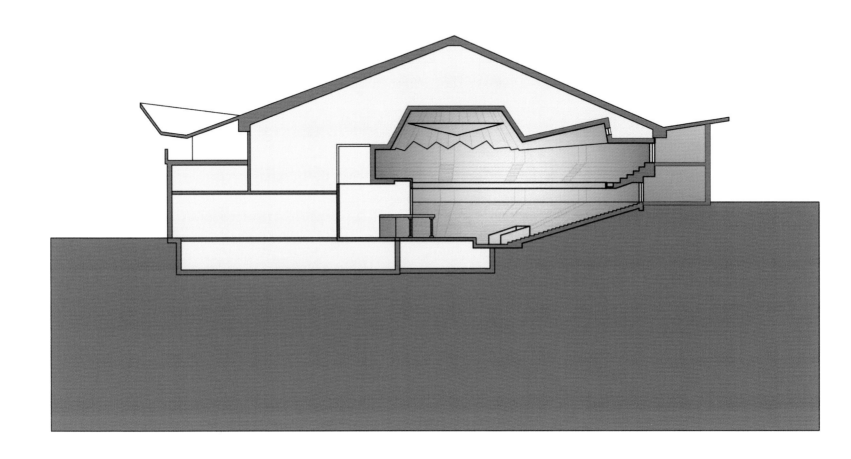

Festival Theatre, Stratford, comparative section

1:500

Kalita Humphreys Theater, entrance

Kalita Humphreys Theater, 1959
Dallas, Texas, USA
Architect, Frank Lloyd Wright

David Staples

Sadly, Frank Lloyd Wright died in 1959, a few months before the opening of two of his arts buildings, the Solomon R. Guggenheim Museum, in a dense urban setting on Fifth Avenue in New York and the Kalita Humphreys Theater, on a steep slope among the trees in Turtle Creek, Dallas, Texas. Both were radical innovative buildings that shared features – cylindrical forms and dramatic ramps – and both proved controversial.

The Guggenheim Museum in NY appears as a white ribbon curled into a cylindrical form wider at the top than at its base – a marked contrast with typical rectangular buildings in Manhattan. Internally the most dramatic feature is a gently sloping spiral ramp rising from ground level to the top of the building. The museum attracted considerable criticism; some architectural critics felt the dramatic architecture of the building would overshadow the art displayed. All the art is effectively presented in shallow, concave spaces opening off the spiral ramp. Art works are hung in spaces with sloping floors and ceilings on walls that canted outwards following the external shape. Despite these criticisms the building was widely praised, is loved by the public, and inspired many other architects.

Conceived at a series of meetings in 1954, the Dallas Theater Center was one of the first regional theatres in the United States. A board was assembled with two initial tasks – to find an artistic director and to create a building to house the emerging group. Paul Baker, innovative head of drama at Baylor University in Waco, Texas was chosen as artistic director, a position he held for over 20 years. The idea of a repertory company was new at the time, the only other significant company being in NYC.

Frank Lloyd Wright, who was at his peak and seemingly without competition, was asked to design the new theatre. He was busy with other projects and agreed, as long as he was allowed to draw from two previous unbuilt schemes – for a West Coast theatre that had been subsequently adapted for Hartford, Connecticut.

Kalita Humphreys was a native of Liberty, Texas who, after graduating from Vassar College, worked in Dallas and Texas as an actress before moving to perform on Broadway. She and her husband were killed in a private plane crash in 1953. Her parents made a significant donation to the building project and the theatre was named after her.

Lloyd Wright had developed an organic theory of architecture which emphasised the unification of the building's form and function, and unity with its natural setting. Because Wright's design was based on nature, and everything in nature, he maintained, is at a 30/60-degree angle, the only 90-degree angles in the theatre are where the walls meet the ceiling and floor.

Both Baker and Lloyd Wright were notoriously stubborn and probably enjoyed some creative tensions during the design process. Both

Solomon R. Guggenheim Museum, New York, interior

wanted to move away from or eliminate the traditional proscenium arch, to engage actors and audience in one space and to push the stage into the auditorium, giving a very pronounced curve to the stage edge. At this time there was considerable interest in thrust stages (see the chapter on the Festival Theatre in Stratford, Ontario). The Kalita Humphreys goes some way towards a thrust, with small side stages on either side. It is perhaps an uncertain compromise between an end stage and thrust theatre.

Wright's original plans were for a significantly larger building estimated to cost 50 per cent more than the budget. As a result, the building was reduced in size; there were major cuts to both the public and backstage areas of the building. The 1.2-acre site was tight and led Wright to stack elements of the building. In particular, the workshop was located under the stage, linked to the stage level by two curving ramps on either side of the stage. A rather simplistic vision imagined the sets coming up one ramp onto the stage's large 40-foot diameter revolve before being removed down the opposite ramp. The ramps were steep, narrow, and had limited headroom.

The ramps were the cause of considerable disagreement between Wright and Baker. Eventually, without telling Wright, Baker persuaded

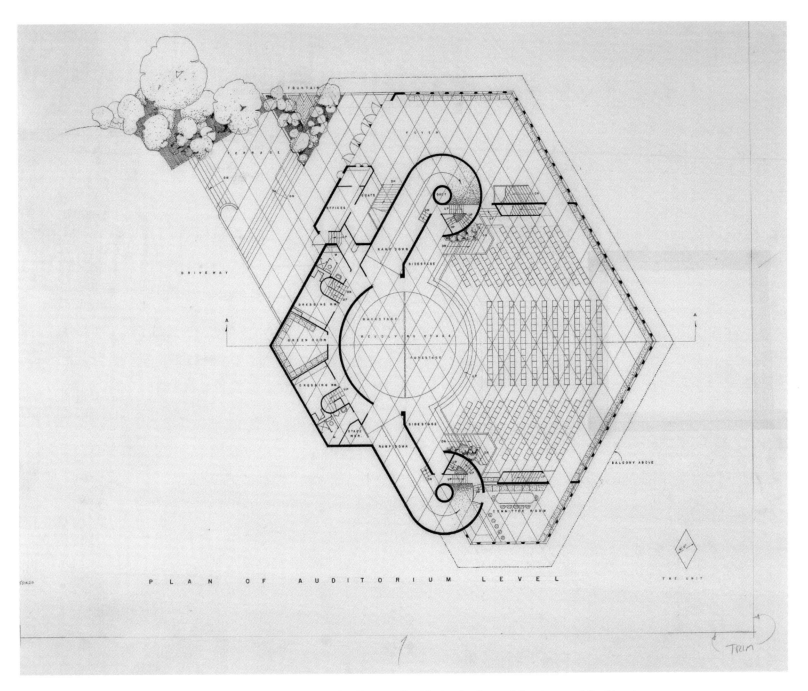

Kalita Humphreys Theater, Frank Lloyd Wright plan showing the 'diamond' grid, circular form of the stage and flanking towers

one of the associate architects to provide a freight elevator in the location where the stage left ramp was intended. Before Wright visited the site, the contractor and associate architect concealed the elevator with scaffolding so Wright would not see it.

Over the stage, a huge cylindrical fly tower rose, cleverly counter-weighted by the backstage structure behind the stage. The original interior of the theatre was gold, with a relatively low ceiling that was not able to accommodate stage lighting and requiring the needed lighting to be hung

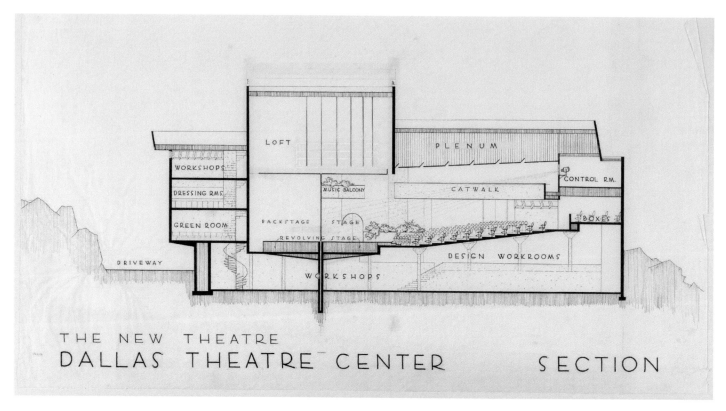

Kalita Humphreys Theater, Frank Lloyd Wright, section

Kalita Humphreys Theater in January 1960

below the ceiling. The interior of the auditorium was very light coloured and unsuited to a theatre; it also had a series of windows at high level that let in natural light, which have been covered for much of the building's life.

When completed, the Kalita Humphreys was hailed as "the most innovative theater building in the country, a great work of architecture, and the product of visionary civic leaders and an avant garde director". Publicity stressed "it permitted a great variety and flexibility in staging".

The theatre is intimate, with a good audience/stage relationship. But by the 1970s the lack of space and support facilities led to negative press and to alterations and additions. Having been initially hailed as a very flexible space, in practice it was a very inflexible space designed for a singular vision of theatre production. The panoramic nature of the stage, with the extended side stages, meant the space lacked focus, the seating rake was increased, and the bright auditorium was controversially painted a darker colour. Overall, the condition of the theatre deteriorated.

In the 1960s and 70s Dallas, like many American cities, suffered from racial problems, leading to the phenomenon of 'white flight', the migration of the white population to new suburban cities north of the LBJ Freeway. The city of Dallas and the developer community determined to try to revitalise the city centre. At the time the city was also looking to bring together several cultural institutions. Following consultant studies and reports, the city decided to establish the Dallas Arts District in the

Dee and Charles Wyly Theatre, Dallas

northeast end of downtown. The Booker T. Washington High School was already in the area, having re-opened as an arts magnet high school in 1967. In 1984 the Dallas Museum of Art, designed by Edward Larrabee Barnes, opened as the first institution in the newly created district.

The city purchased land for the long-term development of the district. The land was planned to be vacant for a number of years and the Dallas Theater Center took this opportunity to create the temporary Arts District Theater, a dynamic, flexible space designed by acclaimed scenic designer Eugene Lee. This space was limited life and planned as a very flexible empty shed. This large volume space was the antithesis of the Kalita Humphreys – it was a large empty space, allowing directors and designers to create whatever environment they wanted for their production. There was only one problem: the cost of operating and using the space. When there is total flexibility and no fixed infrastructure, the space becomes very expensive to operate.

The Dallas Theater Center used both the Kalita Humphreys and the Arts District Theater while planning was underway for an entirely new theatre within the Arts District. The Dee and Charles Wyly Theatre opened in 2005 and the Arts District Theater closed. The Wyly theatre is reviewed in a subsequent chapter.

The Dallas Arts District is today the largest contiguous arts district in America. The original Booker T. Washington School and Dallas Museum

Kalita Humphreys Theater, 2019

of Art have been joined by the Winspear Opera House, the Crow Museum of Asian Art, the Myerson Symphony Center, and a host of other performing and visual arts spaces.

The Kalita Humphreys is a theatre building by a great architect, Frank Lloyd Wright. It is elegantly and carefully integrated into its natural setting and has a distinctive exterior. The project was cut back during design and the internal spaces have always been cramped. Various changes over the years have eased this situation, but it is not a generous building.

The theatre is now in a very poor condition and groups in Dallas are lobbying for its restoration and renovation. Mark Lamster, the architecture critic of the *Dallas Morning News*, wrote an article titled 'It's time for Dallas to save Frank Lloyd Wright's crumbling Kalita Humphreys

Theater' and said "Of all the buildings in Dallas, none has been so consistently misunderstood, mistreated, misused, mismanaged, maligned and generally neglected as Frank Lloyd Wright's Kalita Humphreys Theater."

Frank Lloyd Wright had a particular vision of how theatre should be presented in this room. This led to an inflexible auditorium and stage which, while intimate, is difficult for directors and designers to use. The Dallas Theatre Canter was founded and grew in the Kalita Humphreys. It is now one of the best regional theatre companies in America. After experimenting with a temporary theatre, they created the very flexible Wyly Theatre – the antithesis of the Humphreys. Dallas now needs to decide what to do with the Humphreys: allow it to continue a slow decline or renovate a flawed theatre by one of the twentieth century's most eminent architects.

Kalita Humphreys Theater, proposed renovation with gold color scheme

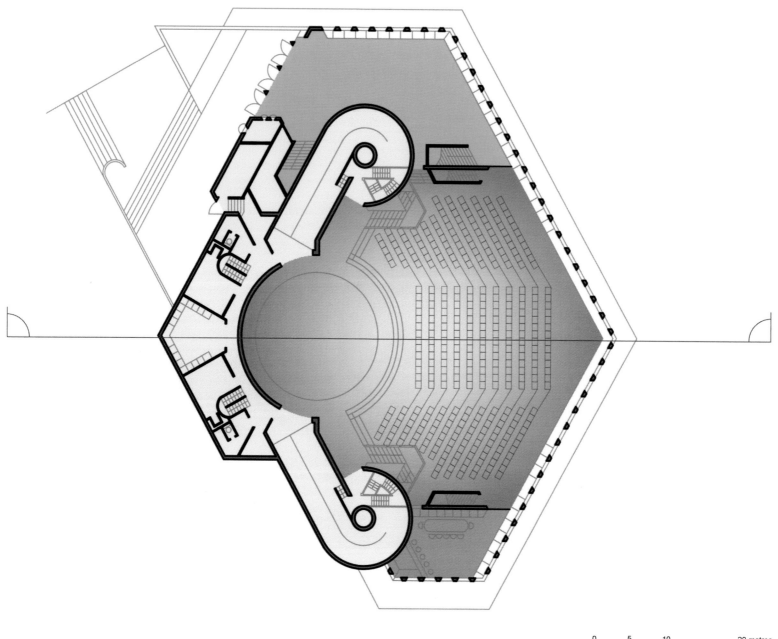

Kalita Humphreys Theater, Dallas, comparative plan

1:500

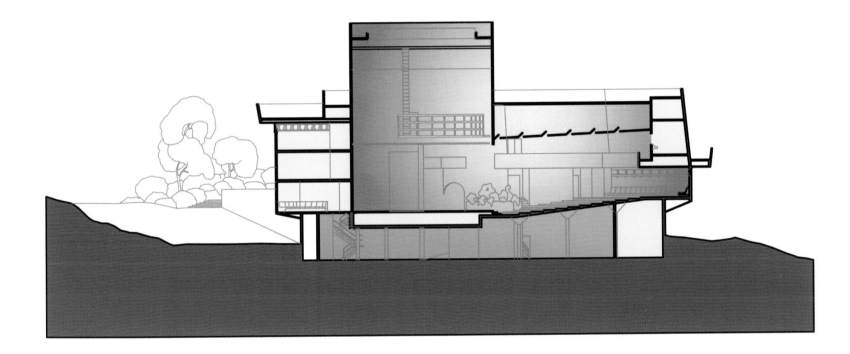

0   5   10   20 metres

1:500

Kalita Humphreys Theater, Dallas, comparative section

Musiktheater im Revier at night

Musiktheater im Revier, 1959
Gelsenkirchen, Germany
Architect, Werner Ruhnau

Elain Harwood

Theatre and opera offered a highly visible repository of moral conscience and cultural reflection to West Germany as it sought to claim political respectability after the Second World War. This was encouraged by the first president of the republic, Theodor Heuss, and by local politicians. The municipal theatre (Stadttheater) had held an important place in German culture from the early 19th century, and some 200 were rebuilt between 1946 and 1967 following war damage, with competitions providing exceptional opportunities for young, local architects to make their name. Funding came mainly from city and regional (*Länder*) councils, with the federal government contributing only about five per cent of the costs.

The Origins of the Design

Harald Deilmann, Max von Hausen, Ortwin Rave and Werner Ruhnau, a group of young architects working locally, won a competition in 1950 to rebuild the war-damaged Münster Theatre, but its construction was delayed until 1954–6. Deilmann quickly left the team, but the other three were still nominally in partnership when in 1954 the city of Gelsenkirchen announced a competition for the rebuilding of its municipal theatre, a 1930s' building that had been completely destroyed in the war. Werner Ruhnau produced a design which was declared the winner in September, but the city council then worried that it was too expensive to build, and quietly turned to the design placed second, by Fritz Bornemann of Berlin. When he learned of the change, Ruhnau protested and was allowed to produce a revised scheme which he proved was more economical to build.

Whereas the first rebuilt theatres, around 1950, incorporated the remains of their previous structures for reasons of economy and austerity, later in the decade complete rebuilding in a modern style took hold. As restrictions on steel and stone were lifted, the young architects took as their models the sleek modernism of the United States, and in particular the buildings by the expatriate Mies van der Rohe – one of their own to admire within the dominating, occupying American colossus. Mies himself was invited to produce a design for the Mannheim Nationaltheater as part of a competition in 1953, but his scheme suspending two auditoria within a wholly glazed foyer was passed over at a second stage in favour of a less radical and transparent version by Gerhard Weber, completed in 1957. There were local objections to so much glass,

Auditorium following 2010 renovation

and Mies could not produce accurate costings for the scheme from the United States. The experience led Ruhnau to take the precaution of moving to Gelsenkirchen to oversee his project and he made the city his permanent home.

Ruhnau sought to regain something of Mies's radical design, whose influence is palpable in the revised scheme for Gelsenkirchen, which – although reduced from that of the competition – retained its original layout and is very large by non-German standards. The site lies across a dual carriageway from a large open square that closes a long (largely pedestrian) promenade through the rebuilt town centre. The American magazine *Arts and Architecture* (vol. 77, no. 3, March 1960, p. 18) commented that 'the integration of the theater with this new plaza has been considered [as] important as the integration and spectators within the theater'. The building is 250m long, and while the competition design

Architect Werner Ruhnau

Musiktheater im Revier, exterior

featured a steel screen, as built the frontage comprises a fully-glazed foyer on two main levels raised over a cloakroom and mezzanine bar that are deliberately kept low. It surrounds the dark drum of the main auditorium, with behind it the main stage and extensive backstage facilities. Ruhnau saw the foyer as a stage for the audience, to be seen both from within and as a spectacle from outside that would attract passers-by to venture in. By day the glass is reflective, and it is possible to see in only when the foyer is illuminated from within at night.

Description of the Building

The foundation stone was laid in 1956 and the theatre was constructed between 1957 and 1959. The main auditorium in the central drum seats 1,050 people in steeply-sloping stalls and in two balconies, revised from three in the original scheme. Each has slips formed of linked *schlitten* – the name given to the staggered sledge-like boxes that are a feature of 1950s' auditoria, at the Royal Festival Hall and Coventry Belgrade Theatre as well as throughout West Germany. Their fronts are finished in glistening aluminium leaf to contrast with the back lining of the rest of the hall that for Ruhnau served to unite the auditorium and stage. The proscenium is 13 metres wide and 9.5 metres high but can be made smaller if required. Behind, a long slab incorporates the flytower within six storeys of dressing rooms, workshops, a scenery construction room, rehearsal space and a ballet studio. On the lowest level, stores and a canteen complete a complex that operates for most hours of the day; the atmosphere backstage is somewhere between a small factory and Broadcasting House. The structural engineer was Guido Schoen, who devised a series of expansion joints along the frame, dividing it into separate sections as some settlement was expected across the site, with deep foundations for the flytower. The building was fully air-conditioned, also a response to the heavy industry and coalmining in the area, for the area suffered severe problems of air pollution at the time (*Architect and Building News*, **vol. 227, no. 10, 10 March 1965, pp. 463–471**).

Externally the studio theatre or Kleines Haus, seating between 350 and 400 people, appears dark where the main theatre is light, but it is glazed at its far end where the foyer makes a visual link to the street as well as a physical one with the auditorium immediately behind. A bridge links it to the main building, with parking between the supporting pilotis. The form of the small theatre is indebted to Adolphe Appia's pioneering open space theatre at Hellerau from 1912 and is unusually flexible, for the stalls and apron areas can be adjusted, theoretically even during the course of a performance. There is one broad tier of seating across the rear.

Ruhnau brought in several major artists to decorate the foyers and exterior. They stayed with him and his family in a three-bedroom flat over the architect's office in a nearby former fire station, which was dubbed the 'Bauhütte' by a local journalist. There, Ruhnau claimed in his autobiography, *Der Raum, Das Spiel un Die Künste/Space, Play and the Arts* (Berlin, Jovis/ Gelsenkirchen, Stadt Gelsenkirchen, 2007, p. 149), 'we achieved the ideal of engineers and artists designing a building together. It was no longer just a question of the individual artistic disciplines – we were building together.' The English sculptor Robert Adams created a concrete relief on the outer wall of the low box office wing that sits in front of the main façade, a foil to the latter's transparency. Most remarkably, Ruhnau was introduced at a gallery opening in Paris to Yves Klein, who produced six blue murals in the foyer after a formal competition was held in October 1957. Two of these are a monumental 21 metres wide by seven metres high, while two more of similar height were made at Ruhnau's behest, using the sponges Klein normally used to apply his paint fixed into gypsum plaster on a wire mesh. They make dramatic splashes of colour in contrast to the deliberately monochrome auditorium. Paul Dierkes decorated the external drum of the main auditorium. Ruhnau's friend Norbert Kricke produced a relief of long, horizontal aluminium tubes for the exterior of the small hall, but his designs for fountains were never realised. Jean Tinguely progressed from the task of acting as Klein's translator to making the mobile behind the bar of the small

Small theatre

theatre. Ruhnau himself designed distinctive chairs for the foyer, which have padded leather seats and arms but no backs. They were remade as part of the restoration of the theatre under Ruhnau's supervision in 2008–9, when the ceiling was raised in the main auditorium to improve the acoustics and new lighting was installed. He retained a keen interest in the theatre and was a regular visitor until his death. The building has been used almost entirely for opera, musical plays and ballet since 1968, as reflected in its modern name, the Musiktheater im Revier.

Assessment of the Building

Gelsenkirchen is the most published and widely admired of Germany's post-war theatres, described by Hannelore Schubert as 'the happiest and most thoroughly integrated example to emerge during the first decade of post-war theatre-building', as well as a dramatic advance on the traditional auditorium at Münster (Hannelore Schubert, *The Modern Theatre, Architecture,*

Yves Klein blue murals

Stage Design Lighting (London, Pall Mall Press, 1971), p. 7 (originally *Moderner Theaterbau*, Karl Krämer Verlag, Stuttgart, 1971)). For G. E. Kidder Smith, 'it abounds with ideas: its over-all planning which includes the eventual development of the entire area; its art which was carefully integrated with the theatre design from the beginning; its clever architectural marriage between auditorium and stage.' ('New German Theatres and Concert Halls', *Architectural Record*, vol. 134, no. 10, October 1963, p. 183.) Victor Glasstone described the foyers as the 'finest, most successful, in Europe' ('Auditoria Galore', *Architectural Design*, vol. 33, no. 11, November 1963, pp. 555–556). Gelsenkirchen offered a successful main auditorium that brought actor and audience close together, together with a very flexible studio theatre. It is also remarkable for the close relationship of artist and architect, for while the French and English artists were personal friends, the programme is contemporary with the rebuilding of Coventry city centre using art students from Dresden. Its influence was limited, however, because of its very size – Peter Moro visited it before designing the Nottingham Playhouse in 1960–1961 but found it too large and its stage facilities too technical for a British budget, although he repeated the basic concept of the auditorium as a decorated drum set within an open, rectangular foyer (personal comment, April 1994).

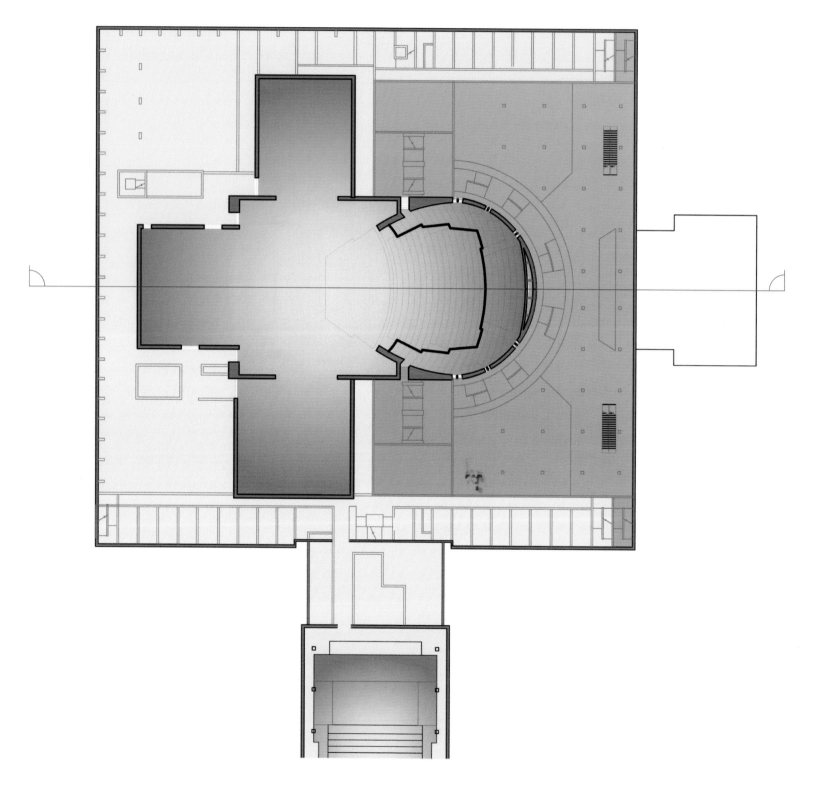

Musiktheater im Revier, Gelsenkirchen, comparative plan

0   5   10   20 metres

1:500

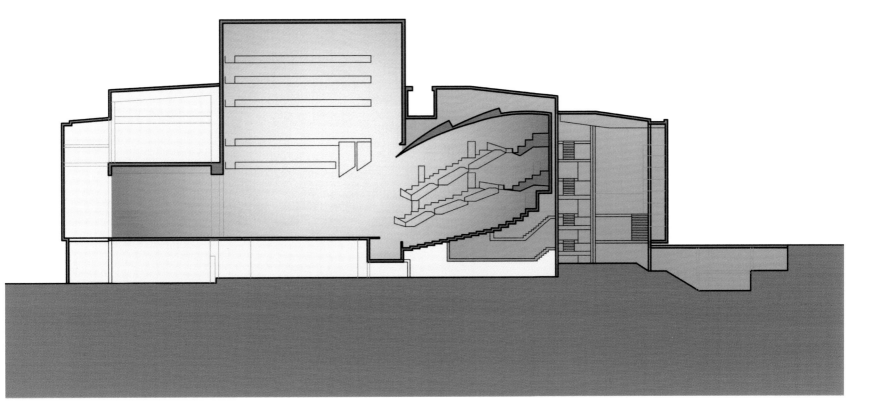

Musiktheater im Revier, Gelsenkirchen, comparative section

0   5   10   20 metres

1:500

1960s
The Sixties

Fichandler Stage, Arena Stage

Arena Stage, 1961
Washington, DC, USA
Architect, Harry Weese

Joshua Dachs

There are few theatre buildings that one can identify that are as completely original and without precedent as the Arena Stage in Washington, DC. When it opened in 1961, it was just the second purpose-built professional theatre in the United States in an arena format, or, so far as I can tell, in the world. And at 800 seats, it was also the largest and most ambitious, by far. Where did this remarkable building spring from?

The proscenium theatre has a familiar and well-documented history beginning in the late 16th century – early 17th century in Italy. The thrust, amphitheatre, or "three-quarter" seating form has been written about a great deal also. Narratives generally trace its lineage to the ancient Greeks and Romans, of course, and later Max Reinhardt's work in Berlin at Zirkus Shumann and Grosses Schauspielhaus in the early 19-teens, Robert Atkins season of productions in an adapted boxing ring in Blackfriars in 1936, and famously Tyrone Guthrie's staging of *A Satire of the Three Estates* in Edinburgh in 1948 before purpose-built buildings like the Festival Theatre in Stratford, Ontario, and the Chichester Festival Theatre (1962) were built. The line of thinking leading to the contemporary "arena" or "theatre-in-the-round" form, in which the audience surrounds the playing area, is much less well known.

Spiritual Progenitors

While the act of gathering around a performer is certainly as old as the human race, the beginnings of arena staging in contemporary Western theatre can be traced to the late 19th century, and its purpose-built structures to not even a century ago. Western theatre, in the late 19th century, consisted largely of professional commercial companies working in the proscenium format, and it was centralized in the major cities and capitals; from there, provincial tours originated. In addition, there was a blossoming interest in amateur theatre, and community theatres featuring local enthusiasts were established in small communities throughout Europe and North America.

By the early years of the 20th century two important themes had emerged that would have profound impact on the theatre:

First, there was a reaction against the commercial dramatic stage, with its emphasis on formulaic drawing-room comedies and sensational melodramas featuring stars. Passionate dramatists and directors were interested in producing more challenging and thoughtful work. A key component of this sensibility was the idea that theatres could offer more compelling experiences if freed from the exclusively commercial need to entertain the broadest possible audience. This soon led to development of a series of professional theatres with very small capacities for a different kind of audience, among them: Reinhardt's Kammerspiele in Berlin with just 300 seats (1906); August Strindberg's Intima Teatern (Intimate Theatre) in Stockholm seating just 161 (1907), Konstantin Stanislavsky's First Studio in Moscow seating 75 to 150 (1913), the Provincetown Playhouse in Greenwich Village that launched the career of Eugene O'Neill, seating only 200 (1916), and even on Broadway, with Winthrop Ames' "Little Theatre," seating just 300 (1912). All these were proscenium-format houses.

Second, there was a growing interest in symbolic and abstract scenography. Designers like Adolphe Appia (1862–1928), Edward Gordon Craig (1872–1966), and Robert Edmond Jones (1887–1954) rejected the conventional illusionistic scenery that filled contemporary stages. In their work, their books and articles, and their drawings and paintings which were reproduced in the theatrical journals of the day, they showed how simple elements, abstract forms, geometric ideas, and sculptural use of light could be very powerful, perhaps illuminating a play's emotional truth more evocatively than traditional approaches. Their work was incredibly influential and is still inspiring to this day.

Beginnings

The world's first purpose-built "theatre in the round" was the Penthouse Theatre at the University of Washington in Seattle in 1940, which is still in use after having been moved to a new site. Having experimented in found spaces with rectangular arrangements since 1932, Professor Glenn Hughes decided to do away with corners in an attempt to bring the audience completely around the stage. He chose an ellipse rather than a circle for the seating, clearly believing that there was something important – or

at least more interesting – in a space with a strong directionality. A 12' × 18' stage (3.65m × 4.26m) was encircled by three elliptical rows; this being the maximum number of rows he thought was possible while still allowing the audience to feel immersed in the action. The stage entrances, down the aisles, connected directly to the lobby, which was treated as a circular corridor running around the outside of the theatre's walls.

In 1947 the director Margo Jones founded a theatre in an old exhibition hall in Dallas. She called it Theatre '47, and each New Year's Eve she would host a re-naming celebration – Theatre '48, and so on – before her untimely death in 1955. Jones' 200-seat theatre had a basically rectangular playing area with three to five tiered rows on a side. The first row was on the same level as the stage. The audience was able to enter from only one corner and climbed aisles in each of the four corners to get to their seats. Actors could enter from three of the four corners, the fourth being unusable as an entrance or exit for anyone due to an idiosyncrasy of the building. Lighting was an extremely important element, together with costume, furniture, and props.

In 1951, Margo Jones wrote the book, *Theatre-in-the-Round*, arguing for the use of the arena form, and set out her ideas for a national network of independent professional theatres. It was a call to arms, and it was widely influential. It was also a good read. There were plans and photos of her theatre in Dallas. Director Alan Schneider wrote that Jones' work at Theatre '47, her speeches and articles, and later her book created a snowball effect: Arena Stage in Washington, Alley Theatre in Houston, and many others owed their existence to her example.

Also in 1951 a 30-year-old Englishman, Stephen Joseph, later himself to write a book called *Theatre-in-the-Round*, would enter a playwriting program at the University of Iowa and took the opportunity to visit several American theatres, including Margo Jones' theatre and Arena Stage in Washington, DC, then still in its first home. These experiences, and Jones' book, would influence him greatly. He would become the leading British advocate for non-proscenium forms of theatre.

Zelda and Thomas Fichandler, Edward Mangum

Having earned a master's degree in theatre from Catholic University in the late 1930s, by the late 1940s Edward Mangum (1914–2001) was operating an amateur theatre group in the Washington, DC area called the Mount Vernon Players and teaching at George Washington University. In 1949, Mangum flew to Dallas and studied Margo Jones' theatre. He later wrote that it was her work with Theatre'49 that inspired him to open the Arena Stage the following year.

By 1949, Zelda Fichandler (1924–2016) had already earned a degree in dramatic literature from Cornell University and acquired sufficient command of Russian to translate Chekov and work briefly in military intelligence. Now, while working on her master's thesis on Shakespeare and the Soviet Union at George Washington University, she got to know Magnum and appeared in several plays he directed. Together they bemoaned the fact that there was little theatre to be seen in Washington – or anywhere else but New York – aside from amateur productions, summer stock, festivals, and touring Broadway shows, and they agreed that the solution was to start their own.

"'I needed to learn as rapidly as I could from as many people as I could," Fichandler said. She asked to meet with Margo Jones. "It was summer and I met her in New York in a hot office where she was sitting on a desk swinging her legs. She had on a yellow cotton dress and no stockings and no makeup. I was awed."

Inspired by Margo Jones' efforts in Dallas and her advice, Edward and Zelda opted for a theatre-in-the-round format. In the beginning, it was a bit of a family affair. Zelda's husband Tom Fichhandler (1916–1997), an economist then working at the U.S. Treasury Department, came on board part-time to help with business matters and fundraising, and soon left his job to serve as full time executive director, which he did until 1986. Edward Magnum's wife Mary ran the box office.

Arena Stage opened in August 1950, having converted the Hippodrome Theatre, a former burlesque and movie house, into a 247-seat theatre-in-the-round along the lines of Margo Jones' theatre in Dallas. It was actually the first racially integrated theatre in Washington, DC, an enormously contentious issue at that time. It consisted of a rectangular playing space of roughly 18 x 24 feet (5.4m x 7.3m) surrounded by up to five rows on a side. Entrances, as in Dallas, were at the corners, on the stage floor level.

In an odd quirk of history, just one month earlier the similarly-named Arena *Theatre* had opened in New York City as a 500-seat improvised theatre-in-the-round inside the ballroom at the Edison Hotel, also following Margo Jones' lead. The *Washington Post* theatre critic Richard L. Coe almost missed the first show at Arena Stage because he was in New York seeing Arena Theatre's first two productions and caught a performance in DC only because it was extended to a third week due to its great success. The headline for Coe's review of the New York company was "It's Just Like Eavesdropping". People were intrigued. The Arena Theatre in NY would last a single season; Arena Stage in Washington has now passed its 70th anniversary.

Mangum would leave Washington just two years later, leaving Zelda, then 28, in sole artistic charge of the company, and she would lead it until stepping aside in 1990, in the 40th anniversary season. She went on to head the Graduate Acting Department at New York University and remained a powerfully articulate leader of the American theatre until her death in 2016.

Arena produced an astonishing 17 plays that first season, many directed by Mangum, and some featuring Zelda in the cast. They went on to present 55 productions before concluding that they couldn't continue with such a small capacity. After a dark year searching for a solution, they relocated to a larger re-purposed space in 1956. This second space was a 500-seat theatre-in-the-round in the Hospitality Hall of the Old Heurich Brewery, and approximated the same physical arrangement as the Hippodrome with a larger number of rows on each side. It was playfully dubbed the "Old Vat" and was on a riverside site that would soon be razed to build a national arts center, eventually known as the Kennedy Center, forcing Arena to relocate once again.

In planning their next move, Zelda and Tom realized that only a new building could address all the challenges they'd discovered in their years working in the format. They also deemed it necessary to increase the capacity to roughly 800 – a far cry from Glenn Hughes' 172-seat Penthouse Theatre, their old home at the Hippodrome at 247 and even a 60 per cent increase over the 500-seat Old Vat. Something would have to be quite different.

In order to raise money for the new building and its ongoing operation, Arena Stage, which had formerly been a conventional commercial corporation with a board of supportive stockholders, was reorganized with the generous assistance of the Ford Foundation, into one of America's earliest not-for-profit professional theatre companies. In a race with the wrecking ball, they worked with the City and managed to secure a site in southwest Washington, DC, which was then undergoing a massive urban renewal effort. In 1959, Arena reviewed 50 architects before selecting 43-year-old Chicagoan Harry Weese (1915–1998) who had never designed a theatre before. Arena recorded six hours of discussions of the company's needs on audio tape, and Weese is said to have played it over and over again in developing his design.

Choices

There are a series of choices that one must make in designing a theatre in the round. Each has implications for directors, actors, technicians, designers, and the audience – and a profound impact on the architecture. The key choices include the overall geometry of the playing space, how the audience will enter, where the actors enter, how steep the rake should be, how large the playing area is, and of course everything is shaped by how many seats are needed. There had only ever been two purpose-built theatres-in-the-round before: the University of Washington's 172-seat Penthouse Theatre in Seattle and the circular 300-seat

Playhouse in Houston, which closed after three seasons in 1954. While in Seattle and Houston the playing space and house were elliptical or circular rather than rectangular, in other respects they mostly conformed to the earlier improvised versions in Seattle, and resembled Arena Stage's own two earlier versions: common entrances for actors and audience at stage level, limited height over the stage, limited lighting positions; no special accommodation for hanging or rigging anything, and nothing flexible about the stage floor itself. Together, Weese and Zelda Fichandler made a series of new choices, and their innovations were very thoughtful.

The Stratford Festival Theatre in Ontario had opened in 1953 with its iconic thrust stage by Tanya Moiseiwitsch and a seating bowl under a tent. Zelda and Tom visited Stratford that first season, meeting Guthrie and Alec Guinness, and it's likely that Weese did too, sometime after he was selected by Arena in 1959. By then, the building had been enclosed with proper walls and a roof. He would have seen the stadium style vomitories, lighting positions in narrow slots in the house ceiling, and virtually no rigging accommodations over the stage. Stratford's bold new example certainly would have been on all their minds at this time.

The decision about basic geometry was probably the easiest. Arena had been working with the rectangular form for nine years and were comfortable with it. The size of the stage, however, was more than doubled to 30 x 36 feet (9.1m x 11m). Since one of the key advantages of the arena form is closer proximity, it was important to keep the number of rows to a minimum, and it would have been impossible to accommodate 800 people around the old stage size without significantly increasing the number of rows and the distance to the last viewers. A balance had to be found between stage size and row quantity. I'm sure they recognized the trade-off in compactness, but also may have viewed it as an opportunity to increase the scale of the work as well, being able to undertake plays with larger casts and more epic scope while keeping the distance to the last seats under 36 feet (11m).

At the Penthouse Theatre the dressing rooms and support spaces all opened into the lobby, which actors had to cross to get to the stage entrances. At Arena they chose to stick with the idea of corner entrances for actors at stage level, but instead of sharing these with the audience, Weese recognized the organizational advantage of placing actors and audience on separate levels. Instead of individual pie wedges of seats divided by actor entrances so typical of the form so far, by entering the seating from above rather than below, all the quadrants of the room could be unified into a single seating bowl. The stage level could be given over entirely to actors and production support, with stage entrances made through stadium-style vomitories. This offered a huge technical advantage; suddenly there could be an unseen wing space for scenic elements, props and furniture to emerge from and retreat to. This space, linking all the voms and ultimately connecting to the dressing room wing, soon became known, quite aptly, as the "run-around". The cross aisle above, in addition to providing audience access from the lobby, could be used as an acting area along with the stepped seating aisles, so performers could still move freely through the house.

Another unique, and ultimately unsuccessful element, was a ring of seating boxes around the outer perimeter. Perhaps they were there to make it clear that the scrappy Arena Stage had left its raw, improvised surroundings and had grown up; it was now ready to offer luxurious accommodations along with the finest traditional theatres. Or perhaps it was to make the space feel smaller, by suggesting there were fewer rows surrounding the stage than there actually were. A cross-aisle was placed behind the eighth row, giving access to all quadrants of the room and to the lobby. Behind this was a series of 11 raised boxes, tucked under the descending roofline. Of 786 total seats, 132 were in the boxes. By being outboard of the cross-aisle, up some narrow steps, and in small concrete alcoves, these seats always seemed disconnected from the audience and the performer – they seemed to be seats for watching an audience

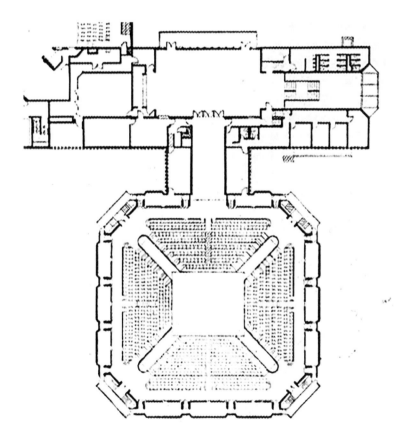

Harry Weese and Zelda Fichandler with Arena Stage model

Arena Stage plan

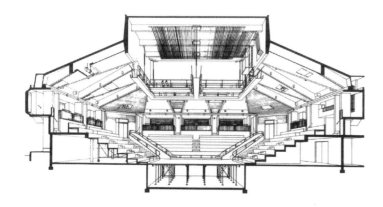

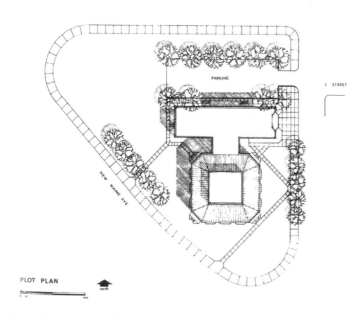

Arena Stage plan and section

watching a play. In later years, they were blocked up with temporary panels and used for storage, and in 2010 we blocked them up permanently as part of a large expansion and renovation project designed by Canadian architect Bing Thom.

Being a new building, they were also able to plan a trap room beneath the stage, a first for a theatre in the round, but an obvious move. In an arena, the topography and decor of the floor itself is a critical design element. The entire stage floor footprint was treated as a trap room and the stage itself was made of platforms to allow any height or configuration. Actors could even enter from below. Sadly, it was not quite eight feet

(2.4m) below stage level, most likely for reasons of cost, something that we would alleviate somewhat in our renovation and expansion in 2010.

Overhead they devised a sort of pop-up loft above the stage. This carried roof steel that could support rigging loads, and there was a grid of catwalks that could be flown up and down as a unit as needed. Within this grid certain catwalk segments were cleverly designed to slide back and forth to allow them to be located where needed. Over time this was modified into a two-level grid of catwalks; a fixed upper level to support spotline rigging activities for flown or suspended elements, and a moveable lower level for lighting. In addition to the lighting catwalk system over the stage itself, some small slots were integrated into the sloping auditorium ceiling. They were difficult to get to and far too limited in extent and led to a variety of improvised work-arounds until this could be better addressed in the 2010 renovation.

Since one of the selling points of the arena format was ostensibly that there was comparatively little need to spend much on scenery, space for construction and painting was kept to a minimum, anticipating mostly props and furniture. The scene shop was just 1200sf (111sm), divided into three small workshops with a low eight-foot (2.4m) ceiling height, barely larger than the costume shop and laundry. Here their experience in found spaces may have led them astray; the new tall space overhead and the trap room gave designers free rein to use the vertical dimension aggressively for the first time, and this led to moats, tiers, and pools below, and branches, ceilings, and skylights above to be built, rigged, and painted. Ten years later, when a second, smaller frontal theatre was added to the building, a new, larger scene shop was built, and the old scene shop became the prop shop.

The building was simply but beautifully detailed and proportioned. Weese, who would later design the famed Washington Metro system with its gorgeous concrete vaults and curvaceous stairs, had a way with concrete, wood, and steel. The high-quality concrete work throughout was exposed as the finish surface, and in the auditorium wood boards were fitted between the triangular concrete ribbed vaults of the roof over the seats. A continuous thin black metal railing traced the outline of the playing area and the voms; just a foot above the toes of the first row at the edge of the stage, then rising along the edge of each vomitory, making a

Arena Stage, exterior, showing the addition of the frontal Kreeger Theater and a scene shop in the early 1970s.

graceful curve at the top before coming back down the other side, adding a thin sinuous line to the room. The interior wasn't painted black; it almost glowed in a calm, warm silver grey, and does to this day.

The new building opened on October 30, 1961 with Bertolt Brecht's *Caucasian Chalk Circle* directed by Alan Schneider. Both the production and the building were met with enthusiastic reviews. A *New York Times* article described it as understated while declaring it a new cultural landmark. One article mentioned the punch-card automated lighting control system! The boxes were even praised as "luxurious".

In 1967, Arena was the first regional theatre to transfer a production to Broadway; *The Great White Hope*, with its original cast of James Earl Jones and Jane Alexander in the lead roles. In 1973, it was the first regional theatre invited by the U.S. State Department to tour behind the Iron Curtain, which gave Zelda an opportunity to dust off her old Russian language skills. In 1976, Arena Stage became the second theatre outside New York to receive a special Tony Award for theatrical excellence. So far, 21 other Arena productions have had a subsequent life on Broadway, including *Dear Evan Hansen* (winner of the 2017 Tony Award for Best Musical) and *Sweat* (winner of the 2017 Pulitzer Prize for Drama).

Arena's example, and those of its predecessors, have been carried forward in several ways. Larger-scale venues over 500 seats like the Royal Exchange in Manchester (1976) and Stephen Joseph Theatre (1996) clearly drew directly on Arena's example in various ways, but there have been relatively few of those. Others were devised in existing, as well as new, buildings to work at smaller capacities, such as the White Theatre in the Conrad Prebys Theatre Center at San Diego's Old Globe Theatre (2009) or The Cockpit Theatre in Marylebone, London (1970). Central staging is most commonly used, I suspect, in spaces that are designed for flexibility – either the thousands of small studio theatres that are arranged as needed, or theatres that are normally arranged in three-quarter seating but where the fourth side is added for certain productions, as in The Octagon Theatre, Bolton (1967), the Neuhaus Theatre at the Alley Theatre in Houston (1968) or the Circle in the Square Theatre on Broadway (1972).

Zelda Fichandler earned a well-deserved reputation as a founder of the American regional theatre movement, and was always an articulate advocate in the press, in speeches, and in testimony before congress for the importance of supporting live theatre. Harry Weese went on to design the Washington Metro system, several more theatres, including a performing arts center in Milwaukee and the Actors Theatre of Louisville. The brilliance of their very original theatre, today called the Fichandler, is still evident today. It stands there, completely intact, within the enormously transformed and expanded complex designed by Bing Thom now known as the Arena Stage at the Meade Center for American Theatre. It is a fitting concrete legacy for two pioneers, Zelda Fichandler and Harry Weese.

Fichandler Stage following renovation in 2010

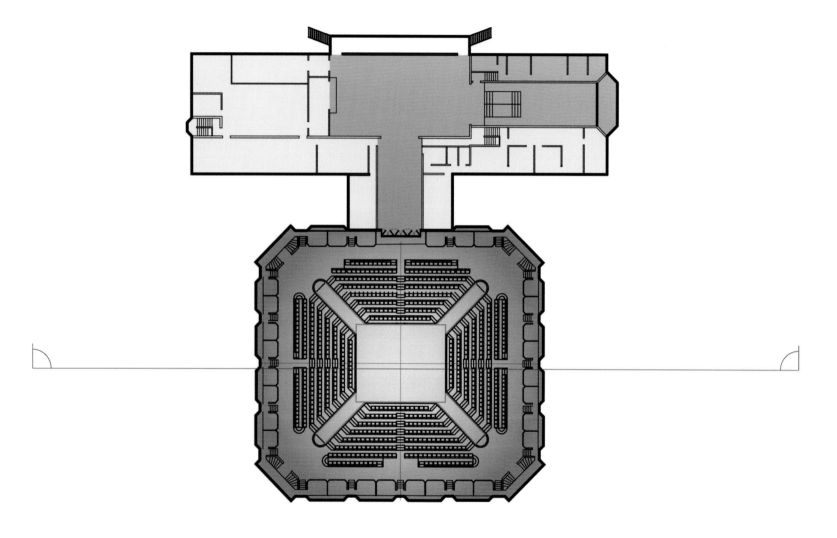

Fichandler Stage, Arena Stage, Washington, comparative plan

0   5   10   20 metres

1:500

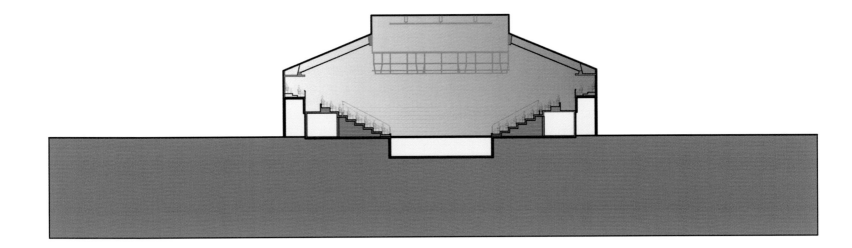

Fichandler Stage, Arena Stage, Washington, comparative section

0   5   10   20 metres

1:500

Tokyo Bunka Kaikan, main auditorium

Tokyo Bunka Kaikan, 1961
Tokyo, Japan
Architect, Kunio Maekawa

Shozo Motosugi

Being shocked by the last "Confession" chapter in Le Corbusier's *The Decorative Art of Today*, a man left Tokyo in 1928 on the Trans-Siberian Railroad to visit Corbusier's studio in Paris. The man was architect Kunio Maekawa, who was to design Tokyo Bunka Kaikan (TBK). Avoiding the growing militarism in Japanese society, Maekawa left Japan as soon as he graduated from the university in pursuit of the architecture of humanism under freedom and equality. He apprenticed for several years in Le Corbusier's studio in Paris. Corbusier designed the National Museum of Western Art in Tokyo's Ueno Park. Thirty years later his former pupil, Maekawa, designed TBK in the same park.

Tokyo Bunka Kaikan is a multi-purpose hall which opened in 1961; it has been one of the most important and influential music and cultural venues in the reconstruction period after World War II. TBK was commissioned by the Tokyo Metropolitan Government in response to public demand for a venue to enjoy classical music, opera and ballet in Tokyo, and to commemorate the 500th anniversary of the city.

Kunio Maekawa designed TBK as a city square in a large park because he believed that a theatre should be both a place open to the public for social interaction and a place presenting art and cultural events. A number of TBK's features give expression to this vision, including the public sequence from the lobby to the foyer, whilst linking to the surrounding environment; the design of the audience space where people can equally enjoy the action on stage and interact with each other; the creation of an auditorium and stage with technical capabilities and acoustic qualities suitable for both concerts and operas; and the arrangement of the stage and the audience seats in a manner that is successful for both performers and the audience.

The first opportunity offered to this young man was the competition, held after World War II, for Kanagawa Kenritsu Toshokan/Ongakudo (Kanagawa prefectural library/concert hall) which opened in 1954. This was commissioned to memorialize the "Treaty of Peace with Japan". Maekawa grasped the potential significance of the new building in supporting the revival of culture saying, "now is the time to provide people with a place where they can enjoy music calmly to give themselves strength towards tomorrow". His work on this project was so well received it led to his appointment to design TBK. The construction of TBK took place under the political wave caused by ratification of U.S.–Japan Security Treaty (1960), the signing of which caused mass demonstrations in Japan. Both projects are symbolic of Japan's post-war recovery.

Nonetheless, the appearance of TBK looks the opposite of the quieter style of Kanagawa prefectural concert hall. The size itself is huge, and the stretch of land in front of the building is also different. Compared with

Le Corbusier's National Museum of Western Arts, Ueno Park, Tokyo

the Kanagawa hall, which has a plain façade made with glass windows and walls and simply presents the necessary functional volume; TBK has a stronger and massive expression, being rather exaggerated or boorish, with its large upswept pent-roof, a lot of heavy vertical pillars, and exterior wall panels inlaid with crushed marble.

And yet, there are common concepts. For example, the pent-roof (balcony) emphasises its horizontal character, the open-ceiling space or high pillars arranged on the periphery conversely highlighting the vertical nature, huge glass surfaces extend from the floor to the ceiling in the foyer, the ceramic industrial materials found in the perforated blocks and the wall panels with crushed marble. So, whilst having different appearances, these buildings share the same architectural root.

Compared to many European and American theatres and concert halls, TBK is compromised spatially and technically. The depth of the main stage is restricted by the sound reflectors; and the ceiling of the side stage is low due to the foyer garden of the small hall. There are too few fly bars, and they are not correctly located because the sound reflectors interfere. Moreover, their loading capacity is limited. Even with such inconveniences, TBK was the best facility in those days in Japan. Because of

Tokyo Bunka Kaikan, exterior

these shortcomings, new concepts and ideas were sought in subsequent Japanese halls. TBK influenced many future performing arts buildings.

The performances by foreign companies spurred the growth and development of musical life in the city. Musicians, theatre people, and even audiences matured and developed. Of course, such growth was realized not solely by TBK. It was boosted by cultural exchange programs with Western countries which were conducted at public halls, commercial theatres, etc. throughout Japan at various levels. The construction of so-called Japanese-style multi-purpose auditoriums where various programs including operas, ballet, concerts, and dramas are performed spread quickly after this period.

Theatre as a Square

The external appearance of Tokyo Bunka Kaikan is characterised by its large upswept pent-roof, whose height is aligned with the roof of Corbusier's National Museum of Western Art located facing TBK, the height of the Museum dictating the height of TBK. The layout patterns of sashes are also matched with the pavement pattern in the front garden of the museum. The two buildings are like brothers, because the exterior wall of the museum is finished using the precast concrete slabs with boulders, while the precast concrete slab with crushed marble is used for the exterior walls of TBK.

On the initial plans, the large hall of TBK and the museum were not directly opposite each other because a larger building site was originally proposed. The buildings were planned to face each other at an angle with a rather wide square in between. This would have placed the stage along the main traffic line toward the Ueno Park, a reverse positioning compared to the completed scheme. Although the intention to expose the large wall surface of the fly tower along the main traffic line toward the park was not achieved, the idea of locating the stage at ground level and leading the audience to the second floor is rational from the viewpoint of theatre functionality. The site was cut almost in half, requiring drastic changes. New ideas were proposed where the stage and the related rooms such as dressing rooms and rehearsal rooms are arranged in the basement, while other facilities like meeting rooms are in the upper part of the foyer. These ideas allowed the entrance lobby and the foyer of the large hall to be created at the place that used to be the outside square. To hide the rooms on the upper part of the foyer, the large upswept pent-roof was created.

Planning restrictions limited the building height in a sensitive park and the volume above ground had to be minimised to reduce the impact on the green environment. This resulted in the stage being lowered to first basement level which compromised the load-in but allowed good audience entrances and escape. It was fortunate that the theatre was regarded as a place where people would gather, an open space where the flow of people to the space is spontaneous.

The foyer floor of the large hall is inlaid with tiles which have triangle patterns in different colours and look as if studded with fallen leaves. On the dark blue ceiling, lights are arranged randomly, like the Milky Way. Moreover, the main entrance near Ueno station and the façade on the opposite side have similar large glass surfaces and doorways respectively, so people can pass through the building. To access the small hall, on the other hand, people walk up a gentle slope from the entrance hall to the foyer on the second floor. There, visitors find the outside garden linking to Ueno Park.

The auditorium wall facing the large-hall foyer is formed with pre-cast slabs inlaid with crushed marble which continue to the exterior walls that are finished in the same manner. The spectators enter through a ramped passageway created between this wall and a second inner wall to reach their seats. Along the passageway, windows are set here and there. The visitors can look out of the window into the foyer of the large hall, the slope to the small hall, etc. Audience seated on the upper levels in the large hall can go out during an interval to a roof garden.

We can see the intention of the architect that the entrance lobby and foyer should be indoor squares or public places in the city flowing into the park. The architect wanted to create a square where anyone can enjoy music and drama.

The auditorium is characterised by its hexagonal form: the shallow stacked balconies, the side walls which slope inwards, the convex curve of the ceiling shaped to improve the acoustics and the wooden diffusing panels on the side walls.

Maekawa loved music and often went to the opera and concerts during his time in Paris while working at Corbusier's office. He visited and investigated the Royal Festival Hall, London, which had the latest design at that time. As an architect who promoted the modern architecture of humanism, he had to infuse the principle of a modern theatre in which everyone can enjoy music and drama equally with fine sight-lines from any seat by also removing the decorations and box seats from the horseshoe-shaped opera houses typical of the 19th century.

At the time it was designed, auditorium design worldwide was moving away from the historic galleried, multi-level rooms. This was partly influenced by Wagner's Bayreuth Festspielhaus, which accommodates the entire audience on one very large main floor, and by a move away, in many countries, from the apparent elitism of multi-level galleried theatres to seemingly more democratic spaces with only one or two seating levels. This resulted in large, impersonal auditoriums lacking warmth and intimacy. Moving balcony rows forward to give better sight-lines would create considerable depth and place a significant number of audience under the balcony, where poor acoustic conditions would result from the deep overhang. The distance to the stage would also be longer.

Tokyo Bunka Kaikan, foyers

Tokyo Bunka Kaikan, foyers

Maekawa developed the concept of the auditorium with seats spread in a fan shape at the rear sides of the lower level and stacking a series of shallow balconies above. The balcony seats are on the three sides, facing the stage and down the side walls. They are shifted by half a floor-level respectively so that the gaps between the balconies are tightened to fill out the entire wall surfaces with the seats. In this way, the total of 2,340 seats are stacked in a tight footprint.

The side and rear walls of the auditorium are inclined outward by 6.5 degrees to improve the sharp downward line of sight from the audience to the stage and reduce the difference in levels between the seats. Owing to these ingenious arrangements, the maximum distance of a seat from the stage is kept within 38m, even with over 2,300 seats, and good sight-lines are provided. It also helps performers on stage to feel as if they are embraced by the audience.

The balcony fronts have a curved face. The shape was designed to optimise the acoustics of the auditorium, but also to reinforce the significance of the room as a public place where people meet. The interior shapes also suggest the shape of the big eaves on the periphery of the building.

Tokyo Bunka Kaikan, large theatre

Development in Acoustical Design

Amajor design issue was acoustics and an acoustical design team from NHK Science & Technology Research was involved from the earliest conceptual design phase.

The site is close to a railway station, which is convenient for visitors but vibration and the noise of whistles from freight cars using Ueno station was an acoustic challenge. The team measured the levels of noise and vibration to obtain data to identify and solve this problem. A first step was to locate the stage of the large hall as far from the railway track as possible. This resulted in the small hall, originally conceived as a conference hall, being located close to the railway track. To reduce vibration,

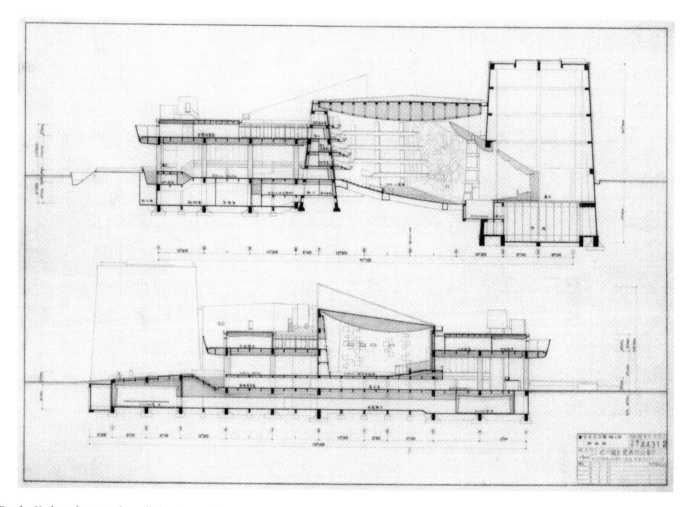

Tokyo Bunka Kaikan, large and small theatre sections

it was lifted to the second-floor level and the sound insulation of the surrounding windows and walls was enhanced.

Repeated sound measurements led to design and construction solutions to minimise the disturbing effects of noise and vibration carried through the air and ground from the railway track. Floating isolating layers were conceived and arranged on the side walls of the stage and the roof of the audience area. Noise and vibration from the heating, ventilating, and air conditioning systems was reduced by resiliently mounting fans and pumps and using silencers and other measures on the ducts and chambers to reduce airborne noise to realize NC-20.

As an early post-war building, detailed acoustic knowledge was limited and the design process was iterative. The only acoustic information available was the experimental results of Haas related to the reflected sound up to 50m, obtained from literature. Considerable effort went into tracking reflected sound based on the hexagonal plan, sloped walls and the shaped balconies. The goal was to identify the optimum routes by which sound from the stage could be reflected and delivered to each spectator equally, and what kinds of room shape and finishing are required to optimise the room acoustics.

The shape of the downward ballooned ceiling of the auditorium was generated through the above process. It was designed to play an important role in delivering the early reflected sound effectively to the entire audience. The ballooned part was made with 50-mm thick light-weight concrete. It is believed that this structure has contributed to "the warm tone" of the hall.

Diffusers or sound absorbing surfaces are attached on the walls to affect reflected sounds of 50ms or higher. The sculpture-like wooden acoustic diffusers attached on the side walls of the auditorium close to the stage and the big white curved ceiling over the orchestra pit are typical examples.

The experience and acoustic experiments in designing and building TBK caused a great step forward in acoustical design in the country and were used in the acoustical design of subsequent multi-purpose halls in Japan. Minoru Nagata, the founder of Nagata Acoustic Inc., and now one of the most acclaimed acoustic consultants, was a member of the TBK acoustical design team. His three key expressions *"silence, good sound, and good tone"* are based on the experience he gained in this team.

A Multi-purpose Hall Satisfying both Concerts and Operas/Ballet Performances

A multi-purpose hall at that time was inevitably a compromise and could not fully satisfy either those who wanted to present symphony concerts or the needs of opera/ballet performances. Maekawa and his design team decided to focus on theatre, opera and ballet uses and to introduce sound reflectors above and around the stage to modify the acoustics for unamplified music, symphony and other classical music. To ensure the best acoustic performance, however, the sound reflectors need to be heavy to properly reflect frequencies in as wide a range as possible from low to high-pitched sounds. These heavy reflectors and other devices had to be easy to deploy and remove. The orchestra pit is on an elevator that can be raised to stage level for concerts extending the stage/platform forward into the room for music performances. Sound reflectors are hung overhead in the fly tower above the stage. A series of panels behind the musicians are stored in the rear stage area while the side acoustic reflectors are lowered below the stage into the trap room area.

The need for many heavy acoustic reflectors frequently clashes with the need for an unobstructed fly tower and stage for theatrical performances. At TBK, the reflectors were originally stored in the three ways described above, but in 1998 the reflectors were re-designed to be stored under the stage and the stage rigging system was completely renewed.

Issues regarding sound reflectors vs. stage rigging that are found in multi-purpose halls have continued to challenge architects and design teams not only in Japan but elsewhere. In a sense, however, the theatre engineering unique to Japan was developed to manage these challenges. How best to arrange and store sound reflectors has been studied and developed following the plans for TBK, and these days many options are available.

Tokyo Bunka Kaikan has been presenting domestic and foreign opera, ballet and orchestra performances for over 50 years. It was one of the first significant post-war theatres in Japan. It is a multi-purpose hall housing fully staged productions like opera and ballet alongside classical music, orchestras and smaller ensembles. At the time it was designed and constructed, there was limited experience or knowledge of such buildings and the architect and design team had to pursue innovative ideas to achieve a successful building. There are inevitably compromises, but TBK remains a significant performing art building for Tokyo and Japan.

Tokyo Bunka Kaikan is well known to the many world-famous opera companies and orchestras who have visited from London, New York, Vienna, Munich and Milan. Just imagine how many people – artistic directors and stage engineers as well as the conductors, players, and singers of classical music and ballet dancers – from outside Japan have stood on the stage and provided Japanese audiences with their wonderful performance!

TBK has contributed to the design and planning of subsequent buildings planned by both private companies and local governments, including Suntory Hall (1986) and the New National Theatre, Tokyo (1997). From the viewpoint of the theatrical construction, the hall was valuable as a building to be imitated, with concepts that were developed and improved in subsequent buildings.

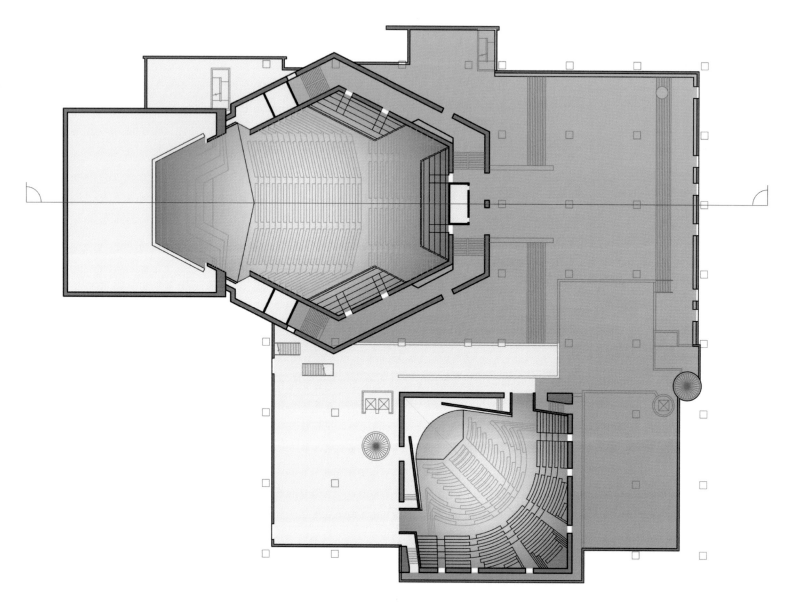

Tokyo Bunka Kaikan, comparative plan

0   5   10   20 metres

1:500

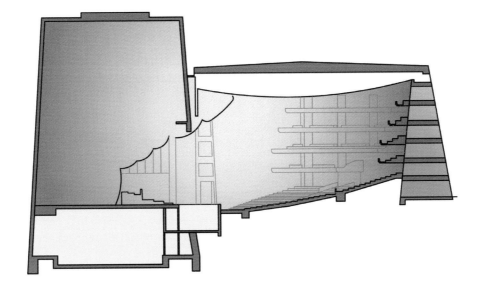

Tokyo Bunka Kaikan, comparative section

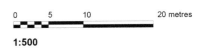

1:500

Philharmonie Berlin

Philharmonie Berlin, 1963
Berlin, Germany
Architect, Hans Scharoun

Karin Winkelsesser

The original home of the Berlin Philharmonic Orchestra (BPO) – a converted ice rink – was destroyed by British bombers in 1944. After a peripatetic existence for over a decade, an architectural competition for a new concert hall for the company was announced in August 1956. It was to be situated in the vicinity of the Academy for Music at the Bundesalle in West Berlin.

Hans Scharoun was awarded the first prize for his innovative concept. However, before construction commenced an urban design competition – Hauptstadt Berlin – was announced and work on the entire project was postponed.

The new site was at the edge of the Tiergarten, a large park in the centre of Berlin. Hans Scharoun was awarded the second prize for this competition. His entry included a cultural forum as a counterproposal to the Museum Island in the eastern part of Berlin. As a consequence of this competition, it was decided to relocate the new concert hall to this site. The concert hall was to become the first, free-standing object in a no man's land still devastated from the war, and the design had to be adapted to this situation where the building was visible from all sides.

From the beginning Herbert von Karajan, Director of the BPO, strongly supported Scharoun's design, which was otherwise widely criticised. Many architects, engineers and acousticians considered the project as unrealisable, but also the concept itself, with a central orchestra in an non-hierarchic auditorium, was new and provocative in conservative post-war Germany.

In February 1959, however, the contract was signed and construction commenced a year later. On 15 October 1963, the Philharmonie Berlin was inaugurated.

Meanwhile the political situation had dramatically changed. In August 1961, the Wall between East and West Berlin had been erected. It passed just beside the Philharmonie. The building now found itself at the border of West Berlin.

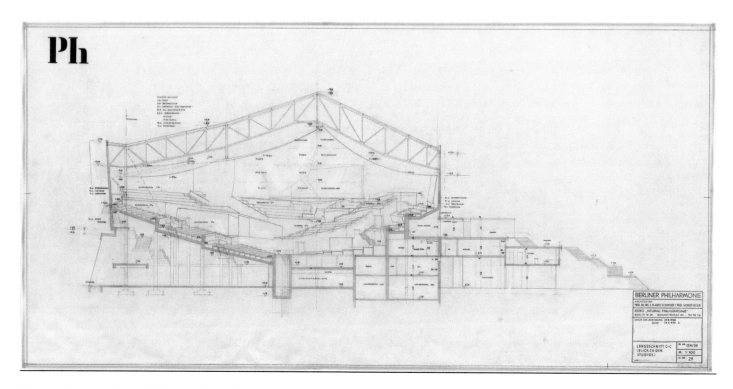

Hans Scharoun drawing of the Philharmonie Berlin

The Design of the Building

The basic shape of the Philharmonie consists of three superimposed, concentrically rotated pentagons, now the logo of the orchestra. For Scharoun, the triple pentagon represented the harmonious unity of space, music and humankind. The main characteristic of the Philharmonie's exterior is its curved silhouette roof. It reproduces the curves of the auditorium ceiling, a tent-like form that culminates in a rooftop sculpture by Hans Uhlmann, called, "Phoenix". It symbolizes the rise from the ashes of the Nazi past.

The auditorium in its polygonal form is superposed onto a largely transparent (large coloured glass walls) substructure housing the box office and foyers, with wardrobes on two levels. A southern building for administration, rehearsal rooms and other facilities is attached to the main building. The staircases and terraces embed the auditorium and give structure to the building. Glass roofs at the west side bring daylight down to the ground floor. They constitute a connection from the auditorium to the adjacent administrative building. The façade could only be realised at a later stage; its pattern, with half circles, corresponds to that of the coloured glass in the foyer.

In the documentation for the competition, Scharoun explained his concept of a central auditorium:

This is a space that is dedicated to music – in which music is to be performed and heard. Solutions that have been found for this architectural task vary largely, but they have one thing in common. Even modern concert halls keep the traditional configuration of the orchestra being placed on a stage and the public sitting in the 'audience', like in a theatre. However, it is certainly no coincidence that, today as at all times, wherever improvised music can be heard, people gather in a circle. Music should be located at the centre in spatial and visual terms. Everything else follows from there on.

This notion, dating back to the ancient Greek theatres, was an important impulse for Scharoun's concept.

Philharmonie Berlin under construction

Another important aspect was the political background. After World War II, a democratic system had to be built up in Germany, and Hans Scharoun was part of a Planungskollektiv that by 1946 had already started to develop an urban design for Berlin based on democratic principles.

For the design of the auditorium, Scharoun also wanted to apply democratic principles instead of reproducing social hierarchies in the architecture. He did not want any loges; all seats should be accessible from any entry; and the acoustic and visual conditions should be equally excellent from all seats.

Scharoun deliberately chose to offset the entrance from the auditorium's axis of symmetry so as to enhance the sense of excitement and confuse the public so that concentration would inevitably shift from everyday life to the music event.

Members of the audience were not expected to locate obvious and immediate routes up through the building. However, as one rises upward, the range of options is reduced, the path becomes more evident, and the goal of the auditorium is within sight . . . And then the moment of entry: at any one of these points, one is offered the most exciting synesthetic experience that modern architecture can provide. This passage, from one cavernous space – the foyer – to another – the auditorium – is entirely without precedent.

Chamber Music Hall

The Auditorium

The auditorium is conceived as a valley. The orchestra sits at the base, surrounded by forcefully ascending plateaus and slopes. Arranged in groups, the rows of seats rise like vineyards around the podium of the orchestra . . . The ceiling reacts (responds) to this landscape like a skyscape; formally, it looks like a tent.

This statement by Scharoun later led to the definition of this type of auditorium as the "vineyard" principle. The tent structure is strongly related to the acoustics that intend to diffuse the sound all over the auditorium. The sound is not sent from one side into the auditorium, it rises from its centre and into the depth of the space before it sinks down to the audience in various ways.

Scharoun hoped to encourage composers to create new and innovative works that would use this space for 4D compositions and develop new ideas to use the space as a constituent artistic element of music.

The auditorium was conceived for 2,440 people. It is structured into 23 groups of seats, each numbering around 128, the size of the full Orchestra. Audience groups and orchestra are thus placed in a commensurate relationship. Moreover, rather than being focused on a single point as in neoclassical space conceptions, Scharoun was interested in notions of modern space with multi-facetted and multi-focal performances.

(*Philharmonie: Hans Scharoun* (O'Neil Ford Monograph)
Ed. W. Wang and D.E. Sylvester).

Philharmonie Berlin, exterior

Most of the seats, however, are in front of the orchestra, and a rather small number (260) are placed behind it. On the whole, about 950 seats are around the orchestra in omnidirectional groups.

The ground plan of the Philharmonie is a symbiosis of a long shape (later to be called shoe box) and a central space.

Acoustics

The acoustics were the main challenge for the project. The success of the acoustic consultant, Prof. Dr. Ing. Lothar Cremer, was at the same time a success for the acoustic sciences, as wrote Prof. Werner Gabler, acoustician himself, in Bühnentechnische Rundschau (Nr. 4/1964): "The success just came in time – in a period where some misfortunes had been exaggerated and our knowledge about acoustic phenomena was questioned."

Daily newspapers wrote about mythical secrets of acoustics, while the experts had earned their success after thorough preparations, model tests and calculations. To them, the result was not a surprise – and if it was, certainly in the positive sense. The fact that this space, which takes 2,400 spectators in a volume of 26,000 m^3 of air and is able to diffuse the sound of even the smallest chamber orchestra or a solo singer to the most distant seat, surprised everybody. The required reverberation time was 2 seconds. In an empty situation, the reverberation time is 2.4 seconds.

Philharmonie Berlin, auditorium

The short journey of the sound waves from the orchestra to the most distant seats was particularly explored. The breaking up of the walls and the multiple forms and inclinations of the vineyard sections and the elevated parquet also enhances the diffusion of the sound to every seat.

The cooperation of architect and acoustician resulted in the actual shape. The seats of the audience are not directly adjacent to the orchestra platform but are lifted onto a kind of terrace. This helps to create acoustic reflection walls around the orchestra. However, the wall is not high enough to enable the musicians to hear one another. Sound reflectors had to be installed for this. The ceiling, between 12mm and 25 mm thick, is conceived as an absorber of basses. The absorption of deep frequencies is necessary, because the clothing of the audience and the upholstering of the seats absorb the high frequencies. Also, the wooden walls and balustrades were conceived as resonating bodies for differently deep frequencies.

To design the acoustics of the auditorium, a model in the scale of 1:9 was built from wood and hardwood. The tests for the diffusion of sound were done with spark gap impulses and registered with echograms from microphones. The reverberation time and the progress of the frequencies however could not be tested; these were calculated in numerous variations.

Chamber Music Hall

One of the most important developments was the construction of a "little sister" to the Philharmonie, the Kammermusiksaal

(Chamber Music Hall). Soloist and chamber music concerts had been performed at the Philharmonie, but they were thought to look somewhat lost on the big platform. In addition, new kinds of modern music required a smaller type of auditorium.

After many fights and controversies, the Kammermusiksaal was inaugurated in 1987. It was designed by Scharoun's disciple, Edgar Wisniewski, who dedicated a large part of his professional career to take care of the heritage of Scharoun's work. It follows the same principle as the Philharmonie and is directly linked to it by a common foyer.

presentations, where parts of the orchestra are placed in the auditorium or where electronic music fills the space in four dimensions, have been performed there – also as world premieres. But artists did not really "dare" to compose music for this space, because it was and is unique and gives them few opportunities to perform them at other places.

The architecture of the auditorium has been copied and modernised in many projects, but the "original" still looks as young as it was in 1963. Once the actual plans for the Kulturforum have been realised, it is hoped that the Philharmonie will be less isolated and become part of a lively centre to enjoy the arts and to meet people.

The Role and Perception: Then and Now

Until the end of 1989, the Philharmonie was the prominent cultural attraction in West Berlin. Famous conductors helped to make this unique orchestra world famous, and their home, the Philharmonie, became equally significant.

After the unification of Germany, the Philharmonie suddenly found itself in the centre of the new capital, and the cultural forum was further developed. A stronger attention however was given to the redevelopment and reconstruction of the historical city centre. Although further buildings such as the National Gallery (by Mies van der Rohe); the National Library (Staatbibliothek), also designed by Hans Scharoun); the Gallery of Old Masters, the Kunstegwerbe-Museum (Museum for Decorative Arts); and the Museum for Music instruments were added to the Kulturforum over the decades, it never became a lively place. Scharoun's concept, which included also artists' residences and meeting areas, was only partly realised. There has always been a lack in social infrastructure – no cafés and restaurants outside the buildings, no attractive open-air areas. Only now, new concepts are being developed.

The Philharmonie itself however remains a very important institution and building. Thanks to numerous educational programmes for young people and people with little music education, the orchestra attracts new and younger groups of audiences.

Scharoun's wish, that new music might be inspired by this building, however, has not be fulfilled. Many modern concerts with 360°

Philharmonie Berlin concert hall and Tiergarten, Berlin

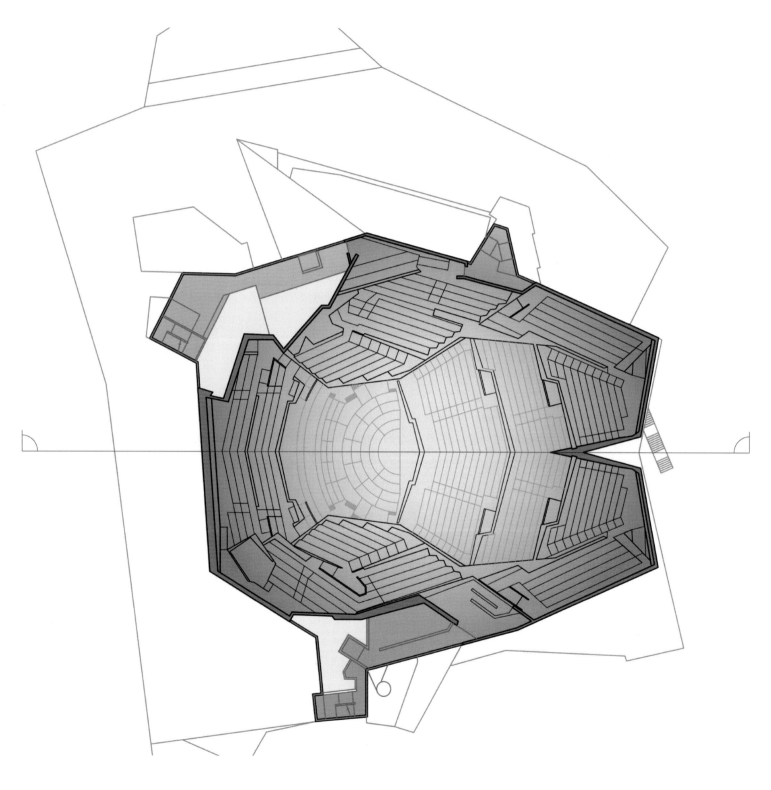

Philharmonie Berlin, comparative plan

0   5   10   20 metres

1:500

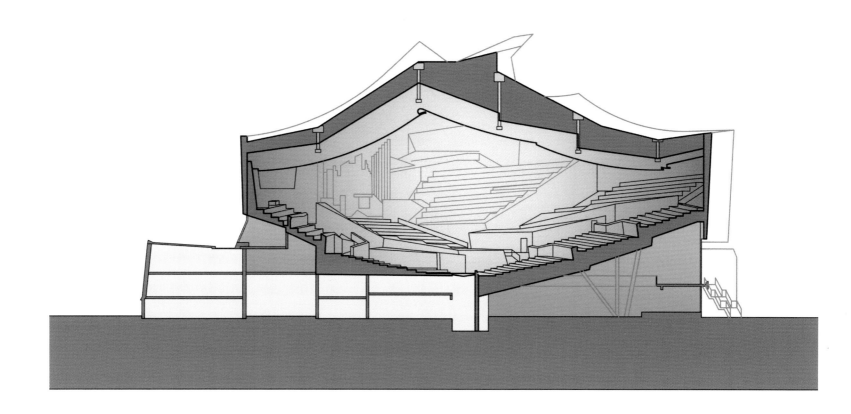

Philharmonie Berlin, comparative section

1970s
The Seventies

Finlandia Hall, façade

Finlandia Hall, 1971
Helsinki, Finland
Architect, Alvar Aalto
David Staples

Many of the chapters of this book were written to the accompaniment of music. This chapter was accompanied and inspired by *Finlandia*, a tone poem by Finnish composer Jean Sibelius.

Finlandia was first performed in 1900, when it was seen as part of covert protest against increasing censorship by the then ruling Russian Empire. When Finland tore itself free from Russia in 1917, the soundtrack was Sibelius's *Finlandia*. When Finland built its national concert hall, it was named Finlandia.

This chapter brings together five or six intertwined people and events – Finland and the birth of an independent nation; Jean Sibelius, the Finnish composer who remains one of Finland's most popular national figures and is a symbol of that nation; Alvar Aalto the architect; Finlandia Hall, designed and planned to be the nation's concert hall; its replacement, the Helsinki Music Centre; and the Aalto Theatre in Essen, Germany.

Finland is a Nordic but not a Scandinavian country. Scandinavia comprises Denmark, Sweden, and Norway while Nordic adds Finland, Iceland and their associated islands and territories. The boundaries are often blurred, and Finnish design is often called Scandinavian. Finland is geographically the 8th-largest and least densely populated country in the EU, with just over 1.5 million people. Part of Sweden from the late 13th century, it was incorporated into the Russian Empire in 1809. This began an unhappy period that saw a strong Finnish nationalist movement grow and increasing use of the Finnish language.

Following independence in 1917, the leaders discussed what the independent country's first building should be. A concert hall received general support. Plans were drawn and a site identified in central Helsinki. But the site was reassigned to build the Parliament building. The civil war in 1918, two Russian wars, and poverty delayed the concert hall project.

Alvar Aalto has been described as the second most famous Finn after Sibelius. Born in February 1898, he grew up in the turbulent period leading to Finland's independence and went on to become one of the 20th century's most acclaimed architects. During his life, Aalto's nationality gave him an air of mystery. He was from a distant, northern nation full of lakes and trees, with an unusual language and a reputation for clean simple design.

Aalto's career started with him designing in a style described as Nordic Classicism before moving, like much of the rest of the world, to a rational, International Style Modernism during the 1930s and subsequently to a more organic modernist style from the 1940s onwards. Aalto not only designed buildings but also furniture, considered Scandinavian Modern, using wood and especially bent chair legs, using new manufacturing processes.

Finlandia Hall, sign

In the 1920s Aalto started holidaying in Italy, from which grew an interest in bringing the materials and spaces of Mediterranean towns to Finland.

He designed the Finnish Pavilion for the Paris International Exhibition of 1936–1937 and three years later another Finnish Pavilion for the 1939 New York World's Fair with a stunning theatrical interior. The free-flowing wooden interior apparently brought to mind Finland's lakes and forests and was the first exposure of many to Finnish and Nordic design.

Decades later, politicians and civic leaders decided an independent Finland needed a central square of its own near the recently completed Parliament House, a building that symbolised the independence won in 1917. In front of the Parliament lay a large railway freight yard,

which was to be relocated. This site would provide a unique opportunity for the realisation of an idea originally suggested by architect Eliel Saarinen after the civil war. By the end of the 1950s, after many alternative plans were investigated and designs were promulgated, discussed, and discarded, Aalto was appointed to formulate a central plan for Helsinki. The resulting master plan, encompassing Töölön-lahti bay, proposed a terraced square with a variety of civic buildings placed along the waterfront, partly on land but also in the water, to allow an open view of the bay through the buildings. The area in front of the Finnish House of Parliament was envisioned as an open central area that acted as a new active centre, providing a focus for the community's economic and cultural needs. However, the plan, after much debate, became a piecemeal development, with only Finlandia Hall being completed, becoming the only building in an imposing position in its relatively natural surroundings. Aalto's master plan, first presented in 1961, would never be carried out in its entirety, although other buildings were constructed, including the Opera House, which opened in 1993.

The first plan for Finlandia Hall was drawn by Aalto in 1961. He modified it in 1964 and 1971 on the basis of criticism from various sources. It was built between 1967 and 1971 and opened on 2nd December 1971. The congress wing was designed in 1970 and was constructed between 1973 and 1975.

Externally, Finlandia Hall has an eastern façade towards the bay, with the bulk of the auditorium rising above the horizontal foyer and public spaces. The western façade shows the building sitting in Hesperia Park; Aalto thought you should always enter a building through nature. The west side faces Mannerheimintie street and provides the main entrance, with a long, elegant canopy.

All the façades are clad in bright, white Carrera marble, which was part of Aalto's attempt to create a Mediterranean feel or link in Helsinki. Unfortunately, thin Carrera marble is a material well suited to mild Mediterranean climates but very unsuitable for use in the harsh northern climate of Helsinki and Finland. Within a few years of opening it was noticed that the thin white marble cladding was bowing because of the cycle of hot and cold temperatures. This is a phenomenon that has come to be called "thin stone façade failure". The marble was failing and after much public debate the entire façade (7,500 m2) was replaced in 1999 with similar Carrera marble. By 2009 it was apparent that the replacement cladding was failing in the same way. A further renovation is being planned to commence in 2022 and complete in 2024. This renovation will also replace many of the technical and mechanical systems that are at the end of their life cycle. More public spaces and amenities will be provided.

Finlandia Hall, foyers

Internally, the building has extensive public spaces, with generous views over the bay and a linear layout linking all the halls and the congress wing.

The main hall seats 1,700 and is essentially fan-shaped in plan, with an asymmetric rear wall to the stalls and asymmetric balcony front. Dramatic side seating blocks cascade down the deep blue side walls and the seating is black leather, providing a strong contrast with the white of the rest of the room. The fan-shaped plan is not ideal for good music acoustics and the hall's section further exacerbates the acoustic problems. Aalto imagined and built a large volume tower above the main seating block. His aim was to improve the acoustics of the concert hall by providing a reverberant space overhead. This volume is hidden from the audience by the suspended ceiling. Aalto hoped it would create a rich acoustic effect. Unfortunately, this experiment did not work, and the hall gained a reputation for poor, muffled acoustics and proved very unsuited for symphonic music. The wide fan shape did not provide side walls able to reflect sound usefully.

Finlandia Hall is considered one of the most important buildings in Finland and has developed an almost iconic status amongst Finns. It is not a successful building – it opened late, missing Sibelius's Centennial by six years. The external cladding has repeatedly failed, and contractors and designers are investigating alternative materials for the latest renovation. Most importantly the hall has poor acoustics for music.

Finlandia Hall, auditorium

Aalto Musiktheater Essen

Aalto went on to design a more much more successful performing arts building, which was eventually named after him, a rare honour for an architect. Aalto was the unanimous winner in Essen's competition for a new Musiktheater in 1959 and continued to rework the design till his death in 1976. The design continued but construction only began in 1983, seven years after Aalto's death.

Essen is an opera house, not a concert hall, but one can see concepts that Aalto brought to both buildings. It has the same clean white exterior, although the inappropriate marble is avoided in Essen. Both auditoriums are asymmetric, the room in Essen having a very dramatic asymmetry. Both auditoriums have a clean white appearance dramatically highlighted with deep blue side walls and, in Essen, blue seating. The foyers exhibit the same clean lines and cool spaces. One unique feature in the Essen auditorium is, the balconies which instead of receding from the stage as they rise are pushed

Aalto Musiktheater Essen, exterior

Aalto Musiktheater Essen, auditorium

forward towards the stage to get the audience as close to the action as possible.

Following a survey of 50 critics in 2008, the magazine *Opernwelt* declared the Aalto Theatre to be the best opera house in the German-speaking countries and awarded the title Opera House of the Year 2008.

Helsinki Music Centre

The acoustic problems of Finlandia did not go away and the user groups started lobbying for a new and better hall. The Sibelius Academy expressed interest in a new concert hall in 1992,

and formal planning started in 1994,, as the two major symphony orchestras of Helsinki, the Finnish Radio Symphony Orchestra and the Helsinki Philharmonic joined the project. A two-part architectural competition was held in 1999 and 2000 for a prestigious site at Töölönlahti opposite the Parliament building and between Finlandia Hall and Kiasma, the museum of contemporary art.

The competition was won by the LPR Architects, with Yasu Toyota of Nagata Acoustics as acoustic consultant. Because of the height restrictions in proximity to the Parliament House, many of the facilities are placed underground. The irregular four-sided building has a clean external design.

The main concert hall seats 1,704 people and is a vineyard form of room, with the audience surrounding the concert platform in

Helsinki Music Centre, auditorium

a number of seating blocks. The walls of the main concert hall at high level are partly glass, allowing daylight from the foyer into the concert hall itself. The glass walls can be closed with curtains located between the glass elements if daylight is not desired during a performance.

Like most concert halls today the acoustics of the Helsinki Music Centre are controversial. Surround or vineyard halls provide visually exciting rooms that excite architects and audiences. They do this by placing the platform towards the centre of the room and surrounding the platform with audience. Inevitably some audience members are seated either behind or alongside the platform. The majority of musical instruments and certainly the voices of soloists are directional. Sound comes out of the front and moves towards audience seated in front of the platform. Those at the sides and behind the platform get a completely different sound and musical experience, which many consider inferior.

The building contains five smaller rooms for 140–400 listeners. These include a chamber music hall, a chamber opera hall, an organ hall, a 'black box' room for electrically amplified music, and a rehearsal hall. The smaller rooms are used regularly by the students of Sibelius Academy for their training and student concerts.

With the completion of the Music Centre, Finlandia Hall is now focused on its role as a congress centre, serving as a venue for government events, trade fairs, and exhibitions.

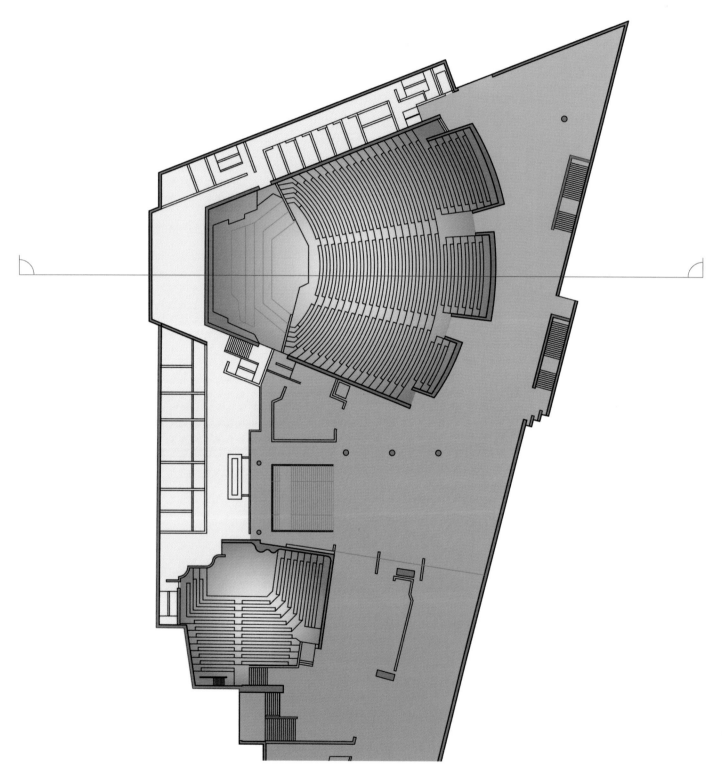

Finlandia Hall, Helskinki, comparative plan

0 5 10   20 metres

1:500

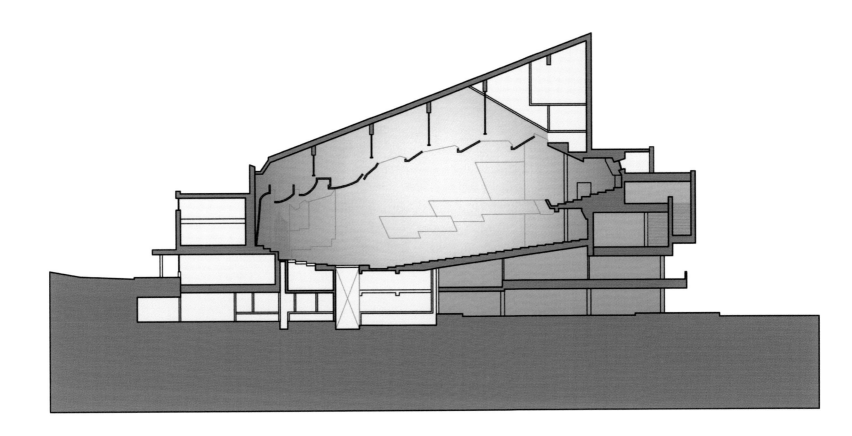

Finlandia Hall, Helsinki, comparative section

0   5   10   20 metres

1:500

Sydney Opera House

Sydney Opera House, 1973
Sydney, Australia
Architect, Jørn Utzon

David Staples

It stands by itself as one of the indisputable masterpieces of human creativity, not only in the 20th century, but in the history of humankind.

> (Expert evaluation report to the UNESCO World Heritage Committee 2007 on the Sydney Opera House.)

Jørn Utzon made a building well ahead of its time, far ahead of available technology – a building that changed the image of an entire country.

> (Frank Gehry in 2003, when awarding the Pritzker Prize (architecture's highest award) to the Sydney Opera House.)

Jørn Utzon won the competition to design the Sydney Opera House in 1957.

He left Australia and the project in 1966.

The building opened in October 1973 to universal acclaim. Utzon never returned to Australia and never saw the finished building, possibly the most famous building of the 20th century. He died in 2008.

The Sydney Opera House is undoubtedly one of the most important pieces of architecture of the 20th century. But as an opera house and a concert hall it is severely flawed.

Planning

Planning for a new performing arts building in Sydney began in the late 1940s; the existing Sydney Town Hall was not considered large enough or suitable for many types of live performance.

Joseph Cahill, the Premier of New South Wales, got behind the project although he initially preferred a different site. The Bennelong Point site was known to the native Gadigal people of the Eora Nation as Tubowgule, meaning "where the knowledge waters meet". This was a location where a freshwater stream carried waters into the sea and provided rich fishing grounds.

Woollarawarre Bennelong was a senior man of the Eora people and served as a bridge with the British settlers. In 1792 he became one of the first Aborigines to travel to England. He returned to Australia in 1795 and acted as an advisor to the governor and held a high position in Eora. The governor built a hut for him on what became known as Bennelong Point.

Cahill declared:

This state cannot go on without proper facilities for the expression of talent and the staging of the highest forms of artistic entertainment which add grace and charm to living and which help to develop a better, more enlightened community . . . Surely it is proper in establishing an opera house that it should not be a "shadygaff" place but an edifice that would be a credit to the state not only today but also for hundreds of years.

Jørn Utzon, a 38-year-old Dane with a small office north of Copenhagen, prepared his 12-page entry for the opera house competition; it was given the number 218 out of the 233 schemes submitted.

Competition

The government announced an international architectural competition and the guidelines were released in February 1956. These called for a large hall to seat between 3,000 to 3,500 persons and a small hall for approximately 1,200 persons. Both halls were conceived as multi-purpose spaces.

Judges and Judging

The jury included Sir Leslie Martin, who had been part of the design team for the Royal Festival Hall in London, and the eminent Finnish-American architect Eero Saarinen.

An oft-repeated, although occasionally disputed, story is that Saarinen was delayed travelling to Sydney and missed the first days

Conditions of Competition

This Competition has been approved by the Royal Australian Institute of Architects and the International Union of Architects.

Throughout these Conditions:

"Promoters" shall mean the Government of the State of New South Wales.

The "Secretary" shall mean the Secretary and Executive Officer of the Opera House Committee, c/- Department of Local Government, Bridge & Phillip Streets, Sydney, Australia.

1. Invitation

The Promoters invite all Architects, who are members of their respective Architectural Institutes in any country in the world, to submit designs in competition for—

A proposed National Opera House, to be erected on Bennelong Point, Sydney, Australia,

in accordance with these Conditions and the Annexed Appendices, which form part of these Conditions.

The winner of the Competition shall become registered in New South Wales as an Architect under the Architects Act, 1921-1946, before he can be appointed.

The qualifications for registration in New South Wales are set forth in Appendix 1.

2. Register

Every intending competitor shall register his name and address in writing with the Secretary, not later than 15th March, 1956.

The register shall be confidential and the names of the competitors shall not be disclosed until the Assessors have made an award.

Competitors may obtain one set of these Conditions by depositing the sum of £10 0s. 0d. (Australian) or its equivalent, with the Secretary. This sum will be refunded to those Architects who submit a bona fide design. Remittances to be made payable to the Government of New South Wales.

Designs will not be accepted from any person other than those whose names appear on the register.

Page 3

Sydney Opera House, competition brief

judging, by which time the other judges had already established a shortlist that did not include Jørn Utzon's design. Saarinen allegedly reclaimed Utzon's drawings from the rejected pile and argued its merits. At that time Saarinen was designing the TWA passenger terminal at New York's Idlewild (subsequently JFK) Airport. The TWA terminal opened in 1962 with a distinctive wing-shaped, tiled concrete roof. There is a considerable affinity between its design and Utzon's opera house.

Saarinen in New York and in some of his other work was proposing a much more organic flowing form of architecture. Utzon in his early sketches was advocating a similarly radical design for Sydney.

In January 1957 Premier Cahill announced the winner was Jørn Utzon, a virtually unknown Dane. The jury noted "because of its very originality, it is clearly a controversial design. We are however, absolutely convinced of its merits". The cost was estimated at A$ 3.5 million.

The Sydney Opera House developed from an architectural competition. This was a loosely structured competition with a broad brief and minimal requirements on the competitors. Utzon won the competition with a series of sketches. Architectural competitions are often intended to identify and develop young emerging talents and Sydney succeeded in this.

The concept for the Sydney Opera House owes much to Utzon's undoubted genius. But he himself acknowledged a number of influences that helped generate his concepts.

As a young man, Utzon was taken by his family to the Stockholm Exhibition in 1930. Gunnar Asplund, a renowned Swedish architect and designer, was at the height of his powers and had a significant influence on the exhibition, which impacted on Utzon and his family. Utzon remarked "Asplund is the father of modern Scandinavian architecture."

Finnish architect Alvar Aalto was also influential. Utzon worked briefly with Aalto in 1945 in Finland. Aalto went on to design the Finlandia Hall in Helsinki and the Alvar Aalto Theatre in Essen, Germany.

In 1949 Utzon received a grant that enabled him to travel extensively in the USA and Mexico, coming into contact with Frank Lloyd Wright, Mies van der Rohe and Ray and Charles Eames. His visits to South America also exposed him to Mayan temples and their influence.

During the competition Utzon apparently pored over maps of the Sydney harbour and possibly images of boats and sailing ships in the harbour, the influence of which can be seen in the roof of the opera house.

Finally, Utzon lived near Kronborg Castle in Denmark. This castle is built on a promontory with some similarities to Benelong Point. Kronborg Castle was immortalised by William Shakespeare as Elsinore in *Hamlet*.

Utzon's winning design consisted of only 12 drawings. It was a sculptural scheme using the stunning location and a building designed to be viewed from all sides. Utzon won the competition on the basis of a few imaginative but undeveloped sketches.

Design

Once design commenced, two problems were almost immediately identified:

- The geology of Bennelong Point had not been fully surveyed before the competition. It was now discovered that instead of good, stable sandstone the site was largely composed of loose alluvial deposits soaked with sea water and unsuitable to support the weight of

Sydney Opera House, Jørn Utzon competition sketch

the structure. Mass concrete foundations were necessary at significantly increased cost.

• The second challenge was a lot of unknowns about the roofs. They had not been designed or engineered in any detail.

Politically there was considerable pressure to start construction as quickly as possible to maintain momentum and avoid political opposition. Premier Cahill was in a hurry; he was 68 when construction began.

It would have been wise to allow time to resolve design challenges and problems but this would have put the project at risk.

In March 1959 construction of stage 1 – the podium – commenced and it was completed in February 1963, two years behind schedule.

The project needed extraordinarily skilled structural engineering and Utzon was introduced to Ove Arup by Sir Lesley Martin and Eero Saarinen. Arup was one of the leading structural engineers of his generation and founder of the practice that still bears his name.

Architects Sir Leslie Martin, Jørn Utzon and Eero Saarinen

The Shells

While the podium was being built Utzon and his design team struggled with the design of the shells. His competition entry had relatively low, linear shells. The auditoriums needed much higher shapes and larger volumes. Utzon had a clear vision of the type of shapes he wanted in the shells, while Arup and Partners in London struggled to devise a structural solution.

Utzon produced the "red book", which contained a complete set of plans and sections for the Government in March 1958; this developed the schematic concept from his competition scheme. But the drawings in the red book were structurally unsound. Each shell was different and

this unique solution would add significantly to the cost and complexity of the building.

As the construction of the podium progressed, resolution of the shells became a critical issue. Utzon struggled to develop a rational concept that could be engineered. A major breakthrough occurred when he observed that they could be derived from a single, constant form – a sphere. This would considerably simplify the sails and allow ease of repetition. The "spherical solution" would become the discovery that permitted the opera house shapes and forms to be engineered and realised.

In January 1962 Utzon submitted the "Yellow Book". In 38 pages of plans and elevations he set out the shapes, details of the ribs and the tiling. The book's cover showed the principles of the spherical geometry.

Sydney Opera House, under construction

Construction and Disputes

With the design of the shells resolved, stage 2 – construction of the roof – began in 1963 and took three years. Utzon had moved with his family to Australia in 1963 but relations with the New South Wales government deteriorated. There were problems over rising costs; originally estimated at 3.5 million Australian dollars in 1959, they had risen to 13.7 million in 1962. There were concerns over Utzon's ability to deliver all of the drawings required for the fitting out and interiors of the project.

In 1963 there were significant changes to the brief for the project. At the insistence of the Australian Broadcasting Commission, which ran the orchestra, the major hall, which was originally to be a multipurpose opera/concert hall, became solely a concert hall. All of the stage equipment needed in this hall to accommodate opera and other types of performance was scrapped, although a significant amount had already been installed.

The minor hall, originally for stage productions only, was now required to house opera and ballet and renamed the opera theatre. It is much too small and totally inadequate to stage large-scale opera and ballet.

Ove Arup stepped back from the project as he moved towards retirement. Arup's Sydney office queried Utzon's ability to deliver the number of drawings needed for stage 3 – the interiors.

A change of government in May 1965 led to further disputes over the cost of prototypes and an impasse ensued. Following meetings in February 1966 between Utzon and the Minister for Public Works, Utzon resigned. There were demonstrations in favour of Utzon and attempts at a reconciliation, but the government moved to appoint a new team led by Peter Hall in April 1966 to take charge of the design of the interiors.

Nine days after Hall was appointed, on 28th April 1966 Utzon and his family flew out of Australia never to return.

January 1967 saw the last pre-cast shell installed, effectively completing stage 2 – the roofs. Stages 1 and 2 had cost A\$13 million to complete.

Interiors

On appointment, Peter Hall and his team found little information on the proposed interiors. They recommended the large hall be designed solely for concerts. Opera was relegated to the smaller hall. In September 1968 Hall and his team advised

Sydney Opera House, Concert Hall interior

the Government it would cost a further $85 million to complete. The cost of stage 3 considerably exceeded that of the first two stages.

Opening

The first production in the Opera Theatre was Prokofiev's epic *War and Peace* by the Australian Opera. British lighting designer Robert Ornbo encountered an opera house without adequate lighting positions and a stage simply too small to house large-scale opera.

The first performance in the Concert Hall was a programme of works by Wagner performed by the Sydney Symphony Orchestra and featuring the legendary Swedish soprano Birgit Nilsson and conductor Charles Mackerras.

One month later, on October 20th 1973, Queen Elizabeth II opened the Sydney Opera House and with British understatement observed that "The Sydney Opera House has captured the imagination of the world, though I understand that its construction has not been totally without problems."

In 1957 the project was expected to cost A$3.5 million and be completed on Australia Day (January 26th)1963. The building was completed ten years late at a cost of A$102 million, some 29 times over the original budget.

Sydney Opera House, Opera Theatre interior

Impact and Resident Companies

The Sydney Opera House is now home to seven significant performing arts companies and is the largest performing arts centre in Australia. It has hosted many performing arts groups from across the world.

Impact on 20th-Century Architecture

The Sydney Opera House is important because it was one of the first buildings to move away from the classical and rectilinear form of civic, public and performing arts buildings. It embraced curves and proposed a challenging structure at the limits of what technology and the construction industry could deliver in the 1960s.

The latter quarter of the 20th century has seen other architects continuing this move away from the ordered, straight line and rectilinear with increasingly audacious projects. The work of Frank Gehry, Zaha Hadid and others illustrates this.

Utzon's Design Principles

In 1999 Jørn Utzon agreed to develop a set of guidelines for future changes to the Sydney Opera House. This was a process of rapprochement between the architect and the building that he had never seen. The goal of the design principles was to enshrine Utzon's vision and provide a framework for the future development and renewal of the building to ensure its integrity. Utzon worked on this with his architect son Jan and Sydney-based architect Richard Johnson.

Part of this process was the re-design and reconstruction of the Reception Hall. This reopened in 2004, renamed the Utzon Room, and is the only interior within the Sydney Opera House designed by Jørn Utzon.

Opera House Renewal Project

2013 marked the 40th anniversary of the opening of the opera house. It was also the start of the building's Decade of Renewal.

In 2016 the opera house announced a series of projects to be enabled by A$202 million of financial support from the New South Wales Government.

Conclusions

The Sydney Opera House resulted from an international architectural competition that illustrates both the merits and risks of such a route to select the architect. The brief for the competition was poor – it asked for two multipurpose halls at a time when the world was moving against multipurpose halls and towards single-use spaces – a concert hall and a separate opera house.

Architectural competitions are intended to offer opportunities to new, young, emerging architects. Jørn Utzon was such an architect and he produced a remarkable building. But architectural competitions also carry a degree of risk that a project will be costly, difficult or delayed. The Sydney Opera House was all three.

Having started with a flawed brief, there were significant client changes to their requirements during the design and construction of the opera house, resulting in massive changes and huge increases in cost. The costs of Sydney Opera House cannot all be ascribed to the innovative roof and shells. The significant cost arose during stage 3 of construction, the fit-out of the spaces.

"Form follows function" is a phrase ascribed to American architect Louis Sullivan. It became a mantra for architects in the 20th century. Utzon conceived and designed extraordinary external shapes for the building; the auditoriums and stages had to be squeezed into these shapes. The performance spaces were and will always be compromised.

The Sydney Opera House is perhaps the most extraordinary building of the 20th century. It preceded many subsequent organic buildings and its influence on architecture in the latter quarter of the 20th century is remarkable.

Could the opera house have been better if Utzon had been retained and had not resigned? An impossible question to answer. The fundamental problem is that the shells are too small. In addition, the client's brief changes compromised Utzon's ability to produce a more singular piece of architecture, but it would still have had practical and functional problems.

Sydney Opera House, at night

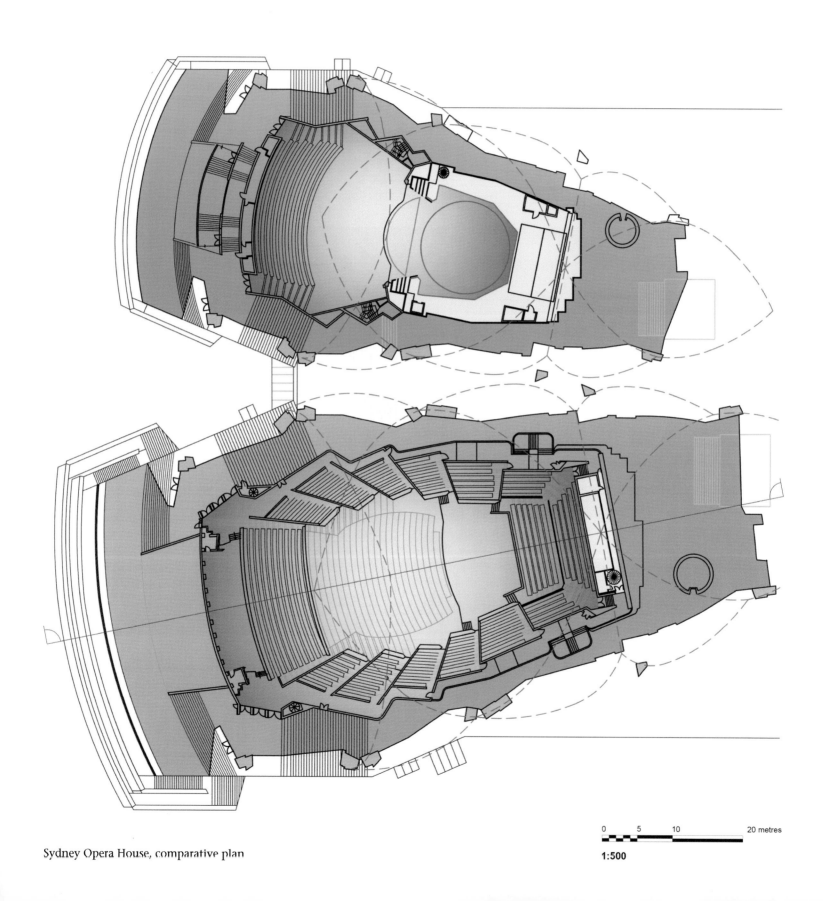

Sydney Opera House, comparative plan

0   5   10   20 metres

1:500

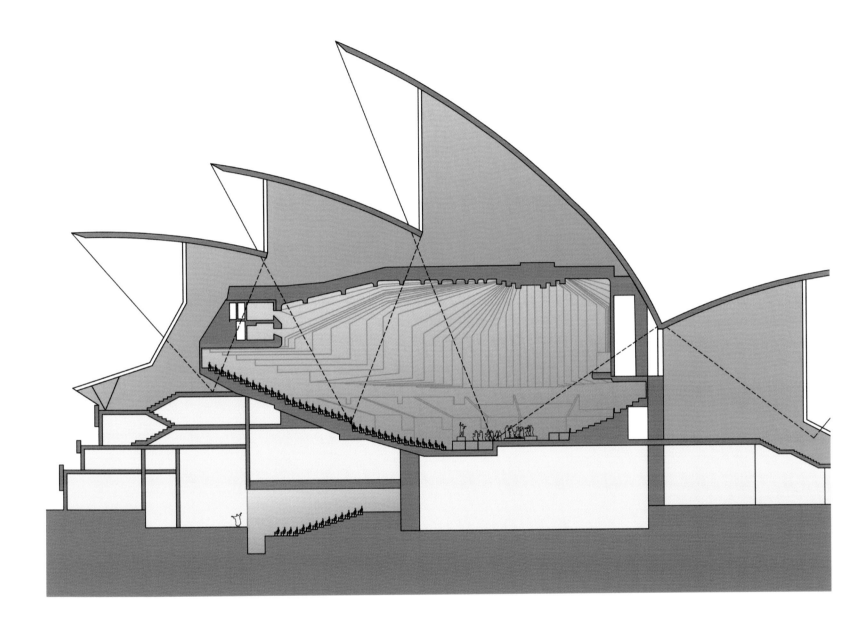

Sydney Opera House, comparative section

0   5   10   20 metres

1:500

Teatro Regio Torino, 1973, the auditorium with the original proscenium

Teatro Regio Torino, 1973
Torino, Italy
Architect, Carlo Mollino
David Staples and Simone Solinas

The cast of characters associated with Teatro Regio Torino (Turin) includes Wagner, Puccini, Richard Strauss, Arturo Toscanini, Maria Callas, and acclaimed architect Carlo Mollino.

The original Teatro Regio was an opera house in the customary form – a horseshoe shaped auditorium with five levels of galleried seating. It was destroyed by fire in 1936 and after a protracted period a new theatre was built and opened in 1973. The new theatre has a radically different form expressed in a unique architecture.

Carlo Emanuele III, the Duke of Savoy, instructed architect Benedetto Alfieri to design a theatre of *great prestige*. There was then considerable rivalry between the Italian city states, with each seeking to create symbols and buildings of greater importance and status. The theatre was completed in only two years and opened in December 1740 with the world première of Francesco Feo's *Arsace*. It seated about 2,000 in the stalls level surrounded by 143 boxes (including the royal box/*palco reale*, placed at the centre on the second level of boxes) with five levels and a gallery (the *piccionaia*).

The theatre was richly decorated with an ornate proscenium and elaborately painted ceiling. Charles Burney, an English music historian and composer, authored *The Present State of Music in France and Italy* (1771) and described the Teatro Regio as one of the most beautiful theatres in Europe. The Regio was a landmark in the European Grand Tour of the time, and Diderot and D'Alembert chose to include this theatre in the new edition of their *Encyclopédie* (1775), with numerous plates and accurate details about the innovative solutions adopted in the building.

The theatre was closely tied to the court and was intensively used until the French invasion of Piedmont in 1798. The Savoy decorations and insignia were removed, and it was successively renamed Teatro Nazionale, Grand Théâtre des Arts and finally Théâtre Impérial.

In 1814 the Piedmont area returned to Savoy rule and the theatre was renamed Teatro Regio and redecorated in neoclassical style by Ernesto Melano and Pelagio Palagi, at the request of King Carlo Alberto. All through the 19th century, great virtuosi of bel canto performed on the stage of the Regio, like Giuditta Pasta and Adelina Patti; serious operas of Rossini, Bellini, Donizetti and Verdi soon became a regular presence in the seasons, and from 1855 the curtain rose for the comic repertoire too. In 1861, the year of Italian unification, a new renovation by Angelo Moja took place: the changes previously made by Palagi were removed and the auditorium got a "neo-baroque" appearance. In 1870 the City of Turin took over ownership of the Regio and began a period full of novel artistic choices.

In 1895 Arturo Toscanini became music director and principal conductor of Teatro Regio for three seasons; the following year he conducted the world premiere of Puccini's *La Bohème* and went on to conduct his

Cross section of the auditorium and the foyer, with view of the proscenium and the curtain (depicting *The Triumph of Bacchus* by Sebastiano Galeotti). The Regio Teatro di Torino opened in the year 1740. Drawing by Count Benedetto Alfieri, chamber gentleman, and prime architect of His Majesty

first symphony concert in the theatre. For the 1898 Italian Expo in Turin, he conducted 43 concerts in just four months. Under Toscanini the theatre became one of the Wagnerian strongholds in Italy, and in 1905 he came back to inaugurate the renovated theatre with *Sigfried*. In 1906 Richard Strauss made his debut in an Italian theatre, conducting here the Italian premiere of his *Salome*.

In the early years of the 20th century there was much discussion about building a new theatre or modifying the Teatro Regio to increase its seating capacity. The latter prevailed: the structural work was entrusted to Ferdinando Cocito and the decorative parts to Giorgio Ceragioli and Giacomo Grosso. The last two tiers of boxes were substituted by three galleries, increasing the overall seating capacity of the auditorium to about 3,000 seats, and the theatre assumed a more "popular" appearance: no

longer a haunt of the aristocracy, but reflecting the social changes that had taken place in the society.

During the night of 8th to 9th February 1936 an electrical short circuit caused a fire which destroyed the theatre after almost two hundred years. The front wall of the theatre, which dates from the early 18th-century, fronts onto Piazza Castello, the most important square in Turin, and was the only element left standing after the fire (it is today part of UNESCO World Heritage together with the Residences of the Royal House of Savoy).

Within a year a competition was announced for the reconstruction. The competition for a 3,500-seat opera house was won by architects Aldo Morbelli and Robaldo Morozzo della Rocca. Despite this prompt initiative, the Second World War and political issues delayed the works for almost 30 years until 1965, when architect Carlo Mollino was appointed to

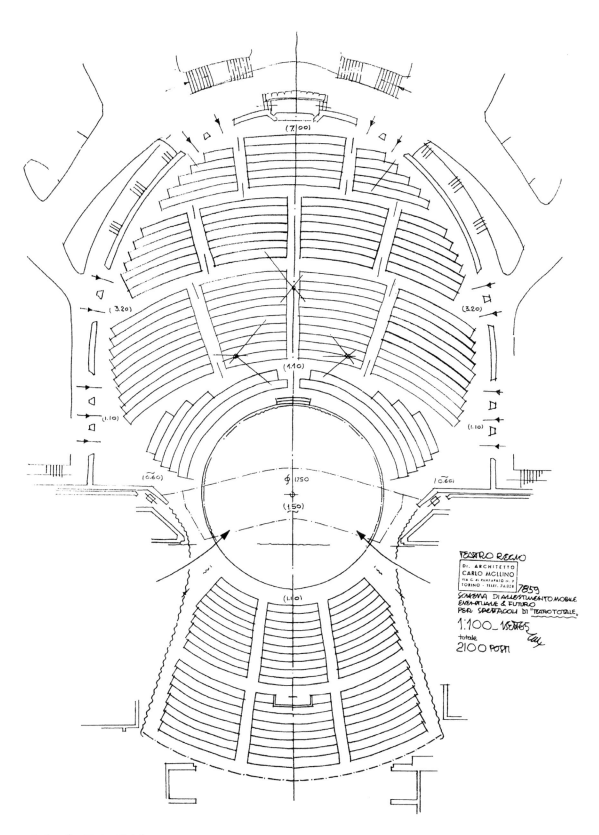

Carlo Mollino concept plan for Teatro Totale

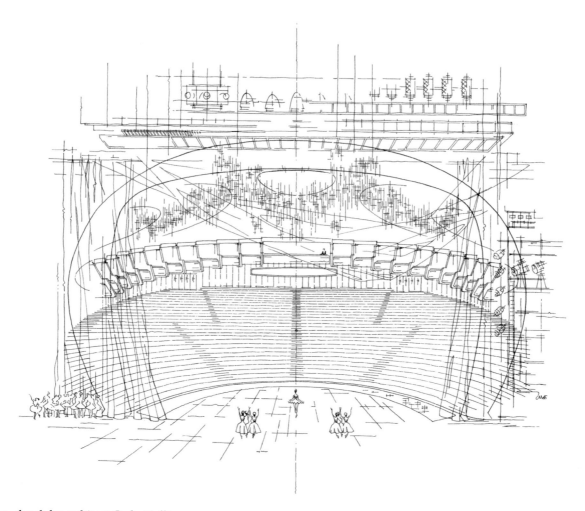

Teatro Regio Torino, sketch by architect Carlo Mollino

design a new theatre with a capacity reduced to a more appropriate 1,800 seats. Mollino was selected by a specific commission, as one of the most acclaimed architects of his time, having been professor of Architectural Composition at the Turin faculty from 1953, responsible among many buildings for the Turin Equestrian Society (1937–40), the Rai Auditorium (1950–3), and the Torino Chamber of Commerce (1964–72). He had eclectic interests in racing cars, planes, streamlining, steel, and was once credited as saying, "Everything is permissible as long as it is fantastic." Mollino had no real experience of buildings for performance or opera houses but he was determined to produce a new form of theatre for Teatro Regio and Turin.

In 1927 Walter Gropius was head of the renowned Bauhaus and originated a design for what he called the Total Theatro. Carlo Mollino also prepared a concept drawing for a "Teatro Totale", illustrated here with his sketch for Turin.

The city authorities wanted to retain the harmony of Piazza Castello and insisted the front façade and colonnade be retained and restored. Mollino kept this element to house foyers and box office. An open space behind led to a completely new glass façade and entrance to the theatre.

The new Teatro Regio foyers have an interesting interplay of levels linked by staircases redolent of those in the Metropolitan Opera in New York. Mollino also picked up the star shapes found in Guarino Guarini's Palazzo Carignano and embodied them in patterns on the foyer walls as on the external, curvilinear side walls, where he juxtaposed cotto tiles and great glass surfaces. The traditional symbol of Turin is a bull and he incorporated a bull in semi-abstract form into a marble ellipsoidal section of the foyer floor in what is now called Foyer del Toro. The predominant colours in the foyers are the red of the carpet (a singular, copyright-registered pattern that mixes red and purple designed by Mollino), the white of the marbles, the golden/bronze tint in the laminated walls and in the balustrade. Everywhere glass walls allow the eye to look at the exterior architecture, in a continuous dialogue with the past, and in total transparency between the people inside and the community. He designed very distinctive lighting, based on frosted globes which are used throughout the foyers, sometimes assembled in shapes that resemble bunches of wisteria flowers.

Although he travelled extensively to review theatre buildings, Mollino devised a truly unique, unusual and challenging auditorium for Turin.

Teatro Regio Torino, foyer with stairway and side glass walls

The auditorium has a wide, deep and quite steeply raked main body of seating. It is surrounded by a single curved row of 37 boxes that rise to follow the line of the raked floor to give, nowadays, a total seating capacity of 1,582. The proscenium was very wide with a purple – Mollino wanted it to be called indigo – curved frame looking as though it was influenced by Radio City Music Hall in NY; it is reminiscent of a 1960s television set. The deep indigo of the proscenium gently fades, through a veining geometrical design, into the white ivory, until the row of boxes. The auditorium is capped with a concave curved ceiling looking like a half-opened shell or scallop which generally is a poor acoustic shape in an opera house. The red colour was carried through from the public areas onto the auditorium seats, with originally red carpet on the floors and running up the walls. From the ceiling you have a dramatic chandelier made up of over 3,600 luminous stems, which creates the effect of an "iridescent cloud".

The stage is a very conventional cruciform with a main stage (24m wide and 20m deep) incorporating six stage elevators under a fly tower 32m high, side stages on either side and a rear stage.

The new theatre opened on 10th April 1973 with *I Vespri sicilliani (The Sicilian Vespers)* by Giuseppe Verdi. It was the first and only stage direction by Maria Callas, together with Giuseppe Di Stefano. The new theatre surprised all the people. Opera houses across Italy had richly decorated historic auditoriums with rows of boxes around the room stacked to very high ceilings. The new theatre was radically different. But the people of Turin took pride in having something different from every other city in Italy and embraced the Mollino project as their own.

Carlo Mollino travelled extensively to research theatres and opera house precedents after he was appointed to design the new Teatro Regio. He visited theatres in Zurich, Warsaw, Malmö, Vienna, Charlottenburg, London, Bucharest, Frankfurt, Cologne, etc. and the Metropolitan Opera in New York. But he was really determined to do something different from what had gone before. His interests in curvilinear forms and streamlining appear to have predominated in his approach to the auditorium.

To deal with acoustics matters, Mollino had a specialist advisor, Prof. Gino Sacerdote, director of acoustics at the National Electrotechnical

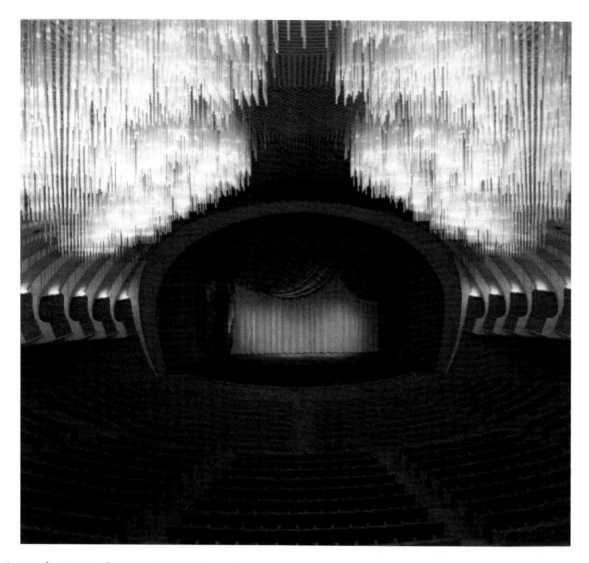

Teatro Regio Torino, auditorium with original proscenium arch

Institute "Galileo Ferraris" (Turin), member of the Acoustical Society of America and of the French Acoustics Association; he was appointed by the commissioning body, the City of Turin. He made a series of tests in 1968, using sound-generator machines and microphones, applied to a gypsum model of the auditorium, based on the executive project. Other tests with orchestra and chorus were made when the auditorium was almost completed.

The auditorium has a generous if not over-large plan area but in section the room has a relatively low concave ceiling and steep rake to the main body of seating – see the comparative section below.

At the time of its opening the new house had difficult acoustics. Singers complained about the difficulty of hearing music from the orchestra pit. The room also had a short reverberation time, giving poor acoustics for the audience, this latter problem being caused by the low concave ceiling and the extensive carpeting on walls and floor. In 1996, the auditorium underwent an important refurbishment, led by Roberto Gabetti and Aimaro Oreglia d'Isola working with German acoustic consultants Müller-BBM from Munich. The intervention, reversible in each part, involved wood-panelling the auditorium, slightly modifying the perimeter walls and stage, and installing a new proscenium over Mollino's structure, which improved the acoustic connection between orchestra pit and stage, and with the stalls.

The acoustics were studied and measured both before and after the renovation. The original "TV" set shape of the proscenium arch did not achieve a balance between singers on stage and orchestra pit and made it difficult for the singers to hear the musicians. A completely new proscenium zone was constructed in front of the original, which narrowed the front of the auditorium and created better reflecting surfaces. To increase the reverberation time in the room, all the absorbent carpet on the floors and walls was removed to expose harder, more reflective surfaces.

Founded in 1740, the Regio is the second oldest theatre still in use in Italy (after Teatro di San Carlo, Naples, 1737). Since the time of reopening in 1973, productive activity has been progressively increasing, right up to the occasions that have left their mark on the recent history of the Regio: in 1990 the 250th anniversary of its founding; in 1996, live on TV, the centennial of the world première of Puccini's *La Bohème*, created at Regio; in 2006 the extraordinary adventure of the XX Winter Olympic Games and its Olympics of Culture, an international event after which the Regio has begun to tour all over the world.

The theatre today hosts both new productions and co-productions, along with repertoire stagings; the most renowned world dance companies present ballet masterpieces too. Teatro Regio also offers a symphonic-choral concert season and has also been used for large-scale musicals – *Cats, West Side Story*, and *Evita*.

Turin is the fourth biggest city in Italy, and its opera house is one of the 14 national lyric-symphonic foundations, financed by the central government, by local administration and by many private companies. Today, the people of this area have a unique opera house, both thanks to the "open architecture" by Mollino (in terms of transparency) and at the same time thanks to the variety of events presented at Regio.

Teatro Regio Torino, auditorium after renovation showing new proscenium

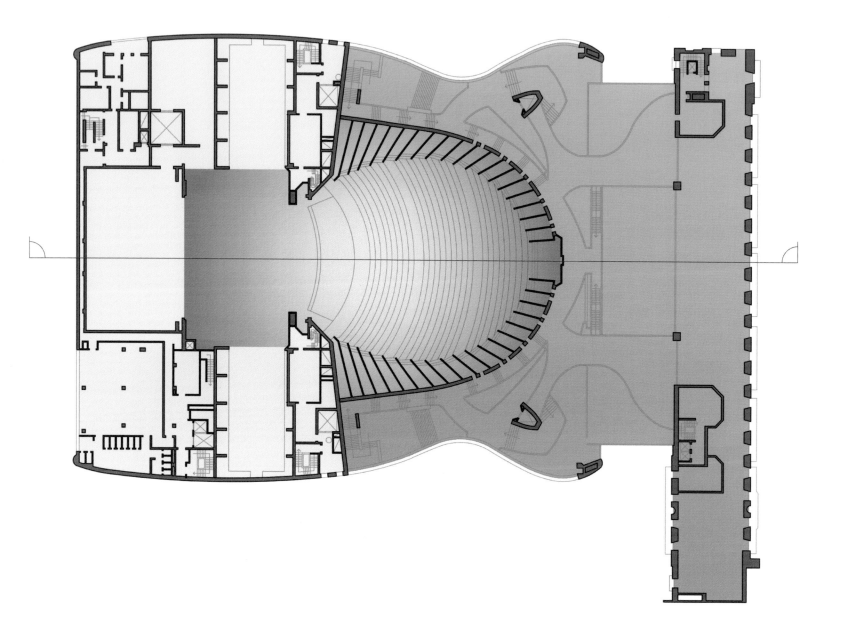

Teatro Regio Torino, comparative plan

1:500

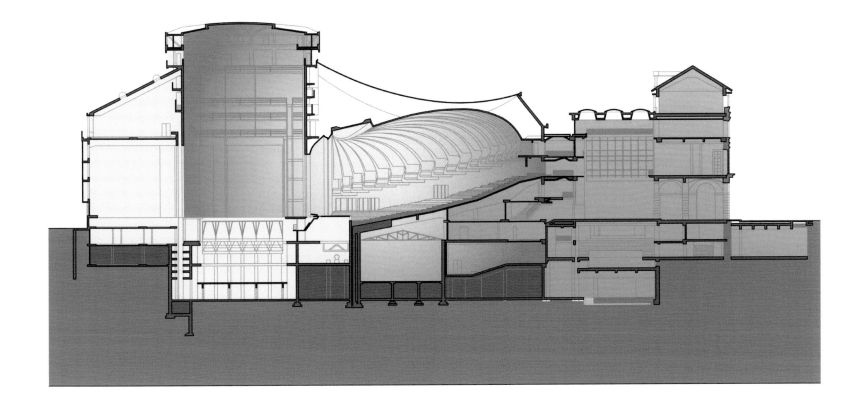

Teatro Regio Torino, comparative section

0   5   10   20 metres

1:500

Laurence Olivier, in the National Theatre's Olivier
Theatre June 14, 1978

National Theatre, 1976
London, UK
Architect, Denys Lasdun

Patrick Dillon

Many buildings experience painful births, but few have suffered like London's National Theatre. Seventy-two years passed between the publication of the first *Scheme and Estimates for a National Theatre*, by Harley Granville Barker, and the Queen's arrival to cut the ribbon in front of a distinguished crowd that included the building's weary architect, Denys Lasdun. Those years involved two World Wars, five sites, four architects, and innumerable different briefs; they saw theatre move on from *The Importance of Being Earnest* to *Zigger Zagger*; and the National Theatre's design morph from a neoclassical palace by Edwin Lutyens to Lasdun's radical experiment on the south bank: an extraordinary, subtle, brutal and challenging building which still divides Londoners, and represents the high point of mid-century concrete Modernism.

Soon after it opened, the Prince of Wales described the National Theatre as "a clever way of building a nuclear power station in the middle of London."[1] "You poor man," his aunt Princess Margaret added cruelly, when she met Lasdun at a party, "What are we going to do about your flagging reputation?" Delayed by the oil crisis, three-day week and national building strike, by hyperinflation, cost cuts, and its own uncompromising technical challenges, the building was completed not in the blaze of optimism in which it was conceived, but in an era which had tired of architects, modernity and concrete. The Pop Art Pompidou Centre opened within a year and wowed crowds. Lasdun's NT seemed out of date before the first show even opened. It has taken London forty years to recognize the concrete ziggurat by Waterloo Bridge as one of its greatest architectural masterpieces.

Strangely, throughout the 70 painful years of its gestation, Harley Granville Barker's founding vision remained substantially intact. In 1904, he promised a "thoroughly dignified and delightful playhouse,"[2] presenting a mix of Shakespeare, revived classics and new plays operating on a repertory system. He wanted theatre-going to be a complete experience, the foyers "ample and dignified," even offering, "light eatables of many descriptions … at moderate prices."[3] Harley Granville Barker was writing at the height of the Edwardian theatre-building boom and reacting against its uncomfortable seats and tortuous sightlines, its cramped foyers and overpriced drinks, its cheap musicals and melodramas presented, ill-rehearsed, to an audience in evening dress. Granville Barker wanted theatre to "bulk large in the social and intellectual life of London,"[4] and to be available to all. Sadly, his *Scheme and Estimates*, however eloquent, attracted little funding. In 1938 a single pile was sunk on a site in South Kensington; then war intervened.

The Second World War made the National Theatre possible. Through the Council for Encouragement of Music and the Arts, forerunner of the

Arts Council, it established the notion that British goverments should fund the arts, and that theatre was an art. Meanwhile, the County of London Plan, formulated by Patrick Abercrombie even while London was being bombed, invented the radical notion that a city could be regenerated through culture, proposing two auditoriums and a bandstand for London's post-industrial south bank. The south bank housed the 1951 Festival of Britain, whose Festival Hall provided many Britons with their first taste of Modern architecture. As part of the Festival, the Queen laid the foundation stone of the National Theatre. It would turn out to be in the wrong place.

The NT's journey had only just begun.

Granville Barker's push for a national theatre would eventually generate both the NT and the Royal Shakespeare Company. In 1932, Elisabeth Scott's Shakespeare Memorial Theatre had opened in Stratford. The RSC itself was founded in 1961, and the National Theatre Company two years later. It had taken over the Old Vic but planned a new home, sustained by a National Theatre Act promising government funds. In November 1963, architectural teams trooped through their interview rooms in St Anne's Gate. Denys Lasdun walked in alone. "Gentlemen," he told the interviewing committee, "I think that my background and my record is sufficient for you to know who I am … so I have nothing further to say to you."[5] "The important aspect," he added to a roomful of mesmerised theatrical visionaries, "is the spiritual one." "Oh, my dear!" Laurence Olivier said afterwards, "We all fell for that!"[6] Lasdun's appointment was announced the day JFK was shot.

Denys Lasdun's model of the original design

Lasdun's site, back then, was on Jubilee Gardens. His brief was for a combined National Theatre and Opera House. No one knew what form the National Theatre's auditoriums should take. The "Building Committee" was chaired by Laurence Olivier, and included an array of theatrical radicals who agreed about nothing. Lasdun, selected partly because he had never designed a theatre, was as pugnacious as they were. Relations soon broke down. The committee's minutes make painful reading – but they also record a fascinating debate between leading theatre practitioners about the nature of theatre.

The main space, which became the Olivier, was understood to be the heart of the NT. The proscenium-arched Lyttelton became the "Any Other Business theatre", while the third auditorium was axed for cost reasons, only later being reinstated as Iain Mackintosh's groundbreaking Cottesloe. Committee and architect soon realised that a hybrid arena/proscenium arch room was impracticable. Lasdun's "Scheme B", an intriguing sketch of a stage in one corner of a square room, gained some consensus. Beyond that they stuck. The committee was seeking to reinvent theatre from first principles, to understand, in Lasdun's words, "What is the relationship between actor and audience, between actor and actor, and between audience and audience?"[7] Lasdun relished Scheme B as "sharp, non-compromising, anti-illusion theatre: blood dripping from concrete walls!"[8] – a vision tailor-made for Oedipus Rex but less suited to Oscar Wilde. A poignant photograph from Lasdun's office shows an entire roomful of smashed auditorium models.

National Theatre, Olivier Theatre

National Theatre, Lyttelton Theatre

In 1965 the project ran into the ground yet again. Arts Minister Jennie Lee axed the opera house, then the Jubilee Gardens site was lost. Lasdun redesigned his National Theatre for a new location on the bend in the river below Waterloo Bridge. Only late in 1967 did he unveil his finished design.

The design was, first of all, a *tour de force* of space planning. Onto a hundred-metre square site, the architects had squeezed foyers, auditoriums, workshops, dressing rooms and offices. The facilities were extraordinary: workshops were large and fully equipped; dressing rooms had windows. Front of house, there were restaurants and ample bars, while generous terraces shelved over the river. The NT's brilliant layout is too little appreciated. But it was in his architectural treatment of a flagship national theatre that Lasdun's design broke new ground.

Theatres are rhetorical buildings: they present an actor's face to the town. Mid-century architecture, however, resisted the idea that buildings should have faces at all. And while traditional theatre design had deployed the full classical repertoire of porticoes, steps and statues, Modern architects had no such language to play with. Lasdun's solution was radical. He conceived the National Theatre not as a building, but as a piece of city – an urban landscape, he called it – whose terraces reached out to merge with the city's pavements, whose foyers were a seamless continuation of public space. "It's not a temple with a door," Lasdun once said. "It's already open."⁰ There were no elevations. The

National Theatre, Cottesloe Theatre

Lyttelton's geometry, while others snapped onto the line of the Olivier, like iron filings obeying a different force-field. Bathed in light through full-height glass screens, the result is a kind of modern baroque, one of the most thrilling spaces in 20th-century architecture.

The reference to baroque architecture was intended. Like most Modernists of his generation, Lasdun knew the classical canon. Uncompromisingly radical as it is, the NT is imbued with historic references. Epidaurus is the most obvious, but the Olivier's grand staircase, parting and rejoining to put audiences on display, recalls nothing so much as Garnier's Paris Opera. Lasdun's ability to fuse contradictory references in one building was possible through the rigorous abstraction of his forms. For all its multiple allusions, the NT always operates on its own sculptural terms. "I don't want anything to come between people experiencing the theatre and your drama," he told Peter Hall. "They have in a way to use the concrete reality of the building, not tarted up in any way."[10]

It was through concrete that Lasdun unified the complex shapes of his theatre. His material palette was ruthlessly constrained: board-marked concrete, a ground plane of black engineering brick; fittings of polished wood, black leather and stainless steel. The foyer carpet was designed by Susan Lasdun to recall the heather colours of a Greek mountainside. The source of so much of the NT's later unpopularity, concrete was also the way Lasdun solved the paradox of a state institution which was also a radical laboratory for young theatre-makers. The NT is often described as 'brutalist', a description its architect rejected. Brutalism, derived from *béton brut*, raw concrete, was shock-art, using an industrial material to challenge and disturb. By contrast, Lasdun's board-marked concrete was made with infinite finesse. The NT is not a machine-age building but a hand-crafted one, built lovingly in timber before its concrete was poured. The 6-inch douglas fir boards were rigorously laid out by the architects. The concrete mix was carefully defined. The result was architecture made with all the craftsmanship a great institution might demand, but in a workaday material that gave theatre's Young Turks the industrial workshop they craved. The NT would be both a palace of culture, and the 1970s punk venue that its opening poster, by Tom Phillips, suggested.

terraces rose like geological strata towards fly towers whose sheer sides towered above the Thames.

Inside, Lasdun raised the main auditorium to second floor level. The Lyttelton remained at ground floor level, enabling foyers and rakes to interlock. Both theatres were symmetrical and axial. Lasdun's masterstroke was to twist the Olivier's axis round by 45 degrees, placing the two axes in tension. The Lyttelton foyer was crossed diagonally by a coffered concrete grid on the line of the Olivier. Some piers obeyed the

National Theatre, entrance (modified in 2015) and terraces

Unfortunately, that opening was still far off when Lasdun completed his design. Ground was broken late in 1969, with an opening promised for 1972. In fact, construction dragged on four more years, during which costs soared, and inflation wrecked an economy staggering from the three-day week and oil crisis. Throughout the grim years in which 1960s optimism came to an end, 'The National' remained a gaunt unfinished shell on the south bank. By the time it opened, concrete was irredeemably associated with blighted housing estates and failed new towns, and the tide had turned on Lasdun's heroic, erudite Modernism. When the National Theatre Act was passed in 1949, people had looked forward to an enlightened era in which governments would sustain a cultured society. A decade after the NT's first show, Margaret Thatcher denied that society existed at all.

The NT's theatrical teething pains didn't help. The Olivier drum revolve didn't work. Innovative computerised lighting desks, designed in the era of Apollo 11, proved hard to bed in. Unionised crew picketed shows. Meanwhile, architectural reception of the NT was decidedly mixed. Prince Charles was by no means its only critic.

Others, though, saw how remarkable Lasdun's building was. John Betjeman, better known as a champion of all things Victorian, wrote to him not long before it opened: "It is a lovely work . . . it has that inevitable and finished look that great work does."[11] Still more encouragingly,

Richard Findlater, reviewing the NT in the *Observer*, noted something that belied descriptions of the building as fortress-like and impenetrable: "Scores of young people – the kind glimpsed all too seldom in West End foyers – at home inside the National, evening after evening … sitting on the floor, propped against a concrete strut."[12]

For Denys Lasdun, profoundly humane in outlook, people would always be the heart of the National Theatre. Without people, the building would never be complete. "I want the feeling," he said, "that the audience – like the tides of the river – flow into the auditoria and become a community within them."[13]

The first remodelling of the building took place only 20 years after it opened, when the accomplished firm of Stanton Williams reconfigured

National Theatre, foyers

the entrance, filling in the overhanging terrace at the front with a bookshop. Lasdun hated the change, which shifted the entrance off the Olivier's axis of symmetry. It was an unhappy experience for everyone. Its only undoubted success was the removal of the road which encircled the building, creating Theatre Square as a place for outside gathering and performance.

The changes which eventually unlocked the NT's potential arose as much from regeneration of the South Bank as reconfiguration of the building. Abercrombie's wartime vision had been of a cultural quarter regenerating the river. It was inspired - but took far longer to achieve than expected. Only with creation of the continuous river walk, and cleansing of the river itself, did the Thames become a public gathering-place. In 2006 the neighbouring Southbank Centre completed a renovation that filled its terraces with cafés and bars. 'NT Future', a regeneration of the NT completed in 2015, was the NT's response to the changes in its surroundings. Designed by Haworth Tompkins, it was a far-reaching re-fit that provided new workshop space through a southern extension, the Max Rayne Centre; reconfigured workshops; rethought the Cottesloe Theatre, reopened as the Dorfman; while carving out space for new education studios. Front of house, the bookshop was moved to re-establish axial approach with a neat entrance pavilion. The north-east river corner originally housed the NT's service yard. When the river walk was extended eastwards past the building, the yard became visible to 12 million visitors a year. NT Future converted store rooms and bin stores to bars and cafés, while the deep overhang east of the entrance was filled with a new atrium derived from the original Lyttelton foyer screen. The result was to capitalize on the soaring buttresses of the north-east corner, which now became a main arrival point for visitors. Landscape was upgraded on every side. Internally, foyer furnishings, lighting and signage were replaced, with careful attention paid to Lasdun's original design.

Whether through these changes, through the dramatic regeneration of the river bank as a whole, or through energetic management of the building, the NT's foyers are now an all-day meeting place for Londoners, constantly filled with schoolchildren, theatre practitioners, tourists and audiences. Granville Barker wanted the national theatre to be a "popular place of resort."[14] Denys Lasdun's masterpiece has achieved exactly that.

Perhaps more problematic are criticims levelled at the NT's three auditoriums.

The smallest, the Cottesloe, is the least troublesome, embraced by audiences, actors and designers, who immediately recognised its flexibility, intimacy and personality. Iain Mackintosh's courtyard form has since been copied in numerous 400-seaters and school theatres around the world. The 2015 refit, which re-opened it as the Dorfman, was a more radical change than most realised, but preserved the Cottesloe's principles intact. Seating was replaced with an ingenious system of folding seats and stage lifts that allowed easier format-changes. Lighting was improved, and displacement ventilation introduced. Moving the internal stairs outwards allowed double rows of seats along the sides, increasing the density of audiences cramming the galleries.

The NT's 'main' auditorium, the Olivier, has proved a thoroughbred space: unpredictable, but at times awe-inspiring. Lighting designers can find it hard to locate the stage's focus; an actor needs extraordinary technique to fill its volume; weak shows die hard in the 'Oli'. On the other hand, for the right show on the right night, the Olivier can provide among the most thrilling experiences in theatre, its curving rows wrapping audiences into an ageless and unforgettable shared experience.

The Lyttelon still struggles to escape its tag as the 'Any Other Business' theatre. It does nothing wrong: its sightlines are impeccable and acoustics fine. Audiences can see and hear everything – just as the NT's forefathers hoped as they contemplated the infuriating conditions of the West End. Yet the Lyttelton's flat balcony creates little contact between audience and stage, and less between different parts of the audience. Since the steep rake, which gives the stalls such good sightlines, pushes the balcony upwards, a rear seat in the circle can be a remote experience, with the stage far away and the stalls hidden from view.

The NT's two main stages remain problematic (although Trevor Nunn's 'Transformation Project', temporarily reshaping the Lyttelton, has not been repeated). Nonetheless, criticism of the NT auditoriums can be overplayed. The National Theatre has been one of the world's most successful companies for the last forty years – which could hardly have been achieved in a theatre with intractable flaws. Each auditorium has virtues; each has housed triumphs. Meanwhile, their backstage design has sustained decades of dynamic repertory, while their technical design has proved visionary. From computerised control systems to large-scale displacement ventilation, the NT pioneered innovations that sustain technical theatre today.

And the same must be said for the building as a whole. The National Theatre has survived its onslaught of early criticism. It houses one of the world's great theatre companies in one of Modernism's great masterpieces. Rethinking theatre from first principles, it experimented boldly with theatre form, and its vision of where theatre needed to go was astonishingly accurate. Other than a lack of digital and education space – two requirements which no one in the 1960s foresaw – the NT prefigured everything a modern theatre needs to be. Its rehearsal rooms and workshops allow complex work to be generated to the highest level. Its democratic layout bonds performers, makers, directors and technicians into an effective company. Front of house, its generous foyers are packed all day long. Attracting visitors and passers-by as its architect intended, the NT has truly become a creative hub for London, dissolving barriers and welcoming audiences, to achieve, as its architect intended, "an extension of the theatre into the everyday world from which it springs".[15]

Notes

1   Speech, May 1984
2   *Scheme and Estimates for a National Theatre*, Harley Granville Barker and William Archer, 1904
3   Ibid.
4   Ibid.
5   *The National Theatre Story*, Daniel Rosenthal, p74
6   Ibid.
7   Conversation between Peter Hall and Denys Lasdun in Complete Guide to Britain's National Theatre, 1977, p26
8   Building Committee minutes, May 1966
9   Conversation between Peter Hall and Denys Lasdun in Complete Guide to Britain's National Theatre, 1977, p26
10 Conversation between Peter Hall and Denys Lasdun in Complete Guide to Britain's National Theatre, 1977, p28
11 John Betjeman to Denys Lasdun, 1973
12 Richard Findlater, Complete Guide to Britain's National Theatre, 1977, p14
13 Conversation between Peter Hall and Denys Lasdun in Complete Guide to Britain's National Theatre, 1977, p28
14 *Scheme and Estimates for a National Theatre*, Harley Granville Barker and William Archer, 1904
15 *Architectural Review*, January 1977, p11

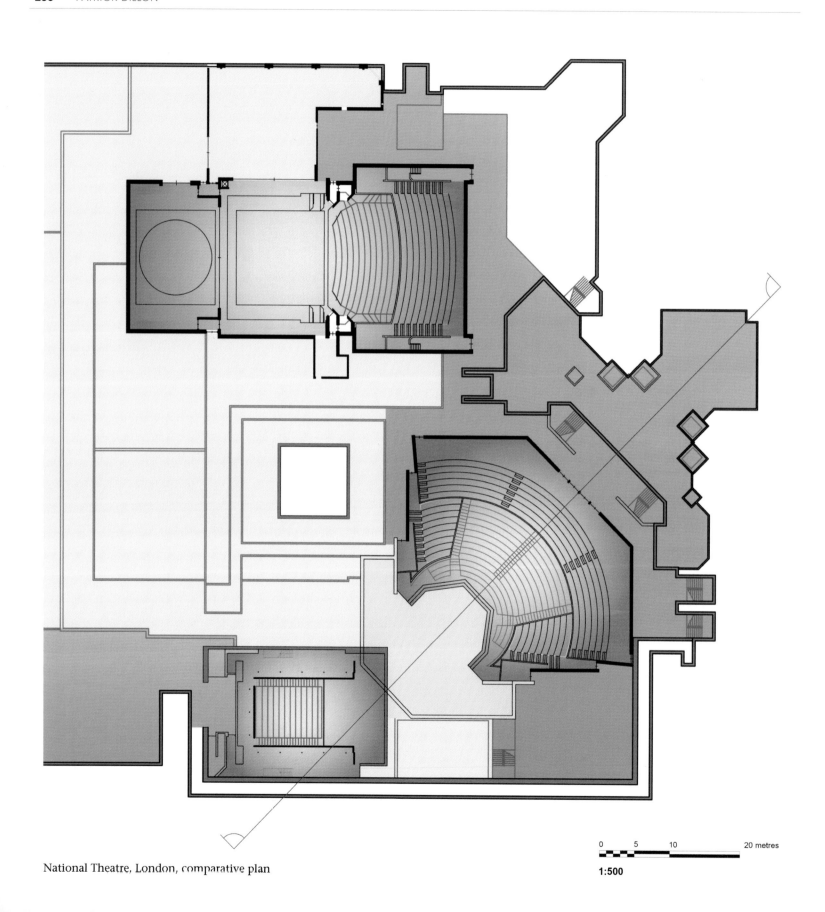

National Theatre, London, comparative plan

0   5   10   20 metres

1:500

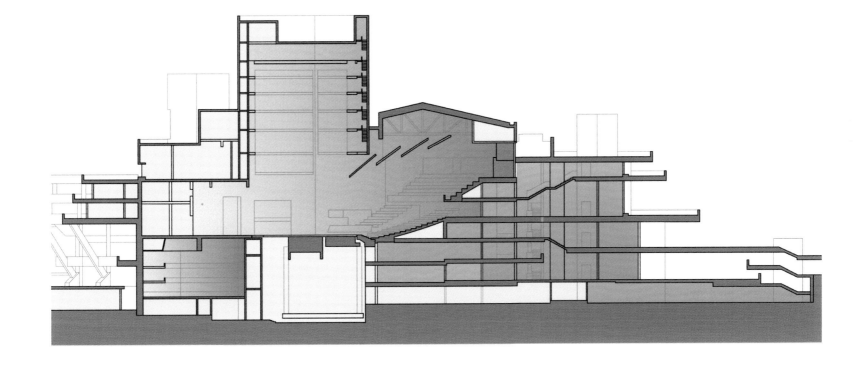

National Theatre, London, Olivier Theatre, comparative section

0   5   10   20 metres

1:500

Royal Exchange Theatre

Royal Exchange Theatre, 1976
Manchester, UK
Architect, Levitt Bernstein (Axel Burrough)

Andy Hayles

Introduction

First came the great plays.

. . . Then they built the theatres out of stone . . .

Irving Wardle, theatre critic for *The Times*, has a personal and private passion for theatres that are provisional in nature.

In common with the Elizabethan playhouses, those spaces built expected to last but a few years, have often housed the greatest theatrical productions.

From the 'Temporary' Young Vic, through Brook's Tramway, Kilburn's Tricycle, the RSC's Courtyard, the National Theatre's Shed, to the Jungle in Calais; the dynamic of a theatre that could disappear any minute and whose very presence seems to be the result of either some benign error of city planning or even a real subversive action by a community, seems to be essential fuel to the spirit of 'This-better-be-brilliant, 'cos-tomorrow-we-might- close…. forever!'

Accepting a direct relationship between a venue's 'temporariness' and its pre-disposition towards striking theatrical brilliance – it's little surprise that Irving's experience of the Royal Exchange Theatre on his first visit for the Grand Opening was one that he describes as 'thrillingly jarring'.

Exchange Hall

As a local lad from neighbouring Bolton attending the opening night, he was at first delighted to see that the old trading hall – so long a monumental presence in the City of Manchester, and, able to accommodate

Trading board in Royal Exchange Hall

9,000 traders, once lauded as the biggest room in the world – had been preserved; even with the relic of the old trading board looming over the St Ann's Square end of the Hall.

And there in the centre of the vast space was a 'spaceship from Pluto, that looked as if it was about to take off back into Space right up through the glass dome of the Hall'.

The shock of the 700-seat theatre Module in the centre of this massive Victorian trading hall still jars today

It's a feat of gymnastic structural engineering, a millimetre perfect fusing of theatrical density and architectural high-tech. Opening less than six months before Paris's Pompidou Centre; for many the benchmark for High-Tech architecture, here is a steel framed structure with glazed infill panelled walls that wears its vertical circulation and its servicing lightly and legibly on its exterior.

And like Pompidou, that still surprises and delights in its discovery buried inside the Parisian Streets, here's a theatre that over 40 years on, still feels like a spaceship that has just touched-down, but is yet to return to worlds unknown. Its aesthetic is certainly more moon-lander than space-shuttle- the architecture of space travel has moved on – and the 90's colour-matching refurb probably strapped the Module down too tightly to its host hall. The constant challenge is how best to celebrate the juxtaposition of this time-limited visitor from Space and its inappropriate Victorian host. And more importantly, how to re-capture a sense that this extraordinary theatre, welcomes ordinary people.

Context and Concept

Much has been written about the dynamic teaming of theatre designer Richard Negri and the director Michael Elliott. This pair formed the heart of the theatre client body for the Royal Exchange; and having shared the cut and thrust of production life together through the formation and operation of Theatre 59, they then collaborated with Casper Wrede and Richard Pilbrow, via Wimbledon School of Art, the RSC, Edinburgh Festival and Manchester University (becoming Theatre 69), eventually landing in the Exchange Hall in a 'tent'.

The tent was a temporary scaffold structure covered with old canvas floor-cloths that inhabited the middle of the hall, and its successful season gave the company the confidence to proceed with building a longer-lasting structure in the space.

Eventually, £1.2m of funds were raised, including significant contributions from the Arts Council and Manchester City Council and from a long list of 30 architects, the then young and lesser known firm of Levitt Bernstein was appointed to collaborate with Negri in the design of the successor to the Tent.

Levitt Bernstein quickly realised that the theatre Module would need to be supported on large trusses spanning between columns (the floor having such poor loading capability due to the arcade of shops beneath.)

Royal Exchange, model

Early eight-sided figures like the cat's cradle model from Axel Burrough's archive indicate how hard it would have been to transfer loads back down through the structure below.

Negri built models of the whole theatre almost faster than the architects could draw! Axel Burrough, the last surviving member of the architectural design team from the original concept meetings, describes how Richard would bring immensely fragile card and rubber band models to design team meetings, few of which could stand up without the aid of human buttresses! Those spanning trusses became the frame that would hold Negri's vessel for people.

This vessel – the Module – stands alone as an island within the space of the Hall; there are none of the traditional backstage support spaces

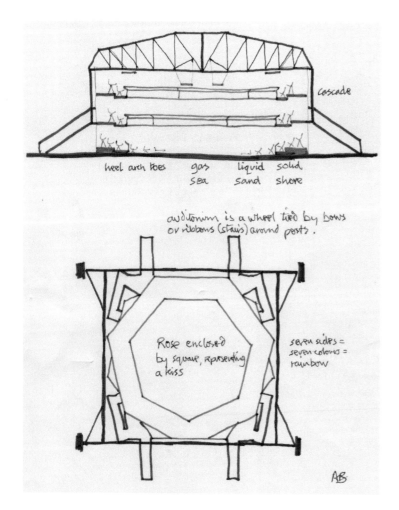

Concept sketches

kept secret and physically concealed from the audience. No corridors or wings or scene docks.

Negri, Elliott and Pilbrow together felt that they had an authority in departing from the traditional separations of backstage and front of house to lead the design team away from the standard theatrical conventions. This was the culmination of a theatrical journey that Irving Wardle believes can be traced directly back to the Vieux-Colombier school of Jacques Copeau and his ideology of 'two planks and a passion'. Peter Brook came to later define this stripping back of theatrical scenery, props, and devices to expose and celebrate the centrality of the actor as 'Holy Theatre'.

Copeau's school concentrated on physically reducing stage sizes and using a minimum of props and scenic devices, removing any obstacle between the actor and the audience so that the text could receive the audience's total concentrated focus.

As disciples of Michel St Denis (who not only attended the Jacque Copeau school, but was also Copeau's nephew), Negri, Elliott and Frank Dunlop (who of course went on to build the Young Vic) shared this deep conviction, honed on the continent, of the primacy of the text, the tight stage size, and the critical connection between performer and participating audience, sharing the same space.

Like the Young Vic, the Module became an exercise in getting as many people as possible to see a modest sized stage at no more than 30' feet away on any level. And to put the actor at its centre literally, physically, and spiritually.

An early Negri sketch, again from Axel's archive, demonstrates Richard's desire for the actor to be 'earthed' in the hall. The actor's delivery of the text is likened to the sea washing up on the shore of the audience. And with those three levels of audience sat at the foot of the theatre being held in its heel, arch and toes!

From Axel's recollections, those other elements of a theatre building (from the lobby to the load-in) were not even supporting cast to the main idea and bravura vision of the centrality of the actor, such was the laser-like focus of Elliott and Negri. The theatre module had to be a perfect functional embodiment of these Copeaution values; everything else would follow.

Royal Exchange Theatre, auditorium and stage

Design Development

The development of the module's eventual form was thus the result of a long period of experimentation between Elliott, Negri and Pilbrow.

The prototype for the Module was built after the discovery of the availability of the Exchange Hall, where another of the company's scenic designers, Laurie Dennett, designed the aforementioned 'Tent' to further test not only their evolving concept, but also, the viability of a theatre in the Hall. Would the audience come? Would they accept an auditorium inside another space?

Unlike the permanent Module, which has no sub-stage, the temporary Tent featured a stage and auditorium raised some 10' above the Hall floor to create a substage trap room. Low-tech, built from scaffolding with an old canvas floor cloth stretched over its frame to enclose the space, the Tent swallowed all of the available floor loading – and was therefore limited to a single audience seating rake, as there was no structural capacity remaining in the floor to support balcony columns.

In fixed thrust format, the Tent was a great success – though the memory of those who attended shows is very much the sense of occasion of the temporary structure within the Hall rather than its interior, which was apparently 'unremarkable'. It appears to have had something of a flavour of Guthrie's thrust spaces.

Enthused by the Tent's success (it was meant to stay for three weeks but lasted ten months!), the company embarked upon designing a more permanent condition. Interestingly, however, as the lease granted to the theatre company for the Hall was to be for a maximum of 21 years, architect Axel Burrough reveals that many of the company believed that they could take plenty of risks with the theatre building – as it was likely to only last as long as the lease!

And until this point, as Theatre 59 and Theatre 69, they had not been resident anywhere for more than a few years.

The Theatre within Exchange Hall

The excitement of provisional theatres that Irving Wardle felt when he first visited the Module is therefore revealed. The Module's DNA is found not only in Copeau and St Denis, but also in provisonality, risk-taking and bold experimentation.

Bold, confident moves were the atmosphere of the time.

Humankind had stepped on the moon for the first time in 1969, just 4 years before the Module design commenced. Supersonic passenger flight on Concord had just become possible; and the Pompidou Centre was in design at the same time.

Axel says that although High Tech was very much the zeitgeist, the architectural team didn't set out to specifically meet its conventions. Rather that it was this bold confidence of the time coupled with the constraints of building in the Hall and the very specific theatrical lead from the company that led to the bravura Module.

Early models featured curves rather than facets, and then Negri tried six-sided and eight-sided forms, overlapping, spiralling and twisting in plan as they rose through the chamber. The eight-sided forms were not pure octagons; but squares with lopped off corners, perhaps inspired by Frank Dunlop's Young Vic (Frank and Richard were at the Old Vic theatre school together and had worked together at the Little Piccolo theatre company in Manchester).

But as the theatre had to be supported by the spanning trusses – this helpfully defined the available area for the geometry in plan.

Inspired by rose petals and numerical sequences in nature, Negri attempted a five-sided geometry within this framework of constraint. But the sides were too long to create a good relationship to the stage, and the angled junctions were awkward.

A seven-sided form was proposed as the best fit by the architectural team; and Negri's ceaseless miniature models began to coalesce with Levitt Bernstein's two-dimensional plan and section drawings and the Module was born. Each level twisted one fourteenth in relation to the level below to emphasise the sharing of one room.

Axel recalls broad acceptance of the structural hangers, the visible services, the celebration of junctions and vents and shock-absorbers by the theatre company. This was a theatre that was proud of its workings. No secrets in its architecture or its theatrical processes. Everything was laid bare.

It must have felt entirely appropriate that the newest and most innovative architectural techniques of the day were the best way for both the demanding combination of the theatrical function and the Hall's geometry to be met.

For all the architectural dexterity, the structural ingenuity, and the theatrical fine tuning – it is perhaps the sheer act of piracy of placing the Module in the Hall that gives the Royal Exchange Theatre its iconic status.

Significance to Architecture and Artists

I think there is a further fascinating context of a strand of 1960s/early 1970s theatre designers who were experimenting with large open stages (the Olivier at the National Theatre – in design in the early 1970s, Sheffield Crucible, 1971, Vivian Beaumont in NYC, 1965, Chichester Festival Theatre, 1962), who had clearly been informed by the fan-shaped proscenium houses in design at the same time (Birmingham Rep, 1971, Colchester Mercury, 1971, Thorndike, Leatherhead, 1969).

The Royal Exchange, the Young Vic and the Cottesloe represented a mid-1970s turning point led by an emerging new vanguard of theatre directors and designers, back towards audience density and compression on smaller stages that then informed theatre design around the world for years to come.

The subsequent Christ's Hospital School, RSC Swan and Tricycle became the next generation inspired by this turning point.

Theatre design had changed forever. And the Module was the tightest, densest auditorium of them all.

Inch-perfect seating design and sightlines, densely packing the audience, it still sets a benchmark for compression and intimacy. And although history would seem to suggest that it's too particular a solution in too grand a collision of circumstances to be repeated, certainly, no one contemplating designing an in-the-round space could do so without studying the Module.

Such is its significance for theatre architecture – but its impact on artists has also been profound.

Impact

The RET is often in any theatre student's top ten theatre buildings. It holds a special place in the heart of theatre designers and architects. It was selected by the Theatres Trust in 1999's *Theatres Magazine* as the most important and influential theatre building of the 20th century.

So it's perhaps something of a mystery that it has not been repeated, copied or improved upon anywhere else. No obvious successor. No evolution of the form.

There's no RET Version 2 with a substage for example. No example using a town square instead of a big hall. No examples of a theatre surrounded by its own backstage (perhaps Ariane Mnouchkine's Théâtre du Soleil comes closest). Not even many seven-sided theatres….

However, so many realised elements of the 1976 Royal Exchange have found their way into critical theatre building vocabulary in subsequent decades. The DNA lives on, even though a clone has not appeared. For example: within Levitt Bernstein's portfolio, Axel cites the celebration of exposed technical bridges and catwalks in their practice's subsequent work at St Luke's and the King's Lynn Corn Exchange.

Pilbrow describes how the Module led to a re-discovery of the importance of three-dimensional theatre, directly informing decades of development of the Georgian Courtyard form, including the 1970s Cottesloe, the 1980s Tricycle and the 1990s Huddersfield Lawrence Batley Theatre. All of these examples feature the insertion of a theatre frame inside a pre-existing volume.

The 2000s Leicester Curve draws on the inspiration of theatres surrounded by a lobby, with transparency provided by large opening walls rather than the Module's glazed panels.

The 2010s Royal Shakespeare Theatre features backstage prop rooms and quick-change areas that wrap around the auditorium.

…and many more besides…

Perhaps after 40 years, something of the original rich influence is starting to fade. And as theatre continues to reinvent itself; other influences have a louder voice.

For example, the original Tricycle is now being altered, the frame removed, the hall that contains it addressed in a different and more direct way. Spaces that are 'found' are celebrating the original host hall in a more complimentary way – the loud insertion of an alien frame is perhaps more aggressive and less welcoming than the relationship between theatre and host than a millennial theatre-maker seeks.

Considering its DNA of provisionality, I wonder if anyone would ever dare to dismantle the Royal Exchange now?

Based on their background in experimentation and provisionality, I wonder if Michael Elliott and Richard Negri would say that someone should…..? Or if the essence of the bold original should somehow be re-examined and re-asserted?

What Next?

Artistic teams will long battle with open and inclusive community access, seeking to demystify theatre, diversify its attendance, and actively be anti-racist. It is a tough mission, not helped by some of the Hall's historical associations with the deplorable exploitation of people of colour that occurred in the cotton trade.

There needs to be an ongoing and sincere rehabilitation of this space and a humble reminder to the city that a theatre company reclaimed this building for the community many years ago with a world-class theatre design. The current and future leadership teams are dedicated to showing the community how accessible and fascinating and relevant the work the company produces in this peerless space is to them.

A building originally for wealthy merchants, that only admitted women in 1946, is open to all.

The spaceship is here for now – and it has claimed this space for you, whatever size, shape, or colour you are.

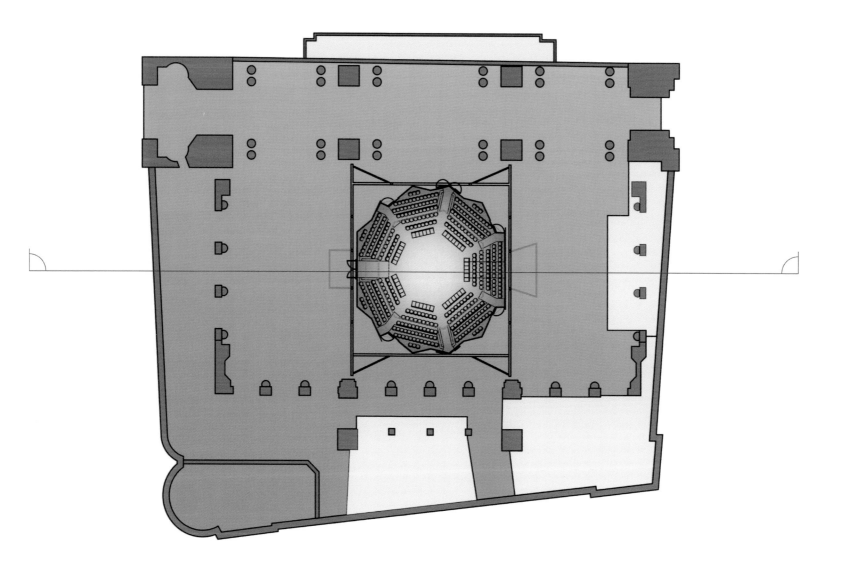

Royal Exchange Theatre, Manchester, comparative plan

1:500

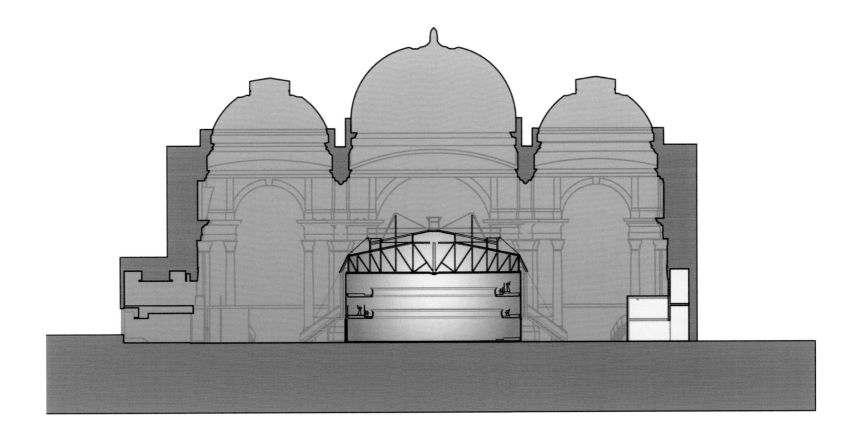

Royal Exchange Theatre, Manchester, comparative section

1:500

1980s
The Eighties

SCHAUBÜHN

Heiter, glücklich und reue

os.*

*aus »Professor Bernhardi«

»Professor Bernhardi«
von Arthur Schnitzler
Regie: Thomas Ostermeier
Ab 17. Dezember 2016

»Der eingebildete Kranke«
von Molière
Regie: Michael Thalheimer
Ab 18. Januar 2017

»LOVE HURTS IN TINDER TIMES«
von Patrick Wengenroth
Realisation: Patrick Wengenroth
Ab 28. Januar 2017

»Toter Hund in der Chemischen
Reinigung: Die Starken«
von Angélica Liddell
Regie: Angélica Liddell
Ab 30. März 2017

FIND 2017
Festival Internationale Neue Dramatik
»Demokratie und Tragödie«
30. März – 9. April 2017

»Peng«
von Marius
Regie: Marius
Ab Anfang

Schaubühne, exterior

Schaubühne am Lehniner Platz, 1981
Berlin, Germany
Architect, Jürgen Sawade

Reinhold Daberto

In 1981, the Schaubühne theatre company moved into a building originally designed by Erich Mendelsohn and constructed from 1926 to 1931, a theatre venue that has been described as a vision and a possible model for the future of theatre architecture.

In the rather conservative, restoration-focused climate of the (actually quite substantial) new building phase of German theatre architecture, the 60s and 70s of the last century, there was, at least regarding the realisation of architectural designs, not much room for utopias; instead, the goal was to meet the population's basic cultural needs.

For the first time in the history of theatre architecture (at least in Germany) – and this is where the remarkable shift in thinking occurs – a theatre space was constructed in accordance with the extensive experience and exact artistic ideas of a theatre company and its directorship. Thirty-seven years later, this article will examine whether the venue has stood the test of time.

However, the renovation, if we may call it that, also raises some fundamental questions on how to deal with structures under landmark protection. Therefore, this question will also be discussed.

Erich Mendelsohn is arguably one of the most eminent architects of the 20th century.

- born March 21, 1887 in Allenstein, East Prussia
- died September 15, 1953 in San Francisco/USA

He was fascinated by the material of reinforced concrete, which for him was an ideal means to realise his expressionist sensibilities.

His most famous and iconic work is probably the Einsteinturm in Potsdam (1920/21), which was conceived as an astrophysics institute.

In 1933, Erich Mendelsohn emigrated to Holland; he worked in London (Cohen House, private mansion, 1935–46), entered a business partnership with Serge Chermayeff and took up residence in the USA in 1940. The USA denied him a work permit until 1945; he kept afloat financially by giving lectures and with the help of a Guggenheim Fellowship.

In Israel, his projects included hospitals in Haifa and Jerusalem (1937–39), and in the USA, he supplied the drafts for the Maimonides Hospital in San Francisco (1946) and for numerous synagogues.

In Berlin, he drafted a development for a large property area on Kurfürstendamm that combined apartments with public functions. Set back from the street front of Kurfürstendamm, apartment buildings designed by Jürgen Bachmann were lined up. Mendelsohn created the public functions. Instead of an indoor pool, as planned, these turned out to be a cabaret and smokers' theatre (!) and the Universum Cinema with a capacity of 1800 seats – the very building that was to become the home of the Schaubühne in 1981.

Einsteinturm, Potsdam

The Schaubühne

Constructing a theatre not for an undefined user, but for a specific theatre company – the Schaubühne – was a task that required the architect to familiarise himself with this institution and its own way of making theatre.

The theatre was founded in 1962 under the name of "Schaubühne am Halleschen Ufer" as a private theatre with a politically and socially conscious repertoire. In 1968, a group of young theatre makers and actors came to the Schaubühne with Peter Stein. There, he staged the "Vietnam Diskurs", a provocation which forced him to leave the Munich Kammerspiele when he collected money from the audience after performances to pass on to the Vietcong.

Against the background of the 1968 movement and driven by dissatisfaction with the municipal theatre system at the time, the idea was to provide an alternative to the German municipal theatres with new forms of collaborative work. The fact that all artistic staff members had a say in selecting the plays and defining the political thrust of the repertoire, along with the paramount significance of a scientific and long-term concept of dramaturgy, enabled the creation of one of the most important acting companies and an extraordinary penetration of society's day-to-day life, as well as highly focused theatre work.

The long-divided city was starved for cultural recognition by the rest of the world, and the Schaubühne was one vehicle to achieve this.

Even today, whenever the Schaubühne is mentioned, the person that immediately comes to mind – along with other artistic forces, and without the intention of exulting him above all others – is Peter Stein. He was the theatre's director until 1985, and now, at the age of 85, he is one the doyens of German directors.

He was a man of the theatre who wanted to break free from the stuffy confines of conventional theatre and scouted for new playing fields. With Shakespeare and his Antiquity Projects or the *Oresteia*, the Schaubühne conquered the large halls. Klaus Michael Grüber, Stein's artistic antipode, even took the company all the way to the Berlin Olympic Stadium with his *Winter Journey*.

The Building

The Schaubühne building is not only remarkable as a type of theatre venue, but regarding its way of dealing with landmark-protected building substance. In the course of the restoration – maybe re-construction would be the better term – this issue stirred up a lot of controversy throughout the project phase from 1976 to 1981. It was a fact that the original building had to undergo substantial changes, as the ravages of fire and war had left almost no substance worthy of preservation.

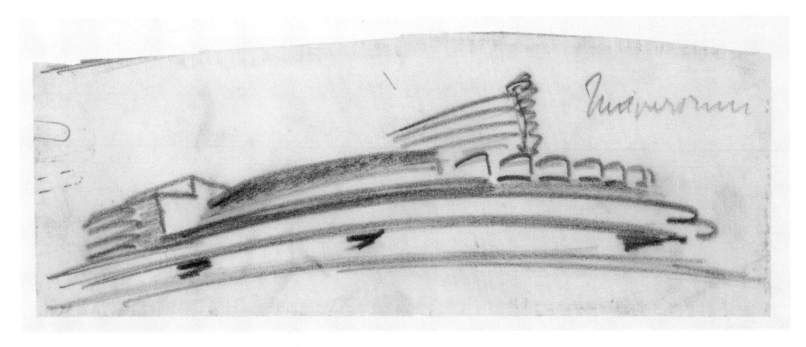

Universum Cinema, Berlin, sketch by Erich Mendelsohn

"Am Halleschen Ufer" is where the Schaubühne originated. Here, Stein staged his legendary, *Oresteia* by Aeschylus among many other things.

But it is "Am Lehniner Platz" that he and his exceptional company made their big splashes, including *The Three Sisters*, which was staged in all three auditoriums, creating a fascinating cinemascope effect over the full length of the space.

Stein belongs to the generation of 1968, whose liberation from their fathers implied a new approach to theatre combined with a unique artistic quality.

Without this status, the project of the Schaubühne am Lehniner Platz would probably never have come to pass. Mind you, Berlin was divided by a wall; on both sides, the political players strove to demonstrate the advantages and achievements of the respective system by championing exceptional projects.

The Schaubühne's concept is that of a laboratory that works in dialogue with other disciplines such as architecture, visual arts, music, literature and film to develop a new theatrical language.

The Schaubühne's unique, distinctive profile that has been obvious since its inception has been further enhanced by its consistently contemporary repertoire and confirms the Schaubühne's reputation as one of the leading German-speaking theatres in Germany and abroad. This shows itself in the fact that the Schaubühne regularly has more than 100 international engagements per season.

What Were the Schaubühne's Demands Regarding its New Home?

Because the Schaubühne's way of staging plays in its original venue "Am Halleschen Ufer" usually entailed massive building code violations and special permits were only granted on a time-limited basis, finding a new venue for the Schaubühne was a vital necessity.

Schaubühne, empty auditorium

The company looked at many buildings that offered the potential to be converted to suit the work of the Schaubühne. The list of potential sites also included Tempelhof Airport. However, the allied forces wanted to be able to dismantle all installations within a 48-hour period in order to be able to have their personnel airlifted out of Berlin if the Soviets were to attack Tegel Airport – a distinctly Cold War scenario.

After weighing the options and on the recommendation of architect Jürgen Sawade, who was a friend of Managing Director Jürgen Schitthelm, the Berlin Senate offered the Mendelsohn Building on Kurfürstendamm, which stood empty after its many conversions, to the Schaubühne.

The Schaubühne troupe was not keen on moving from Kreuzberg in the eastern part of the city to the bourgeois west. However, architect

Jürgen Sawade recognised the opportunity of transforming this building into a highly versatile theatre venue.

The Schaubühne was broke and called on Dr. Stein, the Senator of Culture at the time, to ask for a budget increase. In an act of forward defence, a new venue was demanded as well.

In 1975, the Senate asked the Schaubühne to submit a theatre concept offering solutions for all technical, personnel-related, spatial and organisational problems.

The innovation of the concept presented by the Schaubühne was to do away with the separation between the auditorium and the stage areas. In addition, the option of having simultaneous performances in separate rooms was introduced.

In 1976, the Berlin Senate approved a budget of 40 million Deutschmarks. In return, the Schaubühne was to conclude 10-year contracts with its most important artistic staff members. With this move, the Senate wanted to make sure that this immense investment of public funds into a theatre venue for a private theatre company would yield continuous dividends.

The artistic directorship rejected this demand as unrealistic.

Meanwhile, the project's spatial conceptualisation was further developed.

The remaining building substance of the Mendelsohn building, which was only of minimal use, and the way this issue was handled, stirred up controversy.

Was there anything left to renovate at all? Was it not precisely the remaining original substance of the frequently converted building that was ripe for demolition?

Art historian Vittorio Lampugnani called it "renovation by demolition" – and he was not wrong.

The idea was to create the option of setting up the stage area at any location within the hall, thereby enabling a wide variety of configurations and audience arrangements.

The total space of 67.5 by 21 m was to be used as either one large hall in various layouts or as three separate halls. It was planned to use two double-shell rolling panels to divide the large hall.

With this arrangement, three different performances could be staged in one evening, or the stage designs could remain in place, without necessarily having to perform the same play successively for long periods of time. The idea was to have the option of performing three different shows in the course of one day without having to dismantle the set-ups of the three compartmentalised halls.

Having parallel performances or parallel rehearsals in the individual divisions required a sophisticated soundproofing solution. For this purpose, double-shell rolling panels with one-metre gaps with a T-30 fire resistance and total sound insulation of 60 dB were installed. The original plan to use multipart hydraulic gates would have been too expensive.

The costs soared above the originally approved budget of 40 million DM; the budget was first increased to 68.6 million DM in 1979 and then to 71.1 million DM in February 1980. In March 1981, there was a final increase to 81 million DM.

The 76 lifting platforms in the hall area, each of them 7 by 3 m in size, cost almost 5.0 million DM more than planned. Instead of these lifting platforms, it was originally planned to install a kind of modular system, which would have required a large number of stagehands to shift – the personnel costs, not to mention the conversion times, would have surpassed the investment costs for ten years of operating time.

These lifting platforms covering the entire hall area were the key element for the idea of staging plays with continuously changing audience layouts – at least, that was the intention at the time.

But these 76 lifting platforms turned out to be the weak spot in the intended flexible usage concept. The problem lay in their dimensions of 3 by 7 m, with the length of 7 m being the dimension that is aligned with the main staging orientation, which, while not fixed, is somewhat determined by the room layout.

This resulted in the necessity of gradually raising the auditorium with manual podium extensions. While this is not exactly the modular system as planned originally, the number of podium extensions would turn out to be one of the main obstacles to frequent changes.

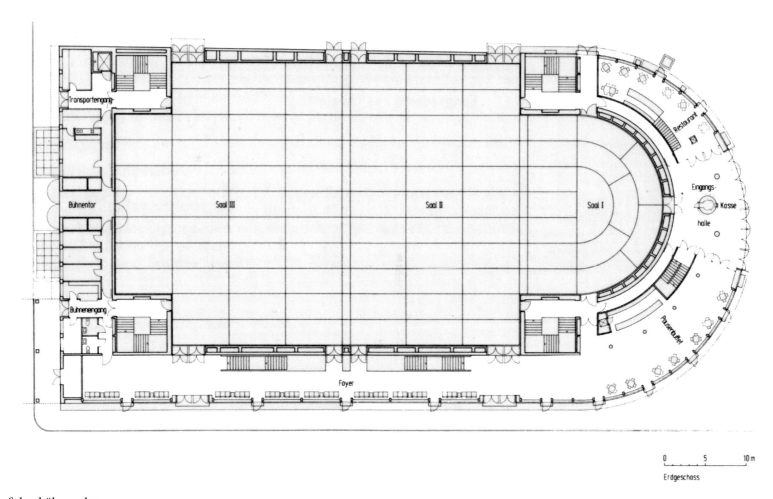

Schaubühne, plan

How do artistic designers interact with this unusual venue that had already lived through several long eras? Jürgen Schitthelm served as Managing director for over 40 years, from the foundation of the company until 2000. Peter Stein stayed until 1985, and after shorter periods of different artistic leaderships, Schitthelm appointed the young director Thomas Ostereier in 2000 as artistic director. He has stayed until today and has had great success also in making the company known at international festivals.

Jan Pappelbaum, who came with Thomas Ostereier, comments:

The Schaubühne is a fantastic and extremely versatile venue. It's easy to explain this in guided tours for visitors from all over the world and to beautifully illustrate it in books. However, in practice, changing the

sets takes too long and costs too much. The Schaubühne has been designed as a repertoire theatre. If we had to reset the halls again and again during an ongoing season, the whole operation would come to a standstill for days at a time.

When we first saw the naked walls, we just loved it and wondered why they had been covered (with fabric) under the old directorship. Or why the then three halls had been set up with a relatively fixed seating scheme. Today, we know that naked walls are a passing attraction and cause some very bad acoustics. At first, we accepted the bad acoustics despite complaints from the audience because the visual impact of the naked walls felt like such a stroke of liberation. Nowadays, though, people would rather understand what's being said again, and productions like *The Duchess of Malfi*, which was plagued by exactly

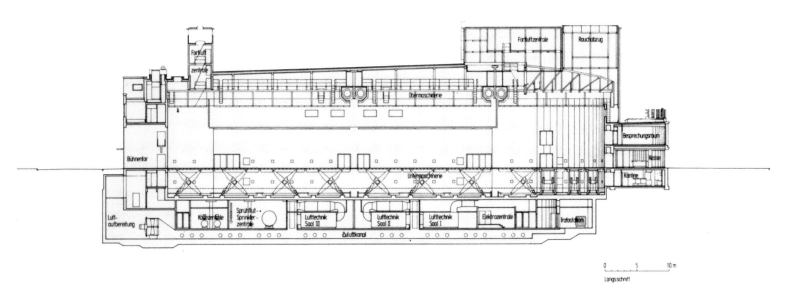

Schaubühne, section

this problem, are not accepted anymore. We also have returned to the setup of three halls with a basic seating scheme – anything else would be unrealistic.

This basic seating scheme described by Jan Pappelbaum is also owed in part to Berlin's financing principle that pays according to seating capacity, i.e., per offered seat. This is why the Schaubühne now permanently offers a hall with 500 seats in Hall B.

Nevertheless, the space, the spaces, represent the possibility of continuous innovation for Jan Pappelbaum, who is an architect by trade:

Being able to work in these rooms is a stroke of luck, and ultimately it was probably this factor that tempted me away from returning to architecture. First, a fundamental decision about spatial configuration must be made, and only then the actual set design is developed. First, we have to create a stage – a stage on which the actors have an opportunity to unfold their performances within a large, open basic space. . . . Spatial experiments always reverberate back to the epic. Because with these stages, the basic configurations – the stage, the auditorium, and above all the viewers themselves – are by default

thematically involved as well. The performance, too, becomes three-dimensional. This is also a problem of acting training. A certain physicality – such as Meyerhold's biomechanics, for example – that would enable actors to perform to three sides of the stage is hardly ever taught.

Has the Venue Lived Up to Expectations?

What has stood the test of time over the course of the last 37 years? Certainly, the principle of having three stages side by side, which provides the repertoire theatre with the option of leaving set designs in place to offer the audience a varied repertoire. Another feature that stood the test of time is the option of combining the three divisions into one large hall for large theatrical productions.

One flaw is that the decision to equip the entire hall with 3 by 7 m platforms, which nearly blew the budget, nevertheless still turned out to be too roughly divided in practice. The fine-tuned topography must be supplemented with manually set-up podium systems for gradually raising the audience space. The personnel and time needed for manually setting up and taking down these podiums presents an obstacle to frequent and regular changes and complete reconfigurations.

Another time-tested feature is certainly the iconographic shape of the robust concrete construction that pushes set designers to continuously develop new perspectives and interpretations.

This approach was a radical one. It was a departure from the well-designed, pleasantly furnished seating arrangements of conventional theatre halls. Peter Brook's empty space was evoked without compromise.

Another radical step was the decision to forego the options of transformation offered by the traditional theatre, with its separation of the stage and fly tower on the one hand and the auditorium on the other.

Schaubühne auditorium showing elevators

Eliminating these options put the focus on the versatility of the stage design itself.

Why did the paradigmatic change launched by the Schaubühne venue not result in any subsequent examples that could possibly have surpassed the state of the art of 1981 and the spatial divisions defined here?

One explanation may be found in the relatively rigid municipal theatre system of mid-sized cities in the German-speaking area. Here, repertoire theatres are not in the habit of offering any variability in the relation between auditorium and stage.

The Schaubühne company demanded this variability. Other companies content themselves with the venues they are offered.

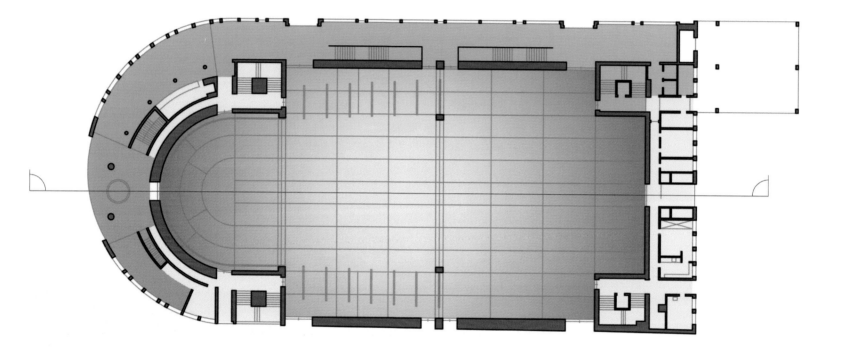

Schaubühne, Berlin, comparative plan

0   5   10   20 metres

1:500

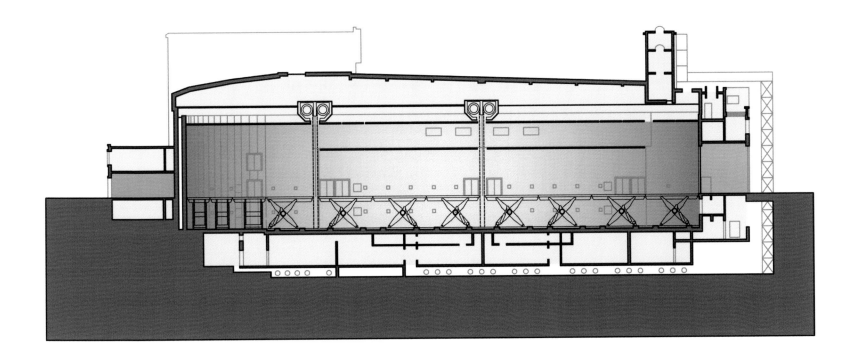

Schaubühne, Berlin, comparative section

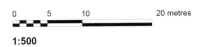

1:500

Aerial view of Arts Centre Melbourne

Arts Centre Melbourne, 1982
Melbourne, Australia
Architect, Roy Grounds
Tim Brinkman

The Greatest Show on Earth

Australia was barely 30 years old itself when prominent voices came to the fore demanding some form of arts centre in Melbourne to extend the established museum and gallery provision. It is typical of Australia that the vision was bold and ambitious.

Melbourne's Arts Centre was spearheaded by newspaper magnate Sir Keith Murdoch and the composer Margaret Sutherland. Murdoch had been on the Board of Trustees for the National Gallery and Museum of Victoria since 1933. Inspired by the trend in the USA for arts to have an extended role by incorporating lecture theatres for educational talks and small recital halls for concerts, Murdoch encouraged the National Gallery to experiment. They agreed to 'combine pictorial and musical arts' by holding chamber concerts in the National Gallery. By 1944, he had gathered enough political interest for a new art gallery to be built on a riverside circus site, which would include a small recital studio and a theatre for 'high-class drama and other cultural activities'. Meanwhile, Margaret Sutherland had more ambitious plans. She lobbied for a building that would be 'grouped around a courtyard to avoid any institutional character and to create a friendly place for instruction and enjoyment'. Her vision would include a 1000-seat theatre, a lecture hall for 200, small recital studios, an arts library and a restaurant.

Murdoch's vision for a new art gallery and Sutherland's dream of a combined arts centre came together in 1946 with the passing of the *Melbourne South Land Act* which set aside the circus site for a National Art Gallery and a Cultural Centre. It took 14 years to finally persuade one of the Victoria State's Premiers to take on the risk of supporting the venture. Observing the difficulties being encountered by the Sydney Opera House Building Committee, most Victorian politicians viewed the project with suspicion. Finally, in 1960, with the liberal government's support, Roy Grounds was contracted to design the Gallery and Cultural Centre. Grounds produced a master plan presented with drawings of the interior spaces and views of the exterior from Prince's Bridge. He wanted the National Gallery and the Cultural Centre to contain a rectangle, a triangle and a circle.

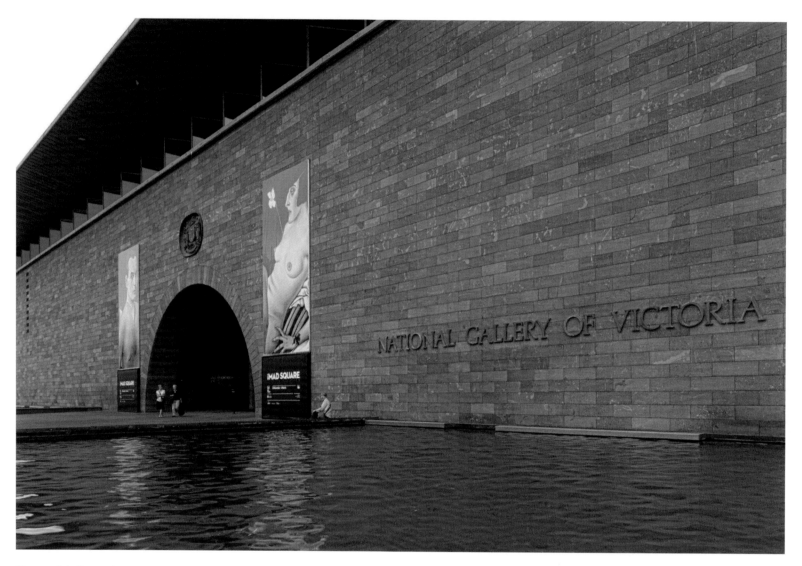

National Gallery of Victoria in Melbourne, architect Sir Roy Grounds

Cheese Cutters and Floating Piles

The rectangular National Gallery of Victoria was completed first in 1967. The design and construction of its next-door neighbour, the Cultural Centre, was another story. The triangular design was created by a tall copper spire. A music auditorium, lecture theatre, fly tower and small experimental theatre would lie beneath the spire, underground and grouped around a central foyer. However, by the time Grounds had completed the National Gallery, he was astonished to discover that in the nine years since he produced his master plan, 'the arts in this country had grown prodigiously' and government subsidy of the arts had been established. The plans and budgets changed several times to find a compromise between the needs of the newly formed Victorian opera and ballet companies and those wanting a major concert hall (echoing the conflict taking place at the same time in Sydney).

Finally, it was agreed that there was to be: a 1500-seat opera and ballet theatre with orchestra pit; a 750-seat drama theatre; a 2500-seat concert hall which could also be used for lectures and a 400-seat experimental theatre. The 5000 audience members would all be up to 40 metres underground, beneath the spire and they'd be in by March 1977.

From the beginning there was conflict of design versus the needs of an arts centre. Grounds was determined to have a sweeping view across an open piazza all the way to the river. From the city, the perspective would take the eye past a soaring copper spire to a great rectangular bluestone National Gallery beyond. Nothing was to distract the eye along the way, certainly not the uncompromising bulk of a flying tower.

Engineering consultant John Connell assessed the riverside site for the theatres and declared 'Below ground at this particular location is beyond belief!' The National Gallery was built on Silurian mudstone, a material solid enough to build on. Just by the river was a basalt outcrop and between the two, along the course of an ancient river and at precisely the place intended for the underground theatres was 40 metres of 'custard like' Coode Island silt. The brief for the massive job of constructing the Cultural Centre's foundations required that builders use a new technique to freeze the silt down to the bedrock 40 metres below then carve it out in chunks 'like cheese'. The tenders were on the Premier's desk for approval in October 1970 when a 367-foot span of the West Gate Bridge being constructed over the River Yarra collapsed, killing 30 workers. Premier Henry Bolte would not now consent to a building project with such complicated engineering and the 'deep hole' plan was abandoned. It was agreed that only the three theatres would be built partly underground, the fly tower would be above ground beneath the spire and the concert hall would be a separate building right next to the river. This was the first of three major compromises forced upon Grounds during the construction of the Arts Centre

In 1974, 329 compression piles were sunk to bedrock to support a 3-metre-thick concrete foundation slab and perimeter walls were built to form the open spaces for the three theatre auditoria. Known as 'the bath tub', it had a strong propensity to float up and out of the ground, so several tension piles were needed to hold the building down and prevent it from floating away. Another pile used, affectionately known as 'the confused pile', began life as a tension (holding down) pile and then transformed itself, as the weight of the superstructure took over into a compression (holding up) pile. In addition to these engineering problems, it was discovered during construction that the aquifer and the ground water lying 8 metres below was highly corrosive to the steel reinforcement in concrete. This meant that construction of the foundations had to be reassessed and new techniques developed to protect the steel and concrete. Working with BHP, the engineers developed solid billets of specialised steel low in energy and tension which would

Arts Centre Melbourne, Spire

Arts Centre Melbourne originally known as the Victoria Arts Centre under construction

corrode less rapidly. Anchors were driven into bedrock and protected by a precast concrete 'sleeve' until the building was completed. Then a corrosion protection system was put in place to provide a continuous electrical current passing through thousands of sets of high energy, zinc anodes 'like strings of sausages' attached to the steel piles, defusing the corrosive properties of the water and protecting the piles. The building has two sources of back-up power to protect these in turn. The anodes, which have a built-in safety factor of 300 per cent, are closely monitored for signs of wear.

Smashing Eggs whilst Designing a Symphony Hall

The concert hall for the newly named Victoria Arts Centre was now to be built next to the theatre's spire on the basalt rock foundation. Knowing there was a precedent in Toronto's Roy Thomson Hall, Grounds was determined to complete his geometric concept and have a circular building, partly underground.

His design concept for the building used the analogy of an egg. The auditorium was the yolk, the foyer the white and the dressings rooms and services protecting the egg from environmental intrusion was the shell.

He decided against the usual procedure where 'acoustic consultants have to advise on how to re-design the architect's schematic or preliminary plans to inhibit the best acoustical design' and invited acoustic consultants Bolt, Beranek and Newman (BBN) to design the yolk, after which the architectural team would take over and produce the design for the egg white and shell. Neither Grounds nor Connell knew how to design the 'egg', so they consulted specialist concrete engineer Professor Pier Luigi Nervi. Meanwhile there was strong political pressure to get started on the concert hall as the theatre building's construction was dogged with construction problems, delays and union strife. The design and a budget of $10 million was approved in 1974 and excavations started in 1976.

The difference between the two sites was astonishing. 'At one end we had powder monkeys blasting basalt rock and at the other end, labourers were being paid mud money.' The proposed theatre building opening date of 1977 slipped by in the mud.

By 1979 financial restraints were being imposed on the Building Committee by the State Government who were not happy with the blow-out in the cost of a state-of-the-art flying system for the State Theatre. With the external structures nearly completed, budget cuts could only be made to the interior finishes. Grounds' design was therefore modest and sober, containing wooden panelling, pebble mix flooring, bush-hammered concrete walls hung with tapestries and glass panels etched with images of Australian flora and fauna. The Building Committee were aghast, they had wanted a 'classy building, not a government building' so they turned to academy award winner film and theatre designer John Truscott to design interiors with a 'sense of occasion.' Truscott set up a large design studio, laboratory and model-building workshop on site and got to work. He planned everything from auditorium walls to the toilets, the carpets, the rubbish bins, the coffee tables, and the waiters' uniforms, laying samples out on the architects plans and elevations like set designs. Knowing that people would want to forget that they were many metres below ground, he created mirrored surfaces to reflect outside light down to the stalls foyer and using suffused lighting behind opaque glass, produced an impression of windows and twinkling lights to reflect on the brass railings all the way up the stairs and escalators. His concert hall design included a Michael Santry sculpture of acrylic, mirror, brass and stainless-steel sculpture to cascade down through the foyer levels to 'act as a shimmering guide to the descent underground'.

Truscott entirely revised Ground's lighting design even though much of it had been installed and brought in young Hollywood lighting designer Dan Flannery to introduce lights that were unknown to Australia at that time: down lights, up lights, glow lights and warm wall washes. For the concert hall, a new paint was used on the bush-hammered concrete to achieve a striated, mineral rock effect on the walls of the concert hall and 3230 leather hides were procured to create curved upholstered leather panels and furniture. Vast new paintings were donated and acquired at

Arts Centre Melbourne, State Theatre

little cost due to Truscott's great powers of persuasion. Although many were irritated by Truscott's time-consuming insistence on everything being designed from scratch and custom made and the budget being blown, the result was a perfectly proportioned, spectacular design. The concert hall opened as Melbourne Concert Hall on 6 November 1982, two years before the troubled theatres building and despite commencing construction two years after it.

In 2010, as I prepared to fly out to Melbourne to oversee the art centre's programmes, the concert hall, now named Hamer Hall (in honour of Victoria Premier, Sir Rupert Hamer), was closed for renovation. The ravages of time compounded the faults with the original building and there were many. The acoustics were not ideal; only one person had a good word to say about them and he was the original acoustician. The sole small services lift couldn't cope with modern demands; musicians and instruments were kept waiting whilst rubbish was being collected. Movement around the "egg" design was scrambled. Retail spaces were not ideal. The striking interiors by John Truscott were flaking around the edges and the 1970s designed state of the art building no longer cut it in the new millennium.

The two-year major upgrade cost $135.8m and was the single biggest project to take place at Arts Centre Melbourne since it opened. It aimed to connect the building with the river, simplify FOH circulation, upgrade every aspect of the facility from new seats to repainted walls, provide state of the art technical facilities and, most importantly, transform the auditorium acoustic to one that could be appreciated by all.

These improvements were implemented by a design team headed by ARM Architecture, Schuler Shook Theatre Planners, and acousticians Kirkegaard Associates and Marshall Day Acoustics. To improve the acoustic envelopment and sound clarity, the width of the stalls was reduced. The balcony wings were eliminated creating a seamless transition from the auditorium's side walls to the stage surround. This improved the flow of sound around the room. New timber chairs with vibrant brushed velvet orange fabric replaced the old. They were chosen for their acoustic qualities as much as for comfort and style. A bit of magic was performed here, with modern materials allowing the seats to be wider with no reduction in leg room. Above, stalactite lighting can vary colour to augment any mood.

Schuler Shook and Wagner Biro brought more magic to the party with newly designed theatre technology incorporating acoustic intelligence. A new technical zone was suspended above the platform housing rigging, lighting and sound equipment. A new system of acoustic reflectors suspended within folds like the wings of a butterfly to improve the acoustic conditions for a performance and to conceal the technical zone. Replacing the timber panelling surrounding the stage, an elegant bronze stage surround bounces a clearer sound to the audience.

With a view to financial sustainability, more restaurant options were added including at the river level where for the first-time patrons can easily take in the city scape. An open scenic promenade has been installed along the front of Hamer Hall's completely new face from Princes Bridge to Southbank. The new team kept faith with the original vision, retaining the cavern theme to the treatment, going so far as to retain the original paint team from 30 years before for the repaint of the subterranean effects on the new auditorium walls. Eagle-eyed architectural historians will appreciate the new team's snake-like design to the water frontage, which keys in with Ground's proposed indigenous themes, which included serpent-like shapes through the interiors.

It's often said that Australia has the best arts centre in the world; the outside is in Sydney and the inside is in Melbourne. It's worth a trip to Arts Centre Melbourne to check out if that is true.

Arts Centre Melbourne, Hamer Hall

Arts Centre Melbourne, spire

Arts Centre Melbourne, comparative plan

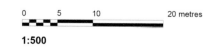

1:500

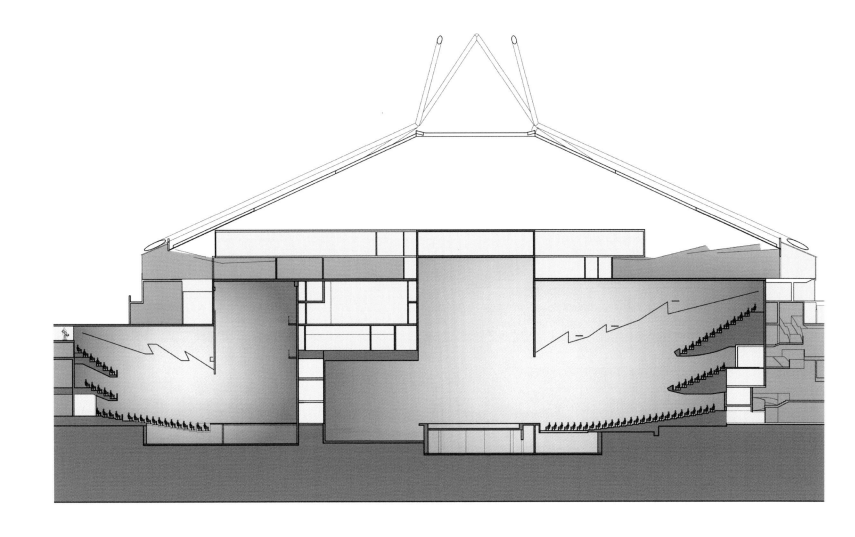

Arts Centre Melbourne, comparative section

0 5 10 20 metres

1:500

Joyce Theater, entrance and marquee at night

Joyce Theater, 1982
New York, USA
Architect, Hardy, Holzman, Pfeiffer (Hugh Hardy)
Elizabeth Bradley

The Joyce Theater – Worked from Day One, and Still Works Today

The season had not gone well. In 1977, the Eliot Feld Ballet presented two weeks of performances at New York City Center, a 2,257 seat theatre on 55th Street. The expenses associated with the presentation – rent, labor and marketing costs – were exorbitant for a company of that scale to bear. The itch to grow and the resulting willingness to take a financial risk to reach a larger audience almost put the Feld Ballet under. Yet the company had outgrown its earlier home – the 300-seat Newman Theater at the Public. Production costs were increasing, and the small capacity of the Newman limited both income and exposure, but City Center was a leap too far. It was also, in terms of ethos, in the "wrong" part of town with an establishment vibe that did not suit the edgier downtown dance audience.

Clearly, in order for the Feld Ballet and companies like it to survive and thrive, a critical need existed for a mid-sized theatre geared specifically for dance. Artistic director Eliot Feld, and Executive Director Cora Cohan knew from the beginning that other emerging contemporary companies would soon come to rely on using such a space, if one could be found and made available. Feld stated, "Our need is to build a dance theater used 40 to 52 weeks a year. We couldn't support a house by ourselves. We were looking for a house that could support dance. That is our motivation."[1]

For months Feld had been curious about a building in the Chelsea neighborhood near where he lived. The Elgin was a deco era movie house that had morphed into an indie theatre showing art house cult films, and porn movies. By 1978, when the theatre was put up for sale, Feld had become convinced that this structure, the only one he seriously considered, was the solution. Robert Goldberg, the son of the original contractor on the project explains the allure:

> The capacity was just under five hundred seats and protected from union jurisdiction, but more than the numbers, the intimacy of the space just felt right. The two mezzanines were like the arms of a chair, the seats like comfortable cushions. And the view of the stage from every seat was excellent.

Now, the formidable challenge for Feld and Cahan was to find a way to both buy the building and then to raise money for the cost of the extensive renovations. Their determination and resourcefulness proved pioneering.

The philanthropist LuEsther T. Mertz, co-founder of Publishers Clearing House and a benefactor of the company who had supported the renovation of the company's studio, underwrote the full $225K cost of the purchase, which closed in January of 1979. (Without hesitation, when petitioned by the pair, Mrs. Mertz sent them a pink handwritten check with a simple note that said: "Here 'tis, kiddos.")

The triage engineered by Feld and Cahan between private philanthropy, local, state and federal government, and especially, the leveraging of monies earmarked for urban redevelopment, has been successfully replicated countless times around the world. They were among the first to successfully made the argument that job creation and neighborhood revitalization were inextricably linked to fulfilment of an artistic mandate.

But even as far along as the early 1980s, with the ownership of the building in hand, the future of the $1 million project was by no means assured.

The distinguished dance critic Anna Kisselgoff described the ensuing scramble for funds in a 1982 *New York Times* article:

By June 30, 1980, the construction budget rose to $1.968 million. A $400,000 Urban Development Action Grant (UDAG) from the Department of Housing and Urban Development had to be matched 3 to 1. Half of this matching sum of $1.2 million was to be met by a bank loan of $600,000 from Morgan Community Development Corporation. But the condition of that loan was a guarantee from the Commerce Department's Economic Development Administration (EDA) of $540,000. The deadline was met when private patrons and foundations made contributions on the basis of the UDAG pledge. LuEsther Mertz, whose involvement has been extensive, provided another $250,000 and the Kresge Foundation gave $200,000. The National Endowment for the Arts gave a two-part matching Challenge grant: $200,000 capital and $250,000 toward operating costs for the first three years. The Ford Foundation paid for a study. The New York State Council on the Arts contributed $22,500 to architects' fees. The budget was seemingly met.

But in February of that year, the EDA funds were frozen. In addition, the construction company's final bid brought the estimated construction cost to $3.5 million.

Faced with the freeze, the Feld staff kept in close contact with Representatives Bill Green and Theodore Weiss and New York's senators. In the end, intensive lobbying by New York City officials led to President Reagan's lifting of the EDA freeze for two New York City projects, the Brooklyn Army Terminal and the Elgin Theater. That May, the budget shortfall was made up by private funds.

The Ford Foundation study surveyed 73 contemporary dance companies and the results supported Feld and Cahan's notion that emerging downtown contemporary dance companies would use the facility if the rent were underwritten at a reasonable weekly rate. (The magic number turned out to be $12,000 a week).

With the capital funding and operating plan finally in place, it was time for the design and build process to kick into high gear. Hugh Hardy of Hardy, Holzman, Pfeiffer who had worked on the renovation of the Public Theater's Astor Place home had been appointed architect. Hardy was a close friend both of Cora Cahan and her husband, Bernard Gersten, the executive director of the Public Theater.

According to Robert Goldberg, who worked with his father on the project, the build was challenging all the way through. The building's footprint was tight. There was nowhere to expand side to side. The cost of securing air rights and building on top was prohibitive. The survey provided to the architects was inaccurate – fully a three-foot margin of error. As a result, all the drawings were incorrect. This caused errors in budgeting and multiple delays. The Joyce Foundation and Hugh Hardy entered into a contractual dispute because of the Foundation's disinclination to increase Hardy's compensation to cover the creation of new drawings and to acknowledge the extra work that ensued. Eventually all involved simply "rolled up their sleeves", both literally and figuratively to ensure that the job would be completed. Hardy insisted on the presence of an "architectural contractor" salaried by the project. This was very much an exception to "normal" working methods, but he was determined to have a staffer from the firm on site to safeguard his business interests and the integrity of the design. Thereafter Charles Gifford worked for Hardy as the rep in the field. Gifford's personal involvement became very hands on, and he was not averse to picking up a tool, alongside the ubiquitous presence of Eliot Feld. For Hardy, preserving the friendship and working relationship with Cora Cahan and Bernie Gersten was extremely important. There were other projects on the horizon that would ultimately contribute to the expansion of the cultural infrastructure of New York City for decades to come. The same team worked on multiple influential projects in a variety of leadership roles.

The Elgin renovation was finished in late 1981, and named the Joyce Theater, in tribute to the "lifelong love of dance"' of the late Joyce Mertz (who died young of breast cancer), daughter of LuEsther T. Mertz, Mr. Feld's chief benefactor. Changes to the building included eliminating the balcony to create a steeply raked one-level seating area. The 67 x 36-foot proscenium stage featured a then "state of the art" sprung dance floor. New construction at the rear of the building provided additional backstage space, and while width and wing space continued to be

tight, there was a "crossover" behind the rear brick wall and a lower level egress also. A range of requirements essential to the staging of contemporary dance had been successfully met.

The audience experience was also positive. The lobby is tight, but circulation is possible. Dispensing with the tradition of a front curtain – an innovation after a flood destroyed the one in use – made opening up the stage and making every part of the experience visible to the audience a signature element of the experience of watching dance at the Joyce.

At its inception, the Joyce's presenting organization rented the theatre for $1 a year plus overhead under the terms of a 35-year lease with Eliot Feld's Original Ballets Foundation. The Originals Foundation owned the theatre and had the priority use for up to 12 weeks per year.

Joyce Theater, auditorium viewed from the stage

Joyce Theater, backstage stairs labelled for visiting international companies

If more companies applied to use the theatre, then a selection panel was to curate the presentations.

All that changed in 2012 when the Joyce Theater bought its long-time home, financing the $22M deal with the sale of a rehearsal and studio building on Mercer Street in New York's Soho district. Linda Shelton became executive director of the Joyce in 1993, shortly after the 10th anniversary of the opening of the theatre, after senior management roles at the Joffrey Ballet and managing touring for the Bolshoi. Under her leadership, the organization's contribution to the field of dance has grown exponentially. The Joyce is a leader in international presenting and also hosted the most highly regarded American companies including Paul Taylor, Camille A. Brown, Urban Bush Women, Garth Fagan, Ronald K. Brown, Martha Graham and many others. The mission requires supporting a diversity of movement aesthetics and traditions and the more than 400 hundred companies that have graced the Joyce stage represent that diversity. The annual budget now runs around ten million dollars and the theatre operates at capacity year-round. The rental subsidy and box office sharing models remain in place. Though the theatre unionized in 2013, operating costs have remained contained. The Joyce presents an annual 45 to 48-week season on its stage, hosting an audience of approximately 150,000 people.

Through artistic residency and commissioning programs, the Joyce gives resources to established, early- and mid-career artists to advance their practice and develop new works for the Joyce stage. The organization also mounts a range of education, school and family programs.

When asked if much had changed physically about the building over the years, Shelton mused wryly, "Not very much at all. We periodically update lighting and sound systems and overhaul the seats when they wear out but there seems to be neither the need nor the space for a radical re-thinking."

The facility perfectly embodies the vision of its founders – "built by dancers for dance" – and demonstrates that it is possible to both operate a theatre and fulfil the mission of contributing to the field of dance.

On a final poignant note, architect Hugh Hardy delighted in attending Joyce performances and revelled in both the dancers on stage and the audience's response. On one such evening, he collapsed in the theatre and died shortly thereafter. Everyone who knew him was convinced he couldn't have planned a better exit.

Joyce Theater, view of the stage from the auditorium

Joyce Theater, entrance lobby

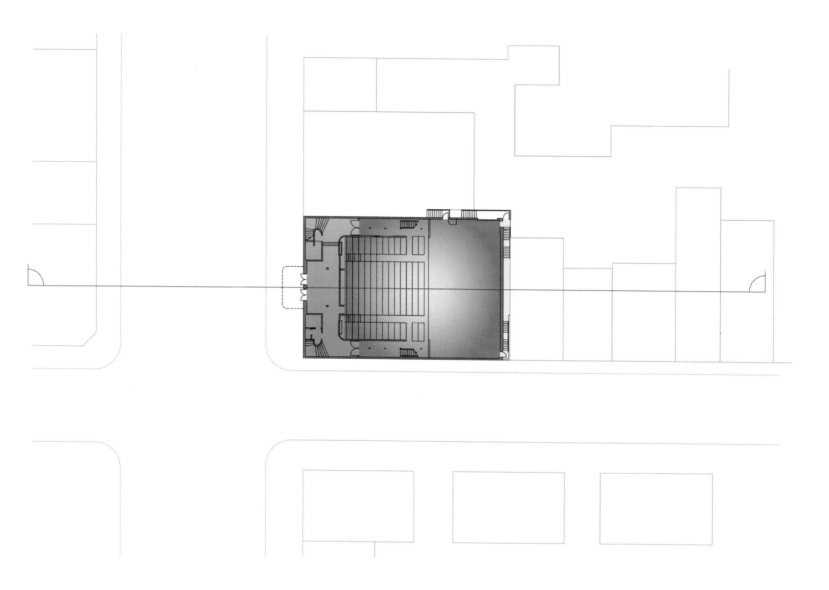

Joyce Theater, New York, comparative plan

0   5   10   20 metres

1:500

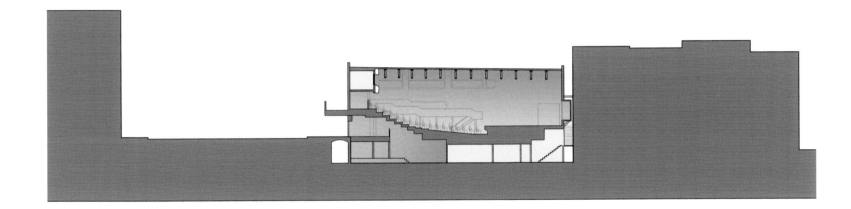

Joyce Theater, New York, comparative section

0   5   10   20 metres

1:500

Derngate, auditorium from the stage

Derngate, 1983
Northampton, UK
Architect, RHWL Architects

Roger Hopwood

Northampton is an expanding town of around 231,683 people some 60 miles north-west of London. Initially a market town, by the end of the 18th century it was booming and prospering when it became a major centre for shoemaking and leather working. The shoe industry declined following World War One and the town only revived with the establishment of a Development Corporation and significant improvements in transport links, particularly the arrival of the M1, Britain's first motorway. Northampton became a commuter town for London. The population grew, as did demand for arts and entertainment.

Northampton had a theatre, the Victorian Royal Theatre, designed by acclaimed theatre architect Charles J. Phipps which had opened in 1884. By the early 1980s the Royal Theatre, with a limited seating capacity (around 500) and uncertain future, was not able to accommodate high quality larger scale music and theatre.

Question: How can a town located in the Midlands of England with a population of 210,000 afford to build:

- a brand new 1500-seat-capacity concert hall expected to host world-class orchestras, soloists and conductors

- a new 1100-seat-capacity lyric theatre fit to host major drama, musicals, opera and ballet

- a conference and exhibition space with 600 square metres for flat floor events

- a function facility with the capability of seating at least 500 covers

- an arena with a capacity of 1200 for boxing, wrestling and presentations

- and last, but not least, an adaptation of the concert hall to allow for the presentation of rock, pop and comedy to a capacity of 1200

Answer: Combine all those requirements into one flexible space and, with the creative utilisation of existing technology from differing disciplines, design a building that can service those performance requirements quickly, on time and cost effectively with an end result that the singular space in each format would appear to have been built for that purpose.

In the early 1980s the local council took the extremely brave decision, in the face of some vocal opposition (white elephant comments come to mind) to invest in the building of a concert hall to serve the population of the East Midlands.

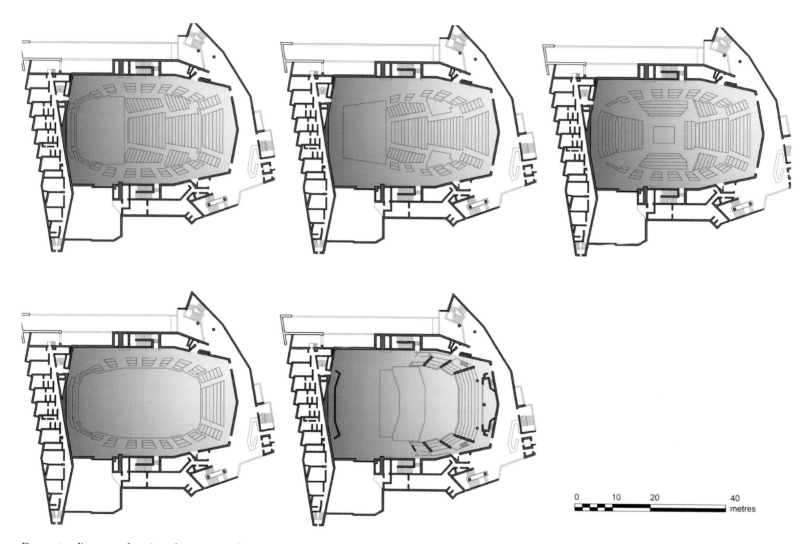

Derngate, diagrams showing alternate configurations

However, it became clear that just providing a concert hall could not deliver suitable financial results and would limit the financial support required, so the provision of a multiform room was mooted and agreed. The hall would be required to service all the differing artistic and commercial needs and the subsequent design resulted in the provision of a quality building providing an innovative solution regarding flexibility and usage.

It has often been said that the secret of the Derngate design success and visual appeal lies in the ability of the space to appear as if it presents itself with an air of permanency in each of the formats it is able to achieve.

Therefore, Derngate was developed, designed and built for a sum of around £7m in response to the demand for a performance space larger than the existing c.500-seat Victorian Royal Theatre with its limited facilities and technical capabilities – incidentally, the longest running operational repertory theatre in the country.

The key driver was the requirement to not only be able to host high-quality symphony concerts but fully staged events such as opera, ballet, musicals, drama and "popular" entertainment.

Scheduled to open in 1982, Derngate came on stream in April 1983 with an opening concert given by Jack Jones, followed by a week of dance drama with Northern Ballet Theatre.

It Did Not Look Back!

Initially requiring a significant subsidy to support the operation and programme, the venues welcomed 314,000 patrons in 2018 with a subsidy of less than 14 per cent of gross turnover.

Unusually, the original business plan also included the need for 50 fully-fledged dinner/dance and conference business events a year – an average of one day a week – and therefore the design also included the capability to remove all the stalls seating and, with the stage, provide 600 square metres of flat floor for up to 600 covers for these events. To service the functions, significant kitchen facilities were provided with a full complement of catering and kitchen staff being added to the staff body. That element was dispensed with very early on as being unrealistic and the venue reverted to primarily live performance/events over the full range of artistic genres.

Therefore, from that blistering start in 1983, even though some of the flexible auditorium elements were still being built overnight for 12 months whilst a busy artistic programme was delivered, the Derngate has provided on average 300 performances or presentations annually, apart from an 18 months closure period to facilitate the development of the site, to over 200,000 ticket buyers a year and for the first ten years undertook over 150 "format" changes a year.

A post-opening development of the space of an "in between" format utilising the auditorium sides and banks of seating in concert format, plus full stage and flying facilities, allowed the presentation of rock, pop and comedy to audience numbers in excess of 1,200 per event.

Format reconfigurations are still numbered at over 100 annually and given that the venue is now in its 36th operational year the design can only be viewed as a brilliantly executed one which more than satisfies its initial brief.

Design Success

The solution to the high expectation was to design and engineer a "multiform room" in which the shape and configuration of the room allowed the necessary changes to suit the differing live performance requirements and resulted in a very practical and low-tech solution that has stood the test of time, with only one performance cancellation in the first 26 years, due to main lift failure.

The elegant solution to the basic brief utilised the lifting and movement capabilities of air castors, developed by General Motors and utilised by them and Boeing, amongst others, to move large, heavy loads allowing all the stalls and side stage components to be moved in large blocks, and when applied to the Derngate auditorium space to be reconfigured into traditional formats that could service productions in their natural "habitat".

Therefore, Derngate offers a unique solution to the presentation of events across differing art forms and commercial presentations and their differing requirements by utilising a multiform room – and changing the shape and form of the room to suit the different events being presented.

Auditorium Flexibility

The flexibility is based on:

- Seating towers – ten auditorium seating towers form the side walls of the room. They are of varying sizes and shapes and incorporate three levels of seating. Each weighs between five and ten tonnes and is moved on air castors.

Derngate, auditorium looking towards the stage

- Auditorium seating units – ten movable seating units, mounted on air castors and with seats permanently fixed to them providing not only the flexibility but the suggestion of permanence. These units having a total seating capacity of approximately 550. It must be said again that one of the successes of this approach is that all formats appear permanent and fit for specific purpose.

- Lifts – two lifts taking up the front half of the auditorium carry the auditorium seating units to and from basement storage. The main stalls lift has a Safe Working Load of 42 tonnes

- Acoustic ceiling – a large, heavy, acoustic ceiling in three sections closes off the fly tower for concert use when flying facilities are not required.

- Air castors – of the low volume high pressure variety, each of the towers has a pair located on each corner, giving 80 large castors in all for the side towers and 48 of the smaller ones. The castors are of the concentric ring, rather than tea-bag, type, and thus almost frictionless movement is achieved on a film of air the thickness of a cigarette paper.

Derngate, two side towers on stage, a seating wagon on the lowered elevator and a further two seating wagons in the under-stage store

The room has variable acoustics designed by Russell Johnson using simple low-tech solutions – acoustic banners along the side walls hidden by mesh screens. (When asked on one occasion how often the acoustic banners were raised or lowered, the answer was "When we knew Russ is coming!") The space provides for two basic configurations involving the auditorium "walls" and auditorium ground floor seating to provide for five major formats and their off-shoots.

Formats and Configurations

The major configurations or formats are:

- **With towers**: wrapped around the stalls seating and stage
- **Orchestral concert hall**: with a 10 tonne, 3-section acoustic ceiling closing off the 22 metre high fly tower. Full orchestral concert hall resulting in a capacity of 1500 (towers wrapped around)

Derngate, configured for a boxing match

- **Choir**: The orchestral format could also include choir seats linking to three permanent rows of seats at the rear of the stage and circle and upper circle levels
- **Concert and choir**: (using pull-out seating) capacity of 1,350
- **Rock and roll**: with all seats available and towers wrapped around
- **Pop concert**: all seats available with towers wrapped round and seating available on side stage – capacity of 1250–1300
- **Sports configuration**: for boxing and wrestling – also used for circus, snooker – in the round with rostra seating to auditorium left and right; 1200 towers in wrap round
- **Total flat floor**: for functions, dinners and conferences
- **No stalls seating**: resulting in a flat-floor space of 603 square metres
- **Lyric format:** with proscenium arch made from retractable sides and the safety curtain for ballet, opera, drama, musicals et al.

All formats require changes to the seating configuration, either to facilitate the change or to be moved to a different presentation position.

Regularity of the Changes

The enduring success of this venue is built around its flexibility and although the original rate of change has reduced from over 150 changes per year to c.120, the ability to provide a home for virtually any production has ensured its survival in changing times.

As you would expect, early in its life individual format changes were taking up to 8–12 hours. However, with practice and by solving some of the engineering problems by applying stagehand solutions to parts of the process, that time has been greatly reduced, so it is not unusual to present a daytime event in one format and a different evening comedy event in the same day.

Staffing costs are also low as changes can now be completed by five people in four hours, although a six-man crew would be more normal. The time taken has reduced from the initial 24 hours to two–four hours

dependent on the change required, with an additional two hours needed for the flat floor carpet layout.

Hosting Differing Events

The flexibility of the venue has enabled it to host many types of artistes, orchestras, comedy, international stars such as Tina Turner, Howard Keel, Tom Jones, companies of the calibre of the Royal Ballet, Birmingham Royal Ballet, Miami City Ballet, Merce Cunningham, major touring musicals such as *Chess*, *Joseph*, *Blood Brothers*, a panoply of world-renowned conductors, with the CBSO and RLPO becoming the "house bands", and long-standing working relationships with conductors such as Rattle and Ashkenazy. Virtually every well-known UK comedian has played the Derngate and it has also seen many high-profile rock & roll and musical acts.

The requirement for a flat floor configuration, whilst useful and still in occasional use today, became secondary to the live performance provision which, in itself, distilled into two distinct groupings to provide the above.

Thus, in its first ten years this unique venue presented over 3000 performances, changed configuration over 1,500 times and hosted classical music, opera, ballet, drama, comedy, election rallies, local groups and schools playing to in excess of 2,000,000 paying customers. And, as I write 35 years after its opening, the venue is still going strong and more than delivering to its planned ambitious aims.

Conclusion

Difficult brief, complex requirements, simple solution, cost-effective, simple operational execution, limited downtime, no expensive technology, simple staff training, demonstrable programming benefit. A building, venue and programme to be proud of and all for an initial investment of £35 per citizen.

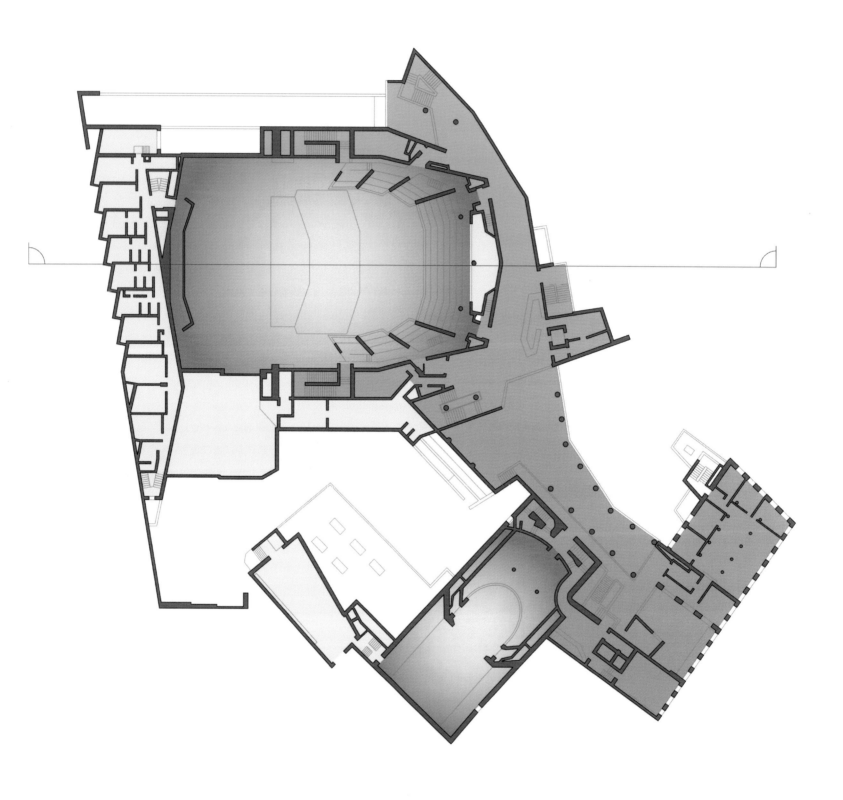

Derngate, Northampton, comparative plan

0   5   10   20 metres

1:500

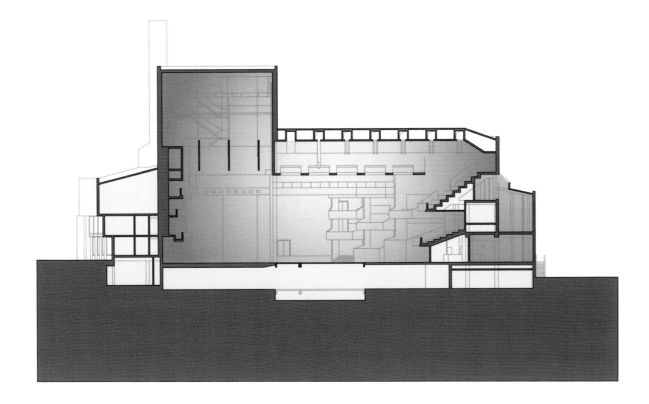

Derngate, Northampton, comparative section

0 5 10   20 metres

1:500

Lucent Danstheater, auditorium

Lucent Danstheater, 1987
The Hague, Netherlands
Architect, Office for Metropolitan Architecture (OMA) Rem Koolhaas
Eric Blom and Lian The

The Lucent Danstheater, which opened in 1987, started out as the Danstheater aan 't Spui in The Hague. The venue was conceived by Carel Birnie, founder and director of the Nederlands Dans Theater (NDT), as a theatre purpose built for the company that he created in 1959. The venue enabled the company to develop and stage their own productions in spaces that were ideally suited to modern dance and that were completely tuned to the artistic ambitions and characteristics of NDT performances.

The building, the first and so far the only fully equipped theatrical building specially erected for modern dance, marked the emancipation of dance, and contemporary dance in particular, as an art form in its own right. The theatre initially accommodated two dance companies, with NDT 1 being the main company and NDT 2 as the breeding ground for talented young dancers. During a period of time, the theatre was able to accommodate even a third company, NDT 3 for older dancers.

Due to sponsorship, the Danstheater aan 't Spui became the AT&T Danstheater from September 1989 until 1996. With the prolongation of this sponsorship deal it became the Lucent Danstheater as the theatre is now mainly referred to. It remained the Lucent Danstheater until demolition of the auditorium, parts of studios and offices and the complete adjacent Dr Anthon Philips Concert Hall in late 2015. This theatre was always planned as a limited life building. The back of house will be demolished in 2021, when the new cultural complex, called AMARE, that is being constructed on the site, which will be the new home of the Nederlands Dans Theater, is expected to be completed.

Running an artistically and also financially successful company, Carel Birnie had been able to save enough funds to convince the City of The Hague to approve building a new venue and also for the City to provide a location for the building. Originally planned in Scheveningen, the City and also the State agreed to allocate required additional funds for the Danstheater, but on the condition it be constructed in the city centre, where plans for a concert hall for the Residentie Orkest, the Dr Anthon Philips Concert Hall, were already in development. Concentrating these separate initiatives in the centre was deemed vital to the lively and attractive inner-city that the City aspired to. Later developments nearby include a cinema and a playhouse, Theater aan het Spui, creating a diverse cultural hub. Combining the two venues on a plot originally allocated for just the concert hall, turned out to be a significant challenge that the development of the Danstheater building had to address and resolve.

For the architectural design, Birnie chose to work with the Office for Metropolitan Architecture (OMA) out of three architectural firms he considered for the project. Contracting OMA in 1980, the firm had not yet completed a project of this size and nature. Without built reference projects in the portfolio, at the time Rem Koolhaas referred to his works as 'paper architecture', plans for the Scheveningen location drafted in 1982–83 proved that the OMA design team were more than suited to dealing with the particulars, also when it came to the altered design brief and challenges. The design had to deal with the limitations of the plot, the design for the concert hall, which the design for the Danstheater had to in some way relate to, and retaining maximum functionality and efficiency of the larger space than was originally planned for Scheveningen, all within the limited budget of the original plan.

The working relationship between Birnie and Koolhaas was stormy at times and increasingly so. The early design process centred on realizing the growing ambitions of Birnie for the building. Convinced more would, or perhaps should be possible, OMA's own ambitions for the building grew as the project progressed. Upon completion of the building Koolhaas dedicated a print to Birnie with the text: "To Carel, for everything you made (im)possible", summarizing his own experience. He later also referred to the completed building as a 'Fata Morgana', an impression of what could have been.

Undeterred by others and other ambitions, Birnie kept the direction of the project solidly in line with his own vision for the building and the requirements that needed to be met. The spatial and technical requirements were drafted by Birnie in close collaboration with the artistic director and house choreographer Jiří Kylián, company members and technical staff. The outstanding works of Jiří Kylián exude purity, clarity and simplicity and the Spartan building was the built expression of such performances. It brought NDT to world class level. The vision centred on creating the ideal setting for rehearsals as well as for the performances. Many spaces were multipurpose, one of the studios could double as foyer space and the large rehearsal studio doubled as a production studio for setting up big decors, easily rolled out to the main stage through a door 3 metres (W) by 6 metres (H). The proscenium width, which at 20 metres across was a novelty at the time, gave maximum artistic freedom. It allowed dancers to move freely and for the performance to be seen by the audience without distraction: all seats were optimally directed at the stage and there was no proscenium arch to frame and limit the experience. Birnie demanded perfect sightlines from any seat in the auditorium of exactly 1001 seats, so that he could jokingly boast about having an auditorium of more than 1000 seats. The original building also housed a small swimming pool, a sauna, fully equipped AVC studio, costume ateliers, a scenery workshop, green room, cafeteria and scenery storage spaces in the attic.

Even though the theatre was purposely built for NDT, NDT was not the only group using the venue, especially after 2005 when after

Lucent Danstheater, entrance

Lucent Danstheater, exterior

having run the building independently, the entire venue, including the Dr Anton Philipszaal, was sold to the City of The Hague. Out of 300 performance days, approximately 40 were performances of NDT. The auditorium proved to be equally well suited to other dance companies, operatic performances and musicals too. The appreciation of performers and of the audience, with Queen Beatrix as a regular in that audience, has been incredibly positive from the start and this remained until the end.

The theatre technology was designed around this same principle of artistic freedom and flexibility. The technical side was quite simple but allowed for maximum flexibility. This benefited the NDT as a touring company. No movable stage floor, no fixed lighting bridges above the stage, but a movable portal bridge and movable side bridges. The grid was made up of 66 fly bars including two side bars. This was originally fitted out as a manual counterweight system. The orchestra pit floor could raise to stage level in order to extend the stage. There were relatively small side stages but a deep backstage. In the auditorium were two fixed lighting bridges. The NDT developed their own stage sets and lighting design to an optimum which could be presented in the Danstheater but could also easily tour all around the world. NDT travelled with their own lighting board, lights and dimmer units. For a long time, this remained unusual for touring companies.

The limitations of the site and the budget constraints were, as is often the case in creative processes, not detrimental or negatives. The positioning on the plot meant that the architect chose not to compete with other buildings on the outside but to focus fully on creating dramatic intensity in the interior. Reflecting the artistic signature of the company, simplicity and maximum efficacy drove the design. It became a masterclass in how to obtain maximum effect with scarce means. Koolhaas blurred lines between theatre and reality and sought to innovate architectural design from within. The building was conceived as a collage of autonomous, sculptural volumes which made it difficult to discern the exact NDT building amongst the other volumes. Where the Danstheater began and ended was not to be too apparent, even though the inverted and overturned golden cone of the restaurant presented a clear delineation between the Dr Anton Philipszaal and the Danstheater. In the design concept for the Danstheater, the whole was more than just the sum of its own parts.

Koolhaas aimed at avoiding traditional boxed spaces, designing the internal layout and volumes to create an innovative spatial experience. Using materials that were not traditionally associated with theatre buildings, such as the steel construction with on the outside the fretted corrugated sheet metal and on the inside simple plasterboard walls. A simple colour scheme of balanced grey tones and stylish door signings add the desired effect. From the Spartan simple spaces back of house, the design front of house suggested more luxury and opulence as spaces became more visible and accessible to the public. In the auditorium six prominently suspended golden reflector panels were the only eye-catching

elements and of course a huge gold decorated main curtain. The building was adorned on the outside of the stage tower on the Spui side of the building by a mural depicting three dancers designed by the artist Madelon Vriesendorp, one of the founding members of OMA. The architectural expression developed by OMA was a balancing act with volumes giving the impression of being mobile or even weightless, such as the gold cone at the entrance of the theatre restaurant.

The unique structural qualities of the venue, although conceived by OMA, would not have been possible without the engineering genius of professor Stefan Polónyi of the studio Ingenieurbüro für Bauwesen Polónyi und Fink GmbH from Germany. The exceptional acoustics were also made possible by him. In the auditorium, the six golden reflectors and the undulating ceiling that referenced the nearby sea delivered the perfect acoustics that Birnie required. The acoustical qualities were such that after a performance of "The Unsung" by José Limon a visitor enquired who the composer of the music was, only to learn that there was no musical score. What he had heard was dance itself: the movements and breathing of the dancers.

In the entire process of design and the subsequent construction period, all requirements were realized in the completed building according to plan except one. Limitations of the zoning plan meant that the required height of the fly-tower could only be managed if the building in its totality would be lowered by one metre, a change that was implemented. This concession was to be the only dissonance in the functional scheme, permanently compromising the loading bay area. During the design development, part of the underground parking area was acquired by Birnie to have the space converted into two additional studios, leading to a total of six, and also additional dressing rooms. These dance studio spaces are significantly lower in height, but functional nonetheless.

Apart from minor changes to ancillary rooms, the space has remained largely unchanged since completion of the building. No major renovations or alternations were necessary, as the building remained as functional to the company as important production house and as venue over the years, while NDT grew and diversified as planned by Birnie at its conception. Technically the only big renovation was the change in accordance with Dutch legislation of the manual counterweight system to a mechanized system using Waagner Biro drives and a Bytecraft control system. Over the years many designers and (dance) companies have visited this unique venue to learn and experience the set-up of the building as an inspiration for other buildings. Many important choreographers have also found the building an inspiration and have created a body of work on this stage that is still being performed in venues around the world. A full reproduction of the unique qualities of the Danstheater has however never been realized. Birnie masterminded a singular unique venue that successfully proved the value and significance of development of a venue completely tuned to the requirements of a single end-user. It was a luxury at the time and one that few have enjoyed since and fewer are likely to enjoy in the future.

This theatre opened in 1987 and was always conceived as a limited-life building. After playing a significant role in developing NDT as one of the world's best dance companies, the auditorium and stage were demolished in 2015. A new building, Cultural Centre AMARE, partially on the old footprint of the Danstheater, is scheduled to open in September 2021.

Lucent Danstheater, auditorium

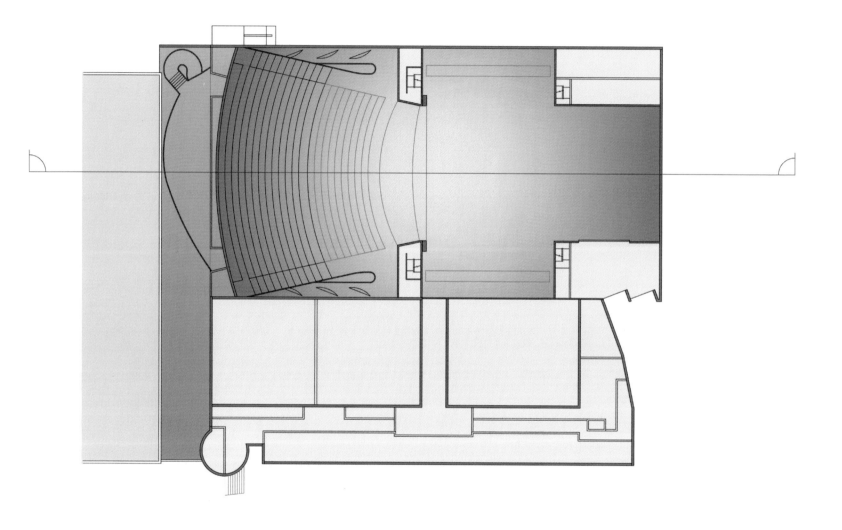

Lucent Danstheater, The Hague, comparative plan

1:500

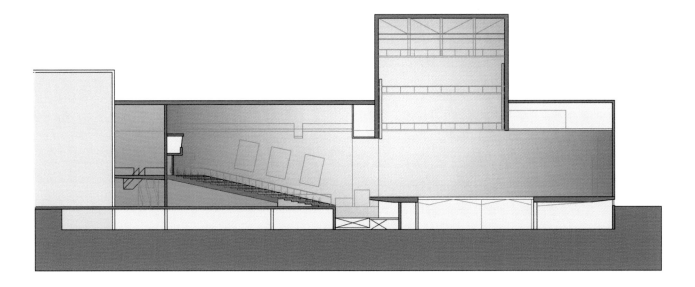

Lucent Danstheater, The Hague, comparative section

Opéra Bastille, exterior with the July Column

Opéra Bastille, 1989
Paris, France
Architect, Carlos Ott
Michel da Costa Gonçalves

Draped in a safety net waiting to be repaired and repaired again, this Parisian opera house sits almost quietly alongside cafés and retail. Its stained white marble façade and corporate glazing gives it a faint appearance of an office building with only the grand staircase, or black stone portal, as lukewarm memorable features. The decaying building is not the 200-year-old historical building designed by Charles Garnier, but the modern Opéra Bastille completed a mere 30 years ago. Praised for the high quality of its facilities and technical spaces, the building equally suffers from the poor quality of its urban and public presence. Its original sin syndrome probably lies in how it was programmed, selected and conceived, making it an internationally acclaimed tool and facility for the Opéra national de Paris company. However it is an unexciting, rather forgettable public experience beyond the shows. If one refutes the Opera as a social experience in a manner passed on from the 19th century, Opéra Bastille achieves its acetic goal of being not much more than a well-functioning auditorium and stages for high quality performance; a generic container.

The name Paris Opera, or Opéra de Paris, justly conveys a tradition of excellence tracing back its history to the Académie Royale de Danse (Royal Academy of Dance) founded in 1661 by Louis XIV. Today, with it's various "corps", including ballet, orchestra, opera and chorus together with invited Artists, the company is mandated to present circa 300 shows annually including opera, ballet and musical concerts (489 shows in 2017/18 Season). Since 1990, the venerable institution is split between two 'houses', the cherished 19th century Opéra Garnier, or Palais Garnier (named after its architect Charles Garnier), and its now official venue, the contemporary Opéra Bastille. This dichotomy of physical places subconsciously supports a qualitative division between the untouchable glamour of the old masterpiece and the tedious efficiency of the unmemorable modern counterpart. Beyond stylistic differences, the comparison between these two buildings demonstrates the evolution of status of performance spaces. In this case the ostentatiously select building for 19th-century social encounters of the privileged versus the function orientated building catering to the modern deconstruction of "higher" art and its democratisation.

However, The Palais Garnier has not always maintained the esteemed position it holds today; it was criticised in the late 1970s for its lack of flexibility, and for its elitist stance, resulting in the birth of an idea for a new Opera for the people. The idea of creating a monument of the arts for the masses can be further traced back to the popular work of leading artists of the time, dancer and choreographer Maurice Béjart, promoter of popular theatre Jean Vilar and the composer Pierre Boulez who famously declared "Blow the opera houses up". Together they authored a report on the renewal of the Opera pleading for a forward-looking institution in opposition to what they claimed was weighed down by centuries of elitist culture. They seeded the idea of a new Opera house which the newly elected socialist regime headed by President Mitterrand from 1981 endorsed as the idea of a 'people's opera' at Bastille. "Opera would be offered to the masses at the very spot the patriciate had first been challenged."

A much-disputed public institution, it seems that from the outset, technocratic and technical approaches led its conception, making it the result of a quantitatively driven exercise. The building's existence emerged from a state mandated study leading to a single-stage anonymous architectural competition with a brick-sized 423-pages-long brief. The brief was so precise that it left very limited leeway for architects to reinterpret the typology, arguably leaving them with only the task of designing a building envelope.

Opéra Bastille was designed by then unknown Carlos Ott who was chosen in November 1983 after an international competition that attracted entries from some 1,700 architects. The International Competition launched under supervision of the ad hoc public body, Opéra Bastille Public Corporation (EPOB) attracted 756 entries. The competition is forever known for its unexpected result and an unclaimed mistake. Rumour suggests that several of the jurors assumed that Ott's project presented anonymously was that of the renowned American architect Richard Meier. Much has been said of the superficial resemblance to Meier's work and the style of Ott's entry. It does however remain an undigested point of departure, which the underwhelming building never overcame. It equally implies the risk taken, and the variability of the results of single-stage competitions which were popular at the time; others resulted in the striking avant-garde Pompidou Centre under the patronage of President Pompidou. There was much political pressure to provide supporting architects and interior designers to work with Ott; this probably ensued from the underwhelming result of the competition. Ott however chose to dismiss this patronage and continue on the project alone.

Following the same presidential tradition, the building is part of the string of projects engaged by François Mitterrand in his "Grand Travaux", or Grand Works, referring to a series of monumental buildings directly commissioned and supervised by the French president during his tenure from 1981 to 1995. It was originally planned to be situated close to the northern edge of the city amongst the "Cité de la Musique" – a cultural and leisure park where now sits the recently completed Paris Philharmonie. It was later decided for it to replace the former train station, Gare de Bastille, decommissioned since 1969, hence assuming a more central and highly symbolic location. The site is in a mostly working-class neighbourhood and marks a traditional point of departure and closure for public demonstrations during the French Revolution, and since, in short, a highly politically charged location for a monument to the arts.

This new location came with its own limitations, where rather than being a stand-alone object, the building would have to negotiate its immediate urban context. Amongst the portfolio of projects of its era within the "Grands Travaux", which included the Louvre Pyramid, Musée d'Orsay, Parc de la Villette (Cultural Park), Arab World Institute (Museum), Grande Arche de La Défense (Monument), Ministry of Finance and the Bibliothèque nationale de France (National Library), the Opéra Bastille does not feature high in public regard. Whilst for example the Louvre Pyramid has achieved international and iconic status, the Opéra is regarded as yet another forgettable public facility.

In so much as the contemporaneity of the Pompidou coincided with its future content, there was an added layer of difficulty for the Opéra Bastille to transmute into contemporary design the repertoire of a centuries old institution. Furthermore, both the Bastille location and the left-wing political "patrons" meant that the project was not devoid of ideologies. In the words of President Mitterrand, the "Building, a modern and popular opera, radically different from the Opera Garnier originally built for the bourgeoisie of the Second Empire." Conceived as the "people's Opera", Opéra Bastille was to be built in the eastern working-class area of the city. In so much as the Pompidou Centre revitalised the slum-like derelict part of Central Paris, Opéra Bastille was to inject grandeur and monumentality amongst former workshops, a neighbourhood of light industry. The site is somehow humbling as it meant for the building to stitch the city in congruence with the obsessive alignment and uniformity of Paris. So, whilst Palais Garnier had been erected as the central urban crown of developing Paris, Opéra Bastille was to be built on an oddly shaped corner site.

The former has the city organised around it in order to stand out, being the focal point of multiple urban perspectives, whilst the latter needs to be grand whilst aligning to an unassuming part of the city fabric

Garnier Opera, exterior

After five years of construction, the official opening concert was fittingly on 13 July 1989 to celebrate the bicentennial of the French Revolution with George Prêtre's "La Nuit d'avant".

The shape of the site for Opera Bastille was characterised by its former use, with a narrower northern frontage to the Place de la Bastille, which gets progressively larger northwardly before intersecting diagonally with an adjacent hospital site. Ott's response covers almost entirely the site with a volumetric composition following the plot's central axis, headed by a semi-circular main volume. Occupying roughly 30 per cent of the site's length, the semi-cylindrical volume contains all the public spaces, foyer and auditoria, and abuts the stone clad stage and back of house (including an unfinished auditorium) using the rest of the 70 per cent in the length and larger part of the site. The glazed curved façade following the semi-circular plan is accented with stainless steel panels composing stair-like areas protruding from the glazed area that are supported by thin columns. These zigzagging elements house the grand staircases climbing along the façade under a glass roof. These "escalier d'honneur" are thought to be homage to Palais Garnier's famous layout.

Thought to signal the principal public and staff entrances, the glass curtain walling and protruding cascading steel elements are symmetrically arranged on the building's site axis; this is not perceived due to a skewed relationship to the circular Place de la Bastille. Therefore, the main entrance is at an oblique to the public piazza and with the main circular volume detached from the adjacent 18th-century building creating a fairly unused shady link to a rear street. To reconnect to the urban alignment and achieve a stronger relationship to its context, Ott placed a freestanding, black-granite portal tangentially to the building's curve. Acting as prominent entrance, it hosts monumental staircases leading to the first-level foyer. However, access to the entrance hall is directly from the square at street level. The monumental external staircase is seldom used, as is the direct underground access from the Bastille subway station that has been closed. From the outset the competition that requested the entrance to be from the Place de la Bastille had defined the narrowest façade as the main elevation, resulting in the long-side elevation along Rue Lyon to remain unanimated and overwhelmed by the sheer bulk of the back of house facilities and offices.

The sheer bulk remains its main characteristic; "The massive Opéra in this residential landscape resembles a beached supertanker (Witold Rybczynski, "A Blight at the Opera", *Saturday Night*, December 1994)."

Covering 22,000 square metres at street level, the building houses a main auditorium with 2,745 seats, a 500-seat amphitheatre, a 230-seat studio theatre, set and costume workshops and offices. The main auditorium covers only about 5 per cent of the total area of the building footprint and works with impressive stage facilities. Palais Garnier was often incapacitated by changeovers between productions so the mission overseeing the project introduced a gigantic turntable system of the main stage's scale, installed deep below the stage, on which several sets could be stored simultaneously, thereby reducing turnaround time and ensuring theoretically that the theatre needs never to close.

The main stage is 45 metres in height, 30 metres wide and 25 metres deep, with an adjustable and mobile orchestra pit which at its largest can house 130 musicians. The stage is in itself made up of elevators allowing several levels to be created and supported by three side elevator systems, which bring scenery up from below stage clearance zones through an automated system of motorised trolleys. In this area, four side and rear stages with the same dimensions as the stage backstage area make it possible to simultaneously mount and store multiple shows, with its scenery turntable allowing for rapid transformation. The hangar-like backstage areas allow complete three-dimensional sets for several productions to be stored on site and brought forward on rails for performances, thus permitting more than one opera to be performed each day. The scene design was led by the German office of Rudolf Biste and EHM for stage hydraulics.

The lower level also includes workshops and a rehearsal stage as well as the 500-seat auditorium, Salle Gounod, with its orchestra pit and dimensions identical to those of the main stage. Several shows can be staged and rehearsed; decors can be rotated to and back from the stages in minutes in a jigsaw manner. In 2023, there is a scheduled opening of the modular auditorium, left as an unfinished shell since the project's inception, together with additional costume storage, painting workshop and rehearsal spaces, which are today located in another building. Operationally and spatially impressive, these facilities, with their interconnecting cathedral-like spaces are the core of the initial political project and remain hidden from an unaware public.

The main auditorium is predominantly frontal, in an arena-like format with a limited number of narrow balconies to the sides. The two steep balconies are divided into five progressively recessing sections. The sidewalls are abruptly vertical, with no relationship to the balcony; thus purposely unlike the vertical horseshoe-shape of the Palais Garnier, Opéra Bastille feels large and lacking intimacy. Once again, the efficiency arguably trumps the sensational with the possible exception of its scale, the acoustics and the cloudy white ceiling. The auditorium uses natural materials, with the prominence of grey/blue granite, black or white stone

Opéra Bastille, main auditorium from the stage

and black ironmongery. The overall sense of uniformity in the decoration is contrasted by a gradient of three colours in the seating – brighter for the top balcony and darker warmer tones close to the stage achieved with pearwood for the seats and oak for the floor. Housing the over-scaled structural trusses, the white glass ceiling is strikingly backlit and also contains longitudinal strips of glass panels which open to reveal/hide technical grilles for lighting and other effects.

Without intermediary support and hence free of sight-line obstructions, the aim is to offer every seat an equal view, with the same level of comfort, and in accordance with the people's theatre motto, no boxes are provided, although two small standing areas were later added.

If one looks at the basic organisational diagram of the building, the main auditorium is not the central element but heads the north end of the site, leading the public to a thin strip along the rounded façade. As the building, or its aggregation, is organised around the site's longest axis, the foyers are left with what looks like leftover space on the northern semi-circular volume. The public areas are vertically stacked corridor-like curved spaces, which due to their simple superposition do not foster interaction between the three foyer levels. The internal decoration is voluntarily restricted in order to achieve the 'Everyman' public spaces desired, in opposition to the Garnier. Conceived to be comprehensible, transparent and welcoming, Carlos Ott has however been quoted to describe the building as "a functional project which is not essentially aesthetic". Is it the failing of the competition through its overly detailed brief, technically driven design and social ambition that conditioned an architectural gesture as an anti-monument?

Famously Palais Garnier gives almost equal room for public space as for the back of house, emphasising the importance of social encounters around the performances. Comparatively, Opéra Bastille is disproportionally made of back of house areas. The 19th-century icon translates a clear sequence in its spatial aggregation of grand space, with the countlessly photographed grand staircase acting as its central piece. With the Opéra Bastille, one feels urged in and out of the dramatic auditorium, as the annexe spaces are not conducive to the flâneur's parading but rather directed at avoiding a lingering audience.

The recurring comparison with the old Opéra Garnier is unavoidable as the people's opera was a riposte to Palais Garnier's aristocratic affectations. It is equally interesting to study the spatial differences as each aims to carry a certain idea of what an opera building should say. Arguably it also demonstrates that at the time of its inception Opéra Bastille arguably lacked an artistic and spatial project for a modern lyrical house. It was instead driven by political intentions translated into quantitative and technological prowess that the architectural competition failed to lift to more than the sum of its parts. In so much as one would accept the pretence that simplicity equates democracy, the building does not reach – maybe does not seek – iconic status. The size of the main auditorium and the advanced technologies of its back of house were seen as a way to bring down the cost of the ticket and ensure a show is on every night, a productivity-driven way to define a performance space. The political ambition of the people's opera quickly failed and has taken a compelling artistic project to achieve the successful institution it is today, somehow beyond the shortcoming of its modern receptacle.

It all comes back to the same conclusion; Opéra Bastille is a highly sophisticated tool without elevation. Paradoxically praised for the functionality of its technical prowess, the Opéra Bastille remains an unloved building when it comes to its public presence. Whilst patina often slowly softens the image of once undesired edifices, here the defect-ridden building has not had such luck. This dichotomy of perceptions between the ones that use and those who experience is one of its many contradictions, stemming from its inception and continuing to this day. For designers around the world, the original sin for the design community still lies in the organisation of the competition, whilst later appreciations reside in the balance between the front and the back of house. Given the task to design what would anywhere be considered an international icon, this Opera House had a convoluted site and the ambition to avoid monumentality, hence the expected result. The building was a technological, but equally social, engineering attempt at bringing back the public to lyrical scenes through economies of scale. Whilst it is finally achieving these goals, it could be time to depose its uninspired architectural wrapping rather than further repair it.

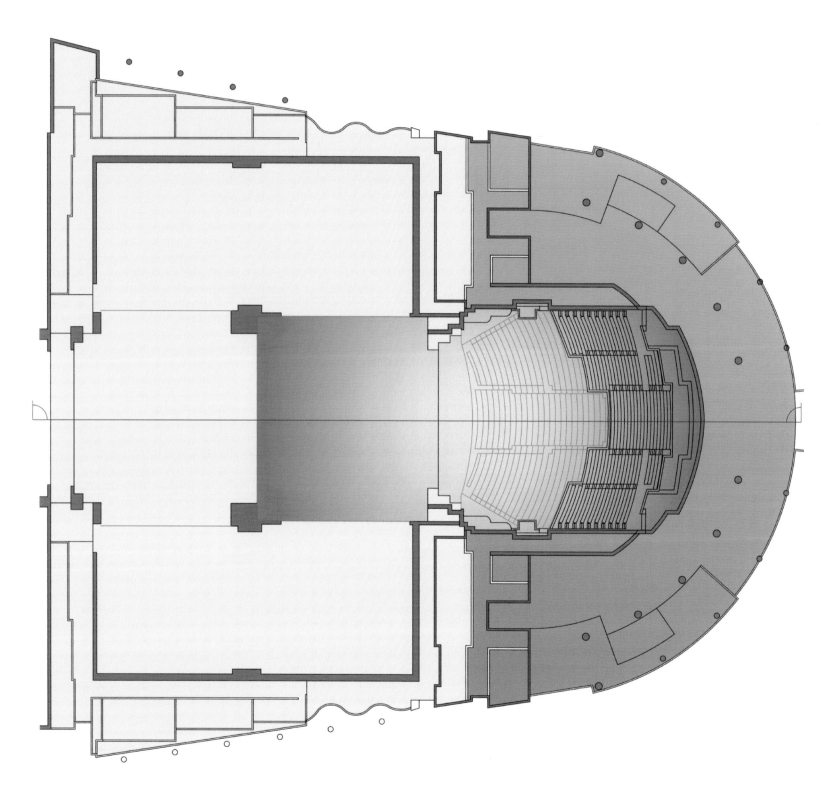

Opéra Bastille, Paris, main auditorium comparative plan

0   5   10   20 metres

1:500

Opéra Bastille, Paris, main auditorium comparative section

1:500

1990s
The Nineties

Sadler's Wells Theatre current auditorium

Sadler's Wells Theatre, 1998
London, UK
Architect, Nicholas Hare
(interiors by Renton Howard Wood Levin)

Richard York

Sadler's Wells is a small piece of land that has been the site of a place of public entertainment since 1683. On a footpath between Islington and Clerkenwell (villages just to the north of the City of London), it was acquired by Richard Sadler, a surveyor, who began digging for gravel to repair the King's highway. An ancient well was discovered, therapeutic qualities were ascribed to the water and Mr Sadler persuaded the gullible to come and partake. Since this involved a good deal of hanging about while the water wrought its magic, he built a Musick-House to entertain the customers and started a history which has run pretty well continuously as one building has succeeded another. Sadler's Wells Theatre has been the home of most forms of entertainment including concerts, plays, masques, naval and military extravaganzas, pantomime, music hall, opera and dance – it even did a stint as an early cinema. Until the third decade of the 20th century it was generally managed for profit by its owners – thereafter it became one of the cradles of state-supported arts as we now know them.

The modern story of Sadler's Wells dates from 1915 when the Victorian theatre, the fourth on the site, closed and drifted into dereliction. In 1928 the remains were rescued by Lilian Baylis, an irresistible force who managed the Old Vic, south of the Thames, as a people's theatre with a programme of plays, operas and dance. Dance was provided by a young Irish dancer named Ninette de Valois (another powerful personality) who had been hired to coach actors at the Old Vic while also running a dance school in the theatre. Miss Baylis, planning to replicate the Old Vic at Sadler's Wells, raised the funds, rebuilt the theatre and opened it in 1931 with a policy of circulating productions between the two centres. Since this proved expensive and the theatre's acoustics were unpopular with actors, by 1939 the Old Vic was focussed on plays and Sadler's Wells on opera and dance – Mme de Valois's dancers becoming the Sadler's Wells Ballet.

The theatre closed in 1940, becoming a shelter for those displaced by the bombing, and its companies spent the rest of the war on the road maintaining their founders' vision of taking the arts to the people.

Opera and ballet returned to Sadler's Wells in 1945. The companies were the mainstay of the theatre, which was also hired to many other dance and opera organisations from the UK and overseas. The ballet company moved to the Royal Opera House in 1946 but Mme de Valois created a new company for Rosebery Avenue, which in turn moved to the Royal Opera House in 1956 as the Royal Ballet Touring Company, although it still held its London seasons at Sadler's Wells. In 1968 the opera company moved to the London Coliseum and subsequently turned itself into English National Opera. After this the Governors of Sadler's

AQUATIC THEATRE. SADLER'S WELLS.

Sadler's Wells Theatre, Finsbury, London, 1813. View showing a horse-drawn carriage and figures fishing along a stretch of water

Wells Foundation resolved that the theatre should focus on being a receiving house, particularly for dance and ballet – a tall order since the number of nights to be filled was great and the money available to support the visitors was small – the Arts Council policy of the day was not to subsidise bricks and mortar. However, the roster of visitors grew, with many overseas companies and some UK ones bringing their subsidy with them. Contemporary dance, ballet and opera with occasional drama and mime provided a substantial and mixed programme.

Ballet Rambert (founded by another formidable woman in the late 1920s – Marie Rambert) became closely associated with Sadler's Wells as it moved from smaller scale classical ballet to contemporary dance in the 1970s and 1980s. London Contemporary Dance Theatre became another home grown dance company which became regular visitors

from the mid-1970s and the combination and number of overseas and UK companies defined the theatre as London's contemporary dance house.

During the 1970s and 80s, the theatre was deteriorating and increasingly unsuitable to meet the ambitions of its managers and their clients. In 1985, a £7 million pound scheme for expansion and refurbishment of the building was prepared with the help of £500,000 from the Greater London Council. Before this could progress, Mrs Thatcher's Government dissolved the GLC and, not only did the scheme stall, but the theatre lost its GLC revenue funding (about £200,000 a year). With help from corporate sponsorship, the theatre managed in 1988 to implement part of its project by building the Lilian Baylis Theatre (a 200-seat studio) and adding a café, a new stage door and some other rehearsal facilities. The

8th September 1933: The Sadler's Wells Theatre in Rosebery Avenue, north London, before the opening night of Puccini's *La Bohème*

theatre staggered on in poor physical and financial state – at increasing risk of trading insolvently and losing its entertainment licence.

In 1994 the trustees recruited a new Chief Executive, Ian Albery, whose family had been theatre owners for four generations. Not only was Ian the perfect candidate to see the possibilities of a new future for the theatre but he had the technical, administrative and personal capacity to articulate it. He gathered a project team around him including architects Renton Howard Wood Levin, whose Arts Team had great experience of re-purposing theatres. A masterplan emerged: to rebuild Sadler's Wells as "The Dance Theatre for London" creating an excellent auditorium, stage and supporting facilities equipped to modern standards.

Redeveloping Sadler's Wells Theatre was a mighty challenge. Not only was the theatre broke, but the nation was just emerging from a down-turn, Housing-the-Arts money was a distant memory, the site was an awkward one, the theatre was protected by a Grade II listing and audience numbers were shrinking. On the plus side was an international reputation for contemporary dance, a clear vision for the project, the support of many potential users – and the arrival of the National Lottery in November 1994. One of the objectives of the Lottery was to fund the improvement of the nation's arts buildings via Arts Council England. Ian Albery was the first theatre manager waiting on the doorstep of ACE's offices with his application on 4 January 1995. A substantial grant

Sadler's Wells Dance Theatre

(eventually totalling £42million) followed after much negotiation, leaving the management team to raise some £12 million from other sources.

The 1931 Sadler's Wells Theatre was not a prepossessing building; it shared the rather lowering qualities of Elizabeth Scott's Shakespeare Memorial Theatre of the same period. Economy dictated that it was a plain building, famously described by John Gielgud as looking like "a denuded wedding cake" (he added that "the acoustics were dreadful"). It had a narrow, deeply recessed proscenium arch, behind a large orchestra pit, very little wing space combined with archaic technical facilities and poor audience facilities.

The building had been Grade II listed since 1950, with the implication that any works to its fabric would be heavily constrained by English Heritage, the listing authority. However, in this instance English Heritage took the view that the building was of limited merit and that it was

the site that was of the greater importance because of its history since 1683. A more or less free hand was given to build a new theatre, although Lilian Baylis's example of utilising the previous building as much as possible was repeated, so the fabric now retains elements of theatres which probably go back to the third one built on the site in 1765. The listing was restored when the new theatre opened in 1998.

The general disposition of the rebuilt theatre is remarkably simple and reassuringly theatrical – full of promise of a good night out. The exterior, designed by Nicholas Hare (Renton Howard Wood Levin did the interior) comprises proud brick walls punctured by deeply recessed doors and windows, and a glass curtain wall revealing a stack of foyers linked by a cantilevered staircase behind a prominent entrance. A central block, to the east of the foyers, evidently contains the auditorium and an obvious fly tower delineates the stage. A canopy over the pavement leads along the street frontage, past the get-in, to reveal a second entrance and foyer – to the stage door, the café and the Lilian Baylis Studio.

While the theatre was unequivocally designed for dance, Ian Albery's vision allowed for other theatrical forms including opera and pantomime (harking back to the gifted clown Joseph Grimaldi who performed at the theatre in the years either side of the turn of the 18th century). Economy of working was considered vital, given the varied and rapidly changing programme imposed by the dance world, best operated by a small but highly trained technical staff supplemented by freelance technicians. The proscenium opening is 15m, the flat stage is 19m wide and 16m deep of sprung stage, with unsprung wing space either side. The sprung section floor modules may be replaced with unsprung panels to enable fixings or unusual loads. An 85-bar power flying system providing full power flying throughout was

installed from the beginning and has recently been upgraded as part of a refurbishment project. The get-in at stage left comes straight from Rosebery Avenue and Sadler's Wells is unusual in having a second get-in on the other side. Given that wing space is very restricted, this must be helpful when productions are being juggled. The orchestra pit may be provided in different sizes by lowering up to three lifts in the front stalls with the loss of up to four rows of seats. The same lifts offer the possibility of a variably sized forestage.

The auditorium is on three levels, with gently curved continental seating in rows of variable length with a maximum of 33 seats. Given the distance from the stage to the back row of the second circle this makes the auditorium feel comparatively narrow, but it does ensure that almost all seats have sightlines to the furthest corners of the stage – except the first and last seats of the front rows of the first circle which are obstructed by

Sadler's Wells, exterior

Sadler's Wells, cantilevered staircase

the people sitting in the corresponding side gallery. Maximum seating capacity is 1568. The comfortable seats are bright red, with greys for carpet and architectural metalwork so the auditorium manages to be visually striking without being distracting during performance and it has a number of hidden virtues – the side walls are masked by suspended metal mesh panels which hang 2m in front of the structural walls and upon which colours and images may be projected. The void also contains staircases which provide ease of circulation for technicians. Some of the panels may be opened to reveal lighting positions and there are clusters of lights at the ends of the circles and the circle fronts as they extend down the side walls. There are lighting positions in vertical slots just outside the proscenium and three lighting bridges in louvres across the ceiling. A section of the ceiling may be lowered to reduce the impact of the second circle if a more intimate ambience is required, although this is rarely used since demand for seats is high.

The 1931 theatre closed in 1996. The two-year reconstruction period was particularly testing and Ian Albery and his project manager, Roger Spence, pay tribute to the theatre's staff for their fortitude, not only in contributing to the project but to managing the Peacock Theatre, with

1000 seats on the east edge of London's West End, leased as a temporary venue to retain both the flow of visiting companies and the audience during the closure. Sadler's Wells still retains the lease and operates the two theatres in tandem. The theatre reopened in October 1998 under difficult circumstances – possibly the first lottery-funded project to be not quite complete on the night and certainly not the last. Press response was rather mixed – a particularly irritating article by the architectural commentator Jonathan Glancey in the *Guardian* was mildly approving of the theatre but nit-picking about the quality of some of the finishes and about the project being done so hastily.

After a splendid opening season, which featured Rambert Dance, William Forsythe's Ballett Frankfurt and Pina Bausch, the new theatre faltered, perhaps dogged by the decline that had characterised its predecessor. Ian Albery retired in 2002 and was replaced by a Frenchman, Jen-Luc Choplin, whose career had been divided between Disney and the Paris Opera Ballet. He didn't stay long and was replaced by Alistair Spalding, who, at the time of writing, is still in post. Spalding's vision is best told by Sarah Crompton, whose book *Sadler's Wells Dance House* records the theatre's recent history:

Sadler's Wells, auditorium from the stage

He decided that Sadler's Wells had been at its best when it had resident companies and new works being created in its walls. This vision paved the way for an increasing number of Associate Artists and for companies producing work in the building. Today Sadler's Wells not only promotes but also commissions and produces outstanding dance.

And Sadler's Wells is even more than that since it still manages the Peacock Theatre and the Baylis Studio, it has an extensive community programme, and "Sadler's Wells East" a mid-scale theatre (with a full-size stage) and rehearsal facilities is being built for it at Stratford's Queen Elizabeth Olympic Park. In 2016/17 it was responsible worldwide for 912 performances played before 750,000 people. In the same year it commissioned 300 UK and international dancers, choreographers, designers, composers and dramaturgs, it toured 18 productions to 35 venues in 21 countries and commissioned or produced 16 new dance works. It turned

over some £25million of which only 10 per cent came from the public purse.

Sadler's Wells is an important theatre – it provides London with a building devoted to contemporary dance and it has contributed hugely to creating a substantial and youthful audience for that art. Dance companies tour the world to and from Sadler's Wells. It is a modern theatre that is fit for purpose and it provides a model for a major capital project – no Act of Parliament, no overblown committee, no international architect, and no city-dominating site. Just a group of people who saw the need and the opportunity, who knew what they were doing because they had done it before and who were able to persuade everyone to let them get on with it. The modern Sadler's Wells Theatre celebrates the 335-year-old theatrical history of the site and provides a memorial to Lilian Baylis and Ninette de Valois, those early adopters of the view that the theatrical arts are a public good that should be available to all.

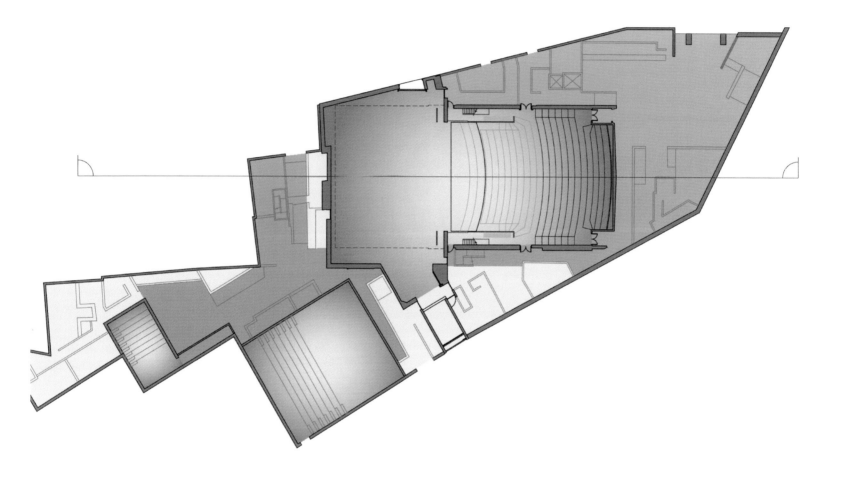

Sadler's Wells Theatre London, comparative plan

1:500

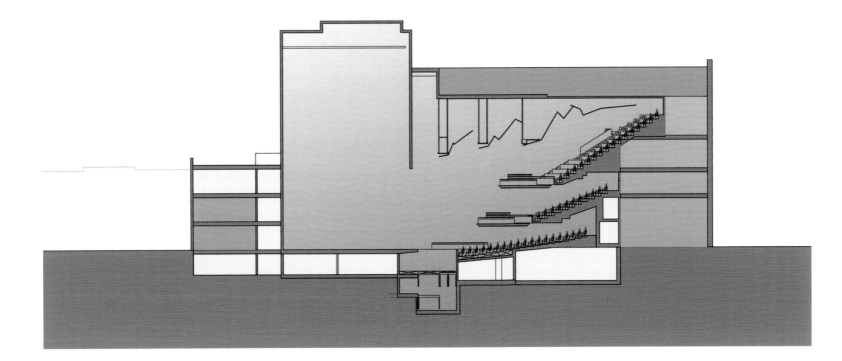

Sadler's Wells Theatre London, comparative section

0   5   10   20 metres

1:500

2000s
The New Millennium

The Lowry, exterior

The Lowry, 2000
Salford, UK
Architect, Michael Wilford and Partners
Alistair Fair

The Lowry is a major centre for the visual and performing arts in Salford, in the north-west of England. Opened in 2000 at a cost of some £58 million and designed by Michael Wilford and Partners, it was one of the UK's flagship 'Millennium Projects', supported by funding from the proceeds of the National Lottery. Its significance relates not only to the scale and ambition of the building, and the prominence of the architectural practice that designed it, but also the intention that a major centre for the arts might catalyse the regeneration of a run-down inner-city area – an aim which has been successful.

Salford Docks were originally built in the late 19th century as part of the Manchester Ship Canal, a purpose-built waterway that connected the city with the River Mersey and the Irish Sea. Changes in shipping patterns after the Second World War eventually prompted the closure of the docks in 1982, and a year later Salford City Council acquired a large part of the site. A Development Plan followed, and by the end of the 1980s the idea of a 'Centre for the Performing Arts' had emerged – along with a drawing showing London's Royal Albert Hall transposed to one of the dock piers as a demonstration of the sheer scale of the site. The proposal, the work of the architect Peter Hunter, enthused local politicians. The 'vision' – inspired by waterfront projects in such places as Bilbao and Baltimore – was that the construction of a major centre for the arts might stimulate further investment. At that time, Salford was one of the most disadvantaged communities in Britain in economic and social terms: the regeneration of the docks was, it was hoped, a way to change its fortunes.

A competition was held to find a master planner for 'Pier 8', on which the nascent 'Centre for the Performing Arts' might be located, and to produce an outline feasibility study for the centre itself. By early 1992 the firm of James Stirling Michael Wilford and Partners had been selected. The aim of the competition had been to secure a designer of some repute to produce the masterplan, in part to add some 'prestige' to the project. In this respect, James Stirling had been a prominent figure within the British architectural scene since the mid-1950s: his practice, initially with James Gowan and later with Michael Wilford, had been responsible for major buildings in Britain and internationally, including several significant cultural projects. By April 1992, they had produced an outline design in which the new Arts Centre would be located at the tip of Pier 8, facing a new public square and various other new buildings.

By June, an outline design for the building had also been produced. It included three auditoria, one of which was located outdoors, perhaps optimistically in view of the frequently wet Mancunian climate. Centred on a 1200-seat, horseshoe-shaped auditorium, the various parts of the centre were gathered together in a typical example of the 'collage' that characterised Stirling's design method. In other words, each element of the scheme was treated as a discrete 'object' or volume whose form often

Royal Albert Hall superimposed on Salford Quays, drawing by Peter Hunter

Stirling died suddenly in June 1992; Wilford and his colleagues continued to work on the project. Over the course of the next three years the design was developed while the 'vision' for the centre itself was refined. The question of exactly how the auditoria would be used had initially been loosely defined: members of Theatre Projects Consultants, appointed in 1993, later recalled that 'there was no brief', with the main auditorium 'varying wildly in size'. It was, after all, being promoted by the local authority, not by an existing arts organisation. There were several options. Should it be used by commercial touring productions, or by local arts groups, or should it be a 'producing' theatre that originated its own shows (and which would require substantial backstage facilities to support those productions)? There were rumours of an 'opera house', and in fact some of the early Stirling/Wilford auditorium designs suggested this use by echoing the forms of traditional opera venues.

An experienced theatre manager, Stephen Hetherington, was appointed to develop the brief while an influential project Steering Group was also set up, chaired by an experienced BBC broadcaster, Felicity Goodey. With several 'producing' theatres already in Manchester, it was decided that The Lowry would be a 'receiving' venue for touring shows – despite nearby Manchester also having several theatres of this type. The argument was made that Salford would appeal to a regional catchment, drawing audiences from across north-west England. The theatre consultants became 'guardians' of the artistic vision in the absence of an 'artistic' client organisation; they were responsible for making sure that the design would work in a practical sense for the kinds of groups who would be likely to perform there. In parallel, it was decided to bring Salford's collection of paintings by the noted artist L.S. Lowry to the centre, giving it its name. Lowry's work was well-known and popular, but not always critically well-regarded, and the move of the collection to the centre ultimately contributed to a broader critical reappraisal of his work.

The launch of the UK's National Lottery in 1994 supplied the project with additional impetus. The Lottery was conceived with the intention that some of its proceeds would be spent on 'good causes'. Ultimately, The Lowry received funding from the Lottery's Arts, Heritage, and Millennium Project funds, with the award being announced in February

had historical resonances, and the complex as a whole was formed by gathering these 'objects' together. Drawings from this time suggest an initial nautical theme with porthole windows and suggestions of funnels, as well as banded stonework of the kind that Stirling had previously used elsewhere. While numerous refinements were subsequently made to the design, both in terms of plan and appearance, the basic parameters had been set.

Concept diagram of The Lowry painted on Salford Quays

1996. Further funding was received from other sources including the European Regional Development Fund (in view of the potential regenerative role of the building) as well as the local authority. This mixture of funding is typical of the major arts buildings constructed in the UK since the 1990s. It can be challenging to manage in practice: each funder may have their own requirements in terms of, for example, reporting and monitoring, and the result can be significant work for the design and client teams in providing funders with information.

The original 'vision' was pared back at various points in the name of 'value engineering', but, as realised, The Lowry delivered most of the facilities originally envisaged. It includes two auditoria (one seating 1766, the other 466), a drama studio, galleries for the L.S. Lowry paintings as

Aerial photograph of The Lowry showing the adjacent shopping development

well as visiting exhibitions, and extensive foyers (with ample toilet provision, a feature insisted upon by Felicity Goodey as something that was integral to a good visitor experience). Clad in stainless steel panels and complex in its massing, the building has a striking appearance. The impression is of a series of discrete but related volumes, suggesting the multiplicity of functions within. The exhibition spaces and foyers wrap around the two auditoria, which are placed stage-to-stage at the core of the building. To the front, a large 'portico' has a suitably civic quality. (Sadly, the buildings which Wilford had proposed for the site opposite The Lowry were not built, with a commercial retail development taking their place and offering a less architecturally satisfactory approach to The Lowry.) Internally, the colour scheme is dynamic, even extrovert. As is the case in many other Wilford projects of the 1990s, bright colours abound, with the foyers, for example, featuring yellow, red, purple, and orange.

Both auditoria, realised with significant input from Theatre Projects Consultants and Sandy Brown Acoustics, possess a certain theatrical intensity. The larger one, known as the 'Lyric Theatre', has three tiers, namely stalls and two curved balconies, and a proscenium-arch stage. It accommodates large-scale opera, dance, theatre and musicals. Although relatively subdued in its finishes, the richness of its purple colour scheme together with dramatic lighting suggests a certain theatrical glamour. Meanwhile the smaller Quays Theatre reprises the galleried 'courtyard' form with which Theatre Projects Consultants has been associated since the mid-1970s, when Iain Mackintosh originated the principles of the Cottesloe (now Dorfman) auditorium within London's National Theatre complex. Narrow balconies – hung from the roof to avoid the use of columns – are wrapped around a flexible area at stalls level, while the stage can be used in proscenium-arch, thrust and in-the-round formats.

The Lowry, vibrant foyers

How should we assess The Lowry, nearly two decades after its completion? We might conclude that, in some ways, it was hardly an innovative type of building. It can be situated within a long tradition of civic 'boosterism' in which the construction of major public buildings demonstrated a municipality's ambition and vision. In this respect, it is perhaps a contemporary reinterpretation of the same spirit that inspired the grand 19th-century architecture of Salford and Manchester. Similarly, we might also understand it as an enlarged version of the new regional theatres that sprang up around Britain between the late 1950s and early 1980s. During those decades, the introduction of Arts Council and local-authority funding for the practice of the arts, and for arts building projects, encouraged new 'civic' conceptions of theatre and the construction of new theatres, typically for resident Repertory companies. Theatre was re-cast as a kind of public service – even a cultural element of the 'Welfare State' – and its buildings were on occasion conceived as prominent structures within the urban landscape. Many offered generous public spaces, and, in contrast

The Lowry, Lyric Theatre

to their older, commercial counterparts, were open all day, with refreshments and exhibitions on offer in a manner not unlike The Lowry.

The Lowry can nonetheless be distinguished from the cultural projects of the 1960s and 1970s in the intention that it might not only embody (and prompt) civic pride but also stimulate urban regeneration. This line of thinking had emerged during the 1980s, when arguments were routinely constructed about the economic and regenerative value of the arts, partly in response to increasingly market-oriented government policies and, in parallel, squeezes in the Arts Council's budget. In the case of The Lowry, these hopes seem to have been borne out. Salford Quays has attracted more than £1.4 billion of investment since the late 1990s, with developments including a large shopping mall as well as the Imperial War Museum North and, more recently, television studios for the BBC and

ITV. The Lowry itself draws a significant number of people to the area, attracting more than 820,000 visitors per annum – a figure which makes it one of the most-visited cultural attractions in the north of England. It supports the equivalent of more than 500 full-time jobs and contributes more than £26 million annually to the local economy. Discounted tickets are made available to the local community, and The Lowry is involved in initiatives including a University Technical College.

Although some actors have reportedly quibbled with aspects of the design, the building itself has received several architectural awards, as well as a generally positive reception from the architectural press. The *Architectural Review* concluded that the exterior possessed a certain civic bravado, appropriate to its function (although it wondered if the design was 'too much an assembly of pieces', and it criticised the

The Lowry, Quays Theatre

abandonment of the original Wilford masterplan for the surrounding spaces). It also praised the interiors, especially the foyers and the exhibition galleries. Writing in the *Architects' Journal*, critic Kenneth Powell was similarly positive, suggesting that the use of colour imbued The Lowry with a welcoming and theatrical atmosphere, and praising the energy of the design. Powell noted the persistence of certain themes from Stirling's earlier work, notably the formal 'architectural promenade' (or sequence) which structures the internal spaces, but also considered that the building revealed that Wilford was developing Stirling's ideas in new directions.

Ultimately, The Lowry demonstrates that 'landmark' architecture need not be incompatible with a functional, successful theatre. It is now an established fixture on Greater Manchester's cultural scene, presenting a varied programme to an audience drawn from across the region. The steady increases in audience numbers achieved during the last decade under Chief Executive Julia Fawcett mean that The Lowry now operates with a low level of subsidy, some 10 per cent of income in 2015. Its success contrasts with the high-profile failure of several contemporaneous 'Millennium Projects', their 'landmark', 'iconic' architecture failing to compensate for over-egged business cases or a lack of content. Indeed, The Lowry's architecture – in its colourful complexity the opposite of cool minimalism – seems to be part of the reason for its success. One visitor in 2007, interviewed by the *Guardian*, thought it 'odd in design, a carbuncle', but noted that 'it grows on you', being 'comfortable and child-friendly'. Such a conclusion would no doubt have pleased Wilford, who, the same article reported, 'wanted to make this place joyful, light, bright, playful, to show people the future, not the past'.

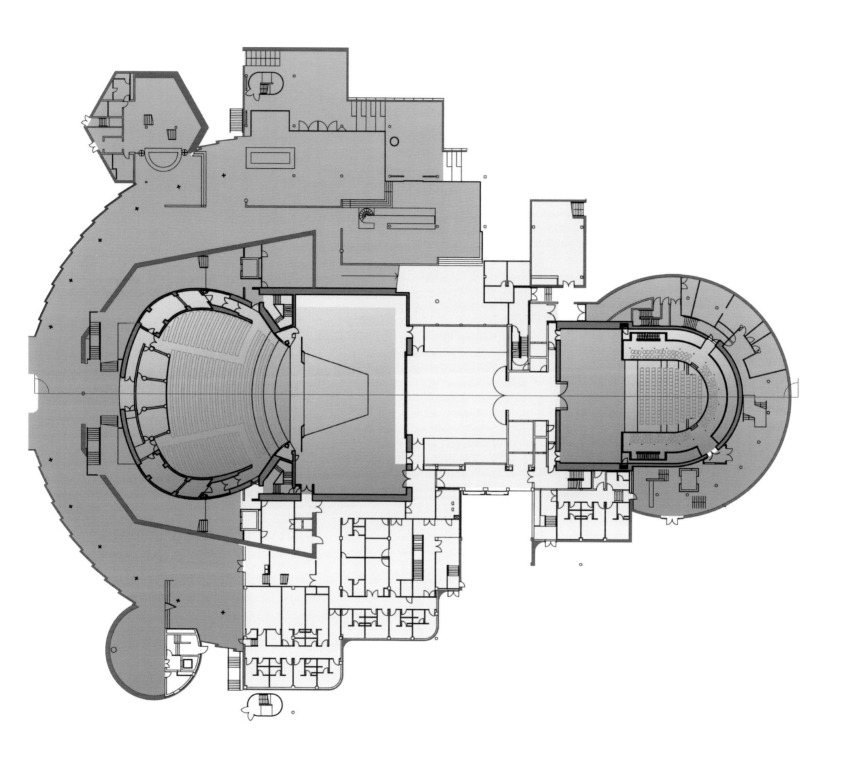

The Lowry, Salford, comparative plan

0   5   10   20 metres

1:500

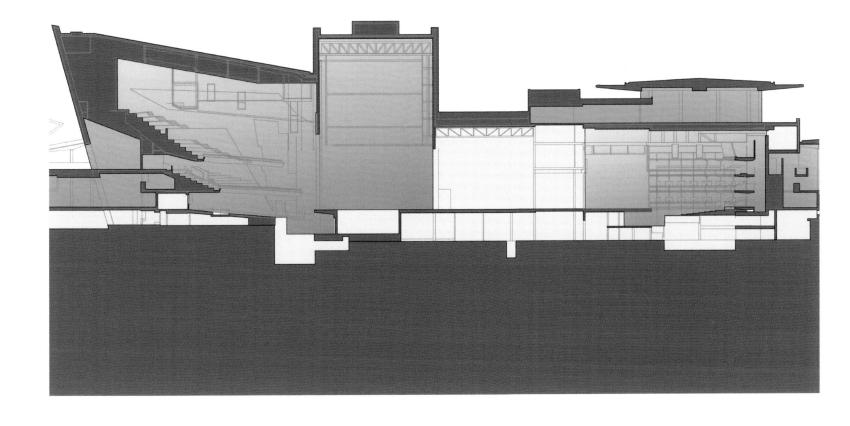

The Lowry, Salford, comparative section

0 5 10 20 metres

1:500

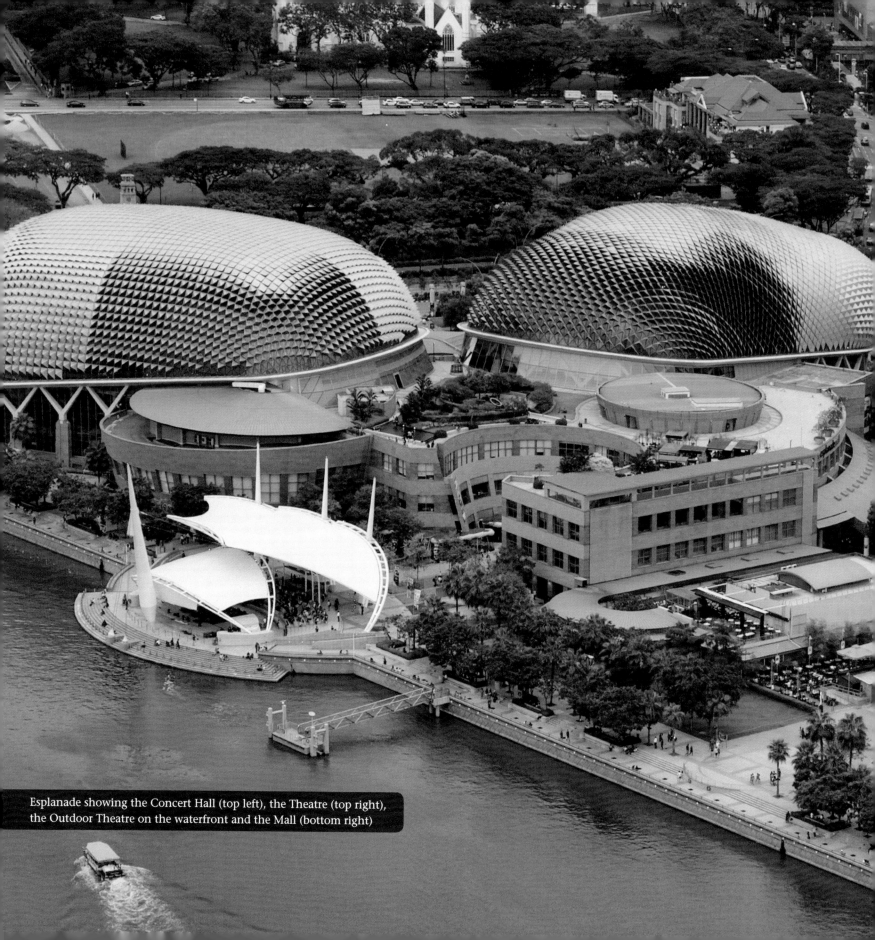

Esplanade showing the Concert Hall (top left), the Theatre (top right), the Outdoor Theatre on the waterfront and the Mall (bottom right)

Esplanade – Theatres on the Bay, 2002,
Singapore
Architects, DP Architects (Singapore) and Michael Wilford & Partners (UK)

Gaurav Kripalani

Introduction

Esplanade is Singapore's national performing arts centre and one of the busiest arts centres in the world. Since its opening in 2002, the centre has presented more than 41,000 performances and activities, drawing an audience of 28 million and 98 million visitors. This architectural icon, with its distinctive twin shells (the Durians, a powerfully smelling local fruit), houses world-class performance spaces complemented by a comprehensive range of professional support services.

Esplanade's vision is to be a performing arts centre for everyone, and its programming is guided by its social mission – to entertain, engage, educate and inspire. The centre's year-long calendar of about 3,500 arts performances and activities span different cultures, languages and genres including dance, music, theatre, and more. Of these, more than 70 per cent are presented free.

Esplanade regularly presents world-renowned companies and artists that attract international attention and add to Singapore's cultural vibrancy. The centre is also a popular performance home for arts groups and commercial presenters who hire its venues to stage a wide range of programmes.

Esplanade works in close partnership with local, regional, and international artists to develop artistic capabilities, push artistic boundaries and engage audiences. The centre supports the creation of artistic content by commissioning and producing new Singaporean and Asian work for the international stage.

History – Envisioning a World-Class Performing Arts Centre in Singapore

The idea of developing a world-class performing arts centre in Singapore was first mooted in the mid-1970s. One of its more vocal supporters was the late ex-President Mr Ong Teng Cheong, who was then the Minister of Culture.

At that time, Singapore was a young country with no natural resources to fall back on. Singapore's leaders knew they had to be pragmatic and accelerate the process of nation-building, focusing on the development of the economy, security, and defence. Infrastructure like roads, housing, schools, and hospitals took priority. But even in those early days of nation-building, Singapore's leaders had recognised the island's unique and rich cultural legacy.

As the nation grew and the economy found its stride, more emphasis was placed on arts and culture. English theatre saw the largest growth because education policies had made English the medium of instruction in schools and English had become the first language for Singaporeans. Some of the key theatre companies which were formed then include TheatreWorks, The Necessary Stage, and the Singapore Repertory Theatre.

Esplanade – Theatres on the Bay, sign

The 1980s saw the formation of national music and dance companies, which continue to play significant roles in Singapore's cultural landscape. The Singapore Symphony Orchestra was set up in 1979, and the Singapore Chinese Orchestra, in 1996. In 1987, the Singapore Dance Theatre was formed.

Following that, the Advisory Council on Culture and the Arts, chaired by Mr Ong, then the Deputy Prime Minister, submitted a report in 1989 which was regarded by policy-makers and the arts community as a watershed in the nation's development of the arts because it led to the formation of key arts agencies in Singapore. It presented comprehensive recommendations designed to make Singapore a culturally vibrant society by the turn of the century. The Report paved the way for the formation of statutory bodies including the National Arts Council, the National Heritage Board and the National Library Board, as well as the development of infrastructure such as the Singapore Art Museum, Asian Civilisations Museum, and Esplanade – Theatres on the Bay.

In 1990, the Cabinet announced its intention to build the arts centre. A Steering Committee was formed to guide planning for the project subsequently, under the chairmanship of Mr Ong. The Singapore Arts Centre (SAC) Co Ltd was established on 26 September 1992 to develop and manage the arts centre.

Calls were made for submissions from architects worldwide and by December of the same year, a design team comprising architectural team DP Architects (Singapore) and Michael Wilford & Partners (UK), theatre planners Theatre Projects Consultants (UK), and acousticians Artec Consultants (USA), was set up to finalise the master plan and schematic design for the arts centre.

The master plan was unveiled on 21 July 1993 to the public in an exhibition "Taking Shape" and an announcement of the name "Esplanade" was made by the Culture Minister BG (NS) George Yeo.

Important study trips were made to gather information relating to the design and construction of world class concert halls and theatres in the UK, USA, and France. Links were also established with the managements of the Queensland Performing Arts Centre, Sydney Opera House, Hyogo Performing Arts Centre, and Hong Kong Cultural Centre to view their facilities and observe their operations. By November 1993, the architects had completed the master plan and the schematic design was completed in March 1994.

Building and Construction of Esplanade

Esplanade's Location, Naming and Branding

In 1989, the six-hectare reclaimed land at Marina Bay was identified as the site for the new arts centre. Situated near the Esplanade Park where the Satay Club used to be, the area that the arts centre sits on was fondly remembered by the people as one of Singapore's favourite haunts for young people and families alike from the 1960s to 1990s.

Which is why, when it came to choose a name for this performing arts venue, Esplanade – Theatres on the Bay beat over a hundred other alternatives. It was found to be the ideal link between the nostalgia for Singapore's past and the exciting possibilities of its future.

On 11 August 1996, construction work began and the traditional "turning of the sod" ground-breaking ceremony was officiated by then Deputy Prime Minister Dr Tony Tan.

On 19 November 1997, The Singapore Arts Centre Co Ltd was renamed The Esplanade Co Ltd to further reflect the company's role in developing and managing the new arts centre.

Initial Design and Façade

Building a world-class arts centre generated excitement among architects, the arts community and the public. Early visions regarding Esplanade's architecture focused on the need for an Asian theme. The overriding sentiment was that a centre that fit with the East Asian Renaissance should incorporate Asian aesthetic elements for a unique blend of East and West. The idea was to continue Asia-centric practices in the performing arts and to build a world-class "stage" for them. Singapore's location and heritage were integral to the design objectives and the needs of Asian arts were to rank equally with those of Western art forms.

Architecturally, the centre was to be "seminal of a new generation of Asian Arts Centres…a reference point like the first Gothic cathedral" (Minister, Information and the Arts, BG George Yeo, 1992). Today, Esplanade is indeed a reference point, having won local and international architectural awards.

The location of the arts centre, which was between the historic/civic districts and the modern city, inspired the initial design of spaces which combined the philosophical heritage of both East and West, traditional and contemporary art forms and their differing technological requirements.

The arts centre was to be friendly and inviting to performers, audiences, and all visitors. It would offer world-class facilities to welcome artists and audiences from Singapore and all over the world, enlivened by shops, eating outlets and leisure activities on the bay.

The actual schematic design was unveiled in March 1994, illustrating the positioning of the venues within the centre and the volume of the structure. Comprising five main spaces: Lyric Theatre (later renamed Theatre), Concert Hall, Medium Theatre, Adaptable Theatre, Developmental Studio and the Wayang Pavilion (later re-named Outdoor Theatre), it evoked many reactions from normally reticent Singaporeans who took the model as a literal representation. It was described as "ugly"

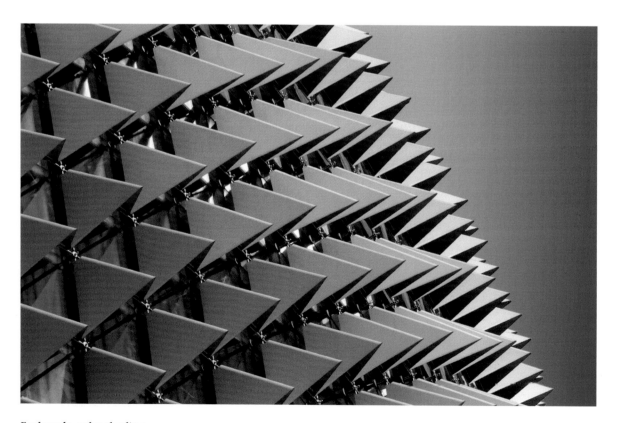

Esplanade, solar shading

and "un-Asian" and was criticised for side-lining the outdoor needs of Asian arts.

Noting that this was the first arts centre of such a scale to be built in Singapore, the architects worked very closely with user groups and incorporated the feedback into the final design. This design was further refined between 1994 and 1996, with the development of the cladding system by British engineering firm, Atelier One.

As the two domes housing the Theatre and Concert Hall were designed in glass, to convey a sense of openness, they would require sunshades to keep the sun out, while offering panoramic views of Marina Bay and the city skyline from the inside. These aluminium sunshades, together with double-glazed laminated glass, were installed on a steel truss frame to form the cladding. The system of aluminium sunshades to keep the heat out from the twin glass domes resulted in its spiky outer shell and gave Esplanade its unique form.

And as with all creative undertakings, the design generated controversy. Nicknames such as "bug eyes," "pineapple," and the most popular, "durian," surfaced. There were also associations with *jali* screens (woven mats of rattan or palm leaf, sometimes used in the building of traditional Southeast Asian houses, as well a carved stone screens common in South Asian architecture).

Esplanade, external form

Construction of Phase I and Deferment of Phase II

Construction was initially to be carried out in two phases, beginning with the Concert Hall and a cluster or village of three smaller spaces in Phase One, followed by the Theatre in Phase Two. This sequence was changed in 1994, when the Government decided that the large spaces – the Theatre and Concert Hall – were to be built first in Phase One, with the studios and the three smaller theatres in Phase Two.

The large halls would, first of all, complete the look of Esplanade. The lack of existing performance spaces of that size and calibre also made their construction more urgent. They would give Singapore an international platform, enable the staging of productions that were never before possible here, offer the best chance for presenters to recover the cost of bringing in world-class productions, and consequently, help the industry to grow.

The change in sequence generated dissatisfaction in the local arts community as the medium-sized theatres were viewed as being crucial to the fringe arts and local arts development which brought them to question if their need for smaller theatres was secondary to the government's desire for an international platform.

The views of the arts community were taken into consideration, and their feedback resulted in the conversion of the rehearsal rooms of the Theatre and the Concert Hall into smaller performance spaces – a black box at Theatre Studio and the Recital Studio.

Esplanade's Facilities

Concert Hall

The 1,600-seat shoe box shaped Concert Hall boasts superb acoustics by world-renowned acoustician, the late Russell Johnson of ARTEC Consultants Inc, USA. The Concert Hall can host a diverse range of musical performances. Acclaimed by top performers around the world, its noteworthy acoustic features include reverberation chambers and an acoustic canopy that enable the hall to effortlessly adapt to different music styles without compromising quality. The Concert Hall also houses a 4,740-pipe organ designed and built by Johannes Klais Orgelbau, one of the world's most established and reputed organ-building families.

Theatre

The Theatre has a capacity of about 2,000 and spans four levels. It takes its form from traditional European opera houses modified to accommodate the Asian performing arts where musicians are often onstage alongside the performers instead of in an orchestra pit. Its horseshoe shape offers a more intimate setting between audience and stage. Housing Singapore's largest performing stage, the Theatre presents all genres of the performing arts from traditional and contemporary dance to intimate or large-scale musical performances or even operatic extravaganzas.

Esplanade, Concert Hall

Esplanade, the Theatre

Recital Studio, Theatre Studio and Annexe Studio

Esplanade's studios provide flexible spaces for intimate performances and rehearsals. The Theatre Studio seats 220 and is well suited for experimental theatre and contemporary dance presentations, while the Recital Studio seats up to 245 and is ideal for chamber music, solo recitals, cabarets, and jazz performances. Located next to Esplanade Mall, the Annexe Studio is a raw and flexible two-storey space, suitable for artist residencies and development programmes, rehearsals, workshops, and masterclasses.

Outdoor Theatre

Located along Esplanade's waterfront, the Outdoor Theatre is set against the backdrop of a dramatic city skyline and it is Esplanade's most popular spot. Tiered steps curve toward a sunken performing stage which features free weekend performances drawing audiences both young and old.

Esplanade, the Outdoor Theatre

Esplanade Mall

While most international performing arts centres are a hive of activity in the evenings and quiet in the daytime, Esplanade however, offers visitors plenty of opportunities to explore other activities before the sun sets, thanks to the integration of a mall within the arts centre. Esplanade Mall offers products and services that directly or indirectly complement the arts, restaurants, cafés and popular watering-holes, and even a performing arts library all housed under one roof.

Vision of Esplanade and its Relevance and Value to Singapore

The arts centre's first vision statement was crafted in 1992 by the Design and Aesthetics Advisory Group which comprised prominent members of the arts community. In 2000, the management of Esplanade re-crafted the vision statement to reflect the next stage of Esplanade's development:

> Esplanade – Theatres on the Bay is a performing arts centre for everyone.
> We will be internationally recognised for our creativity and sense of adventure. We will set exceptional standards of service that will position us as a world leader.

Due to the diverse ethnic make-up of Singapore's community and the fact that Esplanade aimed to be a performing arts centre for everyone, it was decided that the centre would not have a national orchestra or dance company in residence, unlike most arts centres around the world.

Today, as an arts centre with a national agenda, Esplanade's intent is to bring the arts to everyone and influence the aural and visual aesthetic that will help develop audiences of the future, with clear objectives that are relevant to the community it serves. By showcasing a diverse range of presentations of different arts cultures and genres, it serves as a catalyst of social change/growth to help audience and artists in Singapore develop a clearer sense of identity and self, weaving the intrinsic value of arts into an essential part of people's lives.

The Role of Esplanade in Singapore's Cultural Context

Fondly referred to as the "durian", Esplanade has, since its opening in 2002, established a comprehensive arts calendar for Singapore which has helped reinforce a sense of identity for the community and develop the local arts industry.

Esplanade's diverse and quality programmes, which cater to a wide range of audiences, span across all genres to encompass music, dance, theatre, and visual arts, with a special focus on community access and arts education.

The three-week *Opening Festival* from 12 October–2 November 2002 featured 70 ticketed performances and 600 free performances, involving 1,300 artists from 22 countries. Unlike most other large-scale projects of this nature, Esplanade opened on time and according to plan, on the date set by the management team two years before. The scale and range of programmes were also unprecedented for an international arts centre.

Today, Esplanade's year-round calendar, which comprises festivals and programme series, is structured around three key areas: Community and Access Programmes, Audience Development, and Industry Development.

Esplanade's Achievements

In tandem with the growth of its programmes, Esplanade's audience numbers have also increased from 900,000 people attending about 1,500 performances at the centre in its first full year of operations (2003/2004) to more than 1.9 million audiences in 2017/2018 attending about 3,500 performances and activities, both free and ticketed.

Plugging the Gap in Singapore's Arts Industry with the New 550-Seat Waterfront Theatre

To enable Esplanade to achieve these goals in its next phase of growth, a new purpose-built 550-seat waterfront theatre is being built as the arts centre's current venues are fully utilised. This will be completed in 2021. A programmed medium-sized venue at Esplanade can actively produce and present works critical to the next phase of Singapore's performing arts development.

Esplanade's Current and Foreseeable Future

Esplanade has built up strong business fundamentals over the years. Esplanade's revenue streams are not large and are susceptible to external variables as demonstrated in the recent economic downturn. As such, it continues to explore new revenue streams.

As Esplanade continues to grow, it has stated that it will serve the community and industry in an even broader way – by expanding its role and embracing greater responsibility as an enabler of the arts and contributor to social growth.

In order to do that, programming direction and content will have to go beyond just the provision of programmes. Amidst the uncertain global economic climate and despite limited resources, Esplanade plans to continue delving deeper into the creation of content for programmes as well as increase the sophistication of what the arts centre presents. Besides intensifying its focus on developing new works and profiling artists from Singapore, Esplanade will showcase more Asian stories, voices and perspectives through the arts and explore issues of cultural identity and aesthetic vocabulary relevant to Singaporeans today.

While it may be difficult to change the mindsets of the people who have yet to embrace the arts in their lives, Esplanade plays a critical role in working towards transforming society in the long run and bringing the arts to the community so that it becomes an integral part of a better enriched and balanced life.

All this is essential for the next phase of growth for the Singapore arts industry and the evolution of the society, for the arts can engender positive growth in individuals, communities and nations in gentle yet potent ways many other disciplines cannot. It is the fuel that kindles imagination, sparks possibilities, and illuminates life.

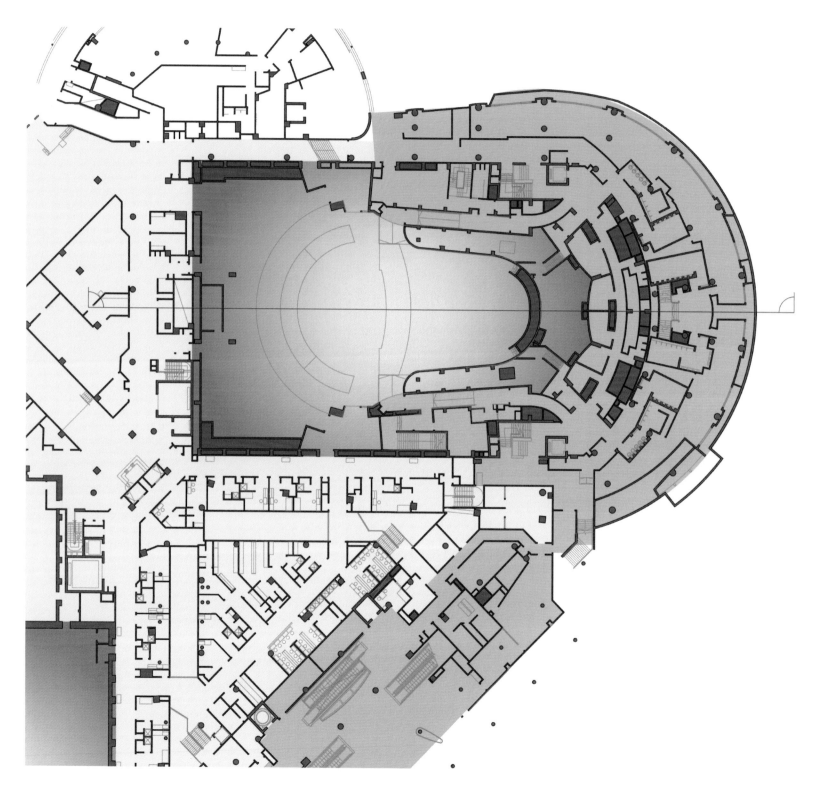

Esplanade – Theatres on the Bay, Singapore, comparative plan

0   5   10   20 metres

1:500

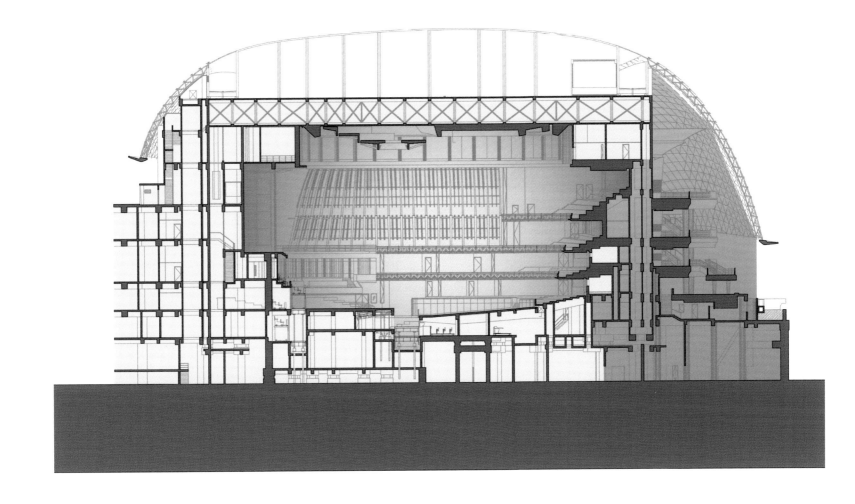

Esplanade – Theatres on the Bay, Singapore, comparative section

0   5   10   20 metres

1:500

Walt Disney Concert Hall

Walt Disney Concert Hall, 2003
Los Angeles, California, USA
Architect, Frank Gehry

Carl P. Giegold

"There is no 'there' there", wrote Gloria Steinem in the 1930s. Her lament about the lost Oakland neighbourhood of her childhood took on a life of its own over the next several decades, becoming a broader statement about the nature of mid-century California and perhaps LA in particular.

In the mid-1980s, LA was looking for a defining architectural landmark (one for the present day) at about the same time that its home team, the LA Philharmonic, was readying to remake itself artistically and awakening to the realization that its home venue was not up to the task. The emergence of the orchestra as a force for new music was concurrent with the design and construction of its new hall, so their stories are best understood when told together.

In the 1860s, Bunker Hill, in LA County, was a largely empty promontory, more of an obstacle to development than an invitation to it. Too steep to climb, it took the construction of the quaint Angel's Flight funicular to make it attractive to the moneyed. The neighbourhood's rise in society was similarly steep, its Victorian peak rather pointed, and its decline into disrespectability slow and relentless. By the mid-1950s, it was slated to go. In a particularly virulent spasm of urban renewal, the demolitionists didn't stop at the buildings but instead kept going until the entire hill had been reduced to more of a mound. A living neighbourhood was thus transformed into . . . not much, but the blank slate at least offered an invitation.

At the time, the LA Philharmonic was labouring away in Philharmonic Auditorium, which was definitely more the latter than the former. Dorothy Buffum Chandler – Stanford-educated, heir to a department store fortune, a director of the LA Times Mirror Company, and a formidable personality in the LA arts community – saw the need for a better place. She led the charge up the depleted hill to top it with Los Angeles Music Center in 1964. The LA Philharmonic and the newly formed LA Master Chorale took up residence in the new facility.

The Music Center was a great leap forward for LA's musical life, but comparisons to Lincoln Center were hard to avoid. It simply didn't present itself as something distinctly of its place, and the multipurpose pavilion that bears her name was never really up to the task of delivering orchestral sound to its audience, or even its orchestra, especially not one that would soon be ignited by a sea change in its executive and artistic leadership. Even before Esa-Pekka Salonen's arrival as Music Director, discussions had begun about the Music Center's missing link – a concert hall to serve as a proper home for the Philharmonic, the Master Chorale, and the still-new smaller ensembles, for which Chandler would have been grossly unsuited in acoustic as well as architectural intimacy.

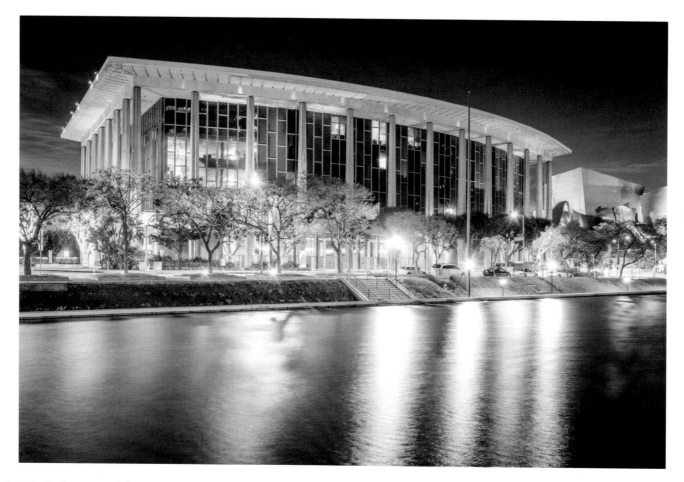

Los Angeles Music Center at night

In 1982, Ernest Fleischman, another powerful personality, began his tenure as General Manager of the LA Philharmonic, bringing a different idea about the nature of the orchestra as an organism. The title of his 1986 commencement address to the Cleveland Institute of Music speaks volumes all by itself: *"The Orchestra is dead. Long Live the Community of Musicians."* The LA Philharmonic's Chamber Music Society and New Music Group with its 'Green Umbrella' concert series had both already been established, drawing from the Philharmonic's community of musicians and pointing it in a decidedly new direction. Salonen made his debut as a guest conductor in 1984 at the age of 26, and his chemistry with the musicians was immediately apparent. Alex Ross of the *New York Times* years later spoke of "an individual and an institution bringing out unforeseen capabilities in each other." He was designated

Principal Guest Conductor in 1989 and became Music Director in 1992. The Philharmonic and Master Chorale were now flourishing as top-flight ensembles with new music in their core missions, distinctly different from the orchestras of the East Coast, but fettered by a venue that neither conveyed this adventurous bent nor delivered a satisfying experience for the musicians and audiences who gathered there.

In 1986, Lillian Disney announced her seminal $50 million gift toward the construction of a concert hall to be named after her late husband. The gift was expected to cover nearly all of the cost of the hall itself under the assumption that the County would separately fund construction of the parking structure beneath the concert hall and its surrounding plaza. Frank Gehry, seemingly against all odds, won the ensuing design competition over Gottfried Böhm, Hans Hollein, James Stirling, and Michael

Wilford. The commission was truly a surprise to Gehry – Ms. Chandler herself had personally assured him that he wouldn't win, and she had veto power over the selection – but it acknowledged that Gehry, the only local contender, was steeped in LA's arts scene, had already become an advocate for the musicians, and deeply understood Lillian Disney's objectives and sensibilities. Tokyo's Nagata Acoustics was selected as acoustician, and Theatre Projects Consultants was commissioned for theatre planning and engineering.

Fleischman advocated what was considered the more democratic 'vineyard' seating arrangement that places the stage more toward the middle of the audience than at the end of the room. The vineyard was pioneered by the acoustically-revered Philharmonie Berlin, a truly seminal hall that had opened in 1963 designed by architect Hans Scharoun and acoustician Lothar Cremer. In contrast to the rather rigid social hierarchy implied by the shoebox form with many of the seats distant from the action and/or overhung by balconies and side galleries, Berlin put everyone out in the open and, on average, closer to the platform. This resonated with Fleischman's community of musicians, gathering the community of audience more closely around it. Skilfully done, it had the potential to create a community of the whole.

Nagata's acoustic work across Japan was well known to the Western musicians and conductors who had toured there in the 1970s and 80s. Tokyo's Suntory Hall in particular had garnered notice for a lush sound in what is basically a rectangular room widened to increase the number of seats flanking the platform (and with a ceiling lifted almost verbatim from Berlin). The architectural idea was rendered in a more refined and organic manner in Sapporo's Kitara Hall, with substantial audience areas flanking the stage and a much-reduced distance to the farthest seat. The two rooms constituted a train of thought compatible with Fleischman's democratic community of music. Yasuhisa Toyota was designated the lead designer for Nagata.

"In the design of a concert hall, the acoustician lays down the rules and the designer then struggles to make architecture of his instructions", a statement perhaps playful, perhaps abject (perhaps both) that could

Hans Scharoun's Philharmonie Berlin

have been made over the last 60 years by any one of a number of architects exploring the concert hall form. These are Gehry's words, spoken in the context of Disney Hall. While a more satisfying aspiration might be a side-by-side exploration of aesthetics that are visually and acoustically symbiotic, Gehry's words do convey the oft-troubled 20th-century relationship between architecture for the ear and that for the eye. While there are wonderful examples to the contrary, the stereotype persists.

Indeed, the ebullient forms of Gehry's exterior are not entirely at peace with the voluptuous rigidity of the concert hall's interior. "Whatever Toyota wants, do it." Gehry, again. Far more influence of Nagata's earlier work in Sapporo is visible in this interior than of Gehry's, but then this was their first collaboration. The delightfully jumbled geometries of the rehearsal spaces in Miami's New World Center, which opened in 2011, suggest an architect and acoustician much more comfortable in their relationship. One can imagine wariness in LA's collaboration growing into friendship in Miami's.

Design and construction were not destined to go smoothly. The construction challenges of the form were clearly substantial, and the roll-out of CATIA software as a tool for complex architectural forms was fraught (it was developed by France's military for the design of aircraft). Seismic requirements changed following the Northridge earthquake, complicating the structural design process. Delay-induced inflation took its toll. By the summer of 1994, the expected cost had more than tripled (the parking structure funded by public bonds was another $100 million still), the private funds simply were not there, and trust amongst the strong wills within the project team was at a low ebb. LA County halted the project, and it would be four years before enough had been raised to restart construction. In the interim, Eli Broad, chairman of the Disney Hall oversight board, questioned Gehry's ability to complete the project. Gehry wrote a letter of withdrawal from the project. Lillian Disney's daughter, Diane Disney Miller, intervened to ensure that

Walt Disney Concert Hall, exterior

Gehry remained, reaffirming the Disney family's commitment to both the building and its architect.

As if in defiance of this turmoil, the Philharmonic and the Master Chorale continued to advance professionally and artistically with Fleischman, Salonen, and Paul Salamunovich (of the Master Chorale) in charge. Salonen's *L.A. Variations* premiered about halfway through the delay. The composition, dedicated to and showcasing the Philharmonic's own musicians, might be construed as a pointed question about the fate of the dormant construction site right next door. The energy of the ensembles was undeniable and only reinforced the imperative for a building of the same calibre, surely playing a role in propelling the project past all of its obstacles.

The hall was finally completed in 2003 at a cost of $274 million (including the garage), following a six-month commissioning period in which the orchestra adapted to the profoundly different acoustics of its new home. Opening night was a triumph, having built upon the musicians' enthusiasm about the hall and their delight with the extent to which the design team had accommodated their day-to-day life in the building, not just their moments on the platform.

One has to admire the simple confidence of Disney's completely fixed volume with the barest scraps of variable absorption in the upper corners of the room compared to the heroic variability of reverberation chambers and concrete overstage canopies found in halls such as Verizon, Myerson, and Birmingham, variability that, in some cases, challenges institutional

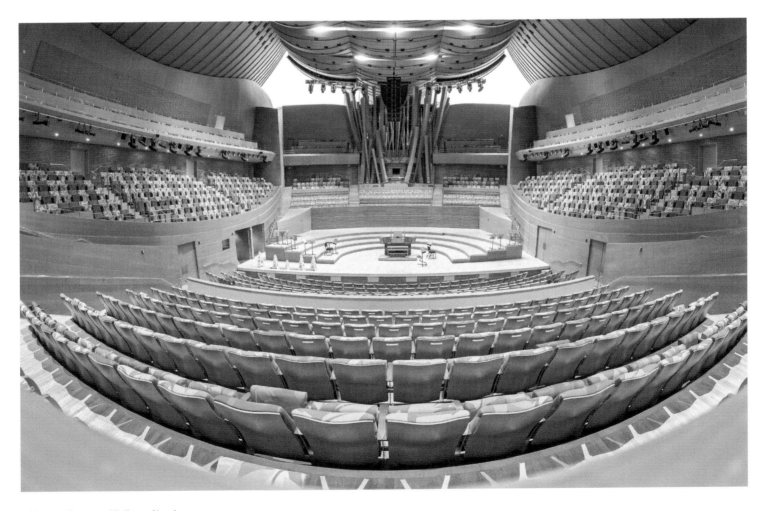

Walt Disney Concert Hall, auditorium

memory as operational personnel come and go. The fixed volume avoids the challenge completely.

In designing the Philharmonie, Scharoun discussed the gathering of musical audiences in circles "as at all times" – the central performer surrounded by an appreciative audience found in all manner of images captured through paintbrush, pen, and camera over the ages. The ready assembly of onlookers in a circle around a street musician is evidence enough of the naturalness of the relationship between artist and audience.

In fact, one can make the case that the structural limitations of masonry, timber, and wrought iron led concert halls of the 18th and 19th centuries to grow longer rather than wider as orchestral music grew in popularity and audiences grew in size, forcing a departure from the natural circular relationship as the last rows grew increasingly distant from the performers. Unfortunately for the traditional circle, composers had the acoustics of these longer, narrower rooms in their minds as they worked. In essence, the music and the shoebox grew up together, and much of the classical canon relies on the narrowness of the shoebox for the music to be heard as the composers heard it.

Berlin's platform is well toward the center of the room, but the circles are rendered in straight rows arranged in rather jagged, tectonic plates. While the audience is indeed arranged around a platform, the circles Scharoun sought to evoke are most readily seen by those charitably inclined to see them.

By contrast, the seating geometry of Disney evokes the circle almost literally, with a sense of embrace that offers a view not just across the hall but also of one's neighbours a few seats down the row. From most places in the hall, it is easy to feel a part of the concentric gathering around the performers, and the effect is warm, social, and satisfying.

Disney's acoustics are well-regarded. Nagata's emphasis on early energy – the earliest reflections to arrive after the direct sound along the line of sight – is well-documented. "He had one rule," says Gehry partner Craig Webb: "Within 80 milliseconds after the concert sound first hits your ear, you need to hear three reflections off three different surfaces of the hall." The hall's ample acoustic volume yields the required reverberation even though that reverberation is not particularly lush by the

standard of the shoebox, but the clarity and transparency resulting from this attention to the earliest reflections yielded acoustics particularly favourable to *ensemble* – the ability of performers to hear each other and themselves while bathed in the whole of the orchestra's sound. Transparency and clarity also lend themselves to the musical detail of the late 20th and early 21st centuries, music in which the LA Philharmonic chamber and Green Umbrella programs are a powerful compositional and performative force.

Anecdotally, visiting musicians citing the hall as a favourite place to play sometimes make the distinction between Disney's acoustics and the experience *in toto*, with the highest compliments reserved for the latter. This bears emphasis: an 'all of us together' experience that celebrates the performers and audience as a community transcends the 'us and them' experience of a traditional shoebox, precisely Fleischman's goal. The designers did not emphasize recreating shoebox acoustics in a vineyard but instead created a venue for musicians and audiences in which the acoustics are allowed to depart from the norm in service of a compelling overall aural/visual/social experience. Disney is not the first to do this, but its excellent sound in an environment that captures such a strong sense of communal experience places it as a benchmark building for projects seeking the same ends.

On the other hand, it is difficult to control a complex form sufficiently to deliver the mandated three early reflections without also delivering unwanted ones elsewhere in the room. For example, from certain vantage points, solo piano is troubled by reflections either too late or from confusing directions. Further, the reflection structure of a room looks entirely different when the source is a loudspeaker 25 feet in the air rather than a musician seated down on the platform. The walls and soffits that serve the orchestra so well, and the lack of retractable absorption to tame the most difficult of them, make the room difficult for amplification. As amplified sound plays a greater and greater role in the life of rooms for orchestra, do such designed-in difficulties do the room a disservice?

In fact, this shortcoming points up a central conundrum of the vineyard form: the grouping of audience around a central stage while embedding surfaces critical to the orchestral experience within that audience

Walt Disney Concert Hall, platform and organ

vastly complicates the delivery of high-quality amplified sound through-out the audience. There is not yet a vineyard that has mastered the challenge, leaving some ground for further exploration and refinement.

Disney nevertheless seems an excellent fit with its resident ensembles. The LA Philharmonic's debut in the building was triumphant (and a testament to allowing an orchestra sufficient time to adapt to the sound of its new building before opening night). The hall has proved a crisp, clear environment for new music offerings, and it presents itself as an example of the power of a distinct experience of music that draws from the primal form of gathering while celebrating acoustics that depart from the traditional.

As part of the package, LA got its 'there'. The Music Center was long established as an arts venue, but Disney gave it an iconic architectural identity and demonstrated LA's commitment to architectural exploration for LA's own sake, catalysing the further development of an extraordinary arts campus. It gave one of the country's most prominent and accomplished orchestras a venue of equal calibre and arguably consummated the Philharmonic's generational transition from the age of Mehta and Giulini to that of Salonen and Dudamel. It traces the path of a powerful idea through the improbable landscape of ego, finance, and politics. And in its success as a *place*, it makes us think differently about the future of performance space architecture.

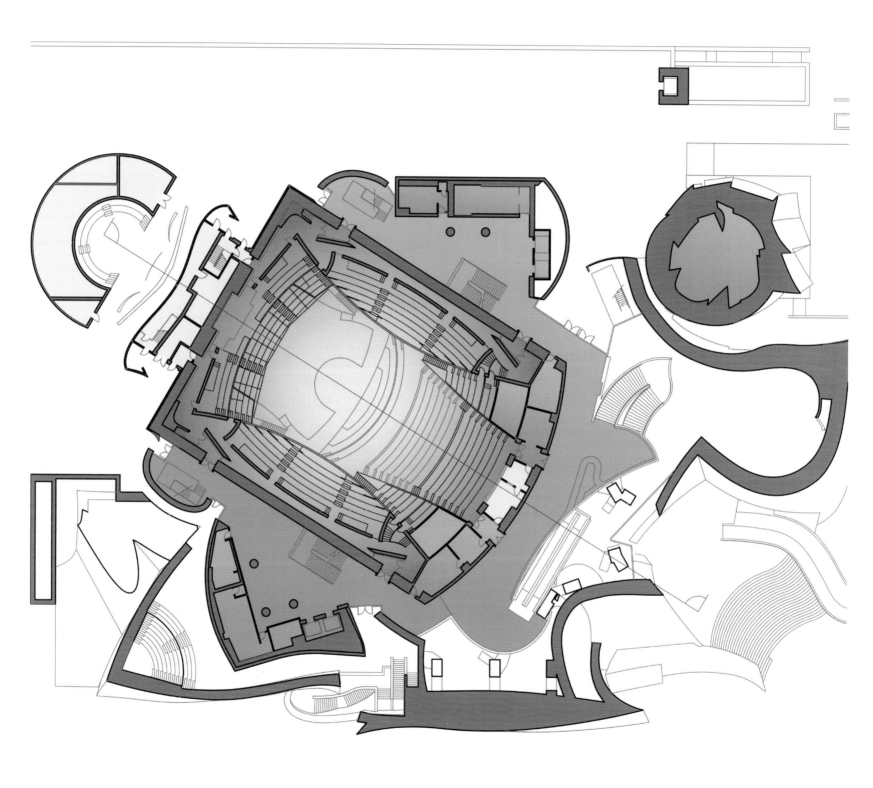

Walt Disney Concert Hall, Los Angeles, comparative plan

0   5   10   20 metres

1:500

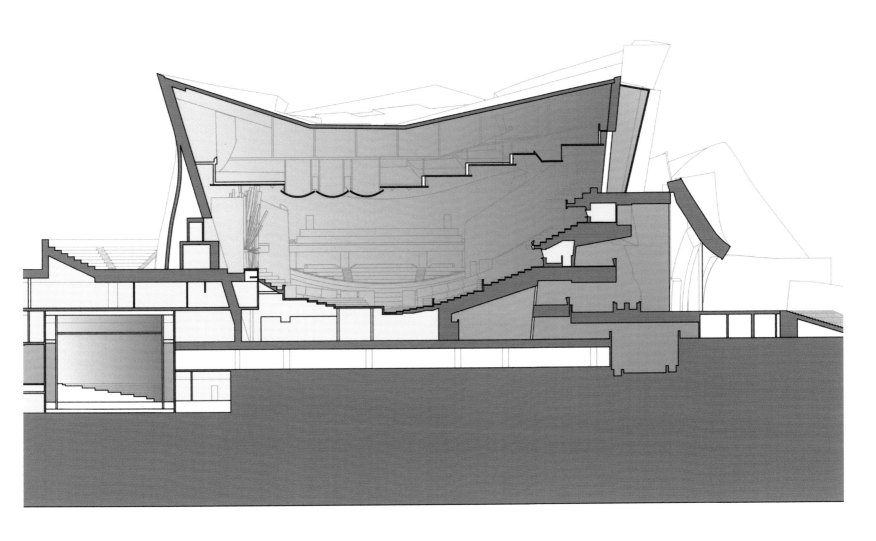

Walt Disney Concert Hall, Los Angeles, comparative section

0   5   10   20 metres

1:500

KÀ Theatre, the Sand Cliff deck tilted and rotated

KÀ Theatre, 2004
MGM Grand Hotel, Las Vegas, NV, USA
Architect, Marnell Corrao Associates and Cirque du Soleil
David Barbour

The KÀ Theatre: Cirque du Soleil's Vegas Apex

The years 1993–2013 constitute the reign of Cirque du Soleil on the Las Vegas Strip. During these decades, the Montreal-based troupe opened eight attractions: *Mystère*, *O*, *Zumanity*, *KÀ*, *The Beatles LOVE*, *Criss Angel BeLIEve*, *Viva ELVIS*, and *Michael Jackson ONE*. These spectacles, each of which created a highly conceptual framework for typical Cirque acts – jugglers, aerialists, and clowns, among others – introduced a new form of entertainment to the city, virtually replacing such old-fashioned showgirl spectacles as *Jubilee!*, and providing robust competition to the headliner shows that were previously the Strip's basic form of entertainment. Such shows required dedicated showrooms.

Founded in 1984 by Guy Laliberté and Gilles Ste-Croix – at the time, a pair of street performers – Cirque du Soleil (CDS) transformed the traditional Ringling Brothers format of touring tent shows, dispensing with animal acts and creating high-concept productions that often feature (however obliquely) narratives, characters, and original musical scores. The company broke through in the American market in 1990 with *Nouvelle Expérience*, which reframed the circus as a chic entertainment suitable for adults as well as children. A quantum leap was made in 1993 with the opening of *Mystère* at Treasure Island in Las Vegas; CDS' first sit-down spectacle, it is still running today. The touring shows have always been staged in the Grand Chapiteau, the company's version of a big top. By contrast, the stage of *Mystère*'s venue is 120' by 70', with a number of lifts built into the deck, including one, 36' in diameter, that comes complete with a 28' revolving stage.

After the success of *Mystère*, CDS continued to populate the Strip with additional attractions, each of which posed new theatre-design challenges. As opposed to many other buildings described in these pages, these venues are not stand-alone architectural achievements; although their interiors are designed to be attractive and comfortable, with good sightlines and acoustics, each is intended to house a single show and is shaped around unique technical requirements. *O*, *Mystère*'s immediate successor, in residence at the Bellagio since 1998, requires a 1.5 million gallon tank for its water-based spectacle. Not every show is on this scale: *The Beatles LOVE*, a relatively intimate piece, at The Mirage, is known for its complex surround-sound system, for the delivery of remixes, by Sir George Martin, of classic Beatles tunes.

The apex of ambition for CDS in Las Vegas was *KÀ*, at the MGM Grand. *KÀ* wraps its visual astonishments around the odyssey of twin siblings lost in a kind of mythical landscape and the technical challenges it posed were mind-boggling. As John Huntington wrote in *Lighting&Sound America's* April 2005 issue, "There is no stage in *KÀ*. There is, simply, a huge pit, from which enormous performance spaces rise, descend, track, lift, and swivel." The scenic elements were conceptualized by the late Mark Fisher, the show's production and theatre designer. Huntington added,

> The enormous 50' x 25' Sand Cliff Deck [which weighs 80,000lb] is actuated by the Gantry Lift . . . a mechanism you'd be more likely to see in an aluminium smelting plant than a theatre. [It] can rotate the Sand Cliff Deck 360° at 2RPM (which is 12° per second), tilt it from flat up 100° (beyond vertical), and track the whole thing up and down vertically nearly 70' at 2' per second . . . The Gantry Lift mechanism itself tracks on two enormous 4'-diameter steel tubes that run from the lowest floor of the building to the roof.

"... A massive 6'-diameter cross tube, called the 'torque tube', connects the two hammerheads," says [former head of automation for *KÀ* James] Tomlinson "which are guided by 75- and 150-ton capacity Hilman rollers traveling on steel wear plates on the columns" . . . Perpendicularly attached to the center of the torque tube is an arm which goes out,

KÀ, performers on the Sand Cliff deck

toward the audience, to a pivot joint called the "wrist," which, according to Tomlinson, "includes a 10'-diameter Rotek bearing typically used in tower cranes," and connects to the Sand Cliff Deck itself . . . "The whole torque tube assembly and arm gets lifted", says [McLaren engineering president Malcolm] McLaren, "by what we understand to be the longest cylinders in North America—a 70' stroke. When they are fully extended, the cylinders are 145' long."

The contracting of the Sand Cliff Deck required a construction design and fabrication team from six different disciplines and included superstructure fabrication, hydraulics, piping, control interface, deck fabrication, integrated peg system and onboard performer access ports, integrated theatrical lighting and dimming, and interactive video deck sensors. Tom Neville, of theatre consultancy Auerbach Pollock Friedlander, led the final coordination of the contractor construction team during the final phase of implementation for MGM.

"The 30' by 30' 75,000lb Tatami deck . . . is supported by a 65'-long two-stage 'drawer slide' mechanism, which is tilted at a 4° rake toward the audience from its anchorage upstage, with 45' 6" of cantilever," Huntington added. "The Tatami deck and mechanism are actuated by 75 and 150 HP electric motors."

KÀ, the Tatami Deck, view from below

The KÀ Theatre is the former home of *EFX*, a spectacle starring Michael Crawford (and, later, David Cassidy), which, in retrospect, can be seen as a kind of bridge between old-style Vegas spectacles and the later Cirque extravaganzas. To accommodate *KÀ*'s engineering feats, the original building was reduced to a shell and a completely new theatre and lobby put in its place.

Fisher's theatre design was executed in collaboration with architect Marnell Corrao Associates, theatre consultant Auerbach Pollock Friedlander (APF), acoustician firm Pelton Marsh Kinsella, production manager Stéphane Mongeau, technical directors Paul Bates and Matthew Whelan, vice-president/production Gabriel Pinkstone, and senior supervisor/theatre projects Don MacLean, among others. Architectural lighting was designed and specified by Auerbach Glasow.

S. Leonard "Len" Auerbach, principal in charge for Auerbach Pollock Friedlander, makes particular note of the strong collaboration among the design team (Cirque du Soleil, Fisher, Marnell Corrao, and the MGM Design Center) as being one of the most creative relationships he has experienced.

Perhaps the biggest challenge of the project was the 50'-deep cavity that is filled with the moving elements described above and replaces a conventional stage. According to Neville, a basement was already in place from the building's previous life, but, he adds, "A fair bit of excavation was required for the gantry lifting columns."

The process began with the removal of the floor area of the stage, creating an abyss housing the five stage lifts, resulting in a total of 4,950 sq. ft. of flexible staging area. The theatre's configuration was altered from a cabaret space, with booths, tables, and chairs, to a theatre that seats 1,951. A new set of catwalks and grid decking over the seating area was added for performer access and front-of-house lighting and technical systems.

The control booth was reconfigured to allow space for the production's extensive lighting, audio, projection, and automation controls. It features 2,850 sq. ft. of space and 170 linear feet of glass.

The building's infrastructure had to be totally reworked to accommodate the new production. All spaces were connected with sound, video, and communications from the stage area. New structural supports were added for the automated rigging system, including an 82'-long hoist-support structure in the arbor pit as well as a 37'-long "battle-hoist" structure on the grid. New company switches were distributed throughout the theatre, for chain hoists, special effects, and specialty gear. A new multi-tiered rigging system was developed at the grid level.

Three high-speed data and communications networks were installed, to ensure that the automation, lighting, and hydraulic systems could function separately and be synchronized. Each system is provided with a minimum RAID-1 shared-drive array to help guarantee system redundancy.

APF developed an infrastructure for the stage machinery, using Cirque's criteria. These included the five stage lifts and 40 individual counterweight-assist automated hoists mounted in the arbor pit area; these automate the operation of lighting pipes, special effects, curtains, and scenic elements. Five 1,000kg specialty hoists were designed for flying human scenery in a circular path over the audience; six 1,000kg specialty hoists handle large scenic transitions.

An additional 16 high-speed acrobatic hoists are used for flying performers and human scenery in a dynamic encounter sequence involving several performers in a choreographed vertical fight scene interacting with the upright Sand Cliff Deck. Each performer controls his or her own hoists via a wireless controller integrated into the costume. One can travel up or down at a maximum of 4' per second. Eighteen high-speed mooring hoists enable the rapid deployment of the safety nets used in the battle sequence. Eighty high-speed scenic pegs are actuated from within the Sand Cliff Deck.

In addition, the theatre's fly tower was rerigged with manual and counterweight-assist line sets. The working areas over the stage and audience were equipped to support motorized sport winches. The lighting system features 40 universes of DMX that can be mixed to any of the 100 double-networked taps distributed throughout the theatre. The system also includes 60 portable nodes, all using power over Ethernet ports. Five wireless data access points were put in place, allowing use of

KÀ, the pageant

handheld wireless remotes and/or a remote wireless notebook for console video displays anywhere in the theatre.

All network equipment was designed to be housed in nine racks interconnected with three fully redundant fiber optic backbones. All network switches/hubs are included for all taps and nodes. Card racks were also located in the racks for use of touch screens for network, house, and worklight controls, and network video distribution electronics for touch-screen feeds. The racks also included space for system file servers and rack-mount consoles. Remote colour touch screens, in both fixed and portable configurations, were located throughout the theatre for use by stage managers and lighting technicians to control cue lights, rehearsal lights, and to view remote stage video feeds.

In addition to a front-of-house sound system to control 144 sources in 184 matrix outputs and a stage monitoring system with a 112 x 80 matrix, an LCS Virtual Room Acoustics Systems (VRAS, now known as Constellation by Meyer Sound) was installed to enhance and augment room acoustics, providing real-time ability to alter reverberation times

KÀ Theatre, seating with integrated loudspeakers

and delay characteristics as needed. APF's principal audio designer Paul Garrity worked with CDS sound designer Jonathan Deans to create an aural experience that seamlessly fits the production's dynamic aesthetic. Customized chairs, by Irwin Seating, "were critical to the integration of a stereo pair of loudspeakers for each patron concealed in the back of each seat," Garrity says.

In addition to an innovative, interactive projection system for the show, more than 25 production fixed-focus and remote-controllable colour video cameras are routed through a modulated video system for monitoring performers, musicians, and critical backstage systems.

The theatre's lighting was designed to usher audiences into the world of *KÀ*. Guests enter from the casino into a dark, low-ceilinged space with lights the colour of glowing embers. Large tree trunks, banded with lights, mark the edge of the main lobby, where the ceiling soars to expose the full height of a wall, which appears to be an inverted, ancient ship's hull. Coloured light plays on the surface of the vessel wall. Before the performance, musicians located in the trees play the strings of a giant harp.

Openings in the vessel wall lead to the concession counters and public restrooms. These spaces have an industrial feel, with metallic painted finishes and glow acrylic panels in the ceiling, walls, and fronts of the counters. Fluorescent strips with dimming ballasts and T8 lamps were mounted so as to be visible behind the acrylic panels. Entering the audience chamber from the lobby, one passes through a sheet of saturated blue light into a glowing blue entry vestibule. In the audience chamber, fixtures are integrated into the post-and-beam catwalk structure, which extends into the audience from the stage wall, while other units are mounted to the technical catwalks above the house.

Upon opening, *KÀ* was a sensation; looking back, it probably represents the height of success for CDS in Las Vegas. *The Beatles LOVE*, which came next, opened to acclaim and sell-out houses, but *Criss Angel BeLIEve*, at Luxor, which attempted to integrate the well-known magician into a typical Cirque show, was poorly received and had a relatively short run of eight years. (That this figure might be considered disappointing is a measure of CDS' extraordinary success—and, perhaps, of each show's enormous cost.) At ARIA, *Viva ELVIS*, a tribute to the entertainer who many see as the patron saint of Las Vegas, ran only three years.

KÀ Theatre, auditorium viewed from lighting position

Michael Jackson ONE has been in residence since 2013 at Mandalay Bay. Since then, the city's ethos, which changes every few years, has shifted toward attracting a demographic of millennials via a series of ever-more-spectacular nightclubs and discos that offer a rather more participatory form of entertainment.

The lasting legacy of *KÀ* is the proliferation of other showroom extravaganzas, most of them in Asia and the Mideast, which also make huge demands on the buildings that house them. *The House of Dancing Water*, which opened in 2010 at the City of Dreams, a resort in Macau, was directed by Franco Dragone, who previously staged a number of CDS shows. Expanding on the scale of *O*, it features the world's largest commercial pool, which is 26' deep and 160' in diameter, holding 3.7 million gallons. It also features 11 stage elevators that rise up to provide the pool with a solid floor. The theatre, designed to look like the inside of a red Chinese lantern, is the fruit of collaboration between scenic and theatre designer Michel Crête, architect Li Chung Pei, and Brian Hall, theatre designer with Theatre Projects.

The Han Show, which opened in Wuhan, China, in 2014, serves as the anchor of a retail and business district, with a theme park nearby. The building, designed by Mark Fisher and his firm Stufish Entertainment Architects with theatre consulting services by Theatre Projects and acoustician Jaffe Holden, is, according to Sharon Stancavage, writing in *LSA's* April 2015 issue,

> a 361' [110m]-diameter cylinder modeled after the traditional Chinese image of the red lantern. It is 71.6m (235') high from the ground to the highest outside point, and 28.5 (84.6') from the ground to the lower basement . . . Prominent on the building's exterior are 18,000 red "bi" discs measuring .78m (2'7")

in diameter each. "The bi disk is a popular artefact [from the Han Dynasty] in China," [Stufish architect Jenny] Melville says . . . the exterior of the theatre is essentially a dimmable low-resolution LED wall.

This is another water show. In this case, however,

> During the performance, while the audience is in place, the seating reconfigures to reveal the performance basin. The orchestra-level seating splits along the centreline and two swing-seat platforms pivot, revealing the performance basin downstage of the dry stage. The balcony lowers into place between the swing seats to complete a thrust configuration, with all seats at the same level around the performance basin and just above water level.

Also featured are three robotic arms on which are mounted 7m by 11m LED screens, each weighing four tons. Each arm has six axes of movement, allowing the screens to been seen in different arrays.

Other attractions of this type include *The Dai Show*, in Southwestern China, designed by Fisher/Stufish in collaboration with theatre consultants Auerbach Pollock Friedlander and acousticians Jaffe Holden, and, in Dubai, *La Perle*, another Dragone show, with a theatre designed by Dragone in collaboration with theatre/show designer Jean Rabasse, architects Khatib and Alami, and consultants Auerbach Pollock Friedlander.

The performance style exemplified by Cirque du Soleil and its successors did not exist at the beginning of the era covered in this book, which spans the years 1950–2020. Indeed, such spectacles were not technically possible six decades ago even if someone had imagined them. The contemporary circus format, which came onto the scene in the 1970s, was destined to burst the boundaries of the traditional circus tent or Grand

Chapiteau, demanding purpose-built theatres designed for individual, very long-running productions.

These complex, expensive, and spectacular shows have been enormously successful (At one time, Cirque du Soleil was the largest theatrical producer in the world). They have spread to many countries, but will they continue? The future of this form of entertainment is unclear; if it begins to fade away, however, it leaves behind an extraordinary legacy, as well as a place in show business history alongside such famed venues as New York's Hippodrome, along with a legion of technical innovations that are likely to appear in other forms of entertainment.

Update February 2021

The COVID-19 pandemic severely affected the performing arts. On 19th March 2020 Cirque du Soleil announced that its 44 shows worldwide would be suspended and over 4,600 employees were temporarily laid off. CDS subsequently filed for bankruptcy protection from which it emerged in November 2020.

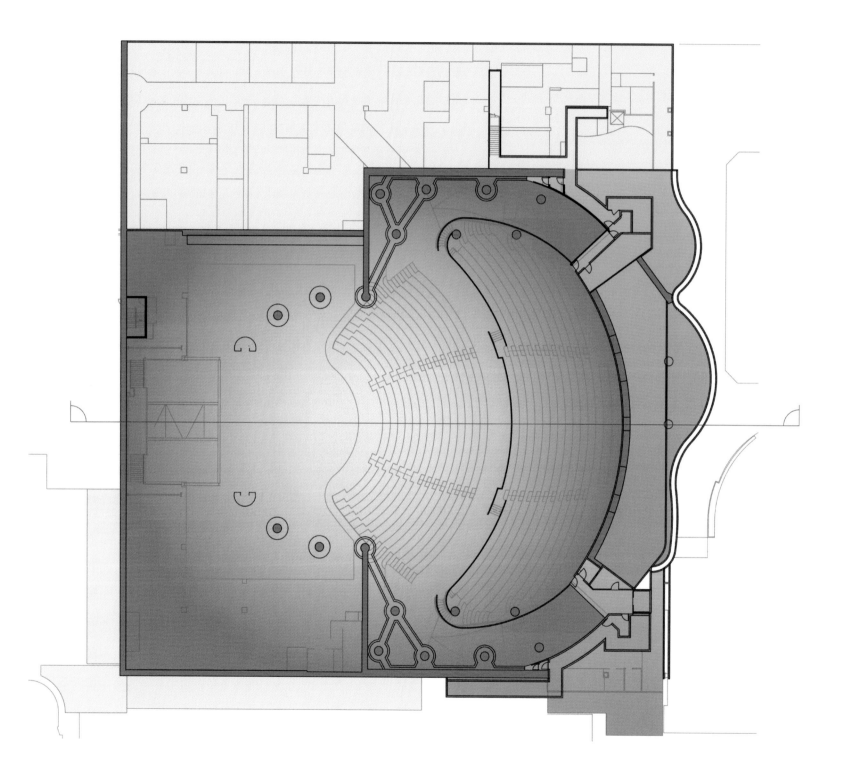

KÀ Theatre, Las Vegas, comparative plan

0   5   10   20 metres

1:500

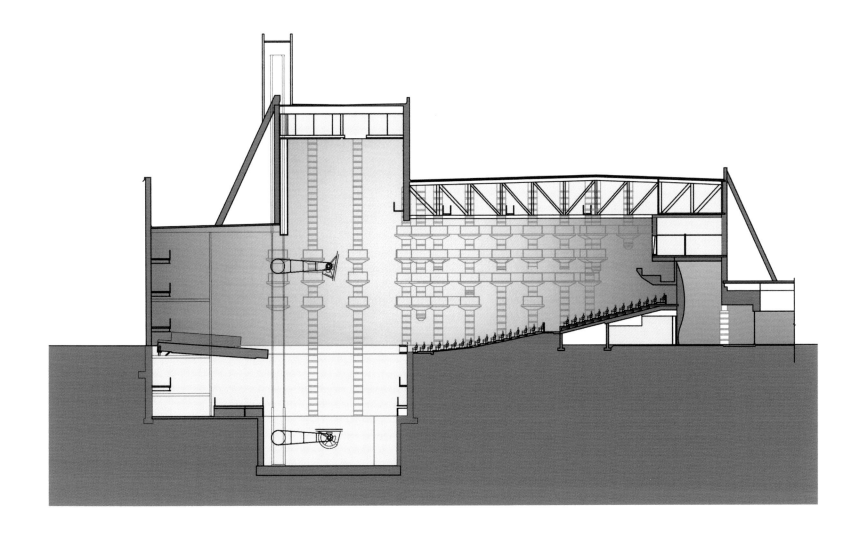

KÀ Theatre, Las Vegas, comparative section

0   5   10   20 metres

1:500

Matsumoto Performing Arts Centre (MPAC) exterior

Matsumoto Performing Arts Centre, 2004
Matsumoto, Japan
Architect, Toyo Ito

Shozo Motosugi

Matsumoto is a mid-sized Japanese city of around 240,000 people located in Nagano Prefecture about 220 km East of Tokyo. It is perhaps best known for the extraordinary Matsumoto Castle, one of five castles designated as 'National Treasures of Japan' and with the oldest remaining castle donjon (or keep). Construction commenced in 1592 and the city developed around it as a 'Castle Town'.

The city had one of the first community schools developed in the region, the Kyu-Kaichi gakko (established in 1876 with contributions from the local people). With many famous summer resorts and hot springs nearby, the town has always been proud of its rich culture. Many highly-educated persons were also born here.

Matsumoto is also the birthplace for the Suzuki Method of music education. Invented by Shinichi Suzuki, the Method encourages music education from the earliest age and has taught millions to play musical instruments.

The Saito Kinen Festival Masumoto was started in 1992 by renowned conductor Seiji Ozawa as a tribute to the magnificent musician and educator Hideo Saito. Saito had been a close friend of Shinichi Suzuki since their school days in Germany and was the teacher of Seiji Ozawa. Operas and various concerts are performed at facilities throughout the city during this festival, which lasts about one month each summer. In 2015, the festival was renamed the Seiji Ozawa Matsumoto Festival (OMF), to mark a new stage in its evolution.

Matsumoto has a rich cultural and music heritage that was poorly served by the inadequate civic auditorium which had opened in 1985 with a concert hall seating 693 with pipe organ and various teaching rooms. The hall had poor facilities, a small stage, unsatisfactory acoustics, poor dressing and rehearsal rooms. The inadequacies of the hall and the needs of the Festival increased pressure for a new theatre.

The City decided to construct a new building and an architectural competition was planned. The brief was for a flexible theatre able to accommodate staged performances of opera, ballet or other events along with the capability to present classical music and symphony concerts. The brief also required a second, smaller theatre and the ancillary spaces required for rehearsal, opera production and to support the performance spaces.

A site was identified adjacent to the old civic hall. Between the hall and the street there was a small square, and an old pond. However, the initial site was not large enough and it was a very odd shape. The site is over 200m long and around 30m wide and is further constrained by a huge old tree that public pressure demanded be retained.

Ten practices entered the architectural competition which Toyo Ito won with a bold plan that reconciled both the brief and the site by adopting a highly creative approach.

Theatres and opera houses have traditionally been symmetrical, axial buildings. The front entrance was typically set in the centre of the front façade. Once into the foyers they were often symmetrically arranged around a grand staircase. The foyers and staircase gave access symmetrically to the auditorium which, with the stage sat resolutely on the axial centre line. Post-war theatres in Asia, the Americas and Europe have largely moved away from this symmetrical and axial approach.

The site virtually precluded such a rigid axial arrangement and Toyo Ito seized the opportunity to create a unique route into and through the building. In his initial draft, the concept proposed lifting a large floor slab to create a new landform below the slab. He was planning to use that rolling landform to create the auditorium and other spaces where people would gather for various purposes. He presented a multi-layered public space in which any spot could become a theatre. The big upper slab would be a flat roof garden open to the sky, and the small lower ground would be full of variety and linked with the town.

The eventual concept created a sequence; a staircase from the entrance rises to an intermediate level where a wide square called

Theatre Park, is open to the public for daily use. Usually, this is a quiet contemplative spot. During festivals or other special events shops in the town open stalls and events like street performances are held here. It is used in various ways as if it were a square in front of a church. The small theatre is also located on this level. The stair continues to rise, passes the stage, enters the foyers and thence to the main auditorium. The main auditorium and stage effectively turn their backs on the public entrance. The staircase continues to a large roof garden and a rehearsal room which can be used for small-scale performances. The rehearsal room has an openable wall allowing it to link to the roof garden and events can be presented in both spaces.

The audience route into the auditorium is a journey through the building unlike the linear approach of many theatres. The staircase follows the curving wall of the building around the stage and side stage to the theatre foyer from where audiences can enter the auditorium.

The logic of public circulation in this theatre is similar to that in the Sydney Opera House. The stage is located on the approach side so that audiences pass around the stage and stage side, make a detour around the auditorium to the foyer which is found after walking up gentle stairs. Both theatres conceal from visitors the bulk and blank walls of the stages as they pass around and into the foyers. The organization of each of the two buildings is markedly different. The stage in Sydney is set about 10 metres higher than the ground level, and the rehearsal rooms, dressing rooms, etc. are arranged below the stage level. In Matsumoto (MPAC) the stage and dressing rooms are arranged on the ground level, and the rehearsal rooms are located above the side stage. The location of spaces in the Sydney Opera House is severely limited by the external shaped "sails" which taper and reduce in size as the building rises. Matsumoto has limited site dimensions but greater freedom in the placement of support spaces. By lifting the public circulation above the backstage spaces, Matsumoto solves the conflict between the two differing activities – public and stage.

The auditorium and stage return to the more conventional architectural language used in an interesting manner. They are symmetrical and axial, and the auditorium has a large stalls or orchestra section

Toyo Ito, architect for Matsumoto Performing Arts Centre

Matsumoto Performing Arts Centre, Toyo Ito plot plan

with a series of narrow galleries stacked above at both the rear and down the sides of the room. The auditorium and stage are planned to accommodate a wide range of performances; not only opera, ballet, musicals and concerts but also Japanese Kabuki theatre.

The first thing performers want to check in a theatre is the stage. It is quite natural for them to see the physical space on which they will act, sing, or play music but they rapidly look out into the auditorium to check how it "feels". How can architects design a space which makes the performers smile as soon as they look at it, and give them an incentive to perform? What kind of theatre can encourage the performers and make them say "Yes, this is the place?" Matsumoto achieves this magic.

Similarly, for the audience as they move from the foyer into the auditorium the space should thrill and amaze them. An auditorium is a place where strangers meet to share a (hopefully) moving and engaging performance. A space where there is a conversation between performer and audience members and between the audience themselves. In a

Matsumoto Performing Arts Centre, aerial view

Japanese context, a space where audience members can bow to each other or quietly acknowledge the other. A great auditorium should raise audience expectations.

Matsumoto succeeds in creating a large (1,800 seat) theatre that works for both performer and audience. From the stage a performer immediately sees and is embraced by the multiple levels of balcony seating extending down the side walls and almost reaching the stage. The performer would feel at the centre and enfolded by the audience. The balconies are slightly inclined toward the stage. This makes the sight-lines better and hides the ceiling of the balcony seats when

Matsumoto Performing Arts Centre, stairs from entrance hall to main foyer

viewed from the stage. Thus, the close contact between the audience and the performers becomes more significant. The theatre successfully creates a wonderful auditorium space that does not compromise the performance and draws the audience's attention to the play, whilst providing a stagy and brilliant atmosphere before the performance starts.

From the stage, performers would notice the color gradation of the seats and walls of the auditorium. The seats are covered with polka-dotted fabric, and the colours gradually change from dark red to bright pink as they go from the stage side to the rear side of the auditorium. Seen by the audience, the colours become darker closer to the stage, becoming almost black near the stage. Ten kinds of patterns are used for

Matsumoto Performing Arts Centre, roof garden and rehearsal room

the seat fabric and arranged at random, which makes the entire appearance very natural.

Another challenge for MPAC's design was finding ways to vary the seating capacity. The maximum capacity is 1,800 seats with a need to occasionally reduce to about 1,000 seats for drama productions. The space and acoustic environment must also be suitable for orchestra concerts. The seating capacity can be varied by vertically moving the entire ceiling of the auditorium, effectively closing off and hiding some of the highest balcony tiers and reducing the usable seating capacity.

As a result, the horseshoe-shaped auditorium with the five levels of balconies including the seats beside the orchestra pit were created. The maximum distance from the edge of the stage to the rearmost seats in the parquet circle is 30m, and that to the further-most seats is 34m.

Three rows of stage lighting bridges are attached to the ceiling of the auditorium. At the centre of the third row, a follow spot room is incorporated. The lighting bridges in the auditorium and side lighting positions are exposed to the auditorium to form part of the acoustic environment.

The orchestra pit can be raised to stage level to extend the stage/ platform into the auditorium for classical music concerts and the first lighting bridge on the stage is used as an acoustic reflector behind the orchestra. This makes the atmosphere more intimate. The orchestra pit lift can also be used as a forestage or lowered to create an orchestra pit. If positioned at auditorium floor level it can carry additional audience

Matsumoto Performing Arts Centre, main auditorium view from stage

seating. The sight lines from the stalls and balconies work to this forward stage edge.

This flexibility works well for Western operas and concerts and is also suitable for Japan's traditional Kabuki performances. For Kabuki, about 300 seats in the front area including the orchestra pit are removed, and the visitors are seated on floor cushions. Removing the seats considerably expands the performing area and allows the performers to move into the audience. Although this theatre is large, the audience are brought close to the stage.

The stage is generous, and the theatre has both a left side stage and rear stage. An additional "fit-up" theatre can be created on the stage by utilising the generous stage space. A set of retractable seats are housed in the rear wall of the rear stage. By sliding and pulling them out, a theatre with about 400 seats which uses the main stage from the opposite side appears. All the stage facilities – lighting, flying, sound, etc. can be used in this smaller theatre. On this occasion, the wall in the back of the stage left and the technical gallery contained therein laterally move to surround the auditorium so that a wall surface symmetric to the fixed wall surface on the stage right side can be framed.

To reach the seats in this theatre on the stage, generally, the audience can enter from the main lobby on the second floor and go down the auditorium tiers. For some performances in this on-stage theatre it isn't possible to enter through the auditorium and the audience are asked to enter from the delivery entrance and go up temporary stairs to the stage level. Some performances are even held in the foyers. The concept of "any place becomes a theatre" is thus cleverly planned and executed.

Sendai Mediatheque (2001), another project by Toyo Ito, was built three years before Matsumoto. Transparency was pursued in making the structure of Sendai Mediatheque. The concept was realised by weaving tube steel frames into nets to form multi-layered floors and cover them with the glass façade.

In designing MPAC, a different route to achieve transparency was pursued. Panels made of Glass-fiber Reinforced Cement (GRC) are used to cover almost the entire building. The GRC panels are inlaid with glass glazing in seven sizes and shapes. Owing to the variety of size and density of the inlaid glass, it appears as if ground water is bubbling, or sunlight filtering through trees. It is just amazing. This appearance seems to be representing the region, which is rich with water, or the place blessed by the trees of a shrine next to the theatre.

The design of Matsumoto places the stage at the centre of the site. Thus, the old tree was preserved, and a waterfront space was created on the south side where the original pond was located. Great public spaces were created, all linked by a gentle sinuous stair lit by glass panels set into the façade. Functionally, the scheme has multiple loading docks with good access and circulation is well integrated into the neighbourhood.

An earlier chapter in this book examined the Bunka Kaikan in Tokyo. Completed in 1961, it was one of the first post-war theatre buildings constructed in Japan. It was an innovative pioneering building setting out to create a flexible theatre that could be used for differing types of performance. Hundreds of theatre buildings have subsequently been created across Japan, many influenced by Bunka Kaikan.

MPAC was completed in 2004, some forty years after Bunka Kaikan. It is probably one of the most successful theatres, a very usable, attractive building with great public spaces achieved on an incredibly constrained site. It departs radically from the traditional formal symmetry of older theatre buildings. Unique public spaces are created both internally and externally, many of which can be used as temporary, improvised theatres or meeting places. An extraordinary sinuous wall provides both a sensual external elevation and one wall of the internal staircase penetrated by small irregular windows. It is amazing all this has been successfully realised on such a challenging site.

Modern architecture has sought after homogenisation and transparency. Plane and abstract spaces have been admired. Architects have made full use of geometry and the best combination in functions, accordingly. Functionality has been significantly improved with advice from theatre experts. Poor theatres with problems like the Sydney Opera

Matsumoto Performing Arts Centre, main theatre staging kabuki

House are rare today. Theatre people demand ever better theatres – demands that also produce better buildings for audiences. Rationality is necessary, but I do not think it creates an unprecedented drama, unexpected dramatic interpretation, or a unique stage. If a drama is established through a fight among the script, music, and actors, should the theatre as architecture also have some power to join the fight?

A theatre is not merely a place to present dramas. Too much listening to theatre people makes architecture boring. Too much enthusiastic architecture would spoil dramas. No creative, no theatre. Art can survive with something seemingly unnecessary or impossible. In that sense, theatre architecture should co-operate and compete, with the performance and audience.

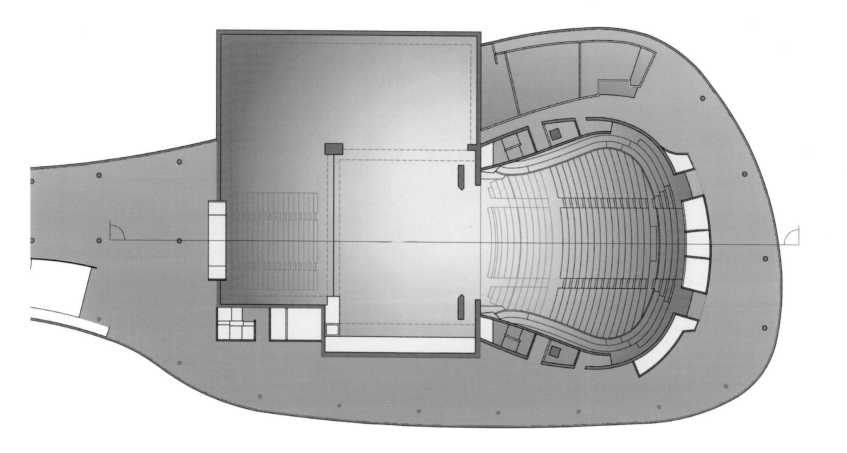

Matsumoto Performing Arts Centre, Matsumoto, comparative plan

1:500

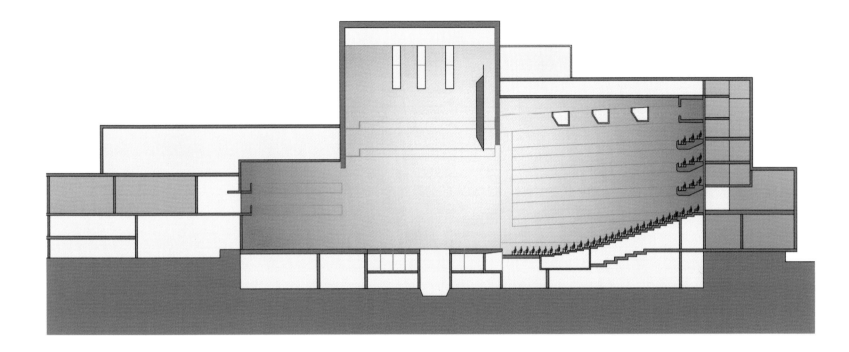

Matsumoto Performing Arts Centre, Matsumoto, comparative section

0   5   10   20 metres

1:500

Casa da Música, exterior

Casa da Música, 2005
Porto, Portugal
Architect, Office for Metropolitan Architecture (OMA)
Rem Koolhaas
Maria Rita Liberal Arnaut

Maybe I shouldn't finish it; maybe it is much more beautiful unfinished.

(Rem Koolhaas)

Porto is not really a city: it is a family. When some evil strikes, everyone feels it with the same intensity; when they desire something, they all desire it at the same time.

(João Pinheiro Chagas, journalist and politician, 1863–1925)

It was in Portugal, pioneer of globalisation, in its second largest city, Porto, that the most iconic artistic and architectonic project of a country was born, reverberating in the rest of the world: Casa da Música.

The building and the artistic vision are inseparable. One can't exist without the other. The building itself is breathtaking – drawing in to question the esthetic sense of the "normal" – the artistic vision giving it life, elevating it. It is its soul.

A building with a polyhedron shape that brought a tremendous change to a city, and naturally became an atypical ambassador of its own country.

A building that evokes the role of the arts center within a metropolis. It forces us to rethink the definition of "viewer", since each observer is considered audience from any perspective. As itself, it is a piece of public art democratically contemplated by each person who encounters it.

Considered by the *New York Times* to be the Dutch architect Rem Koolhaas' most seductive work, Casa da Música catalyzed a discussion about the relationship between a building, an artistic project and its reason for being: the public.

The reason why Casa da Música was created is the essence of its success: to welcome people and bring them closer to Art. It is a human project.

In 2007, Casa da Música was awarded with the Royal Institute of British Architects (RIBA) prize and the jury classified it as an "intriguing, disturbing and dynamic" building.

Rather than struggle with the inescapable acoustic superiority of this traditional shape, the Casa da Música attempts to reinvigorate the traditional concert hall in another way: by redefining the relationship between the hollowed interior and the general public outside.

(Rem Koolhaas)

Within the scope of the candidacy of Porto to be the European Capital of Culture in 2001, the possibility arose to create a building dedicated entirely to music. At the core of Casa da Música's genesis lies a particular and historic preference of Porto's inhabitants: an innate appetite for music.

When the proposal for Casa da Música went from paper to reality, the Portuguese Government and Porto City Hall formed Porto 2001, a society whose main purposes would be to head a series of renovations of the city's cultural monuments and to assume the ambitious mission of edifying the project that would become Casa da Música.

Casa da Música, exterior, east side

Referring to the previous discussion about the type of building to design, Porto 2001 engaged in a great reflection about the artistic project at hand: to build a structure to welcome and inspire the main institutions dedicated to music in the region, and also be able to independently programme music ranging from the polyphonic to the contemporary. The building hosts all the renowned artistic projects of the city within the scope of music.

Currently, Casa da Música hosts the following five institutions:

- Porto Symphony Orchestra;
- Remix Ensemble (project dedicated to contemporary music creation);
- Baroque Orchestra;
- Casa da Música's Chorus;
- Children's Chorus.

With the exception of the last one, all of these institutions have great national and international recognition, with a particular focus on investment in Remix Ensemble, since this is Casa da Música's most distinctive project, *"our star"* according to Paulo Sarmento e Cunha, Casa da Música's current General Director.

There is a very strong investment in the programming and its concept. Every year, at the invitation of the artistic director, audiences are challenged to take an engaging journey deepening their relationship with Casa. Each programming year also features a guest country, which inspires the programming choices. 2018 was dedicated to Austria, for example. According to António Pacheco, Artistic Director, Casa da Música has conquered the confidence of its audiences because there is a continuous effort to offer the most challenging programming, especially regarding contemporary music and live composers. The audience is vibrant and curious about what they are going to learn in Casa.

Given such an ambitious artistic project, combining the will to host and inspire artistic structures together with an emphasis on building a stronger connection with audiences, it became mandatory to construct an iconic building which could support the execution of the project's mission and could reinforce its potential on an international level. There was no other way than to create a building that "(…) would itself be a catalyst to the artistic project", summarises the General Director of Casa da Música.

In this context, Porto 2001 issued a set of invitations to prestigious Portuguese and international architects. In the first phase, 26 participated in the contest, 15 of whom were international.

After several stages of the process, the three finalists were: Dominique Perrault (France), Rafael Viñoly (Uruguay) and Rem Koolhaas (Netherlands).

In July 1999, Porto 2001 – based on the opinion of a jury composed of a variety of public figures from Porto (including the renowned Portuguese architects Eduardo Souto Moura and Álvaro Siza Vieira) – awarded the project to OMA (Office for Metropolitan Architecture), headed by Rem Koolhaas, in partnership with the British ARUP, firm of design and engineering.

According to Paulo Sarmento e Cunha, "there was no doubt in regard to the decision, since it was supported in the compatibility of the project and not in the comparison with the others. The proposal was unquestionably unique." OMA's proposal materialised the most challenging part of Casa da Música's mission: to strengthen the relationship between the Casa and its internal and external audiences, along with a remarkable adaptation to its surroundings: "On the outside it has no color; all the color is provided by the context. This is a very fragile position. It needs these other buildings around it", stated the Architect. Consolidating a project with the belief of the preservation of the others is an act of nobility and humility. It only truly exists if the others exist. This is the principle of harmony in humanity. It is a mindset, a way of life that overflows the mission of a mere building. This predicted the success of the project.

Beyond the development step, it was necessary to invest time and work in the edification of a complex polyhedron: a challenge that caused several people involved in the project to question its feasibility.

The team noticed that some exterior parts of the polyhedron were not freestanding. Consequently, it became needed to project and build special centres, similar to those used in bridge constructions, while the building was being completed. The teams held countless meetings between national and international architects in order to create a complementary structure that would *"hold"* Casa da Música together while its top was under construction, says Paulo Sarmento e Cunha.

The work was planned in 83 sequential steps that depended on the amount of time it took for the concrete to dry, which caused an extension and expansion of the deadline and budget, something that often occurs with such a complex and ambitious project. Casa da Música ultimately opened in April of 2005.

During the working period, there were several episodes that marked its gestation. In 2003, the decision was made to produce the initial performances in Sala Suggia – the main concert hall of Casa da Música, the name of which honors the Portuguese cellist Guilhermina Suggia (1885–1950), from Porto. These concerts occurred while the room was still revealing bare beams and concrete, and the initiative transformed the construction process into a living work of art. One challenge remained: to ensure that conditions were safe enough to make this idea feasible. Part of the machinery and materials of the works were used in the performance, which then as a result became site specific. This experience was so emotionally moving that its own architect Rem Koolhaas admitted thinking: "Maybe I shouldn't finish it; maybe it is much more beautiful unfinished."

Although the funds raised were mainly public, there was a huge effort to bring together private financiers who would commit to supporting Casa da Música's day to day expenses and to participating as external consultants in the strategic decision making, responsible for the project's survival. This achievement allowed for distance from the public financing, protecting Casa da Música from the volatility of national political tendencies, preserving its robustness and impartiality.

Today, Casa da Música is an icon of the city of Porto and of Portugal, consistently making an effort to fulfill its mission. "We seduce people every day", says Paulo Sarmento e Cunha. The Education Department is one of the most significant contributors to this achievement and is a strategic element of the organisation.

Casa da Música has the following spaces:

- Sala Suggia, main room, with 1228 seats, 756,92 m²;
- Sala 2, with 300 seats, 650 standing seats, 326,23 m²;
- Ten rehearsal rooms, some for orchestras and other for small ensembles and soloists, 910 m²;
- Cibermúsica, orange atelier and purple atelier dedicated to the Education Department. These spaces have windows that look onto Sala Suggia's stage, 330 m²;
- Sala VIP, decorated in Portuguese motifs and covered with tiles, furnished with classical Portuguese furniture. It is used for small events, cocktails and press events, 44 m²;
- VIP terrace, 320 m²;
- East and West foyers, 130 m² + 130 m²;
- Suspended bar, 90 m²
- Restaurant and café (430 m² + 250 m²);
- Parking area, 644 vehicles, 26.200 m².

As time has passed, Casa da Música, has become a provider of "new stages": non-traditional spaces of the Casa that are used to host performances. This is made possible by the continuous and arduous work of the technical team, headed by Ernesto Costa, who envisions the Casa as a challenge every day, wanting to bring the best out of each and every corner. The restaurant has its own programming, as does the café, which offers a space and visibility for emerging creators. One example of the way the space is used is the Jazz Summer Series that happens below the main stairs, in the entrance, in a unique and welcoming environment.

Some particular features of the building attracted very unpredictable audiences, who use its facilities in very surprising ways. For example, the "wave", a plaza emanating from the external floor of Casa, immediately started to be used by the skateboard community. The skaters elected this place as the coolest in the city to practise their sport. One of the reasons for this preference is also very human: the Casa da Música's teams' rooms have glass walls with a direct view to the exterior. So, as soon as someone from the staff realises that one of these skaters has been injured, they immediately call the emergency services to provide assistance. Sometimes, an accident happens due to the skates . . . a broken glass, a damaged door, but Casa's team considers this "miracle" of audiences absolutely priceless, so they don't mind fixing these small damages occasionally. And the "sliders" history does not end here . . . At a certain point, the security team noticed that the last parking floors (−2 and −3) were invaded by another exquisite community: a group of beautiful artistic roller skaters. Apparently, the floor of the parking area is very suitable. This fact, combined with a very few number of cars being parked during the week evenings on the lowest floors, results in the perfect conditions for these roller skaters to rehearse. And actually, the security team's work became much more interesting. They feel very special to have the chance to watch these exclusive training sessions.

When Casa da Música was near celebrating its 13th anniversary, the General Director and the Technical Director, being asked about what they would do differently if they had the chance to create the project again from scratch, answered: "Maybe we would rethink the number of stairs in the foyers. Maybe they push people to the outside, while we want to keep them inside", states Paulo Sarmento e Cunha. Ernesto Costa refers to the need to pay attention to the functional side and to the

Casa da Música, staircase, north foyer

production efficiency, saying that there would be opportunity to reduce labour needs.

In sum, according to Paulo Sarmento e Cunha, the greatest lesson from Casa da Música's history is that "a building is crucial for fundraising, attracting audiences, visitors and increasing corporate events". Investing in an iconic building capitalises on the emotional relationship with all visitors: the ones who enter just to appreciate the space, the ones who attend a concert, come to enjoy a meal or merely contemplate the building from the outside. The way in which all involved with Casa da Música maintain their enthusiasm after many years of its existence is strongly connected to the marriage between its artistic concept and the physical building designed by Koolhaas. Casa da Música has become an iconic building, photographed and celebrated by visitors from across the globe.

Casa da Música, auditorium; note the corrugated glass wall behind the stage

Casa da Música, view into Sala Suggia from the purple atelier, education space

Still in a very young stage of its life, Casa da Música's strong personality, present since its conception, has influenced other international projects in multiple ways, including aspects related to its architecture, such as the pioneering and successful usage of corrugated glass. The innovation of using this type of glass has proven its good performance regarding acoustics: it "splits the sound". To ensure the sound diffusion instead of its direct reflexing, several studies were made regarding the curvature of the glass.

Another example is the usage of white concrete on the exterior walls. A lot of chemistry tests and adjustments were made in order to discover the perfect recipe that would make its usage feasible. The usage of white concrete in the walls and the fact that they would be "naked" (not painted)

Casa da Música, corrugated glass walls behind the platform, east foyer

was not a very popular idea amongst the teams, since they would not be able to mark the walls. It was very challenging work to convince them.

Casa da Música as a whole has been taken into account as a model for conceptualising new performance spaces, such as a possibility of building a new concert hall in London. Casa has been cited as a reference because of its choice of a shoe-box for acoustic reasons, innovating in other aspects, which provide singularity to a space.

The world can't live without Casa da Música: a home that needs its neighbours in order to fully exist.

Acknowledgements

Special thanks to Paulo Sarmento e Cunha, General Director of Casa da Música, Ernesto Costa, Casa da Música's Technical Director, António Pacheco, Artistic Director and Óscar Liberal, former Casa da Música Board Member (2003–2005), who kindly invested their time and energy in order to contribute to this article.

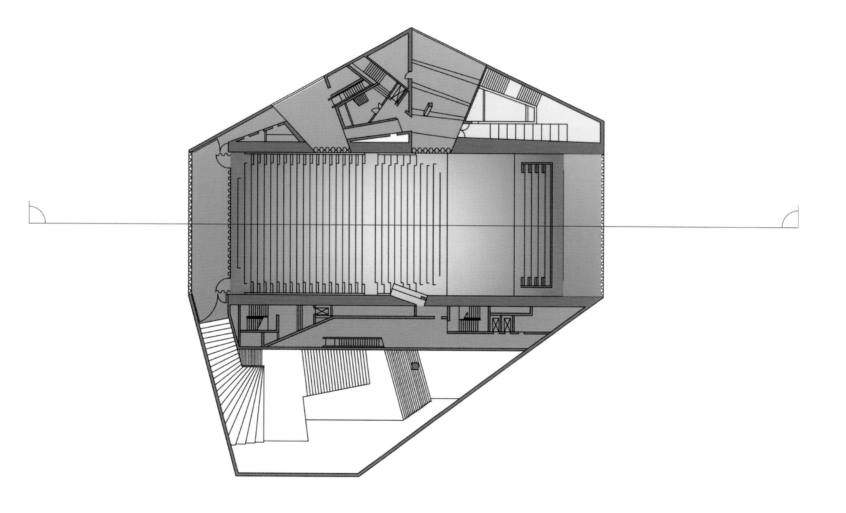

Casa da Música, Porto, comparative plan, 4th floor

1:500

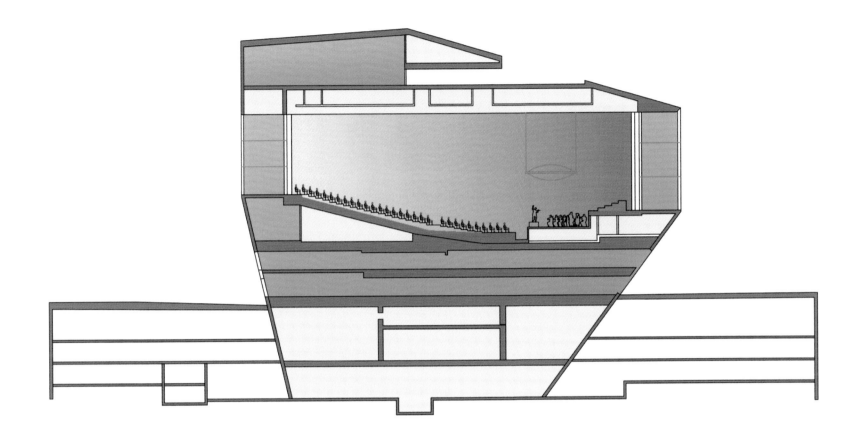

Casa da Música, Porto, comparative section

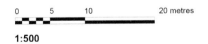

0   5   10   20 metres

1:500

Auditório Ibirapuera

Auditório Ibirapuera 'Oscar Niemeyer', 2005
São Paulo, Brazil
Architect, Oscar Niemeyer
Claudia Toni

With a population of over 207 million, Brazil is the largest country in Latin America and the second largest in the Americas after the USA.

São Paulo is the most populous city in Brazil, with over 12 million people in the city and over 21 million people in the wider metropolitan area. This makes it the largest city in the Americas and the biggest in the southern hemisphere.

For many years Rio de Janeiro was the country's capital and perhaps best known and most prominent city. The decade of 1950 marks the growth of São Paulo city and ensured its position as the most dynamic urban center in Brazil, overtaking Rio de Janeiro in population and in economic prominence. Brazil's surging industrialization started to secure the city's leadership, which stands to this day.

São Paulo had already witnessed the birth of its Visual Arts *Bienal* (which held its 33rd edition in 2018) and of the *Museu de Arte Moderna* (Museum of Modern Art), but the city still had further cultural ambitions. Its 400th anniversary in 1954 deserved to be celebrated with pomp and circumstance. A Commission for São Paulo's Fourth Centennial festivities was formed in December 1951, and they planned on inaugurating the Ibirapuera Park in 1954.

They invited Oscar Niemeyer (1907–2012) to design it; the internationally renowned architect was 45 years old. The park's project included buildings that could host scientific and artistic exhibitions, besides events that contributed to the state's economic affairs, such as agricultural and industrial fairs. Furthermore, as a capital that wished to be modern, its main park should encompass areas for cultural manifestations, sports, lakes, a botanical garden, a zoo, play-grounds, and a venue for the installation of an amusement park or circus, and a theatre.

Oscar Niemeyer was born in 1907 and was allegedly still practising architecture shortly before his death at the age of 104. He was a key figure in the development of modern or modernist architecture. His largest and most famous work is the city of Brasília which became the country's capital in 1960. Niemeyer was part of the Board of Design Consultants appointed to collaborate on the design of the United Nations buildings in New York.

Niemeyer's team consisted of some of the most important architects in the city, in addition to the renowned landscapist Burle Marx. Most of the designed buildings were constructed, although the original project was not entirely carried out. The theatre, however, was left out of the construction plans altogether. Alongside the planetarium – that later turned

Ibirapuera Park overview

Ibirapuera Park overview

into the 'Oca', a venue for exhibitions – it would have been located right at the entrance of the park, forming a square. They would have composed the park's most architecturally complex set of buildings, and Niemeyer's favourite. However, the square was never actually built.

The *Auditório Ibirapuera* plans went through twelve different versions from 1951 to its construction in the 21st century. The projects varied in size, ranging from 3,000 to its current 804 seats. Niemeyer gave a lot of thought to the theatre concept at several times, because he could not accept its absence in the park, nor the absence of a performing arts venue of that size in the city. Therefore, by looking at the design projects from the park's inauguration, in 1951, to the eventual opening of the auditorium in 2005, Niemeyer walks us through his different attempts at convincing mayors and cultural institutions to construct his project (1989, 1993, 1997, 1999, 2000). Fernando Serapião's exhaustive research gathers multiple versions of the *Auditório* and their different variables, a recurring procedure in Niemeyer's record.[1]

Auditório Ibirapuera, rear elevation and door

The auditorium was finally built, and just in time for São Paulo's 450th anniversary. It is shaped like a trapeze, and features big interspaces/apertures, the largest being that of the stage, measuring 50 metres. Its roof sits upon triangular side walls and two pillars that separate the foyer from the audience.

Dedicated to music, the space is no longer a theatre but an auditorium that sporadically hosts dance and theatre performances. It was built of reinforced concrete and it is entirely white. The marquee that gives it access was named *'Labareda'* (meaning "flame"), also conceived by Niemeyer. Painted red, it marks the *Auditório* and distinguishes it from the other buildings in the park.

Internally, the foyer is located by the entrance, in the lower part of the building. There, a red sculpture by artist Tomie Ohtake (1913–2015), hangs supported from the ceiling and front wall. The monumental aspect of the foyer is completed by a spiral walkway leading up to the audience, giving the space a unique and involving atmosphere.

The audience and stage are situated on the opposite and highest end of the *Auditório*, while the dressing-rooms, administrative offices and music school are underground.

Wide and not very deep, the audience is oval-shaped and its walls are lined by wooden slats.

Labareda, Flame

Auditório Ibirapuera, foyer

Auditório Ibirapuera, the auditorium with rear door onto park open

The stage is 50 metres wide, 15 metres deep, 28 metres high and with a 28 metre-wide proscenium line. A 20 metre-high red steel door in the back wall offers a surprising experience to the spectators: when triggered, it rises in 50 seconds and offers an exquisite view of the park. This trick allows the stage to be used from both sides, accommodating 15,000 audience outdoors seated on the grass that surrounds the *Auditório*.

The hall has poor acoustics for classical, unamplified music and it was decided to dedicate the *Auditório* to amplified music. It has the volume for an audience of 1500 people, but with only 800 seats. Being 43 meters wide, it has poor lateral acoustic energy, according to José Nepomuceno, responsible for the hall's acoustic project.[2] The sound system is a collaboration with Anthony Nittoli, from Akustiks. This characteristic limits the offering of musical programming to the audience. However, the foyer

Auditório Ibirapuera, rear elevation

kept to the architect's original plans, resulting in a space with a lot of reverberation/echo.

Located in a central region of the city, Ibirapuera Park is a postcard of São Paulo and hosts thousands of people that visit the multiple attractions gathered there. Some of the most important Brazilian museums are now hosted at the buildings designed by Niemeyer, and the Visual Arts *Bienal* still takes place in one of his pavilions.

Auditório Ibirapuera' s attractions are some of the most sought-after in the city, for they include concerts by popular artists, Brazilian and foreign orchestras, and series dedicated to film, which use the white walls outside the building as projection screens.

Keeping up with a global trend, the *Auditório* maintains a music school that opens daily and guarantees that the beautiful construction is constantly and intensely used. Its 170 students, varying in age between 12 and18 years, are taught by 32 teachers of winds, percussion, singing, and theoretical subjects. The course spans four years and is dedicated to Brazilian popular music.

Auditório Ibirapuera, classroom

The school's space counts with a central hall presenting a large panel, 16 metres long and 2.5 metres tall, painted by Luis Antonio Vallandro Keating (1940), and individual as well as group classrooms. The students' orchestras and ensembles perform regularly at the *Auditório*.

Niemeyer's interest and dedication to the construction of the *Auditório* reveal his respect and concern about the lack of venues dedicated to the performing arts in São Paulo and in Brazil. Nonetheless, he never liked working in collaboration with acoustics and theatre planning specialists when designing performing arts venues. In general, his designs in this area have always been deficient regarding the needs of the artists, whether they be musicians, actors or dancers. To some extent, a good

deal of Brazil's underdevelopment in matters of technology, and our failure to measure our theatres to standards of excellence, especially in comparison to so many excellent theatres around the world, can also be credited to him.

Ibirapuera Park was an amazing project for the city's 400th anniversary. It created a large open space like the grand parks and open spaces found in other major cities. The park has a series of buildings and interventions of which the most dramatic is *Auditório Ibirapuera*. A dramatic white object in the middle of the park with a red tongue to mark its entrance and a dramatic red door on the rear that can open to reveal the wonders being presented inside. The bold exterior is coupled with a dramatic entrance and foyer. Sadly, the auditorium is not of the same quality as the other parts of the building with its over-wide rectilinear shape

Originally named *'Auditório Ibirapuera'*, the building was renamed after its designer following his death in 2012.

Notes

1   SERAPIÃO, Fernando. Oscar Niemeyer: Auditório Ibirapuera, SP – Auditório completa conjunto edificado no Parque Ibirapuera. Available at: https://arcoweb.com.br/projetodesign/arquitetura/oscar-niemeyer-auditorio-sao-14-12-2005. Accessed on March 3, 2017.
2   SERAPIÃO, Fernando. À espera do último ato: as diferentes propostas para o desenho do auditório Ibirapuera. Available at: https://arcoweb.com.br/projetodesign/artigos/artigo-a-espera-do-ultimo-ato-01-12-2005. Accessed on 23 February, 2017.

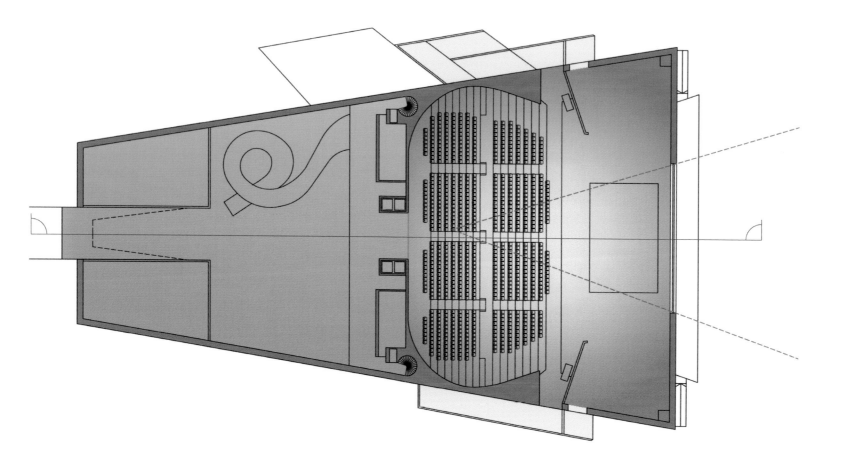

Auditório Ibirapuera, São Paolo, comparative plan

1:500

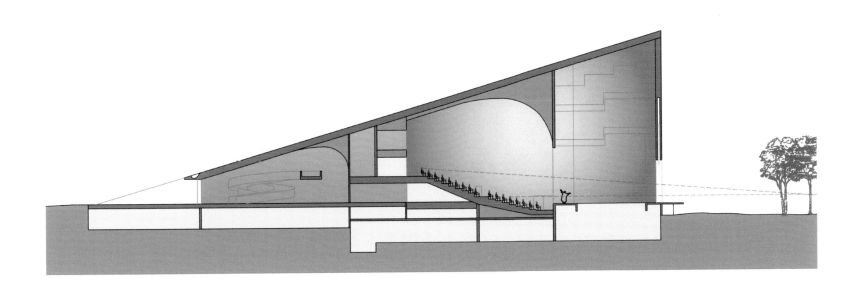

Auditório Ibirapuera, São Paolo, comparative section

1:500

National Centre for the Performing Arts, exterior

National Centre for the Performing Arts, 2007
Beijing, China
Architect, ADP (Aéroports de Paris – Paul Andreu)
with Tsinghua University

Jörg Kümmel

The National Centre for the Performing Arts in Beijing is located on the south of West Chang'an Avenue and to the West of the Great Hall of the People.

This area is one of the most prestigious in China, built around the extraordinary Forbidden City. The National Museum of China, Tiananmen Square and the Memorial Hall of Chairman Mao are all neighbours.

The decision to build a Grand Theatre in an area of such historical and symbolic import clearly testifies to the importance given to this building from the architectural perspective.

The history of the National Grand Theatre reaches back to 1958 when the Chinese government decided to build the "Ten Great Buildings" to commemorate the tenth anniversary of the founding of the People's Republic of China. One of these buildings was planned to be the National Grand Theatre. A design contract was awarded to the Architectural Design Institute of Tsinghua University in Beijing, who completed the preliminary design phase one year later. The appearance of the project was strongly related to the Paris Opera House and the scheme consisted of a 3,000-seat opera house and a 960-seat concert hall; the total area of the Tsinghua project was about 40,000 m^2 and it reflected a distinct Chinese architectural style.

In the early 1960s the project was put on hold due to natural disasters in the People's Republic.

In 1986 the government initiated a new project to create a National Grand Theatre. In 1990 an expert group was established to realise the preliminary studies for a new opera house under the leadership of the Tsinghua University Architectural Design Institute in Beijing. A team of Chinese engineers and experts was established to research and document the state of the art for stage technologies and acoustics of recently constructed, famous opera houses and concert halls worldwide. These Chinese experts closely cooperated with the architects of Tsinghua University for a period of three years to finalise the feasibility study. The conclusion of the study was a brief to create a complex with three theatres and a small multipurpose hall with an overall area of 105,000 m^2.

The country was developing rapidly, and foreign architects were designing many new buildings across China. The Chinese People's Political Consultation Committee again proposed the re-launch the project in 1996.

There is a certain competition between Chinese cities and the completion of the Shanghai Grand Theatre in 1998, designed by French architect Jean-Marie Charpentier and planning for the Jiangsu Grand Theater in Nanjing by the Canadian architect Carlos Ott & Associates spurred planning for the new Centre in Beijing.

An international architectural competition attracted both foreign and Chinese teams. Two competition rounds were held. In the second round the competition jury recommended the three schemes of ADP (Aéroports de Paris) with Tsinghua University, Terry Farrell & Partners with Beijing Institute of Architectural Design & Research and Carlos Ott & associates with the Ministry of Construction of China.

The architect selection process became complex and protracted, with rumours of government interference and meddling. Eventually, some 43 years after the project inception, ADP led by Paul Andreu with Tsinghua University were appointed. Stage planning was conducted by the stage planning department of the National Centre for the Performing Arts and the architectural and structural acoustic of the halls was contracted to CSTB under the lead of Jean-Paul Vian. After his death in 2006 Isabelle Schmich took over the final part of the acoustic design of the project, in close cooperation with their local partner Professor Guonqi Li from Beijing University of Technology.

Their scheme covers a land area of 118,900 m² and its total construction area is 217,500 m² (including an underground parking lot of nearly 46,600 m²). Construction started on 13 December 2001 and the building was formally opened on 22 December 2007, with attention from the whole world.

The main structure of the National Centre is a unique semi-oval shell some 46.68 m high with a further 32.50 m below ground. The long axis of the oval is 212 m, the short axis is 143 m and its perimeter is more than 600 m. The surface of the shell consists of 18,398 titanium panels and more than 1,226 ultra-clear glass pieces. The joint curves of these two materials resemble the curtain gradually opening for a wonderful performance. The main structure is surrounded by an artificial lake with greenery all around to create an atmosphere of comfort, grace, warmth and romance. The deep greenery with the magnificent building harmonises with the political and cultural centre of the Tiananmen area.

National Centre for the Performing Arts, entrance hallway beneath the reflecting pool

The initial architectural idea was that the National Centre for the Performing Arts looks like a bright pearl on water and represents the top performing arts centre of the nation. Somewhat inevitably it was christened "The Giant Egg" by locals. The building is entered through a dramatic tunnel under the lake. This requires audiences to descend into the tunnel before rising into the foyers of the building. This initial descent is unusual in Chinese culture. Normally one only descends to the tombs of ancestors.

Inside the complex, in addition to the performance halls, there are large spaces for exhibitions, little performance spaces in the foyers, shops for handicraft sales and items related to the performances in the halls.

The performance spaces include an opera house, concert hall, drama theatre and multi-purpose small theatre. All the halls are structurally separated from each other and surrounded by foyer areas. The Opera House stands at the centre of the complex.

The style and function of these four halls vary dramatically. The Opera House is the largest and most complex hall and mainly accommodates large-scale opera, dancing drama, ballet drama and large-scale galas. The Opera House was designed using the so-called horseshoe shape with a parquet area and 3 balconies. The total seating capacity is 2,354 seats and with its volume of 23,000 m^3 the Opera House provides an acoustic volume of 9,8m^3 per listener.

The material of the side walls is mainly made of metal mesh, with a fine-scale structured wall behind to ensure diffuse reflections, while the back wall has a heavy absorptive fabric behind the metal mesh. The parquet floor and the ceiling of the Opera House were made of pine wood with a mass of 30 kg/m^2 to ensure strong ceiling reflections of the sound. The volume in combination with the material arrangement inside the Opera House lead to a reverberation time of 1.6 seconds, a perfect value for an opera house of this size.

National Centre for the Performing Arts, Opera House auditorium

The sightlines inside the parquet and the balconies are well planned – so that the direct sound contact to the performers is given – and the colour composition inside the Opera House leads to a warm and cosy impression. The aesthetic and acoustic impression inside the hall fully satisfies the audience, the red and gold of this room being auspicious colours in Chinese culture.

The drama theatre, with 1,040 spectators, follows the Western model, its shape follows that of a cinema. It has two balconies and was conceived for guest companies from abroad, but also for Chinese theatre productions. All four auditoriums were equipped with stage technology of the highest standards, but the drama theatre is a superlative in regard to size and structure of the stage. It consists of a revolving stage that is said to be the largest in the world. 15 lifting platforms of 2.5 x 2.5 m are integrated in this revolve, which has a lifting height of 6.8 m. The upper machinery consists of a sophisticated flying system. The construction follows the German model and was built by a German Chinese consortium. This kind of stage usually serves for repertory theatre, but the Chinese client was very ambitious in getting this technology independent of its use.

The architectural design for the Concert Hall follows the acoustically proven form of the classic rectangular hall – the 'shoebox'. Such halls provide good geometric conditions and produce for musicians and listeners alike a musical sound quality that is not achieved by any other hall shape. This is one of the reasons that the Concert Hall of the National Centre for the Performing Arts in Beijing is widely accepted by most of the high-ranking orchestras around the world.

The floor plan of the hall has an optimal length in the parquet – including the stage – and is due to the early reflections of the rectangular shape in its width appropriate, which suggests acoustically an

National Centre for the Performing Arts, Concert Hall auditorium

optimal distribution of early reflections. Due to the compact arrangement of the listener surfaces and the relatively strong seat row elevation in the individual areas, good visibility is given in all places and due to the associated optimal direct sound propagation, it provides very good acoustic conditions. The maximum distance of the spectators to the soloist's place is just under 30 m. Thus, the proximity of the event, even in the large hall capacity of 1,859 seats, ensures a good ratio of sonic intimacy in smaller-scale concerts of sufficient size for the acoustically optimal unfolding of the tremendous energy of a large symphony orchestra.

The volume of the Concert Hall is 20,000 m³, which creates good conditions for the reverberance of the room. The given volume per seat is 10.5 m³/listener and the reverberation time was measured analog to the volume ratio with 2 seconds in the occupied condition.

The foyer around the Opera House uses metal mesh, with its transparency creating multi-dimensional visual effects and feelings of depth while keeping a light and simple appearance. Looking over the Opera House in the public area, you will see people's movement indistinctly shown, which creates a novel and obscure effect. The strong absorptive structures in red on the exterior of the auditorium are decorated with modern-look metal panels, which echoes with the architecture sign of 'bird's nest'. The warm and vibrant colours of the metal mesh and yellow light belt contain artistic passion.

The National Centre for the Performing Arts held about 950 performances and welcomed 1,800,000 visitors in 2018. The multipurpose use of the complex can be seen from the split of the aforementioned audience numbers. 900,000 people watched performances in the halls, 400,000 visitors came without watching a performance in a hall and 500,000 participated in artistic events or educational sessions. Nearly 30 per cent of the performances are given by foreign groups such as the famous Mariinsky orchestra, which gives three performances each visit.

Grand theatres have been built in various cities across China, but the National Centre for the Performing Arts in Beijing is still the flagship among all these houses.

National Centre for the Performing Arts and Great Hall of the People at sunset

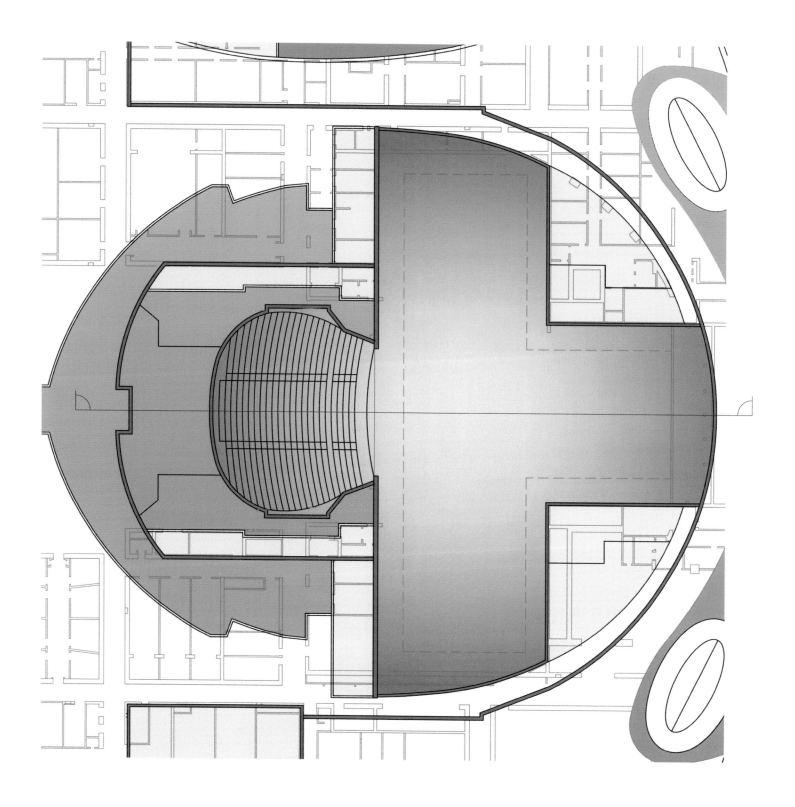

National Centre for the Performing Arts, Beijing, Opera House, comparative plan

0   5   10   20 metres

1:500

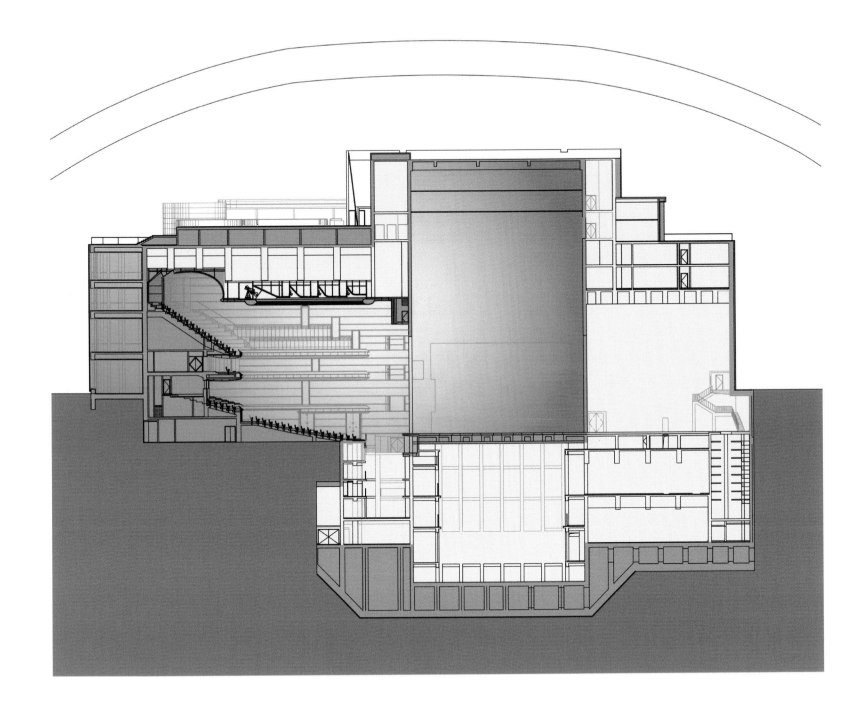

National Centre for the Performing Arts, Beijing, Opera House, comparative section

0 5 10 20 metres

1:500

Operahuset, in the winter

Operahuset, 2008

Oslo, Norway
Architect, Snøhetta

David Turnbull

Yes!! She punched the air . . . the winners were Norwegian! This mattered, a lot. I was in a group, taking a tour. I had been to the home of the Norwegian National Opera and Ballet in Oslo many times, but I wanted to hear the stories that are used to describe the building to the thousands of people from all over the world who visit, who want to get to know the building, who, like me, have read about it, have seen photographs in books and magazines, in print and online.

The winners were Snøhetta. It was 1999. The competition was international. Two hundred and thirty-nine teams had entered. The prize was the commission to design and supervise the construction of the building . . . the most significant public building to be built in Norway for generations . . . that would be completed within the first decade of the next Millennium. She smiled. She was radiant with delight. I could understand. I have been in Oslo on National Day. I have witnessed this spectacle of Norwegian pride and Norwegian loyalty . . . and I love the ancient songs, the myths, the sagas, assembled, edited, written and rewritten, in the 13th century by Snorri Sturluson (1179–1241), that, in my mind, remain essential, providing persistent images that define 'the North' . . . from the Norse Myths, the Kalevala, the Poetic Edda, the 'Heimskringla' . . . particularly the stories of Magnus Olafson's journey from the West (1035) . . . the songs of Sigvat the Skald (995–1045) . . .

the crusade (1107–1110) of Sigurd Jorsalfar . . . sailing to Lisbon and the islands of Iviza and Minorca, his long stay in Sicily, his voyage across the 'Greek Sea' to Palestine . . . riding to Jerusalem, to meet the second Crusader-King, Baldwin I, successor to Godefroy de Bouillon (1060–1100) . . . his expedition to Constantinople and eventual return to Norway, overland . . . through Bulgaria, Hungary, Pannonia, Suabia and Bavaria, 'where he met the Roman emperor, Lotharius' . . . stories . . . about pre-Christian battles for territory, and Christian battles of belief . . . 'dry swords moistened with blood' . . . the deception of 'pretenders', the fragility of identity, stories that can be told and retold.

This matters. As I listened to her stories, I recognised a multitude of narratives, some very old . . . some new . . . ancient myths reconciled with contemporary ideals, dreams infused with reality, or reality as a dream. Listening to her was like listening to the wandering singer Loddfafnir's chant, from his 'chanter's stool . . . by the wells of Urth' . . . about the past, from the past . . . in the present.

I have seen the building in every season, and at every time of day, as a visitor from another land, who cannot speak Norwegian. This matters too, because the building communicates, without words, directly, as an accumulation of material facts, and mental images. It communicates, as a distillation of dream-thoughts, an avatar of the gods, the material incarnation of mysteries, that can be articulated

Operahuset, roof in the evening

in relation to Norwegian identity, and the magical atmosphere of the North, as it is understood around the World . . . gathering associations from the creation stories, the mysteries, stories of the sea, of storms, and epic voyages, of magical runes, Giants and Elves, Gods and Kings, mountains, forests and islands, of snow and ice, and fire, of wars, and the Valkyries, who select the warriors who will be granted eternal life, and those who must die.

The building transformed the reputation of Norwegian Opera and Ballet internationally, as much as it projected optimism about the future of Norway, Oslo and, specifically the Bjørvika district on the Oslofjord, occupying land that had been part of a busy port for centuries and a container terminal for two decades, in the 'Golden Era' of economic growth, that included the catalytic discovery of oil in the Norwegian continental shelf, in 1969. The liberalisation of credit regulation in the 1980s, the relocation of the port to Sørhavna, the construction of new roads and tunnels, a new airport at Gardermoen, and new rail lines created the circumstances in which new places and new images of civic life could be nurtured, and flourish.

Operahuset, the auditorium from the stage

When it opened in 2008, the 'Oslo Operahuset' set a standard against which all future developments in the Fjord City would be measured. When it was imagined, when the brief was written, before the competition to select an architect was announced, it already set a standard, as an exemplary collection of performing arts venues, with ambitious expectations, and an unusual insistence that no compromise would be accepted that might affect the quality of life in any part of the building, including the back of house, working areas. The social-democratic legacy of 30 years of national reconstruction after the trauma of the Nazi Occupation of Norway from 1940–1945, perhaps, but also socialist and liberal feminism, and student protests in the 1970s, informed the construction of a milieu in which equality and cooperation are expected, and a duty of care was obligatory. Equally, critical decisions about the scale of the auditoria were clearly given a level of attention that reveals an extraordinarily balanced understanding of the benefits associated with intimacy rather than commercial optimisation, as it pertains to dimensions, from balcony to balcony, between the stage and the most remote seat, sight-lines and reverberation time. Before the site was selected, before architects and engineers around the world considered the arrangement of the programme as a constructed artefact . . . the

Operahuset, auditorium looking towards stage and safety curtain

'rooms', the stages, the equipment, the volume and distribution of functional areas . . . the apparatus that would allow the Norwegian National Opera and Ballet companies to achieve prominence internationally, was designed. If accommodating a Romantic-Classical repertoire within a recognisably romantic setting, with a proscenium, parterre and progression of balconies became inevitable, the determination that the seat count in the opera-house would be less than 1,500 was remarkable, as was the decision that the capacity of the second auditorium would be limited to 400 seats.

The technical brief, developed by David Staples and Statsbygg (the state property agency), over many months of consultation with the Opera and Ballet companies, captured their dreams, desire and hope, in a catalogue of requirements that was simultaneously practical, intellectual and emotional. It set limits, established parameters and declared preferences, addressing general considerations of orientation and access, with implications, affecting the physical form of the building, the most plausible location of the fly-tower, relative heights of side-stages, smaller rooms, loading docks and stage-door.

The challenges faced by the architects were profound . . . a tabula rasa as a site in an astonishing location on the Fjord, on land that was close to the central station but disconnected from the city . . . significant engineering work on roads and tunnels nearby . . . the ad-hoc appropriation of neighbouring sites for interim uses . . . an unsettling combination of hubris and uncertainty about the future . . . considerable international attention . . . the unequivocal obligation that the building would be a declaration to the city, the country and the world, that Bjørvika would be a cultural centre as much as a new commercial and residential district.

Snøhetta's proposal was a paradox. While it was self-evidently a large object, it avoided the problematic formal consequences of the brief, that established a vast block of a more or less uniform height, with vertical projections associated with the fly-tower and the upper levels of the largest auditorium, and the upper level of the smaller second auditorium, and an indeterminate foyer, cloakrooms and toilets, box-office, shop, restaurant and cafe, by introducing a plane, an accessible 'carpet', sloping up and away from the water to cover and enclose the building, through which one complex vertical object could pass, and one simple rectangular form.

The dressing rooms, workshops, wardrobe rooms, fabrication and assembly areas were arranged as a 'factory' with a courtyard, daylight to almost every room, wide corridors and a three-storey high covered street connecting the stages, loading areas, freight elevators, stage door and vertical circulation – a backstage village. The brilliance of the schematic design was clear. It eliminated a lot of organisational complexity while maintaining flexibility, and the capacity to nuance the detailed design in consultation with everybody who would work in the building. It transformed the large amorphous volume into a singular, white, geological formation, that could be immediately understood as a vast snow-covered hillside, a glacier or an ice-floe in the Fjord, eternal, archaic and yet, entirely new. It belonged . . . as a public place. It belonged to the sea, to the long cold winters and warm summers, to the sky, to the

Operahuset, the slope

Operahuset, the 'factory'/backstage 'street'/stage door

Nordic light. It belonged in Oslo, in Bjørvika, with or without neighbours. It belonged in the social media that were being launched as the building was being designed, and it would transform the way that people interact with places.

Snøhetta understand the logic of images and the power of stories, particularly intricate narratives, that draw on shared memories or myths. Between 2000 and 2007, as the building was designed in detail and built, these memories became more involved, implicated in architectural decisions of many kinds, a form of folklore, that was semi-autonomous, provided direction, and remains in the collective imagination of the people who are involved in making and operating the building.

My guide's stories revealed how important this can be, encompassing big ideas and the smallest detail . . . from the form of the building to the colour of a wall. As I have learnt more about the building, I have become intrigued by the way that multiple narratives are sustained, and manifest as discrete layers of construction, related to the spatial organisation and structural systems, directly. While watching a rehearsal I experienced an astonishing moment of clarity in which the National Romanticism of the setting on stage, a gilt-edged, fictional place that resembled so many palaces that I have seen or imagined, revealed the balconies, with their curved and folded profiles, their timber surfaces, darkened with ammonia, appearing burnt or weathered,

Operahuset, foyer

mysterious, like the interior of an ancient tree, a ship or a wooden cave . . . and the seating, the fiery colour of the upholstery invoking the warmth of the hearth, or the celebratory flames of winter and summer night-time festivals. I imagined the balcony shapes and seats as distinct forms . . . separated from the walls, and the external envelope of the auditorium, walls, ramps and galleries, itself a complex construction of oak, brighter than the interior timber surfaces but with the same grain, separated from the white surfaces of the foyer, characterised by Snøhetta as the 'wave wall', the angled props supporting the roof . . . the public slope . . . 18,000 square metres of 'Carrara' marble paving, laid out as a carpet with a weave, a pattern that seems to avoid repetition, like a cloud formation . . . and realised the complexity of the synthetic assemblage that had been dissembling in my mind. Involutions in the wave, transforming the cut, knotted, roll of timber into layers of signification corresponding to layers of construction, construction sequences and contractual procedures . . . a spectrum of meaning from the legal to the cosmological. Looking up, into the 'Height' according to the gods, the elves' 'Fair Roof', the dwarfs' 'Dripping Hall' . . .

Operahuset, foyer, interior walls by Olafur Eliasson

the Giants' 'Up-World' . . . or, as the Vanir called it, the 'Weaver of Winds' . . . Heaven . . . dream-images coalesce . . . ice and snow, the Oak, the Ash, the forest and the Fjord . . . the cauldron, roaring . . . the Crucifixion . . . a fragment of the Cross, Baldwin I's gift to Sigurd Jorsalfar . . . the 'Eikthynir', an 'oak-thorned' hart . . . a Swan's skin, a Valkyrie's disguise . . . a Caryatid singing, skaldic verse.

Operahuset, at dawn, in the snow

The foyer holds a secret, a magical atmosphere . . . immediately apparent . . . spontaneity mixed with eternal echoes, from 'the wells of Urth'. Reflected from the sea and sky, transmitted through vast planes of suspended glass . . . drawn from fossil-water and ice, transmitted through the crystalline, fractal geometry of internal walls designed by the Danish-Icelandic artist, Olafur Eliasson, the quality of the light is extraordinary at any time of the day or night, in any season.

Soon there will be many public buildings facing the Fjord. For decades there was one, the Rådhus, Oslo City Hall, designed by Arnstein Arneberg (1882–1961) and Magnus Poulsson (1847–1934), an extraordinary building that has been loved and hated and loved again. Imagined in 1915, built slowly, fitfully, with fortitude and uncertainty, completed after the Second World War, after the Occupation, it is in so many ways an exquisite counterpoint to the 'Operahuset'. I thought that I should compare them, and then I didn't need to, or want to. Five years after the liberation of Norway in 1945, a fresco was completed, in the City Hall, on the east wall of the Rådhushallen, by Alf Rolfsen (1895–1979) and Henrik Sørensen (1882–1962), depicting Norwegian life during the Occupation. In the centre of the wall, a white marble caryatid, her eyes blindfolded, her hands behind her back, witnesses the destruction of cultural institutions and artefacts, as members of the Resistance are lined up, and shot.

I returned to the 'Operahuset' at dawn, on the day after my encounter with her and a companion, a second caryatid, seen in the foreground, in pieces, her neck broken. Haunted. It was snowing. The building was covered with a thin layer of crystalline snow-flakes, its whiteness more extreme, becoming blue. The foyer glowed. The oak surfaces of the auditorium warmed the light. The tragic scene, recalled in the Rådhus, remained in my mind, but, remembered, in the snow, in the morning, was restored, as a gift . . . the darkness, redeemed. I understood why this building was so significant. As I stood in the snow, I returned, in my imagination, to 'The Poetic Edda', to 'Hovamol, the Ballad of the High One', stanzas 139 to 147, concerning the 'Tale of the Runes'. I had read one stanza many times: 146.

> Better no prayer_____than too big an offering,
> By thy getting measure thy gift,
> Better is none_____than too big a sacrifice

The first line is clear. There is a pause, a moment for reflection . . . a breath . . . between two ideas, prayer and offering, and the consideration of scale, scope and imagined impact. The middle line held my attention, as I thought about the architecture of the Norwegian National Opera and Ballet, about Snøhetta's extraordinary offering to the city of Oslo, to Norway. 'By thy getting' . . . 'measure thy gift' . . . the syntax is challenging, as written, or rather as translated, there is no pause. I thought about the responsibility associated with the design and construction of any public building, the representational burden, and the opportunity. In that moment I understood the genius of the ancient wisdom and the brilliance of the 'Operahuset' as a gift, precisely measured . . . perfectly judged.

Footnote

The architect and writer Christian Norberg-Schulz died one year after the architectural competition. His book on Nordic Building, 'Nightlands' was published three years before. He lived in Oslo. He had been the Editor-in-Chief of 'Byggekunst', the most important architectural journal in Norway. He taught at AHO, the Oslo School of Architecture and Design, where he had been the Dean. He had inspired generations of Norwegian architects. The book ends with a provocation that Nordic architecture is of relevance because it had made regionalism a living reality . . . and, the 'traditional lounging for the South' had been supplanted by a 'renewed interest in the North. For him, the Kalevala's 'interwoven natural forces, divine manifestation, and the role of humans in a total, functioning world-picture' provided 'the strongest expression' of Nordic identity. Nordic existence lies in the 'unceasing search for discovery rather than in the consenting acceptance of the given'.

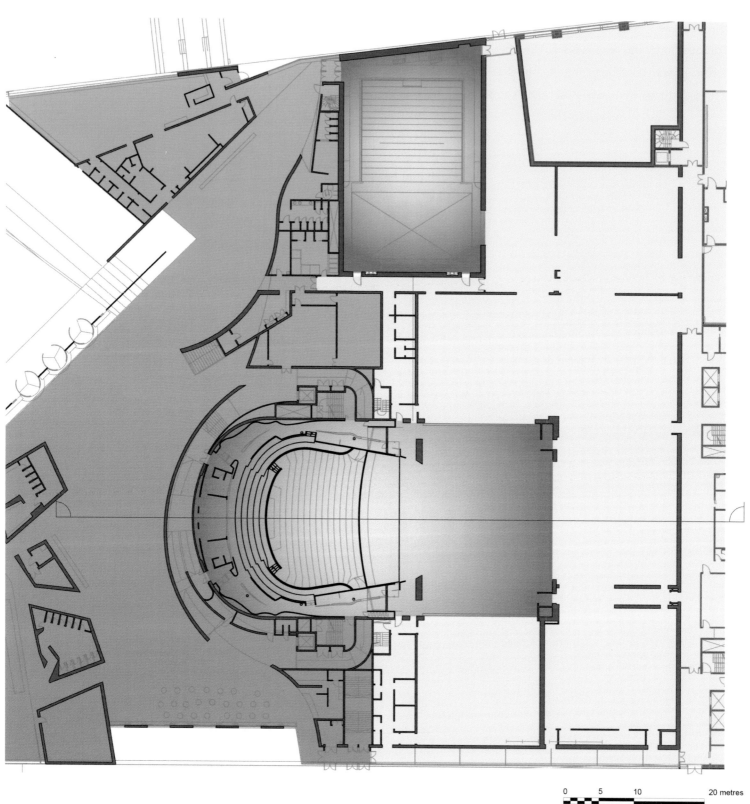

Operahuset, Oslo, comparative plan

0   5   10   20 metres

1:500

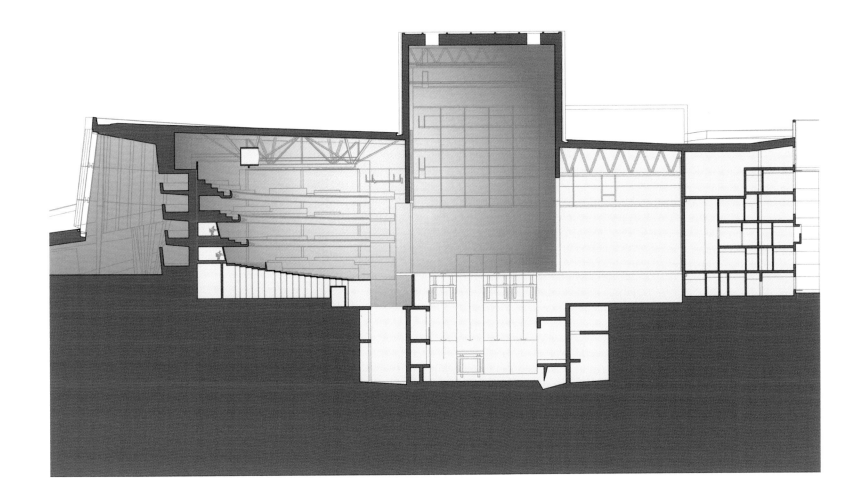

Operahuset, Oslo, Norway, comparative section

0   5   10   20 metres

1:500

Wexford Opera House, main entrance

National Opera House, 2008
(originally the Wexford Opera House) Wexford, Ireland
Architect, Keith Williams Architects

David Staples

The United Kingdom and Ireland have many issues that divide the two countries but also much in common. One of the common features is a tendency to create opera festivals and opera houses in unusual locations and settings, sometimes in someone's back garden or in an extremely small town. The Irish have a reputation for doing things differently and the creation of their National Opera House is possibly a prime example of doing things differently.

Wexford is a port and small town of 20,000 people in the south-east corner of Ireland. In 1950, Sir Compton Mackenzie, the founder of *Gramophone*, a monthly magazine devoted to classical music, was invited to give a lecture to the Wexford Opera Study Circle. This group listened to operas on gramophone records and Mackenzie suggested an opera should be staged in the existing Theatre Royal. Dr Tom Walsh led a group who planned "A Festival of Music and the Arts", which was held at the end of November 1951; from this the Wexford Festival Opera grew. In the inaugural season, a little-known Irish opera was presented and the performance of little-known and "lost" works has always been an important part of the Festival's programmes. Tom Walsh became the Festival's first artistic director and subsequent years saw more high-quality productions of rare or forgotten operas.

The Theatre Royal originally opened in 1832 and was located in the heart of the town, surrounded by small-scale buildings and roads. The theatre had a chequered career, including a spell as a cinema in the 1940s, before being purchased by the Festival Trust. Although the Theatre Royal served the Festival well as a venue for many years, its limited size and lack of facilities led to plans being developed at the beginning of this century for a new purpose-designed opera house.

The Irish Government's Office of Public Works (OPW) undertook initial studies reviewing alternative sites, including the possibility of a standalone building on Ferrybank, a location that might have allowed the creation of an iconic waterfront opera house similar to Sydney. It would however have cut the Festival's close links with the medieval heart of the town (and exposed audiences to the frequently wild Irish weather). The project reverted to the Theatre Royal site, which was doubled in size by the acquisition of the neighbouring *People's Newspaper* premises.

The brief was written by theatre consultants Carr and Angier, working with OPW and Arup Acoustics. OPW prepared an outline design and obtained planning permission to test the opportunity and potential to fund the project. Architects were selected through an open interview and credentials review process, resulting in the appointment of Keith Williams Architects.

Even with a larger site, it was a logistical challenge to fit all the spaces required in a logical, effective manner, while creating interesting public spaces around a high-quality auditorium. The overlay drawings in the illustrated section by Keith Williams Architects shown here show both the old and new theatres in section.

Externally the theatre has virtually no elevations, being entirely ringed by small- scale houses and retail units. It is astonishingly well integrated into the townscape and has possibly the most modest front entrance to be found anywhere. While many opera houses are designed to make a statement or to be signature buildings (Sydney, Oslo, Copenhagen, Dallas, etc.) Wexford has a delightfully small scale. If you are able to step back far enough or view the Opera House from the outer edges of the town, it is possible to see the fly tower and upper parts of the building.

The public spaces/foyers are stacked with an elegant staircase encouraging audiences to rise to higher levels. The scheme also manages to fit hospitality areas into the limited space available.

The heart of the building is the John and Aileen O'Reilly Theatre, which seats 771 when the orchestra pit is in use in "opera mode". While the Festival is a major user, they only present opera on twelve nights a year, so while the auditorium and stage are optimised for operatic use, the theatre must be able to present other types of performance including comedy, concerts (of all music genres), dance, musicals, drama, and family programmes. At the front of the auditorium a large elevator lowers to create the orchestra pit. When no pit is needed, this can be raised to auditorium floor level and additional seating brought in to increase the capacity to 855 seats. The elevator can be raised further, to stage level, to create a forestage and extend the stage into the auditorium. Architect

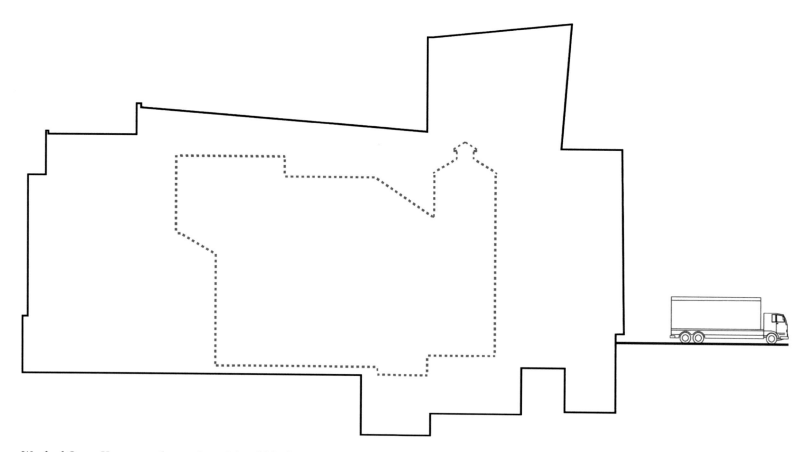

Wexford Opera House, overlay section of the old (red) and new theatres

Wexford, view over the town showing the fly tower of the theatre

Keith Williams tells of consultant Peter Angier creating a full size mock-up of the orchestra pit in a freezing garage in Dublin, allowing artistic director David Agier to stand on a box (representing the conductor's podium), wielding an unused welding rod as a baton to gauge the size and shape of the proposed pit.

The design of the room was influenced by many earlier opera houses, with an underlying "horseshoe" form coupled, as architect Keith William notes, to the form of a cello. Audience seating is on a main floor with a single row of raised seating down either side. The founders circle above has three rows of seats at the rear, a single row of seats, and three six-person boxes on either side. The upper circle repeats the side wall arrangement but has eight rows at the rear. Audience seats are considerably larger and more comfortable than those in the previous theatre.

Wexford Opera House, John and Aileen O'Reilly Theatre viewed from the stage

The room is panelled in North American black walnut which, coupled with seating in pale purple leather, gives a warm, rich ambience and the room has a reverberation time of 1.25 seconds.

The main theatre has a very practical stage, with 40 overhead fly bars (reputedly more than any other theatre in Ireland). Backstage can be found rehearsal rooms, dressing rooms, and other support spaces.

The Jerome Hynes Theatre has 176 seats and is a small, flexible space that can be used for theatre, concerts, comedy, etc. All the seating can be removed to create a flat floor space for rehearsals or other events.

A key requirement was to minimise the closed time, to avoid too much disruption to the Festival. Despite the tight site and limited access, this was achieved, with the theatre closing immediately after the last performance of the 2005 Festival in the Theatre Royal. The new house opened two years later in time for the 2008 Festival.

Wexford is a small harbour town of 20,000 people, the 22nd biggest urban area in Ireland. Dublin, the capital, has a population approaching 1.2 million. But Wexford has an opera house and Dublin doesn't.

When constructed, this theatre was called the Wexford Opera House. In 2008, at the official opening of the 63rd Festival, the Irish Government's Department of the Arts, Heritage and the Gaeltacht announced the renaming of the Wexford Opera House as Ireland's National Opera House. At a stroke, Ireland acquired a National Opera House.

The Wexford Opera Festival is a success story. It stands out among many larger festivals for its presentation over decades of high-quality productions of lost or rare operas in south-east Ireland.

It combines high quality professional leadership with a dedicated core of volunteers. It exists and thrives in a small harbour town and over 40 per cent of Festival visitors are from overseas.

The Wexford (or National) Opera House is also a success story. Carefully integrated into the urban grain of a small town, the auditorium is a warm, elegant interpretation of the traditional opera house.

Wexford Opera House, John and Aileen O'Reilly Theatre looking at the stage from the Founders Circle

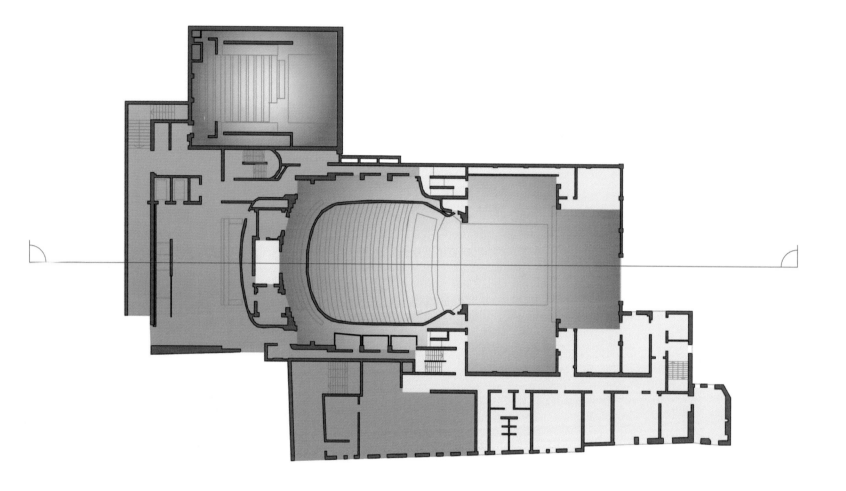

National (Wexford) Opera House, comparative plan

1:500

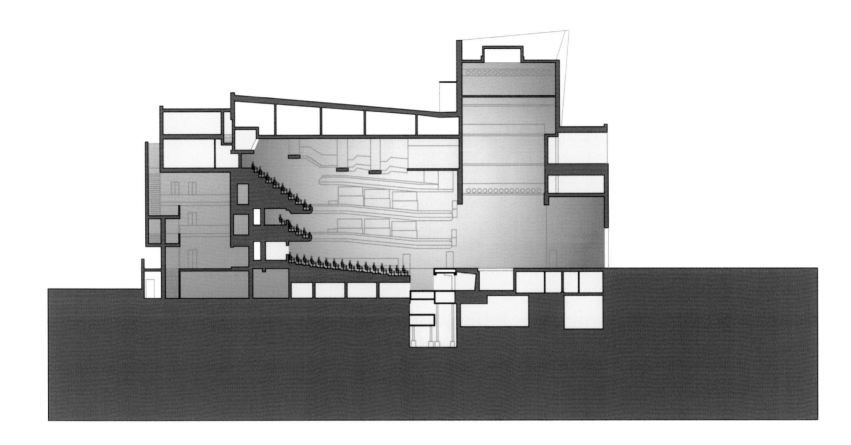

National (Wexford) Opera House, comparative section

0   5   10   20 metres

1:500

Guangzhou Opera House, by Zaha Hadid Architects

Guangzhou Opera House, 2010
Guangzhou, China
Architect, Zaha Hadid Architects
David Staples

The Guangzhou Opera House in Southern China was rapturously received when it opened in May 2010. The biggest performing arts building in Southern China, it was praised nationally and internationally. British newspaper the *Guardian* carried the headline "Move over Sydney: Zaha Hadid's Guangzhou Opera House". In his article, Jonathan Glancy said "The world's most spectacular opera house has just opened in China" while his video sang its praises.

The *New York Times* welcomed it as a "Chinese Gem That Elevates Its Setting", describing it as "the most alluring opera house built anywhere in the world in decades . . . " But it also noted the very poor quality of construction.

Within months Britain's *Daily Telegraph* newspaper headline was "Guangzhou Opera House Falling Apart", noting large cracks in walls and ceilings, leaks, falling glass panels and problems with the external cladding.

Rarely can a new building have fallen from grace so quickly.

Russell Johnson, the doyen of 20th-century acoustic consultants suggested a six-year period was required after a new performing arts building opened before a true and fair evaluation of the building was reached. He suggested:

- Years one and two, everything is wonderful, the building is open, money has stopped flowing out, and the pain is over.
- Years three and four, everything goes wrong – the artistic director leaves, the roof leaks and the deficit is much bigger than anyone anticipated.
- Years five and six, sufficient experienced and knowledgeable people (conductors, critics, musicians, architects, etc.) have visited for a fair assessment of the building to be made.

In a time of rapid social media commentary, instant opinions and fake news, this leisurely six-year period has been condensed into a matter of months or weeks. The acoustics of the Elbphilharmonie in Hamburg were attacked by critics after one (opening) performance.

The Guangzhou Opera was an ambitious project in a rapidly developing Chinese city. Zaha Hadid, the Iraqi-British architect, designed a wonderfully sensuous flowing exterior and interior that was built rapidly in a country with poor construction standards.

Guangzhou, the capital of Guangdong province, was traditionally known to Westerners as Canton, the romantic terminus of the maritime Silk Route. Over 2,200 years old, it is today the third most populous city in China (after Beijing and Shanghai), with a city population of around

Zaha Hadid 1950–2016

The Hadid scheme proposed shapes like "pebbles in a stream smoothed by erosion, the Guangzhou Opera House sits in perfect harmony with its riverside location". The opera house is surrounded by the commercial office towers that have played their part in the economic success of the city. The commercial buildings are generally sharp, rectilinear forms. The jury were presented with a radical contrast in the organic Hadid Opera House. Woody Yao, the Associate Director for ZHA, noted they produced a very sensual wooden model for the competition which illustrated the iconic nature of the building and the contrast with what was happening elsewhere in Guangzhou.

Zaha Hadid had previously won a competition for a new opera house in Cardiff, Wales. Her design was radical and after the first round a smaller group of architects were asked to submit further developed designs. Subsequently, a further third round was introduced. Zaha won all three rounds but the project christened "Crystal Necklace" was controversial, failing to attract public support and openly attacked by the media. After a year of controversy, the British Government eventually withdrew financial support for the scheme and the project died. It was succeeded by the much more pragmatic Wales Millennium Centre.

Many have argued that Cardiff's loss was Guangzhou's gain and that Guangzhou was influenced by Cardiff. However, they were "seven or more" years apart and, in spite of both being opera houses, Hadid's design ethos had changed radically in that time. Cardiff was a very angular building with sharp, straight lines set at acute angles. Guangzhou is a much more organic, flowing building.

The opera house is located on the water-front and is surrounded by a huge new commercial development area. The master-planned urban area is full of rather ordinary, predictable commercial buildings. Fronting an urban park, the opera house shows how one building can lift a rather boring urban experience.

Adjacent to Haixnsha Park, the approach up a ramp or grand staircase leads past the smaller boulder housing the second theatre to an entry plaza giving access to the main hall. The boulders are clad with some 75,000 granite slabs that should join to create a smooth exterior to the building. The problem is the slabs are badly made and poorly fitted,

13 million. Located on the Pearl River, it is a significant port and part of the Pearl River Mega City, with a population of 44 million.

A rapidly developing and growing urban area, the city government decided to create a significant performing arts centre. An international architectural competition attracted detailed designs from Coop Himmelb(l)au, Rem Koolhaus and Zaha Hadid and in November 2002, Zaha Hadid Architect's (ZHA) design was declared the winner.

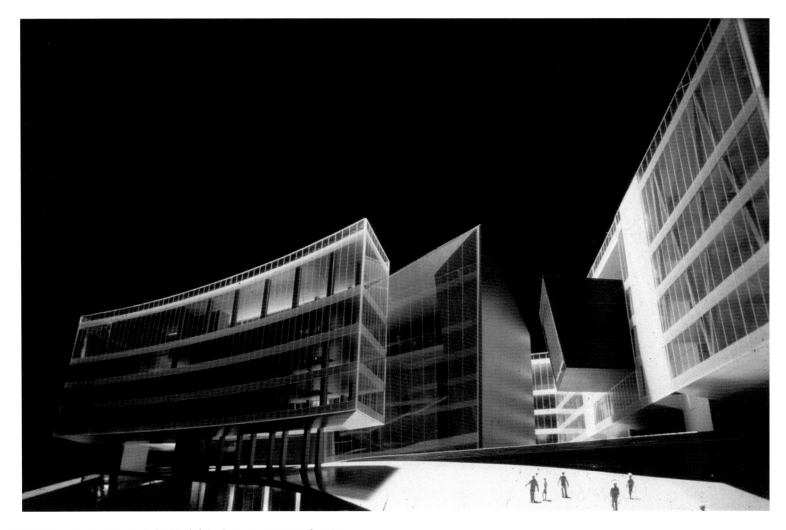

Cardiff Bay Opera House, Zaha Hadid Architects, concept drawing

giving a far from smooth surface. Many have already been replaced. Externally the building looks better at night when floodlighting covers up some of the imperfections and the boulders are reflected in the surrounding pools. The interplay of spaces creates some interesting routes around and between the boulders.

The foyers and public spaces are high spaces with dramatically curved and faceted balconies confronting glazed external walls canted at acute angles.

The large auditorium is an entirely curvaceous space that some have compared to a Gaudi-like structure. It is softly coloured, with a complex interplay of balconies in an asymmetric auditorium.

The main theatre seats 1,800, facing a proscenium arch. Acoustics were designed by Marshal Day using an ODEON acoustic model and a 1:25 scale physical model produced and tested by the South China University of Technology.

The main theatre has a very conventional large Germanic stage with a main stage, two side stages and rear stage. It has extensive elevators and wagons with a full power flying system suited to a major producing opera house. The room is however largely used for touring events – concerts, musicals, and the occasional touring opera.

Given the dramatic nature of the exterior, the dynamic foyer spaces, and the organic main theatre, the second space is frankly a boring

Guangzhou Opera House at night

rectangular room. Labelled the Experimental Theatre, it has some flexibility but is a space lacking imagination.

As with any major project in China, the foreign architect and consultants must collaborate with an LDI (Local Design Institute). Woody Yao notes the close collaboration between the ZHA and local teams. ZHA had several staff resident in Guangzhou during the design and construction periods. While the design collaboration was good, the subsequent execution was poor and ongoing maintenance of the project is also weak.

The Guangzhou opera has some dramatic but slightly disorientating rehearsal and practice rooms. The absence of straight lines or verticals,

which is a strength in the exterior and other parts of the building, is unsettling in a rehearsal room where performers are focused on orientation and position.

Today the Guangzhou Opera House presents a mixed programme of events; the large auditorium is a wonderful flowing, exciting space that provides a positive addition to the cultural life of Guangzhou. The second space by comparison is weak. The exterior was conceived and designed as an iconic addition to the architecture of China's third city. The execution and subsequent lack of maintenance leaves it presenting a disappointing appearance to visitors and the city.

Guangzhou Opera House, foyers

Guangzhou Opera House, large auditorium

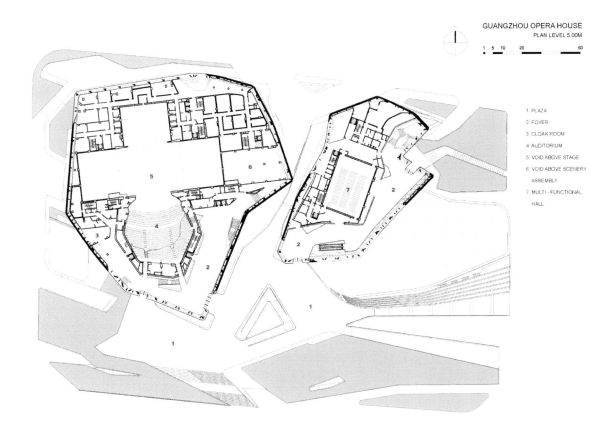

GUANGZHOU OPERA HOUSE
PLAN LEVEL 5.00M

1 5 10 20 50

1. PLAZA
2. FOYER
3. CLOAK ROOM
4. AUDITORIUM
5. VOID ABOVE STAGE
6. VOID ABOVE SCENERY
   ASSEMBLY
7. MULTI - FUNCTIONAL
   HALL

Guangzhou Opera House, plan

Guangzhou Opera House, rehearsal room

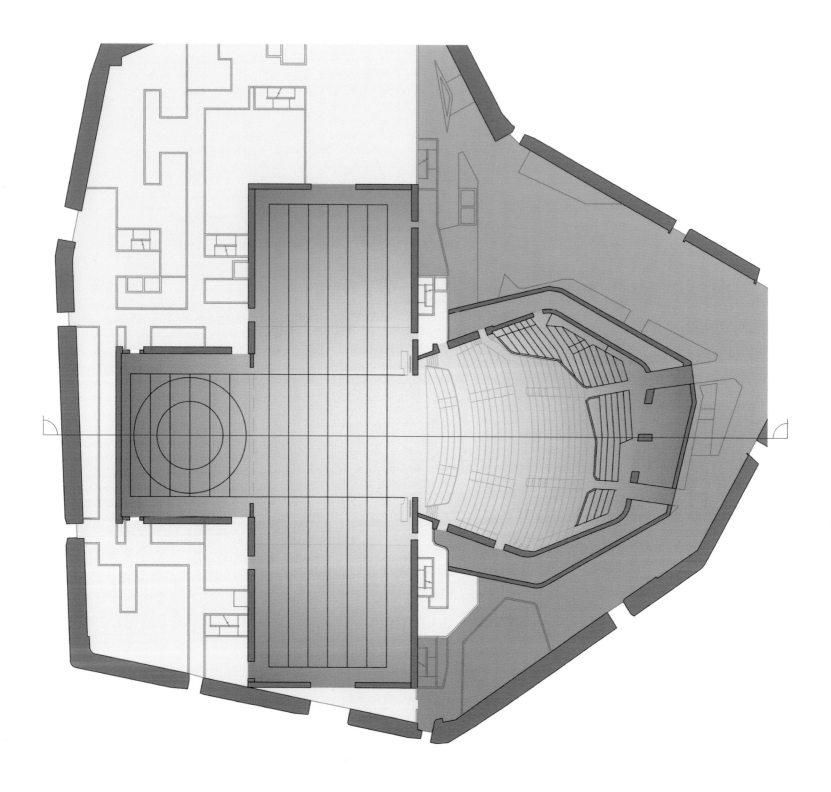

Guangzhou Opera House, comparative plan

0   5   10   20 metres

1:500

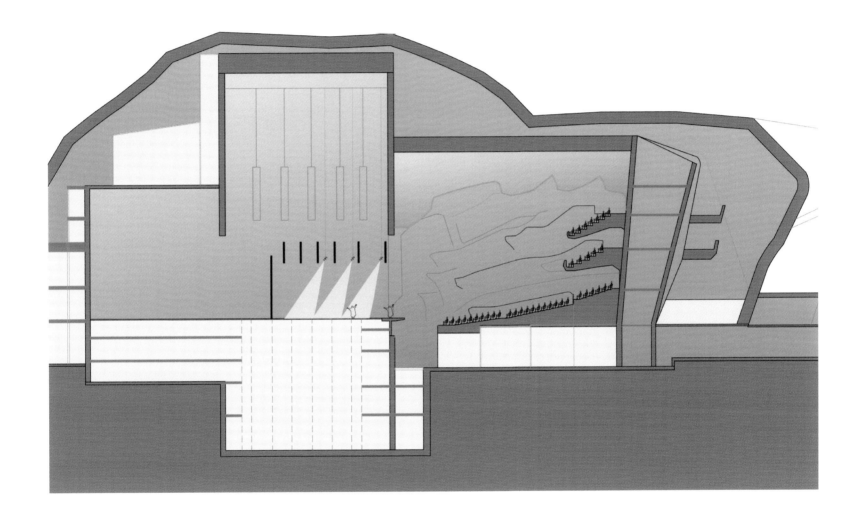

Guangzhou Opera House, comparative section

0   5   10   20 metres

1:500

PART 3.00

SNAPSHOTS OF TWENTY
RECENT THEATRES
2009–2020

9.00

Introduction
David Staples

The original intention was to conclude the *Modern Theatres* initiative with theatres that opened by 2010, to allow sufficient time after opening for a fair evaluation and appreciation of the building to be made.

The last few years have been a rich period for new theatres of all scales and types. While construction may have slowed a little in Europe and North America, the Middle and Far East have experienced a building boom, not only in theatres but in almost every other type of building.

It was therefore decided to add snapshots of 20 further theatres, a selection of those scheduled to complete between 2011 and 2020, and a couple from the two years prior that we felt also deserved a mention. As soon as the term "a selection" is used, disagreement will result about which buildings should be included. The editor consulted with several individuals and differing views were expressed. Some suggested the work should conclude as originally intended in 2010. Others suggested an inclusive approach to try to feature most of the theatres from this decade. Eventually a consensus emerged suggesting we attempt to focus on theatres that are distinctive and differ from the norm.

The theatres chosen will hopefully be of interest to readers. The commentaries are perforce more concise than those for the 'Thirty Significant Theatres' and only two photographs on each are possible. Due to publication deadlines it has not been possible to visit all the theatres and some reviews are based on published information. Readers may disagree with the choice and there is scope to express your opinions on the website www.moderntheatres.org.

Dee and Charles Wyly Theatre, exterior

Dee and Charles Wyly Theatre, 2009
Dallas, Texas, USA
Architect, OMA (Rem Koolhaas) and
REX (Joshua Prince-Ramus)

Karin Winkelsesser

An earlier chapter discussed the Kalita Humphreys Theater in Dallas, the only theatre designed by legendary architect Frank Lloyd Wright, which opened in December 1959, some months after Wright's death. It became home for the Dallas Theater Center, one of the first regional theatres in the United States. Although designed by Frank Lloyd Wright, the theatre company found the theatre difficult and inflexible and with poor functionality.

During the 1970s the City of Dallas undertook a number of studies to determine how to best accommodate the growing number of performing and visual arts groups emerging in the City. At the same time the City was faced with "white flight", the migration of people from the inner cities to predominantly white suburbs. Commercial property owners in the center of Dallas realized the danger of decline and determined to take steps to make the city centre more attractive and assisted in establishing the Arts District Consortium. In 1982 the Sasaki Plan outlined an ambitious plan to create a new Arts District on vacant land on the Northern Edge of downtown. A further study identified the performing arts facilities that might be constructed in the arts district. The City of Dallas purchased land for the future development, understanding the land would not be developed for several years, giving opportunities for temporary uses and structures.

The Dallas Theater Center took advantage of this opportunity and scenic designer Eugene Lee designed a flexible flat floor space – the Arts District Theater. After the inflexibility of the Kalita Humphries, this temporary space was an empty shed in theory offering almost total flexibility although the high costs of effectively creating a new auditorium for each production made the space very expensive to operate.

Dallas Theater Center had grown to become one of the largest regional theatres in North America and needed a new space and planning started for what became the Dee and Charles Wyly Theatre.

Design commenced under Rem Koolhaas's practice OMA. During design Joshua Prince-Ramus, the partner in charge left OMA, and started his own firm, Rex; together, the two firms completed the project working with Theatre Projects Consultants. One essential idea was to build a theatre that would be more flexible than the Kalita Humphries.

Externally the building is a multi-story cube clad in corrugated aluminum panels with large windows, some of which open into the auditorium inside. The architects rejected the conventional ground level layout of theatre buildings and created a 12-storey high block in which foyers, auditorium, production, rehearsal and office spaces are ingeniously stacked. Openings and windows permit views up and down into different parts of the theatre.

The auditorium is probably the most imaginative element. It has large areas of glazing, allowing natural light and views into the room when required. It can be reconfigured into several arrangements. All the seats can be removed to create a flat floor space for functions and events. The floor has a series of elevators that can raise and lower seating wagons or create a stage floor. The elevator tops can rotate the seating wagons to face in different directions as required. The room can be set in end stage format or changed to a thrust or arena stage. Several audience seating towers are stored in void spaces over the auditorium; these can be lowered to surround the seating on the main floor to create a galleried space.

While the photographs show two of the auditoria configurations, they cannot capture its considerable flexibility. This is best seen be viewing animations and time lapse videos that can be found online by Googling /Wyly/Dallas/Video.

The Dee and Charles Wyly is certainly one of the most innovative and flexible theatres created in recent decades. It fulfils the exceptional requirements of the producing theatre company for which it was built. It is a successful experiment that works for this specific user.

Dee and Charles Wyly Theatre, auditorium

Onassis Cultural Center, 2010
Athens, Greece
Architect, Architecture Studio
Karin Winkelsesser

The Alexander S. Onassis Foundation was created by Greek shipping magnate Aristotle Onassis to honour the memory of his son Alexander, who died at age 24 in an airplane crash in 1973. The foundation is one of the largest in Europe, using its assets to create scholarship and prize programmes, endow Greek studies chairs at universities, and support other projects. It has also built several projects including the Onassis Cardiac Surgery Center in Athens.

In 2004 the Foundation decided to construct a cultural centre on Syngrou Avenue in Athens, a major thoroughfare running from the Acropolis in Central Athens to the Port of Piraeus. The goal was to create a place of culture that could host events and activities across the artistic spectrum, from theatre, dance, music, cinema and art to digital and hybrid art and letters. The mission is to promote modern culture, support Greek artists and cultivate international collaborations.

An architectural competition led to the appointment of Architecture Studio, a leading French Architectural practice who worked with XU Acoustique and Theatre Projects Consultants on the planning of the performing arts spaces.

The site is a full city block of limited dimensions that led to a stacking of the facilities. At the lowest levels a significant exhibition space was created. The public spaces are multi-level. They wrap around but are separated from the main auditorium to allow the external shape of the auditorium to be clearly expressed as a gold object within a larger volume. Further up in the building the visitor will discover a second smaller auditorium and a library. The rooftop is fully accessible to take advantage of views to the Acropolis, Lycabettus and the Saronic Gulf. A 200-seat open air amphitheatre shares the rooftop with a Michelin starred restaurant.

Externally the building is a simple, elegant cube clad in bands of Thassos marble above a glass base. From a distance the cladding appears opaque; as visitors approach it becomes more open and transparent. The white marble offers unique opportunities for lighting and projections onto the exterior of the building.

A second selection process led to the appointment of Burrell Foley Fischer, a London-based group of architects and urbanists specialising in cultural buildings, to undertake the design of the two auditoriums and the front of house areas.

ALL WE HAVE IS WORDS.
ALL WE HAVE IS WORLDS.

ONASSIS
CULTURAL
CENTRE
ATHENS

Onassis Cultural Center, exterior

Onassis Cultural Center, auditorium

The large theatre is a proscenium arch room seating 880 for opera, symphony concerts, music theatre, drama and dance with conferences as a secondary use. The audience seating has three tiers and wraps down the side walls to link the audience to the action on stage. The shape refers to the traditional horseshoe but translates it into a modern aesthetic. The balconies have a pale wooden finish and the auditorium walls are panelled in wood and fabric. Overhead a ceiling of metal strip provides a warm and rich environment but also hides the technical functions of an auditorium. A conventional orchestra pit and stage are provided, allowing the presentation of a wide range of performances.

New World Center, exterior showing park in foreground and projection wall on the right

New World Center, 2011
Miami, Florida, USA
Architect, Frank Gehry

Karin Winkelsesser

The New World Center in Miami Beach goes back to 1987, when Michael Tilson Thomas, one of the most eminent conductors of his generation, founded the New World Symphony Orchestra. He has worked with and led many of the world's greatest orchestras including spells as Principal Guest Conductor of the Los Angeles Philharmonic Orchestra and Principal Conductor of the London Symphony Orchestra. He is currently Music Director of the San Francisco Symphony.

Tilson Thomas has a passionate interest in music education. He is also interested in digital technology and new media and in 2009 worked with YouTube to create the YouTube Symphony Orchestra. These interests in music, education and technology came together in 1987 in Miami Beach, Florida when Michael Tilson Thomas founded the New World Symphony Orchestra. It is an orchestra that provides opportunities for musicians who have graduated from distinguished music schools or conservatoires and assists them to make the transition from music education into a professional career in music. Significant initial funding came from Ted Arison, the founder of Carnival Cruise Lines.

As the orchestra developed and grew, the need for a purpose-built home emerged. Frank Gehry, the Pritzker Prize-winning architect was appointed with Yasu Toyota from Nagata Acoustics and Theatre Projects

Consultants to develop the " New World Center"; this team had previously collaborated on the Disney Concert Hall in Los Angeles. The goal was to create a campus to support the music and educational activities of the Symphony by producing "a unique musical laboratory for generating new ideas about the way music is taught, experienced and presented".

At its heart is a very flexible 756-seat performance hall with innovative design and technologies. This is a vineyard form of room, with the audience on steeply banked seating surrounding the concert platform. Perhaps the most distinctive features in the room are a series of billowing, sail-like, acoustic surfaces surrounding the audience. These reflectors also act as screens for high-definition projection.

The surround nature of the hall and the projections can create an immersive experience for audiences, with video projected to complement or support the music being performed.

The room can be easily reconfigured. Ten elevators allow the shape and size of the concert platform to be changed. The platform and auditorium can be levelled and cleared to create a flat floor and allow events and functions to take place.

The New World Center also has a landscaped public park adjacent to the building. The park includes the SoundsScape area, where visitors can sit or stand to view and hear live "wallcasts" on a 7,000 sq. ft projection wall, with 167 loudspeakers providing sound. The public can choose to pay and watch a concert or event in the air-conditioned, comfortable and exciting performance hall or watch the event free outside on the big screen in the usually mild Florida climate. During performances, QR codes can be displayed on the screen, audiences can scan the codes and get more information about the work being presented.

The Centre has many rehearsal rooms, studios, practice spaces and offices stacked around a central atrium. Several of these rooms are glazed, allowing the public to experience the rehearsal process without disturbance (shades can be drawn if privacy is required). The facilities allow distance learning – a teacher in Vienna working with students in Miami and online real-time global collaboration.

The New World Symphony Orchestra offers three-year fellowships where students study many diverse aspects of classical music including finance, management, media relations, and teaching alongside the development of their skills as musicians.

The exterior of the New World Center is understated for a Frank Gehry building. The exuberant, exciting shapes are internal, in the atrium, in a jumbled stack of rehearsal rooms, studios, offices and especially the acoustic reflectors in the performance hall.

Miami Beach has one of the most advanced places for music performance, exploration and education. The quality of the building is complemented by creative programming.

New World Center, auditorium and platform showing acoustic reflectors/projection screens

Royal Opera House, 2011
Muscat, Oman
Architect, WATG

Karin Winkelsesser

The history of the Royal Opera House of Muscat, Oman, is closely related to the late Sultan Qaboos bin Said al Said . He was possibly the only head of state in the world who played the pipe organ. His love of music is said to stem from his education in England. Supported by the British, he came to power in a bloodless coup d'état in which his father was overthrown on 23 July 1970. The coup was an important moment in Omani history as Sultan Qaboos swiftly set in motion numerous wide-ranging, modernising reforms in the kingdom, transforming Oman from a backwater and underdeveloped state. His passion for music includes several music ensembles which exist as part of the Royal Guard. The Royal Oman Symphony Orchestra is a full Western-style orchestra, created in 1986 with young Omani musicians. The Eastern Band is an Arabic, folkloric music and dance ensemble with over 200 performers.

Oman has an oil and gas industry but does not have the abundant reserves and huge oil wealth of neighbouring countries in the Gulf. Its development has therefore been more measured and considered than some of the other Gulf Cooperation Council countries.

The country pursued a considered development of basics – infrastructure, education, health, etc. In 2001 Royal Court Affairs was instructed by Sultan Qaboos to create a theatre initially called the House of Musical Arts and subsequently renamed the Royal Opera House in Muscat, the capital of Oman. In Europe an opera house is typically regarded as a home for a resident opera company (and frequently an associated ballet company) with all the staff, production and rehearsal facilities needed to produce and present operas or ballets. In the Middle and Far East, there was no tradition of Western European opera, so the term opera house has come to mean a large theatre in which many types of performance can be presented with companies or groups from all over the world visiting.

Planning for the new theatre proceeded and it became apparent that as the only significant theatre in a relatively small city (Muscat's population is around 1.5 million) the theatre would need to house a wide range of performances, including opera and classical music, alongside more popular and Arab performers. The concept of a multi-form theatre was developed in which the auditorium and stage could be changed architecturally from a shoebox concert hall into a proscenium stage, with full stage facilities, flying and orchestra pit to enable opera and staged events to be presented.

The pipe organ by Orgelbau Klais of Bonn is constructed on a huge wagon that also carries the side walls and ceiling that surround the

Royal Opera House, exterior

orchestra or ensemble when used in concert mode. This structure weighs over 500 tonnes and is mounted on railway tracks, allowing it to be moved into a rear stage when the stage needs to be cleared for an opera, ballet or similar event needing a flytower and full stage facilities. Elevators in front of the stage can be positioned to extend the stage forward into the auditorium or lowered to create an orchestra pit. The audience seating boxes at the front of the auditorium can be repositioned. For a concert they are moved wide and become parallel 20 to 22m apart. This effectively creates a shoebox concert hall. For a staged production they can be moved in to create a proscenium arch (14–16m wide).

The Royal Opera House opened on 12th October 2011 with a production of *Turandot* conducted by Plácido Domingo and directed by Franco Zeffirelli. The theatre presents a diverse programme of opera, dance and all types of music including jazz, symphonic and Arabic. Recitals are given on the massive pipe organ. The Royal Opera House has become a lively cultural link between Western and Arabic music tradition.

Royal Opera House, auditorium

Harpa, exterior showing glazing by artist Olafur Eliasson

Harpa, 2011
Reykjavik, Iceland
Architect, Henning Larsen Architects
David Staples

Harpa is Iceland's largest performing arts building. Indeed, it is probably one of the largest (and most expensive) buildings in Iceland's capital Reykjavik. The development, design and construction of Harpa is inseparable from the 2008 global financial crisis.

Reykjavik is a capital city with a population of only 128,000 in a geographically huge country with only 350,000 people. Iceland is the most northern and most sparsely populated country in Europe. Located in the Atlantic between Europe and North America it was dependent well into the 20th century on fishing and agriculture and was one of the poorest countries in Europe.

Things improved after World War II with the Marshall Plan and the development of the fishing industry. Iceland became wealthy and one of the most developed countries on earth, until 2003, when the Government privatised the banking industry, effectively creating three significant banks. At this point the emphasis switched from fishing, at which Icelanders were extremely proficient, to banking and finance, in which they lacked expertise. The economy, banking sector and personal wealth boomed.

The Government decided to rejuvenate Reykjavik's old and largely defunct harbour area with the East Harbour Project. A 2004 international masterplan competition was won by Icelandic Batteríð Architects, the Danish architectural practice of Henning Larsen, and Artec acoustic consultants. The huge scheme proposed a concert hall, conference centre, wellness centre, academy of fine arts, bank, cinema, shopping street, residential/commercial units and a five-star hotel.

At this boom time a brief was developed for a full concert hall and conference centre with an array of other facilities. Design and then construction of what became Harpa commenced.

Construction stalled when the global financial crisis hit Iceland in 2007–8. The three banks defaulted in late 2008 and Iceland experienced a severe economic depression and one of the largest banking collapses relative to the size of country. Unemployment and emigration soared.

The new concert hall project could have died along with the rest of the ambitious East Harbour Project but amid significant criticism the Government decided to finance completion of the project that opened in 2011.

A very strong triumvirate contributed to the design of Harpa. Externally the building is a warped cube, with a dramatic façade by light artist Olafur Eliasson, working with the architects. A series of glazed hexagonal tubes made of coloured glass and mirrors is lit by LEDs at night to give the foyers a sparkling, crystal-like feeling both by day and evening.

Acoustician Russell Johnson and his colleagues led on the design of the halls. Eldborg, the 1,800-seat concert hall, is described as "world class" and is one of the last of a successful series of shoebox (rectangular, parallel sided and high ceilinged) halls by Johnson. The room has reverberation chambers and acoustic banners to allow the acoustics to be changed to suit the event being presented.

Norðurljós is a recital hall that can accommodate up to 540, optimised for chamber groups, jazz bands, as well as other types of events. The seating can be cleared to give a flat floor for banquets and other functions. Kaldalón, the smallest hall, with 195 seats, has seating on a single steeply raked block and is designed for all types of music, as well as conferences, meetings, screenings and lectures. There are a series of other halls, meeting rooms and exhibition spaces giving huge potential as a conference centre.

With Eliasson leading on the façade design and Johnson on the halls, the architects linked the two with foyers in dark concrete. Inevitably, visitors and critics have drawn analogies between elements of Harpa and the Icelandic landscape – the fiery volcanic appearance of Eldborg, the grey foyers hinting at lava fields, and the façade catching, reflecting and sparkling like Iceland's sun and light.

Harpa is a large performing arts centre, a very ambitious project for such a small city and country. That it was completed in the face of an economic crash is a tribute to Icelandic determination and spirit. Recent years have seen a huge boom in tourism (more than 10 per cent of GDP in 2017), which might generate visitors for Harpa and delegates for conferences.

The Iceland Symphony Orchestra have a great new home – a world class concert hall. The Icelandic Opera present opera in the concert hall but it was designed without stage or fly tower. There is little international programming presumably due to the cost of bringing ensembles to Iceland in the aftermath of the crash. This underused world class concert hall could have had greater flexibility to allow opera and other staged events to be more readily housed.

Raising the funds to build a new performing arts centre is challenging. Finding ongoing funding to finance the operations and programming is a second and often more difficult task. Harpa is a huge performing arts centre for such a small country – too big? It is a striking and unique building not only in an Icelandic but also an international context.

Harpa, Eldborg, the concert hall

Royal Shakespeare Theatre, 2011
Stratford-upon-Avon, UK
Architect, Bennetts Associates
Alistair Fair

The Shakespeare Memorial Theatre, Stratford-upon-Avon, opened in 1932. Designed by Elisabeth Scott as the replacement for an earlier theatre gutted by fire, the theatre was the first major public building in Britain by a woman architect. For this reason, as well as the prominence of the project at a time when Britain had no National Theatre, the theatre attracted much attention. Its elevations of plain brickwork suggested the influence of contemporaneous Scandinavian and Dutch design and made a clear statement of architectural modernity. However, the auditorium was not universally well-received. The theatre – renamed the Royal Shakespeare Theatre in the 1960s – had a fan-shaped auditorium, which Scott believed would result in good sightlines and acoustics. Seats, arranged in the stalls and two galleries, faced a proscenium-arch stage. There were concerns almost from the day that the theatre opened that the actor/audience relationship was poor, with little sense of contact, especially for those sitting far from the stage in the upper gallery. Various alterations were made over the years to try to remedy the perceived problems, but by the late 1990s the Royal Shakespeare Company (RSC) had resolved to build a completely new theatre. The architect Erick van Egeraat secured the job, but his design was controversial.

Following changes in the RSC's leadership, it was officially abandoned in 2004.

In March 2005, a new design team led by the architects Bennetts Associates was appointed. The brief had been revised, now comprising the reworking of the 1932 building rather than its replacement. A detailed conservation analysis of the building was carried out: in 1971, it had been 'listed' as a structure of architectural and historical significance and by 2004 was listed at Grade II*. Comparatively few 20th-century buildings are listed, and most are listed at Grade II rather than the higher grades II* and I. Negotiations were held with heritage bodies, such as English Heritage, in order to identify where alterations would be acceptable.

Executed between 2007 and 2010, the £112.8 million 'Transformation' project comprehensively remodelled the Royal Shakespeare Theatre. The auditorium was stripped back to its walls; the roof was removed. Within this space, a new, compact galleried thrust stage auditorium was constructed, with 1,018 seats (fewer than the old theatre). Whereas some seats in the old auditorium had been 27 metres from the stage, no seat in the new theatre is more than 15 metres from the action. The layout, which in some ways resembles the smaller and much-loved Swan Theatre (created in 1986 within the shell of the first Shakespeare Memorial Theatre), was worked out collaboratively, with significant input from RSC staff, who generated the initial concept, and the consultants,

Royal Shakespeare Theatre, exterior showing new tower to the right

Charcoalblue. A prototype was realised in the form of the temporary 'Courtyard' Theatre, built nearby to designs by Ian Ritchie Architects in order to serve as a home for RSC productions while building work was underway. The 1932 proscenium arch survives at the end of the thrust stage: it was integral to the structure and could not be moved, and so it now connects the thrust stage to a large rearstage/backstage area. The RSC's historic foyers and the most significant external elevations have been restored, with decades of accretions being stripped back to clarify Scott's original design intent. A generous new foyer has been created along one side of the building, connecting the main RST frontage with the Swan Theatre and opening up new links with surrounding streets.

A new tower acts as a landmark while also offering views over the town. Throughout the building, old and new sit productively alongside each other, with traces of blocked doors, removed floors and dismantled staircases making it possible to 'read' the building's history in often playful ways.

Involving the reconstruction of a substantial listed building on a riverside, town-centre site, and with a complex technical brief, the project was challenging. The result has been well-received; the theatre was shortlisted for the 2011 Stirling Prize. It retains (and celebrates) the gravitas, even the monumentality of Scott's original design whilst re-thinking what a theatre for Shakespeare can be in the 21st century.

Royal Shakespeare Theatre, auditorium

Heydar Aliyev Center, exterior

Heydar Aliyev Center, 2012
Baku, Azerbaijan
Architect, Zaha Hadid
David Staples

Rivalry between cities and states has existed since the earliest communities emerged. This competition has manifested itself in many ways – wars and trade, obviously, but also culture. Royal courts and nobility sought the most famous painters and composers. This led to new work being commissioned and buildings to house the art being constructed. Italy in the 17th century had royalty and wealthy individuals who commissioned operas and music and constructed theatres and opera houses in which to present this work. Such extravagance was a way of showing off your success, wealth and culture.

Countries also wanted to display their success and importance. The Palais Garnier has been called "probably the most famous opera house in the world, a symbol of Paris like Notre Dame Cathedral, the Louvre, or the Sacré Coeur Basilica". Standing at the head of one of Baron Haussmann's grandest boulevards the opera house undoubtably provided a wonderful venue for Parisians and visitors to see and be seen. It also makes a significant statement about the French reverence for arts and culture. The British have always been slightly more ambivalent about asserting their cultural buildings. The Royal Opera House in Covent Garden stands on Bow Street, a small, unassuming street and for many years faced a police station and the Bow Street Magistrates Court.

In the United States during the 20th century, as cities prospered and grew, they frequently sought major professional sports teams to reinforce

their status. As cities sought to attract business and investment, they proclaimed their attributes, including land, skilled and educated employees, tax advantages, etc. These were primary attractors. Secondary but still important factors for relocating businesses and employees were quality of life issues including sports and cultural facilities. Many prospering communities built significant new museums, concert halls and sports facilities alongside airports, schools, hospitals and universities.

The second half of the 20th century and first decades of the 21st saw similar development in rapidly emerging and economically significant cities and countries. In some cases, this is fuelled by mineral, and especially oil and gas resources. The concept of "Global Cities" has been developed and researched in recent times. Sometimes referred to as world cities or alpha cities, there are many league tables often and most easily listed by economic or quantifiable factors. But cities and countries are also aware of the need to focus on softer aspects that are crucial in attracting and retaining talent.

Azerbaijan is an oil-rich country of nearly 10 million people, with a high level of economic development which, on the Human Development Index, ranks alongside many Eastern European countries. The country has also been accused of human rights abuses, with limitations on press freedom and high levels of repression.

Against this complex background Azerbaijan has and is investing in infrastructure and architecture, including the Heydar Aliyev Cultural

Centre in the capital Baku. Named for the third President of Azerbaijan, the centre was designed by Zaha Hadid Architects (Zaha Hadid and Patrik Schumacher, with project architect Saffet Kaya Bekiroglu) who were appointed following an international design competition. The centre, which opened in 2012, is designed to become a centre for the nation's cultural programmes and houses a 1,000-seat auditorium, exhibition spaces, conference facilities and a museum.

Externally the building is an extraordinary white, fluid, wave like object. A series of folds define entrances and the elements within while allowing natural light to penetrate the building. Zaha Hadid's earlier Opera House in Guangzhou attempted a similar flowing external form and while the design is inspired, the execution was poor, with mis-fitting granite panels that have rapidly deteriorated. The centre in Baku has a much better detailed and constructed exterior with joints on the surface that echo the computer drawings and topography used to produce these shapes.

The building rises dramatically from a landscaped park and is an astonishing contrast to the boring Soviet era buildings that surround it. The entrance leads to an equally bright, gleaming white curvaceous series of public areas, foyers and staircases.

After the astonishing white exteriors and public spaces, the proscenium arch auditorium is a rich warm space, with seamless curves that dramatically rise up the walls into a ceiling that steps down to the front of the room to create the proscenium. The overall effect is to dwarf anything presented or any performer on the stage. A conventional rectangular stage with fly tower is concealed under the flowing skin.

Some may scoff at the exuberant new performing arts buildings being created in the Middle East, China and, in this case, the South Caucasus. Some are underused follies while others are bringing music, performances and entertainment to growing communities. They are modern-day projects to proclaim a nation's – or a city's – success, wealth and culture.

Heydar Aliyev Center, auditorium

'A'ali'ikūhonua Creative Arts Center, 2012
Seabury Hall, Makawao, Hawaii, USA
Architect, Flansburgh Architects
David Staples

World Architecture News (WAN) claims to be the largest provider of news and information to the global architectural community. An online internet magazine, WAN also runs an annual awards programme. Projects are either judged by building type, e.g. affordable housing, civic buildings, education, healthcare, or by some specific aspect – use of colour, wooden buildings, façade, etc.

For several years WAN has had a category for performing arts buildings. Each year several new projects are submitted for consideration. They are rigorously assessed by a judging panel made up of architects, and consultants with knowledge and expertise in theatre buildings. Judges also include theatre managers and practitioners.

In 2013 a number of projects were assessed from China, the Middle East, Europe, North America, etc. These ranged in scale but featured many large projects of regional or national importance. The jury deliberated but kept returning to the smallest project considered and unanimously selected the 'A'ali'ikūhonua Creative Arts Center at Seabury Hall in Makawao, Hawaii, USA.

Makawao is a community of around 7,000 people located on the slopes of Haleakalā, a massive volcano that makes up 75 per cent of the island of Maui. Haleakalā is perhaps best known as an important site for ground telescopes because of the clarity, dryness, stillness of the air, its elevation and the absence of lights.

Seabury Hall is a private college preparatory school for middle and high school students that was established in 1964. As the college grew, new facilities were required, and Flansburgh Architects from Boston were appointed to design a new creative arts centre to replace an outdated building. The site on a promontory overlooking the Pacific Ocean and surrounded by rich vegetation is a significant part of the buildings' success and character.

The buildings are simple, with a barn-like character echoing architectural themes seen in upcountry Maui. The two buildings are arranged around an open courtyard which can be used as foyer or an informal outdoor performance space. It is used by day as a work space.

The pavilions have large sliding windows to create a strong, open connection between the indoor and outdoor spaces. One pavilion houses a large dance studio while the other has a 400-seat theatre with retractable and movable seating, allowing the space to be reconfigured. A tension wire grid runs overhead, and the room is fully equipped with lighting and sound systems. There is a limited use of colour both internally and externally but the red seats and walls with the charcoal-coloured steel

'A'ali'ikūhonua Creative Arts Center, Seabury Hall, exterior

'A'ali'ikūhonua Creative Arts Center, Seabury Hall, auditorium

structure are intended by the architects to reference the Haleakala volcano.

The theatre can be used for many different types of performances and events, both those originated on campus and performances by visiting groups and artists.

The 'A'ali'ikuhonua Creative Arts Center has won other awards, from the American Institute of Architects and the United States Institute of Theater Technology. It is an elegant small-community facility.

Musiktheater am Volksgarten, exterior and entrance

Musiktheater am Volksgarten, 2013
Linz, Austria
Architect, Terry Pawson

Karin Winkelsesser

Does a city of 200,000 inhabitants really need an opera house? In the city of Linz in Upper Austria, this dispute lasted over 20 years before the "Pros" of a new opera house prevailed and the building could be inaugurated in April 2013. British architect Terry Pawson wanted it to become the new "living room" of the city, linking the theatre to its urban surrounding and opening the building with much light and a clear structure.

In spring 2006, the Government of Upper Austria awarded the first prize in an anonymous international design competition to the office of Architect Terry Pawson, working with the Austrian offices Architektur-Consult and the "archinauten" architects did the execution design. Theatre Projects, London, and GCA Ingenieure, Munich, were responsible for the technical aspects.

The site of the theatre was rather problematic, located next to the railway and separated from the city. Pawson won the competition with a radical idea: he proposed to move a street and to integrate the tramway into the building by lifting the building and effectively putting the tram underground. Terry Pawson explains:

When developing the ideas for the Musiktheater, it became obvious to me that the Volksgarten (people's garden) was a very important, yet under-used place in the city of Linz. The park

(had) the potential to become a new focus at the other end of the city centre. This placed great responsibility on the new Linz Musiktheater to make an ongoing operational contribution to the park and the wider city, not just as a theatre venue, but as an open public forum.

The public face of the building is organised with the foyer spaces spanning right across the front façade looking directly onto the park. A more complex design challenge was developing the back of house spaces to be equally simple and clear. Pawson's idea was to have a primary circulation corridor that repeats on all levels, with three naturally lit atria that are cut through the building along the length of the main corridor, thereby spatially linking together all the levels.

The architectural language for the façade has been designed with a strong vertical emphasis that refers to both neoclassical architecture as well as the rationalist language of modernist buildings. This vertical emphasis also reinforced Pawson's parallel idea of using the metaphor of a continuous curtain drawn around and unifying the site, which is then opened up toward the park: the entrance portico becoming like a proscenium arch and the foyer being like the theatre stage – an appropriate architectural concept for an opera house!

Internally, the spaces reflect the scale and architecture of the exterior and the layering of a vertical curtain is also a concept that is taken throughout the public areas of the building.

The auditorium and stages presented the biggest challenges to the design and client team. In modern theatres, the horseshoe shape is reappearing again; it was also chosen in Linz in order to achieve a close relationship between audience and artists. The walls are covered with acacia wood; gold-coloured handrails in the galleries, red seats and a huge chandelier are eye catchers. One characteristic is striking: in order to increase the volume of the auditorium, the stairs connecting the tiers were moved inside the auditorium. Vertical brass bars constitute a visual separation between staircases and the auditorium. A main challenge was to create excellent sightlines and satisfactory acoustics. As for now, all reports by visitors and critics have been positive.

The repertory system required a sophisticated solution of the stage area. Following the Frankfurt model, the client had asked for a 34m-revolve to facilitate repertoire operation and on occasion scene changes in view of the audience. The revolve was the largest, most complex and most expensive piece of technology and went through many changes and iterations during the design process. Eventually the concept of a 6m-deep revolve with elevators built into the thickness of the revolve surfaced and was adopted for the project.

The dispute whether a city like Linz needs an opera house still goes on, now with the emphasis on the subsidies to be allocated – or not. Albeit (despite this), the Musiktheater has established itself as a lively cultural centre, bringing new audiences and tourists to the city. This surplus value is one reason not to ask if a city *can* afford a theatre but rather if it *wants* to afford a theatre.

Musiktheater am Volksgarten, auditorium

Everyman Theatre, 2014
Liverpool, UK
Architect, Haworth Tompkins

Alistair Fair

The £28 million reconstruction of Liverpool's Everyman Theatre was awarded the Royal Institute of British Architects' Stirling Prize in 2014, essentially recognising it as the best British building of the year.[1] Designed by Haworth Tompkins (a practice which has dominated British theatre design in the early 21st century) with a team including theatre consultants Charcoalblue, this building accommodates a theatre company whose work has been recognised nationally since the 1960s but which fell on hard times in the 1990s. The new theatre thus embodies the rebirth of the Everyman and supports the company's further development. It sits on the same site in Liverpool city centre as the old Everyman, a converted chapel which was well-liked by actors and audiences. A keynote of the rebuilding project was to maintain a sense of continuity with the forms, materials and welcoming atmosphere of the old building whilst remedying its technical deficiencies. The stakes were high. A local taxi driver told architect Steve Tompkins that he need not return to the city if he messed things up.[2]

The street-facing front of the theatre is substantial in scale, confirming that the Everyman is a decidedly 'public' building. It is dominated by three tiers of adjustable metal sun shades, which carry images of ordinary Liverpudlians in deference to the Everyman's history as a theatre whose work is rooted in its local community and which welcomes all comers. Behind, generous foyers offer space for daytime coffee and food, and for pre-performance gathering. Tough board-marked concrete is juxtaposed with areas of warm-coloured brickwork; the bricks were recycled from the old theatre.

The 400-seat main auditorium has two levels of seating wrapped around a flexible thrust stage. The stage is unusually wide, a feature carried over from the old theatre which was seen as being germane to the Everyman's identity. The introduction of a gallery in the new auditorium helps to bring the audience closer to the action on stage than previously was the case. A smaller studio space has also been provided, while backstage areas are generous in terms of space and robust in their finishes. Sustainability was important in the design brief. The reuse of 25,000 bricks from the old theatre in the new auditorium was thus intended not only to suggest continuity and to imbue the space with personality, but also as a pragmatic move. In addition, the theatre is successfully naturally ventilated by means of four giant stacks at roof level, nicknamed John, Paul, George and Ringo in deference to Liverpool's musical heritage.

The Everyman represents a real meeting of minds. The client team, led by Deborah Aydon and Gemma Bodinetz, had a strong vision of the building they wanted: democratic, welcoming, full of personality, and with clear echoes of the old theatre. The architects, meanwhile, were keen to explore in an all-new theatre the questions of atmosphere and memory which had long been central to their work on existing buildings,

Everyman Theatre, exterior

Everyman Theatre, auditorium

such as the Young Vic in London (2005). Tompkins has spoken of the need for buildings which 'frame civil society', for foyers to have dark corners 'to perch in' rather than being uniformly brightly lit, and for theatres to offer a rich sensory experience with materials which become 'beautiful' rather than 'tawdry' as they age.[3] The result at the Everyman, as Bodinetz has concluded, is a wonderfully 'humane' building.[4]

Notes

1   For a full account of the Everyman, see Alistair Fair, *Play On: Contemporary Theatre Architecture in Britain* (London, 2019), pp. 66–83.
2   'Steve Tompkins: a theatre should behave like a good host', *Observer*, 16 October 2016, online at <https://www.theguardian.com/stage/2016/oct/16/steve-tompkins-architect-haworth-tompkins-q-and-a-national-theatre-liverpool-everyman> (accessed on 5 April 2019).
3   Ibid.; Steve Tompkins and Roger Watts, interviewed on 19 April 2018.
4   'Stirling interview: The Everyman Theatre is quite gobby', *Architects' Journal*, 23 October 2014, online at <https://www.architectsjournal.co.uk/news/stirling-interview-the-everyman-theatre-is-quite-gobby/8671449.article> (accessed on 5 April 2019).

Han Show Theatre, exterior

Han Show Theatre, 2014
Wuhan, China
Architect, Stufish

Karin Winkelsesser

This book examines a 70-year period from 1950 to 2020 during which huge change took place in society, in the performing arts and in performing arts buildings. Much of the change in the performing arts was evolutionary but one type of entertainment – circus – was completely reinvented. The Han Show Theatre in Wuhan, Central China, is an outstanding example of this phenomenon.

Contemporary circus emerged in the 1970s in Canada, Australia, France, America and the UK. Cirque de Soleil was founded in Quebec, Canada in 1984 initially as a group of street performers and then developing shows presented in a big top. It grew rapidly and started touring internationally with huge success. Cirque partnered with hotels and casinos in Las Vegas and subsequently other cities and countries to create permanent shows in purpose-built or adapted theatres.

The Italian artistic director Franco Dragone had directed many of the Cirque de Soleil shows before forming his own company – Dragone. When Wanda Group, a Chinese, multi-national conglomerate with interests in many differing businesses including development, entertainment, hospitality, technology, finance, etc. decided to build a major development in the city of Wuhan in Central China, Dragone were appointed to conceive and develop a show for Wuhan alongside Stufish Entertainment Architects who designed the building to house the show.

The project includes hotels, retail, a movie park and a theatre to house a circus spectacular show.

Wuhan is known as the city of rivers; it lies at the confluence of the Yangtze and the Han Rivers. In the centre of the city, there is a big lake with a surrounding park that looks like an oasis. Many festivals take place here on the occasion of the cherry flourishing, the autumn flourishing or the plum flourishing in winter. The mild climate, many historical attractions and a young university make the city a popular tourist destination. The development in the city centre wants to offer a new and lively district on the lakes.

Both the building and the show drew inspiration from Chinese culture and history, especially those of the Han people, the largest Chinese ethnic group. The exterior of the building was inspired by the traditional Chinese 'red lantern'. Stufish wanted to create a widely visible Chinese symbol that would be a shell for the auditorium and the stage tower. The "lamp" itself is built in a way that it functions in two ways. Seen from far over the lakes it can be perceived as pure symbolic form. Closer, it becomes clear that the shell consists of thousands of panes, each of them illuminated individually from the inside and the outside. In the foyer, the glass roof offers a fantastic view into the 56m-high lantern structure.

The auditorium is designed very specifically for the show conceived by Dragone. It is a highly effective water show, referring to the river Han.

Han Show Theatre, auditorium and stage (both solid and water)

The audience enter a seemingly conventional 2,000-seat theatre with seating at stalls and circle levels facing a proscenium stage. Within a few minutes all the seats move with the audience in place to transform the theatre. The seats in the stalls part and move through 90 degrees to sit either side of a thrust water stage. The circle level of seating descends to form the third side of the thrust.

The stage is not a conventional thrust; it is a series of elevators with perforated floors that can lower into a ten-million-litre pool for a water spectacular to be presented. The sophisticated floor is complemented by a fully automated flying system overhead. The stage is surrounded by three large (7m by 11m) LED screens carried on articulated robotic arms, allowing the screens to pivot and move.

The word unique is used elsewhere to describe some of the theatres featured in this book. The Han Show Theatre is the only theatre in which all the audience seating moves during the show with the audience in place. Roman circuses sometimes flooded the circus to allow naval battles to be re-enacted. The Han Show Theatre has an 8m-deep tank of water allowing similarly spectacular events.

Harbin Opera House, 2015
Harbin, China
Architect, MAD Architects

David Staples

Many young architects have made the pilgrimage to a nondescript school building in Clerkenwell to work for Zaha Hadid Architects. Few have achieved such rapid success in their subsequent career as Ma Yonsong. Born in Beijing in 1975, he founded MAD Architects in 2004.

China has been a magnet for Western architects drawn by the opportunities for major and signature buildings afforded by China's rapid development. In 2014 Ma was the first Chinese architect to win a competition and commission to design an overseas cultural landmark. The Lucas Museum of Narrative Art was originally planned for Chicago; it was subsequently redesigned when the museum benefactor George Lucas decided to build the project in Los Angeles.

The city of Harbin has a population of five million, with over ten million in the metropolitan area, making it the eighth most populous Chinese city. Its location in the far north-east of the country gives it the coldest and longest winter of any major Chinese city, with an average daily winter temperature of −19.7 °C (−3.5 °F); temperatures below −35.0 °C (−31.0 °F) are not uncommon.

Harbin took advantage of this extreme climate by establishing a traditional ice lantern show, which has grown into the Harbin International Ice and Snow Sculpture Festival, the largest annual ice and snow festival in the world, featuring huge ice sculptures, many the size of actual buildings. The 2017 festival attracted 18 million visitors.

MAD Architects won the international open competition for Harbin Cultural Island, to create a master plan for an opera house, a cultural centre, and the surrounding riverside, wetland landscape along Harbin's Songhua River. The site is surrounded by rivers and accessed by bridge.

The exterior of the building is a series of curvaceous, undulating forms clad in white aluminium panels reminiscent of snow-covered hills. The snow illusion is reinforced by a white plaza and entrance routes to the building.

The external language flows into the building where the floors, flowing walls and ceiling of the lobbies and public areas are also a stark white except for the walls surrounding the Grand Theatre, which appear carved from warm rich wood. Audiences and the public can ascend staircases to a rooftop viewing platform and external performance space.

This wooden appearance carries into the 1,538-seat Grand Theatre, where the audience is housed in 12 seating blocks. At stalls level a main body of seats is surrounded by five parterres. The circle and upper circle/boxes are let into the curving wooden walls. These walls merge into a sinuous ceiling and sweep down to the front of the room to create an

Harbin Opera House, exterior

Harbin Opera House, auditorium

unusual and somewhat dominant proscenium frame. Chinese planning authorities mandate a large stage with two side stages and a rear stage for new opera houses built in China. Harbin follows this model, which seems to be based on a traditional central European concept of opera house staging. Hopefully, one day a project in China will break from this rigid view of what constitutes an opera house or Grand Theatre stage.

The smaller theatre seats 414 and is much more conventional, with straight rows of seats facing a wide-open end stage without proscenium arch. The rear wall of this stage is a massive window that visually links the theatre and exterior.

Knowing that Ma Yonsong worked with the Zaha Hadid team, it is easy to understand some of the inspirations for this building. A previous chapter commented on Zaha's Guangzhou Opera House, where strong flowing external shapes are let down by poor execution. Harbin is a later building and much more successfully executed.

Dubai Opera with Burj Khalifa behind

Dubai Opera, 2016
Dubai, UAE
Architect, Atkins (Janus Rostock)

Karin Winkelsesser

A Music Ship Drops Anchor

The opera house in Dubai was inaugurated in 2016 as the centre of a new quarter in the booming city state. Dubai had a population of only 90,000 in 1960 and was an underdeveloped sleepy desert sheikdom. Today it is one of the fastest growing countries in the world. At the moment, the population is about 3.3 million. A new quarter was built in one piece, Downtown Dubai. This is where the new opera house was built as a nucleus of this quarter.

While Dubai boomed, the performing arts, entertainment and culture lagged some way behind. This is not to say the area is devoid of activity. In Dubai, 37 per cent of the population is of Indian origin and that community has many events based on traditional and contemporary Indian music and dance. International groups like Cirque de Soleil are presented regularly in the Emirate. Finally the city decided to build an opera house, to be used as a multi-purpose building. Dubai has a number of large companies which are independent but closely related to the government and ruling family. One of the largest is Emaar Properties, which has grown to become a global property development company. Its signature project is Downtown Dubai, a mega-development covering 200 hectares. At its centre is Burj Khalifa, the world's tallest building. Immediately adjacent is the Dubai Mall, the world's largest shopping mall. These both adjoin the Dubai Fountain, the world's largest choreographed fountain. The district houses several major hotels and extensive residential properties.

The internationally renowned architects Atkins, in cooperation with architect Janus Rostock, designed the opera house that is embedded in the new quarter. The outer shape of the building close to the sea has the form of a dhow, the traditional Arabian sailing boat. The large, oversailing roof creates a large field of shadow which also serves the surrounding area. The foyer is oriented towards the exterior; it is enclosed by a large glass wall, only "interrupted" by wooden panels to shade the sun.

The auditorium itself has been designed in a classical horseshoe shape. In the upper gallery, boxes with large floral decoration serve for local social purposes, whereas Atkins has taken up the European theatre tradition in designing it with dark red seats and warm wooden materials covering the walls.

Emaar's vision for the opera house was to create one of the preeminent venues among the international touring circuit, competing with the likes of London and New York. The team was charged with creating a multi-purpose facility that can host not only spectacular shows, but also accommodate a wide range of performances from classical music and opera to more popular entertainment. Theatre Projects worked with Emaar and project managers Mirage to develop a sophisticated concept for the new project.

The auditorium and stage were conceived as having three different forms or modes. The theatre mode was anticipated as the most frequently used form. An auditorium with 1800 to 1900 seats depending on detailed configuration faces a large stage to house musicals, opera or ballets. A flexible proscenium arch allows the width and height to be varied, and in front of the stage two elevators can be used to create a small or large orchestra pit or extend an apron stage into the auditorium.

In concert mode, for all types of music ranging from full symphony orchestras with choir to soloists and traditional Arabic music, the proscenium arch can be opened or removed entirely to open the concert platform to the audience.

A more unusual mode is flat floor. All the seating can be taken to storage below the auditorium, creating a large flat floor extending unbroken from the rear wall of the stage to the back of the auditorium, an area of over 1,800 m2. This large space can be used for banquets, weddings, ceremonies, exhibitions and any other event. The theatre technology, lighting, sound and acoustics had to be adapted to the multiple configurations of the auditorium, which led to a series of innovative solutions.

·Feedback from audience and touring companies has been very positive. For Dubai the Opera House is a new landmark, inviting tourists and the multi-ethnic population to mingle.

Dubai Opera auditorium

Stavros Niarchos Foundation Cultural Center, 2017
Athens, Greece
Architect, Renzo Piano Building Workshop
Karin Winkelsesser

Greece, the cradle of Western theatre and democracy, has recently undergone many political and economic crises, culminating in an imminent state bankruptcy. To stay in the EU, the country had to undertake a harsh savings programme imposed by the European Union and the IMF. The budget for culture was reduced continuously, although theatre and opera play an important role in cultural life.

In 2008 the Stavros Niarchos foundation stepped in. Founded for the promotion of the arts by the Greek shipbuilder (1909 to 1996), one of the richest men in the world and a renowned art collector, the Foundation offered to finance a new cultural centre in Athens. An opera house and a public library were badly needed for the growing city. In agreement with the city of Athens, the foundation started to develop the project of a cultural centre with Renzo Piano Building Workshop from Genoa. The Greek government provided the site in Kallithea on the seaside. As one of Athens' earliest seaports on Faliro Bay, Kallithea has always had a strong relationship with the water. When design started, however, despite its proximity, there was no view of the sea from the site. To restore this connection, an artificial hill has been created at the south (seaward) end of the site.

The cultural and educational project was built on the coast in the newly created landscaped park. The sloping park culminates in the cultural centre building, giving it spectacular views towards the sea. The site comprises the National Library of Greece and the Greek National Opera.

Both opera and library are combined in one building with a public space, known as the Agora, providing access and connections between the two main facilities. The opera wing is composed of two auditoria, one (1,400 seats) dedicated to classic ballets, symphonic music and traditional operas and the other, the so-called Alternative Stage (450 seats) for more experimental performances, ballet, opera for children, theatre, music.

Renzo Piano's preference for steel, light concrete and glass has made the foyer transparent and clear, bringing natural light into the building. The foyer consists of a steel and glass structure and rises over six floors, with open stairs leading to the upper galleries and to smaller venues and studios.

In the auditorium, however, Piano goes back to the 19th-century model. In cooperation with Theatre Projects Consultants and Arup Acoustics, they designed a traditional horseshoe shape – in contrast to the futurist architecture of the surrounding building. The intimate ambiance is underlined by the wooden structures of the balconies and tiers in light colours. The opera house will also serve for concerts, musicals and other types of performances. A sophisticated stage technology includes a variable size orchestra pit, three platforms and a wagon system allows quick changes of sets for different configurations of the stage.

Stavros Niarchos Foundation Cultural Center, exterior

The Alternative Stage was conceived for contemporary and experimental pieces. It is a flexible space where the seats can be drawn out of the wall and be arranged on the floor according to the artistic needs.

The library is intended as not only a place for learning and preserving culture, but also as a public resource, a space where culture is truly accessible to share and enjoy. The entirely glass-walled library reading room sits on top of the building just underneath the canopy roof. A square horizontal transparent box, it enjoys 360-degree views of Athens and the sea.

The site's visual and physical connection with water continues in the park, with a new canal that runs along a north–south, main pedestrian axis, the Esplanade. The canopy roof provides essential shade and has been topped with 10,000 sq. m of photovoltaic cells, enough to generate 1.5 megawatt of power for the library and opera house. This field of cells should allow the building to be self-sufficient in energy terms during normal opening hours. Wherever possible, natural ventilation has been used.

Even before the official opening, in 2016, the The U.S. Green Building Council (USGBC), the organisation that has developed the leading international certification system for green buildings, awarded the SNFCC it's Platinum-level LEED certification, the highest possible rating for environmentally conscious and sustainable buildings. It was the first cultural building of this size to receive this award, and the Greeks were so enthusiastic about "their" new cultural centre that they insisted on the opening of the building even before the auditorium and library were ready. Culture giving back courage and optimism to the people with an architecture oriented towards the future – this is the best purpose a building can serve.

Stavros Niarchos Foundation Cultural Center, Opera House auditorium

Boulez Saal, auditorium

Boulez Saal, 2017
Berlin, Germany
Architect, Frank Gehry

Karin Winkelsesser

The innovative Boulez Saal in the historic centre of Berlin was inaugurated on 4 March 2017. It is the showplace for the Barenboim-Said Academy, housed in a converted part of the Berlin State Opera's former scenery store. Frank Gehry designed the hall, whose layout can be changed according to the requirements of different types of music performances.

The Barenboim-Said Academy is the brainchild of Daniel Barenboim, lifetime chief conductor of the Berlin State Opera, and Edward Said, a Palestinian literature and arts expert 1935 to 2003. They founded the West-Eastern Divan Orchestra in 1999, to bring together young musicians from Israel, Palestine and Arab countries for concerts each summer.

Following Edward Said's death, Barenboim founded the Academy, with the help of public and private funding, to extend the orchestra's function to a permanent base for joint learning. The Academy is built within the shell of the Berlin Staatsoper's old scenery store. The 34-million-euro construction cost of the Academy was two-thirds funded by the German government, which also helps finance the running costs. It was realized within the cost and time limits.

The building has two parts – the Boulez Saal and the Barenboim Said Academy, which has classrooms and studios that were placed within the 20m high space. Architects HG Merz used the structure of the existent building to keep alive the ambiance of a theatre working place.

Circulation galleries and huge steel doors remained. They are especially visible in the foyer linking the academy and the Boulez Saal.

The Boulez Saal bears the hallmark of three friends and grandees of the arts world: Barenboim had the idea, while internationally renowned architect Frank Gehry of Los Angeles created the design pro bono together with acoustics expert Yasuhisa Toyota. The hall is named after the composer and conductor Pierre Boulez (1925–2016), a close, lifelong friend of both Barenboim and Gehry.

An expressive sketch of ovals was the inspiration for this space, which encompasses a full sweep of 360 degrees. The two artfully interlocking ellipses of the tiers create an impression of awe-inspiring weightlessness. It is a modular construction which, by reconfiguring its tiers and the ground floor with a combination of fixed and flexible seating, can create a variety of spatial correlations.

The hall seats up to 682, and each guest is seamlessly integrated into the space. The setting can adapt to the number of musicians and, above all, to the repertoire being performed. Each vantage point offers a different take on the concert, and even the performing artists will constantly discover new perspectives within the space. The intimacy of the hall allows solo musicians to appear on stage with the same integrity as chamber music formations, while comfortably fitting a medium-sized orchestra.

Acoustics and Architecture

To create the necessary acoustic isolation, the hall was built according to the "box within a box" principle. Three windows each on the south- and east-facing facades forge a visual link with the outside world. In this way, the visitor has a sense of being in a room right in the middle of the city. Three openings along the west side link up the atrium and the music academy. On the ground and first floors, these are light- and soundproof, and on the second floor they form a visual connection between the hall and the atrium.

The upper circle is arranged like a bridge, set into the new concrete walls that are hidden behind the north and south-facing facades. The balcony consists of a steel support with a trapezoid cross-section. The openness factor for the acoustics is 35 per cent. The open side of the construction is lined with acoustically transparent materials, like a loudspeaker grille, which allows sound through and reflects it from the main walls into the hall.

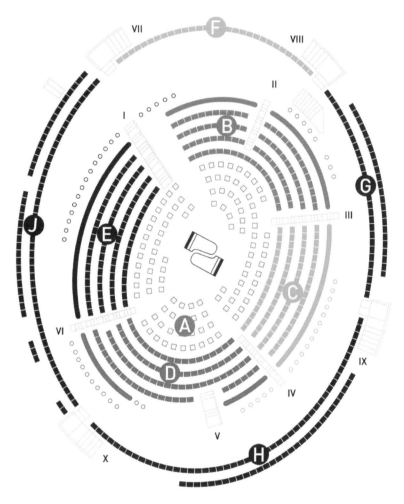

Boulez Saal, seating diagram showing a central stage

Outlook

Frank Gehry was so enthusiastic about this late work that he came from Los Angeles to celebrate his 90th birthday at the Boulez Saal in March 2019. Indeed, the hall has established itself as a lively place for music encounters and lectures. The intimacy that the elliptical form offers however has its price. From the upper tiers one can hear well, but the sight is very restricted (partly due to German regulations on handrails) and the stairs are steep. The 360-degree stage means that more than half of the audience sees the performers from the back. In solo concerts, the performers (and the musical instruments such as pianos) turn by 180 degrees after the pauses to offer equal quality to all. However, the intimacy of the space and the experience of a close relationship between performers and visitors make a visit always a unique event.

Elbphilharmonie, 2017
Hamburg, Germany
Architect, Herzog & de Meuron

Karin Winkelsesser

What seemed like a never-ending project finally reached completion in January 2017 – Hamburg's Elbphilharmonie. Much talked about from the outset, initially owing to its bold design, it was later the delays, cost increases and scandals that made headlines. But the result was extraordinary, and Germany eventually got its lighthouse venue, placing it on the map of internationally famed architecture.

Did Herzog & de Meuron have any idea of the implications of operating a concert hall at dizzy heights when they presented their winning design? It all started with an empty dockside warehouse: *Kaiserspeicher A*. It is part of the former harbour of Hamburg, with brick stone warehouses from the late 19th century. The warehouses are listed as UNESCO World Heritage Sites and since the 1990s have been transformed into a residential area with luxury apartments, shops and offices.

Kaiserspeicher A, the largest warehouse, had been built in the 1960s and was in use until the end of the century. Herzog & de Meuron's design envisaged turning the warehouse into a car park supporting a concert hall, hotel, restaurants and luxury apartments. A public viewing platform linking the two parts of the complex and offering wonderful 360-degree views, dubbed the "plaza", was incorporated to ensure it would also be populated during the day.

The design of the new building is informed by the shape of the Kaiserspeicher; it is identical in ground plan with the brick block of the older building, above which it rises. However, at the top and bottom, the new structure takes a different tack from the quiet, plain shape of the warehouse below: the undulating sweep of the roof rises from the lower eastern end to its full height of 108 metres at the Kaispitze, the tip of the peninsula. The Elbphilharmonie is a landmark visible from afar, lending an entirely new vertical accent to the horizontal layout that characterizes the city of Hamburg. There is a greater sense of space here in this new urban location, generated by the expanse of the water and the industrial scale of the seagoing vessels.

The glass façade, consisting in part of curved panels, some of them carved open, transforms the new building, perched on top of the old one, into a gigantic, iridescent crystal, whose appearance changes as it catches the reflections of the sky, the water and the city.

Reconciling form and function within a building complex where the key facilities are high above ground level called for inventiveness and flexibility on the parts of the planners and, later, the executing firms. The complete building is organized in the vertical. For the concert hall, this means stacked foyers and stairs and inside, steep stairs and accesses. The only access to the concert hall is via one escalator and some lifts. For the staff, there is one elevator but no staircase, and all the material (musical instruments, projectors, etc.) has to be transported via one cargo lift. Some changes had to be made to assure the safety of visitors.

Elbphilharmonie, exterior

The main concert hall, seating 2,100 and built at a height of 50 metres above ground level, forms the heart of the Elbphilharmonie. For the purpose of noise insulation, it was built with a double-shell construction, detached from the rest of the building. Following the "vineyard principle", the orchestra is centrally positioned, with tiers of seats rising steeply all around. No listener is further than 30 metres from the conductor. In this way, listeners are close to the music, despite the size of the hall. The main hall is not, then, defined purely by its architecture but also by the people who gather there to experience the music.

Acoustics were, of course, an essential consideration. For optimum sound in the main hall, Herzog & de Meuron worked with internationally renowned acoustics specialist Yasuhisa Toyota and his company Nagata Acoustics to develop a specially-tailored wall and ceiling structure: the wall construction consists of gypsum fibreboard with 10,000 perforations, individually milled to the millimetre according to acoustic calculations, which reflect and scatter the sound. The hall is mainly intended to host classical concerts, but modern, electrically amplified events are planned here, too. In addition, the reflector hanging from the ceiling helps disperse the sound evenly across the stage. But like a chandelier, it also functions as the central light fixture and contains some important technological components.

The small hall, Kleiner Saal, seating up to 550, is situated on the eastern side of the Elbphilharmonie. Designed in the classic shoebox style, the hall is 30 metres long and 20 metres high. Several smaller studios serve for school classes, music courses and other activities to make the Elbphilharmonie attractive as a lively centre for music.

The vertical structure of the building has proved difficult in many ways. Like the opera house in Sydney, the lighthouse effect (iconic structure) probably compensates for operational problems with the interior. Time will tell if it works for the Elbphilharmonie.

Elbphilharmonie, Great Concert Hall

Bridge Theatre, entrance

Bridge Theatre, 2017
London, UK
Architect, Haworth Tompkins

David Staples

The Bridge Theatre has possibly one of the most extraordinary locations in London. On the banks of the River Thames, it is directly opposite the Tower of London. Look to the right as you leave, and the view is dominated by Tower Bridge. Some might object that it is 'not in the West End'. True, but a branch of The Ivy, the legendary Covent Garden restaurant, has opened in the same building as the Bridge.

The Bridge has bright red signage, which is the only external manifestation of the theatre; it is buried deep inside a brand-new residential development. A prime riverfront site has been developed into upmarket apartments, called One Tower Bridge, by Berkeley Homes, one of the UK's leading property developers. A planning requirement called for the creation of a "cultural" space within the development. A large, clear span space was created at ground and basement levels into which the cultural component had to be fitted. Various uses were considered – exhibition space and at least one London orchestra considered using it, but eventually Nicholas Hytner and Nick Starr, respectively the former artistic and executive directors of the National Theatre, were selected to fit out and operate the space. They had set up the London Theatre Company, which faced three challenges – to create a new theatre within the shell space, to create a new theatre producing company and to operate without public subsidy.

The very experienced architects Steve Tompkins and Roger Watts of Haworth Tompkins were already experimenting with the design of an "ideal" courtyard. They were appointed to work with the London Theatre Company's creative and technical teams on what was essentially the fit out of a found space. The foyers at ground level look out to the Tower of London across the River. They are generous, warm, comfortable spaces that lead easily into the auditorium.

The auditorium itself is an exciting, high-quality space that can be reconfigured into different formats and seats around 900 depending on configuration. The auditorium is essentially a large 'courtyard', as mentioned in Tim Foster's earlier chapter. The side and rear walls are lined with three shallow levels of audience seating, making full use of the restricted 10m headroom in the space. There was limited time to design and fit out the spaces, and techniques from the rock industry were used to create the galleries and interiors of the auditorium in factory conditions off-site for rapid delivery and erection. The auditorium has been used in a number of its configurations. Shakespeare's *Julius Caesar* was presented as a promenade production 'in the round', which is probably the most successful format used to date. The thrust form is successful but in end stage configuration the room feels very long.

The London Theatre Company had/has three challenges. To create a successful new theatre building – the new theatre is very good. To create a new producing theatre company – the leadership have good address books and are attracting very high-quality talent. Finally, to operate without subsidy – flexible theatres can be expensive to operate, presenting high-quality theatre for relatively short runs can also be expensive. Time will tell.

Bridge Theatre, auditorium in end stage configuration

National Kaohsiung Center for the Arts, 2018
Taipei, Taiwan
Architect, Mecanoo Architects (Francine Houben)

Karin Winkelsesser

At the opening of the National Kaohsiung Center for the Arts, it was proudly proclaimed to be the largest cultural centre in the world under one roof. While three to four venues under one roof exist elsewhere in Asia, this roof is special: Mecanoo Architects from Delft have been inspired by the large Banyan trees of the area and the shipbuilding industry in Kaoshiung.

The theatre is built in a corner of the Weiwuying Metropolitan Park, a former military base in Kaohsiung in the south of Taiwan. Francine Houben, architect of Wei Wu Ying, found the inspiration for the shape of the building in the banyan trees that can be found in the park. This tropical tree has a very distinct form. From the branches of the tree, air-roots are formed. When these roots touch the ground, they grow into the soil, thus forming new branches and trunks. Kaohsiung has a very warm climate and the banyan tree offers a welcoming shade that is used by the people of Kaohsiung for tai chi lessons or maybe a siesta. The architect used the idea of the banyan tree to create a similar space that offers shade and a nice sea breeze. The auditoria are the big tree trunks and the covered space in between, called Banyan Plaza, can be enjoyed by the public during the day.

Whereas the inspiration for the building was found in the park, the material to build the theatre was found in the nearby harbour, with its shipbuilding industry. The organic forms of the building posed no obstacle for the shipbuilders. In this way, the know-how of the shipbuilders also influenced the architecture and construction. This reminds us of the history of European theatre: when the republics of Genoa and Venice lost their power at the end of the 16th century, many of the unemployed sailors found work at the numerous courts. The fashion for enclosed theatre buildings developed, and the construction of the backstage areas was done by the sailors, using their knowledge from shipbuilding.

The design team of the theatre was led by Mecanoo Architects from Delft, the Netherlands, who worked together with theatre consultant Theateradvies from Amsterdam. What convinced the jury in the competition phase was its strong focus on functionality. All the stages and loading docks are on one and the same level, with three loading bays on one side of the building, two loading bays on the other side and a very wide corridor in between, functioning as the logistic backbone of the building. The curved metal roof connects all spaces and effectively hides the stage towers of the opera house and the theatre, and it protects from heat and thunderstorms. The two concert halls are situated on one side of the building, the theatre is placed at the other side and the opera, a mix between theatre and music venue, is in the middle.

The vineyard-style concert hall seats 2,000 people. The focus for the concert hall was to achieve excellent acoustics, a goal that was

National Kaohsiung Center for the Arts,
exterior

reached by acoustic consultant Albert Xu from Paris. The second goal was user-friendliness and functionality. To reach that goal, Janssen designed a range of stage equipment that enables the technical staff to facilitate the different kinds of concerts being performed in this auditorium.

The auditorium of the opera hall has a traditional set-up with three balconies and a total of 2,300 seats. The red and violet seats are decorated with a Taiwanese flower pattern. The auditorium has been designed for Western opera, ballet and traditional Chinese opera. The stage technology has been designed to be functional and user-friendly to allow considerable flexibility.

This also applies to the playhouse. It is a combination of a traditional proscenium-style theatre and a classic thrust stage. The combination is achieved by making an elevator of each row in the pit. The rows can be staggered to make a proscenium style auditorium, but they can also be raised to stage level to make a thrust.

The Performing Arts Center of Kaohshiung presents itself as a space to experience culture, to relax but also to work in comfortable conditions, starting from the outer spaces and then continuing to the auditoriums to the stage. "Today Kaohsiung is known for its industrial development", said President Tai at the official opening. "In the future, it will also become a famous cultural city." The start was very promising.

National Kaohsiung Center for the Arts, auditorium

The Shed, The Bloomberg Building

The Shed, The Bloomberg Building, 2019
New York, USA
Architect, Diller Scofidio + Renfro

David Staples

Many of the flexible theatres in this book would be better explained by video or animation. The Bloomberg Building, The Shed in New York, its movement and capabilities are almost impossible to comprehend without benefit of an animation. Readers are strongly recommended to internet search on the words The Shed/New York/Diller Scofidio/Animation and then play the resulting file.

The Shed is both a new building in New York City and a new organisation which "commissions original works of art across all disciplines for all audiences". It opened in April 2019 with five events to showcase the diverse spaces, each billed as "A world premiere Shed commission". They were each created and/or performed by some of the world's leading musicians, performers and visual artists. In the opening week six or seven performances and events were scheduled each day.

The Hudson Yards redevelopment on Manhattan's West Side is the largest private real estate development in the history of the United States. It was made possible by plans to create a platform over the 30 rail lines in the area and use the air rights to create a mixed-use development with offices, retail, residential, etc. The project was made possible by City approval to rezone the area to permit such a massive development and the Metropolitan Transport Authority (MTA) decision to issue a Request for Proposals to developers for the 26-acre (11 ha) site. The authorities required the project to include a significant cultural component which became The Shed.

The site is also adjacent to the High Line, the brilliant transformation of a disused elevated railway line into a linear public park that meanders through the city. The High Line was designed by New York-based architect Diller Scofidio + Renfro, who were also architects for The Shed, working with Rockwell Group as collaborating architect.

The starting point for The Shed is the platform or plaza. Below this are several levels permitting truck access and servicing. At one end is a relatively conventional Base Building which includes two levels of gallery space, the Griffin Theatre, and the Tisch Skylights, which comprises a rehearsal space, a creative lab for local artists and a skylit event space.

The base building is straddled by a movable outer shell that can retract to closely cover the base building, leaving an open public plaza which can be programmed with large-scale visual or performing arts events. The movable shell is carried on a series of large wheels and bogies that can drive it forwards over the plaza to create a huge indoor performance space, the McCourt. This 17,000 sq. ft. (1,600 m²) space is light, sound and temperature controlled and can have a seated audience of around 1,200 depending on configuration or 2,000 standing.

The Shed is said to have cost $475 million, with a $550 million fundraising target to include funds to support the first three years of commissions and organisational start-up costs. The City of New York gave $75 million and a further $75 million came from philanthropist and former Mayor of New York Michael Bloomberg, granting him naming rights.

The name 'Shed' for this building is a misnomer. To many the word shed will conjure up images of a small, simple, immovable building in a back garden or on an allotment. The Bloomberg Building, The Shed is an expensive, very sophisticated, complex 200,000 sq. ft (18,500 m²) building and moving structure in the middle of Manhattan. It creates a unique and controversial place for the performing and visual arts.

The Shed opened in April 2019 to mixed reviews and some very bad ones for the neighbourhood. The *New York Times* has hailed The Shed as "a project that could reshape and redefine the city's physical and cultural infrastructure" and "one of the most significant additions to New York City's cultural landscape in decades". Some hometown boosterism from the local paper.

The institution and building seek to create and present new works and commissions of the highest quality. The scale of The McCourt, its largest space, suggests and perhaps demands large scale and therefore expensive works. The costs of operating and programming will be high. But this is a project in NY, one of the wealthiest cities on earth – it will hopefully attract on-going financial support to help make it a success. But it is a radical, expensive experiment, it could be a folly – time will tell.

The Shed, The Bloomberg Building

Xiqu Centre, 2019
Hong Kong
Architect, Bing Thom Architects + Ronald Lu & Partners
David Staples

When completed, the West Kowloon Cultural District will be one of the largest cultural districts in the world, with 17 core arts and cultural venues. It has also had one of the longest and most troubled gestation periods.

A 1996 study by the Hong Kong Tourism Board showed that visitors thought Hong Kong lacked cultural opportunities. A subsequent study by eminent architect, Dr Tao Ho, examined four possible sites for a new cultural district – the site of the old Kai Tak airport, HMS Tamar, the British Royal Navy's shore station on Hong Kong Island, Shatin in the New Territories, and the reclaimed West Kowloon site. The government decided on West Kowloon.

A design competition was held but the design was scrapped due to public opposition. Development companies were invited to submit proposals for the district with a requirement to include some ambitious cultural facilities. After a process of examination, public and press comment, the competition was aborted. An extensive public consultation process to determine the needed Core Arts and Cultural Facilities led to master plans being prepared by three architectural teams and the master plan by Foster+ Partners was selected. Further public consultation and studies were undertaken before design of any of the facilities could proceed.

Xiqu is the Chinese name for Chinese Opera. The Xiqu Centre was planned to be the first major performing arts building to open in West Kowloon. An architectural competition was held which was won by Bing Thom Architects (now Revery Architects) and Ronald Lu and Partners.

During this planning and design period a temporary Bamboo Theatre was constructed on the site.

The Xiqu Centre opened on 20th January 2019, some 20 years after the site was selected. The exterior of the building is a large, warped cube with a stunning façade conceived as a giant curtain with the apertures as a parting of the curtain. Inside is a large atrium, a multi-functional public space giving access to rehearsal rooms, studios, a seminar hall, dining and shopping facilities.

The Grand Theatre seats 1,000 and is situated at the top of the building flanked by two outdoor sky gardens with views over the harbour and city. Lifting the theatre freed up space below for the public atrium and foyers. The theatre is also raised to improve acoustic isolation from ground and underground train noise. The theatre itself is a very conventional proscenium arch space. Chinese opera was traditionally performed in the open air. It moved indoors into many types of space but often tea houses, end or proscenium arch spaces. The Grand Theatre in the Xiqu Centre is a rather bland auditorium with little relevance to Chinese opera or Hong Kong. This is not a plea for dragons and red lanterns in the decoration. It seems a failure to create a unique theatre for Hong Kong and Xiqu.

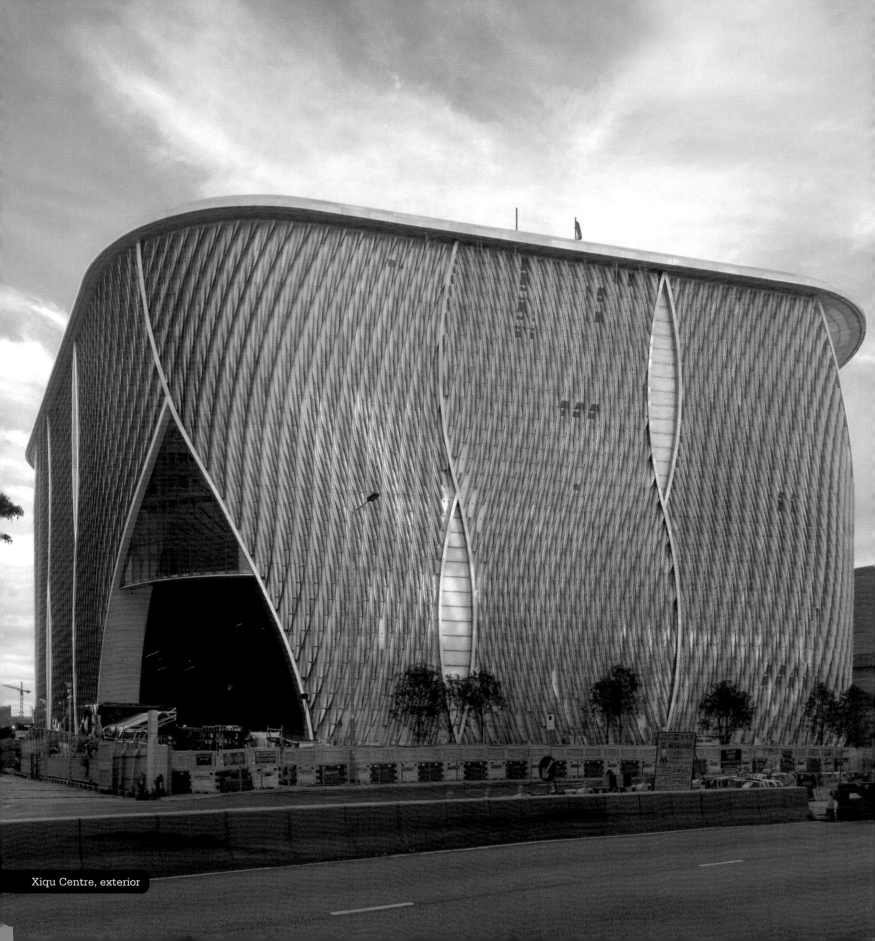

Xiqu Centre, exterior

The smaller 200-seat Tea House Theatre appears much more successful, derived from the traditional Chinese tea houses.

In 20 years, the West Kowloon Cultural project has produced one temporary Bamboo Theatre and the new Xiqu Centre. The Xiqu Centre will be a great asset and help the Chinese opera groups if agreement can be reached over rents but is perhaps a missed opportunity. The management of this project and process has been very bureaucratic. There are further significant buildings to come; perhaps a looser approach could produce some world-class buildings.

Xiqu Centre, Grand Theatre

10.00

Conclusions

David Staples

This is the final chapter and it is customary to try and draw conclusions from what has gone before and to suggest what might happen in the future. Over the past 70 years some remarkable theatres have been designed and built. Theatre technologies have evolved. The world has changed. New cities have emerged and developed. It is difficult to draw conclusions looking back. It is not only difficult but foolhardy to try and make predictions. Television was presented to the American public at the 1939 New York World's Fair and the *New York Times* famously (and incorrectly) predicted:

> Television will never be a serious competitor for radio, because people must sit and keep their eyes glued on a screen; the average American family hasn't time for it.

This book is a collaborative effort – some 40 leading thinkers from 14 countries have contributed chapters. Their research, knowledge and insights are welcomed and appreciated. In this final chapter, the editor draws on what has been written by others and is informed by over 40 years working as a theatre consultant in 67 countries. It is nonetheless a personal view. Over the next few pages, I shall discuss some of the major changes in process, environment, technology and the buildings themselves.

Process

Creating a new performing arts facility is a complex process involving innumerable people. Many clients proclaim their plans to build a new theatre. And for all the often-contagious enthusiasm of those who proclaim their intention to build some mould-breaking new theatre, bitter experience tells us that these ventures fail far more often than they succeed.

Planning

There has been a huge growth in the number of consultants offering feasibility studies for new buildings. Such studies can be invaluable in analysing the need, identifying options, evaluating costs and benefits. A good study can help affirm the need and be used to build support for a new building.

Studies are good at testing hypotheses, not so good at fostering innovative and radical approaches. Too often they simply ask, "What do you want?" then give pragmatic answers based on limited experience.

A successful theatre cannot be based simply on studies and analysis. There must be a passion to create a new, innovative space.

Brief and Budget

The brief is probably the most important document in the life of the project. The brief can vary from a simple requirement for, say, a 2,000-seat theatre, to something detailed, prescriptive and possibly weighing several kilos. Such a comprehensive brief may guarantee the client gets what they want but it can also restrict the design team and limit their freedom to think creatively.

Allied to the brief is the budget. Brief and budget should reconcile, but they often don't – which is when a project proceeds on an unsound footing and will probably die.

Team Selection

There are innumerable methods or routes to select a design team. Projects that rely on government funding usually require bidding and tendering to be within clear and equitable criteria, so that no single bidder is favoured. Privately funded projects have greater freedom.

Major projects have often run architectural competitions to select architect and design teams, and such competitions can help to publicise and build support for a project. The Sydney Opera House is probably the most famous – or infamous – example of this. The Government decided to have a competition, which was won by a virtually unknown Danish architect called Jørn Utzon. The upside of open competitions is they allow unknown architects to shine and win – but this is also the downside, and Utzon proved not to have the resources to deliver a project the size of Sydney.

By contrast, some recent competitions have invited eminent architects (*"Starchitects"*) with mature practices to compete. Although this approach may appear to reduce the client's risk, it can lead to ambitious briefs and stunning designs that break the budget and fail as a result.

In future, clients must surely look to cast their nets wide while taking care to protect inexperienced competitors by giving them the support of a dedicated project team capable of fulfilling the brief.

Design Teams and the Construction Industry

Architecture, design and construction have all become more complex as modern buildings have brought with them new legislative constraints and requirements – hence the dozens of people who often come to design and project meetings. Architects have inadvertently withdrawn from their traditional position as design team leader and the client's principal advisor. Project managers' roles have expanded, and they are now increasingly team leaders and project managers. Their principal role had been to deliver the project on time and budget – they are not renowned for their creativity. Clients who want creativity and efficiency need to do everything they can to streamline and simplify the process. If in doubt, they could do worse than consult *Theatre Buildings – A Design Guide*, edited by Judith Strong and published in collaboration with the Association of British Theatre Technicians.

Environment

Naturally, performing arts buildings must work within their physical surroundings, which in turn are hugely affected by what is happening around them. In 1950 much of the world had just emerged from a devastating war, and the immediate priority was to rebuild cities, infrastructure and theatre buildings. The next significant change came after the 1973 oil crisis, with the sudden emergence of a bunch of wealthy, rapidly growing city states in the Middle East and elsewhere, determined to make a mark in the world. In such an environment, a theatre building was as much a statement as an amenity.

The transformation of Asia and especially China in the post-war period has been somewhat different. Phenomenal economic growth and the development of a significant middle class have powered the development of some of the largest and fastest growing cities on earth. There have been huge construction booms in cities in China, the Far and Middle East, but many of the projects have been poorly designed and executed. With occasional exceptions these cities have generally not produced world-class architecture, although some have produced impressive civic buildings, museums and performing arts facilities. More theatres have probably been built in Asia and the Middle East in the past 25 years than in the traditional markets of Europe and North America.

Although some successful theatres have been built in so-called Global or Alpha cities, we have also seen how cultural buildings can play a role in the regeneration of declining cities. Bilbao is probably the outstanding example of this phenomenon, as the Guggenheim Museum has stimulated tourism and civic pride to transform a declining, post-industrial city in the Basque region of northern Spain.

Technology

Mark Ager in his essay suggested the invention of the transistor was the most important innovation in stage engineering and certainly it and its semi-conductor successors have transformed not just theatres but human existence. In 1950 stage systems were barely mechanised and control was crude. The past 70 years have seen the development of high-quality control systems allowing the easy repetition of cues and movements. At the same time the winches and devices controlled are faster, safer and can carry, lift or move much heavier loads.

This technology allows directors and designers to create ever more complex effects for their shows – allowing, among other things, the effective reinvention of the circus. We can expect to see that trend continue, with technology making more things possible, at ever-lower cost. The stage engineering industry will certainly provide artists with many more creative options.

Nowadays, lighting is such an important feature of any stage production that it is hard to imagine that just 70 years ago, lighting was a rudimentary task carried out by the chief electrician. Alongside the emergence of the lighting designer, the technologies have also changed, as Mark White noted in his chapter. New light sources have been developed and deployed. Lighting control desks and systems have been automated and refined. Techniques from the rock industry have been assimilated in mainstream theatres, opera houses and concert halls. The future probably holds more evolutionary development – control desks will become ever more sophisticated, moving lights will become smaller, quieter and more powerful.

In 1950 sound effects were still being produced by stage managers manually. Then came tape recorders, which allowed creation, editing and playback. Now the tape recorder is obsolete, replaced by ever more sophisticated digital means of creating, processing and reproducing effects. Microphones and loudspeakers are smaller and more reliable, allowing the discrete amplification or enhancement of a voice or instrument.

New technologies are affecting every part of theatre buildings and their operation and design. Social media are deployed to help sell tickets and build new relationships with audiences. Your mobile phone will provide access to a concert; printed paper tickets seem to be going the way of newsprint.

Virtual reality and computer modelling are not only proven technologies for architects, engineers and designers to use in the planning and design of new theatres; they can also be incorporated into the performance itself – as Raj Patel explained when he called for technology to be used as part of the story-telling process.

The Metropolitan Opera in New York has often led the way. In 1910 it transmitted the first opera by radio, with the broadcasts reputedly being heard in New Jersey. Since then it has been at the forefront of broadcasting or streaming opera. Today, its performances are offered not only on large screens to members of the public gathered in neighbouring public places, but also to remote audiences either at home or in large auditoriums. Now many theatres, opera companies and orchestras round the world are following suit.

Theatre Buildings

Much of the development of theatre buildings has been evolutionary, with two major trends emerging over the past 70 years. The first trend has been the re-discovery of three-dimensional theatre spaces, like theatres-in-the-round or thrust stages but also proscenium arch and end stage rooms that paper the walls with people. This has particularly affected drama theatres and concert halls but also opera houses. The second has been a realisation that quality is directly proportional to seating capacity. For a period, concert halls and theatres got larger and larger, especially in North America – the Metropolitan Opera House being the largest repertoire opera house in the world, seating approximately 3,800. Eventually practitioners realised that the quality of the experience reduced as the seating capacity got larger. Concert halls, drama theatres and opera houses are simply better when audience and performers are within close range of each other.

Some final words about each type of theatre.

Opera Houses

The term 'opera house' has developed two different meanings. The traditional European meaning is a place with an auditorium, stage and other facilities for the presentation of opera and usually ballet. The European opera house typically provides a home for an opera company, its performers, orchestra, production and management team, rehearsal and production facilities – often working alongside a closely linked ballet company.

In the Middle and Far East, by contrast, when people talk about an 'opera house', they usually mean a large auditorium (often with 2,000 plus seats) and a generous stage. In China they are sometimes called Grand Theatres. These buildings do not have resident opera and ballet companies. They are typically mixed-programme touring theatres presenting occasional opera or ballet alongside musicals, popular entertainment, large-scale spectacle and events.

In this book, we have been chiefly concerned with the auditorium, and in this respect, the basic plan and section of the European opera house has barely changed in nearly 400 years – a horseshoe-shaped auditorium with many levels of audience seating in boxes or galleries confronting a rectangular stage across an ever-larger orchestra pit.

There have been experiments with different forms of opera house – Carlo Mollino designed a new house for Turin (opened 1973) to replace the previous theatre that had been destroyed by fire. Aldo Rossi designed a house for Genoa that opened in 1983 replacing the previous theatre destroyed by bombing in the Second World War. Both are interesting experiments but tend to confirm the superiority of the traditional horseshoe shape as seen in the recent Oslo and Copenhagen opera houses.

Nonetheless, the opera house has evolved and improved over the last 400 years – the technologies are better, the auditoriums have improved, the acoustics are better but in their basic form they are unchanged. Nicholas Payne suggested earlier that the major change in opera houses was the introduction of supertitles displaying the sung lyrics as the opera proceeds either in the original language or in translation. Supertitles and seat-back titling have made opera more accessible to audiences who do not need prior knowledge of the opera or to read a synopsis to understand the plot.

Supertitles are a way of enhancing the performance for an audience. Increasingly, modern audiences want access to information on their smartphones while a performance proceeds. Too often, audience use of smartphones and tablets during a performance is seen as a problem to be managed, whereas these screens (or smart glasses) should really be seen as an opportunity to present additional information to the audience. The technologies of augmented reality will be increasingly deployed in opera houses.

Another interesting development, which applies to concert halls and drama theatres too, has been the growing number of productions presented in non-traditional or found spaces. Live streaming is another way of taking performances to audiences in cinemas, on the internet or on large external wallcasts.

Drama Spaces

In the 1950s most new drama theatres had a two-dimensional end or proscenium stage. But drama is possibly the most innovative performing art when it comes to using different spaces and formats, and in North America and Britain (though curiously not in central Europe) it wasn't long before theatres-in-the-round and thrust-stage theatres were constructed. The Arena Stage in Washington, DC is a very successful theatre-in-the-round that was copied, with varying degrees of success, on many university campuses across America. In the UK directors and designers soon followed suit, notably with the Royal Exchange Theatre in Manchester which opened in 1976. Theatres-in-the-round and arena stages bring the audience much closer to the performer and action than more conventional two-dimensional theatres.

Thrust stages have the audience on three sides of the stage, again much closer than normal. The director Tyrone Guthrie worked at the Assembly Hall in Edinburgh from which the idea of thrust stages developed with projects under his guidance being constructed in Stratford, Ontario and Minneapolis. Thrust-stage theatres followed elsewhere, notably the Chichester Festival Theatre and the Crucible Theatre in England.

The Cottesloe (now renamed Dorfman) Theatre at the National Theatre in London was one of the first 'courtyard' theatres. These are generally smaller 400–500 seat spaces with flexible audience seating on a main floor and in two or more galleries around the room.

In Western Europe many big theatres added smaller 'black box' spaces with flexible seating, while smaller companies built their own spaces with flexible seating for more experimental work. Perhaps the most famous is the Schaubühne in Berlin presented in an earlier chapter.

For generations, drama theatres have depended on actors' voices to carry from the stage to the rearmost seats. But by 2020 the quality of sound and amplification systems has improved to the extent that discrete amplification of plays is now accepted.

Dance Spaces

Although many theatres accommodate dance performances as part of a mixed programme, few theatres are built specifically for dance. Sadler's Wells in London is hugely successful. The Joyce in New York is a very effective conversion of a 1940's cinema. Lucent Danstheater in the Hague was a limited-life building built to create a home for the Netherlands Dance Theatre. It is now demolished, with a new theatre being created.

Concert Halls

Concert hall design and acoustics have probably seen more change in the past 70 years than any other type of performing arts building. Concert halls and rooms for music have traditionally been rectangular 'shoebox-shaped' rooms with high flat ceilings. The Musikverein in Vienna and Concertgebouw in Amsterdam are perfect examples. This form continues to be built today and many good halls have been constructed in the past half century. The eminent acoustic consultant Russell Johnson worked with clients and architects for more than 30 years to create successful shoebox halls in many countries.

In 1963 the revolutionary Philharmonie Berlin opened, designed by architect Hans Scharoun with acoustics by Lothar Cremer. Scharoun wanted to place the orchestra in the centre of the room with the audience surrounding the musicians on the concert platform. Philharmonie Berlin is a brilliant creation, and possibly the most important performing arts building of the post-war period. The auditorium is complex, with small irregular blocks of seats surrounding the stage. Scharoun was the first to use the term 'vineyard' to describe this type of auditorium. The auditorium is subtly asymmetric. Scharoun wanted the blocks of seating to approximate the size of a symphony orchestra with around 120 seats in each block. The foyers are below the auditorium, accessed by dynamic staircases designed to optimise views and excitement.

The Philharmonie Berlin is an attractive model for architects, clients and musicians. It is more dynamic and a more exciting architectural form than the traditional shoebox – although it took a full 20 years for its potential to be realised. Today vineyard or surround halls have all but replaced the shoebox for large concert halls, with Yasu Toyota of Nagata Acoustics leading the chase.

The briefs for many new concert halls mandate a surround hall, while a few still request "either a shoe box or vineyard hall". While the surround or vineyard hall is undoubtedly the more dynamic architectural form, there are growing questions about its acoustic qualities. Some recent halls have placed significant numbers of audience behind the concert platform or taken the asymmetry of the room to extremes – despite many musical instruments and the voices of soloists being fundamentally directional. Audiences that are placed alongside or behind the platform tend to experience less good acoustics. Typical surround halls lack walls close to the musicians and are criticised for a lack of envelopment.

Concert halls in the future will need to balance the visual excitement of a surround hall with the more predictable acoustics of shoebox rooms.

Recital Rooms

Although there has been real change in the shape of large rooms for music, smaller rooms seem stuck in a mould with an essentially rectangular shape (often with a gentle concave curve to the side walls), a high flat ceiling to create adequate volume and a pale wood-panelled interior. These rooms of say 400 to 800 seats are neat, well-mannered and frankly boring spaces. They are almost indistinguishable from one another. Two exceptions are the New World Symphony Center in Miami and the Boulez Saal in Berlin, both by architect Frank Gehry with Yasu Toyota doing acoustics. Here's hoping they prove to be the vanguard of a new wave of innovative and inspiring recital rooms.

Looking Ahead

Future change in buildings will be largely evolutionary. The trend to build smaller, more intimate venues will continue. On the other hand, there will be demand in some areas for larger, more spectacular shows. Buildings and managements will continue to offer better 'experiences' for audiences.

There will be more use of high-quality sound reinforcement in theatres, opera houses and concert halls. Projection and display technologies are becoming cheaper, better and more flexible, and gradually more popular. Streaming and remote presentation of performances will grow. Virtual and augmented reality will become more important in the design and planning of performing buildings. They could become a significant factor in performances, or they could be a passing fad. It is crucial that live performance stays as live performance and does not become a cinema experience.

The Philharmonie Berlin was probably the most revolutionary change in the last 70 years. It fundamentally changed the nature of spaces for music. Will there be a comparable change in the next 50 years?

Ghost light at Sydney Opera House

Postscript – "The Ghost Light"

David Staples

The ghost light is a single bulb, often in a wire cage on a floor stand, which is left burning on stage overnight when a theatre is empty.

As I write this in February 2021, COVID-19 continues to ravage nearly every country on our planet, killing thousands and affecting societies and economies in ways not yet fully grasped. It has forced the temporary closure of every theatre in this book, with many uncertain about when they will be able to reopen. The performing arts are devastated.

The practical reason for a ghost light is safety. It avoids people tripping on an often-cluttered stage or falling into the orchestra pit. The more romantic reason is to appease the ghosts. Many theatres are reputed to be haunted. Some maintain the ghost light is left burning to placate the ghosts, so they do not cause mischief; to avoid them being left in the dark or to allow them to perform on stage.

For many months, the ghost light has been the only light burning in most of the world's theatres. The pandemic and social distancing regulations make it almost impossible to operate a performing arts building economically. Much has gravitated online, with heroically exciting innovations beginning to emerge. But buildings and performers alike need audiences.

I have no doubt that the ghost lights currently burning in the world's theatres will soon be extinguished and the bright lights will shine again. Audiences will once again experience the unique wonders of live performance in beautiful buildings designed to showcase artistry, delight our senses, and give expression to our humanity.

This book has been created by people passionate about theatre buildings and that same passion and creativity will bring forth whatever changes and design innovations the new pandemic age requires.

David Staples

London

27th February 2021

Contributors

The following people have generously contributed their time and expertise in the preparation of *Modern Theatres*.

Mark Ager completed an MA in Physics at Oxford University, after which he joined the Royal Shakespeare Company and became Systems Engineering Manager at the Barbican, primarily responsible for the maintenance of one of the first power flying systems installed in the UK. Mark set up Stage Technologies with John Hastie in 1994, to produce specialist theatre automation systems. He was directly

Mark Ager

involved with the development of the Acrobat control system, a computerized control system allowing multiple groups of axes to be controlled from a single console. Stage Technologies was acquired by TAIT in 2013. Mark has lectured at many colleges and industry conferences and devotes considerable time to promoting awareness of engineering as a career and is involved in the 'Make Your Mark' campaign that actively promotes engineering in schools and colleges around the UK.

Maria Rita Liberal Arnaut is a consultant for the arts market with more than ten years of experience. She is focused on audience development since her purpose is to bring art closer to people. She develops projects in Portugal and Africa. Her academic background in management and marketing is considered a plus in this sector. She is member of ISPA since 2009. Maria Rita has studied at the Portuguese Catholic University, where she was awarded with a McKinsey Prize.

Maria Rita Liberal Arnaut

David Barbour is editor-in-chief of *Lighting&Sound America*, which he co-founded in 2004. Previously, he was editorial director of *Lighting Dimensions* and *Entertainment Design* and, before that, editor of *Lighting Dimensions* and *TCI*. He reviews theatre for *Lighting&Sound America*'s website and is currently co-president of The Drama Desk, an organization of journalists responsible for the annual Drama

David Barbour

Desk Awards. He edited Richard Pilbrow's memoir, *A Theatre Project*, and has contributed to many other publications.

Christopher Blair is Principal/Chief Scientist at Akustiks, LLC. His primary responsibility is room acoustic design, providing acoustic concepts for many new venues in North, Central, and South America, among them Sala São Paulo (Brazil), Teatro Mayor (Colombia), Sala Placido Domingo (Mexico), Schermerhorn Symphony Center (USA), as well as for major

Christopher Blair

renovations to Cincinnati's Music Hall and New York's David Geffen Hall at Lincoln Center. Also active as a conductor he has led important orchestras in Brazil, China, Venezuela, Bulgaria, and the USA.

Eric Blom has from the late 1980s worked for many different theatre companies. In 2008 he applied for his current position as technical director at The Nederlands Dans Theater (NDT). Over a period of more than 30 years Blom has toured to more than hundred theatres and venues around the world. Since 2012 he has been theatre technical advisor in

Eric Blom

the development of a new cultural centre in The Hague, The Netherlands. Blom created several lighting and set designs for dance and theatre productions.

Elizabeth Bradley is Arts Professor and former Chair of the Department of Drama at New York University's Tisch School of the Arts. She is an educator, independent international theatrical producer, festival curator, presenter, and theatre critic. She was previously head of the School of Drama at Carnegie Mellon University and served as Senior Artistic Associate at

Elizabeth Bradley

Canada's Stratford Festival. Bradley was CEO of the Hummingbird Centre in her native Toronto and is a past Chair of the International Society for the Performing Arts (ISPA), an organization that links leaders in the arts from 59 countries. A Broadway League accredited theatre critic, Bradley writes regular reviews for Broadway.News.

Tim Brinkman was the founding director of touring company Pilot Theatre Company and went on to become Assistant Drama Director of the Arts Council of Great Britain. He oversaw the rebuilding of the Haymarket Theatre, Basingstoke and in 2000 became the Director of Hall for Cornwall in Truro in the UK's far South West. Following that he

Tim Brinkman

spent three years at Arts Centre Melbourne in charge of all its arts activities and produced the reopening events for Australia's top concert hall, the Hamer Hall. After a spell running G Live in Guildford he is now working in Mumbai planning the opening of a major new performing arts centre. Tim is active in ISPA, serving on the board, its subcommittees and Co-chairing the Planning Committees for the New York congresses in 2015 and 2016.

Reinhold Daberto has a rich background as a theatre consultant and architect with projects in Germany, Austria, Switzerland, Greece, Italy, China and Uzbekistan. He has given lectures and presented papers on theatre equipment and installations to the DTHG, VPT Holland, Showtech and Stage Set Scenery in Berlin and various universi-

Reinhold Daberto

ties. He is active for DTHG (Deutsche Theatertechnische Gesellschaft), a member of OISTAT, and between 2004 and 2012 he was chair of the architecture commission of OISTAT.

Joshua Dachs is recognized as one of the world's leading theatre planning and design consultants and has led Fisher Dachs Associates' practice for over 30 years. Drawing on his background as a violinist, architect, and theatre set and lighting designer, he has helped plan and design opera houses, concert halls, and regional and Broad-

Joshua Dachs

way theatres. A graduate of the High School of

Music and Art in NYC, he holds a Bachelor of Architecture from Cornell University.

Patrick Dillon is a writer and architect. A specialist in theatre architecture, he led NT Future, the extensive regeneration of the National Theatre, London, completed in 2015. He is the author of nine books, including Concrete Reality, a monograph on Denys Lasdun and the National Theatre. Paddy is a trustee of the Theatres Trust. He sits on the casework committee of the Twentieth Century Society, and the editorial board of the International Theatre Engineering and Architecture Conference.

Patrick Dillon

Alistair Fair is Lecturer in Architectural History at the University of Edinburgh, and a specialist in the history of British architecture since c.1945. He has written extensively about post-war British theatre architecture, considering not only how these buildings were shaped by changing ideas of performance but also how their conception, design, and reception all reveal broader themes in the period's social, cultural, and urban histories.

Alistair Fair

Tim Foster is the founding partner in Foster Wilson Architects. He has been an Arts Council Lottery assessor in England and Scotland and is currently chairman of the ABTT Theatre Planning Committee and the OISTAT Architecture Commission. He was elected a Fellow of the ABTT in 2012 and was a trustee of The Theatres Trust from 2009 to 2015.

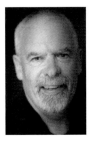

Tim Foster

Chris Full began his career in 1984, since when he has had the pleasure of working with many of the industry's leading new and established theatres, directors, producers and creative teams.

Chris Full

Past UK and Worldwide credits include *Les Misérables*, *Mamma Mia*, *Cats*, *We Will Rock You*, *Evita*, *Grease*, *Oliver!*, *Joseph*, *Into the Woods*, *Cabaret*, *Sweeney Todd*, Fiddler on the Roof, *Rock of Ages* (London and UK Tour), *Shrek* (London), *The Gondoliers*. Arena tours include *Walking with Dinosaurs* (Europe & Asia) and How to Train Your Dragon (Worldwide). His sound design for *Guys and Dolls* (UK and Australia) and *Ragtime* were award-nominated.

Chris has extensive experience of live broadcast events, including *The Marriage of Figaro* for the BBC that won an award for best sound.

Chris is a pioneer in the emerging field of immersive audio on projects like the opera *Death and the Powers* (Pulitzer Prize 2012 Nomination & critically acclaimed for sound), *Ladies and Gentlemen* with film director Jonathan Glazer, 5DX and Sonic Topology (Tate). Most recently Chris spent the summer broadcasting and recording the beauty of Garsington Opera's season and working on *Rocky* Hamburg and *Motown* in London's West End.

Carl P. Giegold, FAIA, has spent 35 years in architecture and acoustics, work which has involved leading the acoustic design for scores of performance and educational buildings in the United States and the United Kingdom, including the renovations of Royal Festival Hall, the Barbican Theatre and Concert Hall, and LSO St. Luke's in London. He earned a Bachelor of Architecture from Virginia Tech in 1982, specialized in acoustics in 1995, and co-founded Threshold Acoustics in 2006.

Carl P. Giegold

Miles Glendinning is Director, of the Scottish Centre for Conservation Studies and Professor of Architectural Conservation at the University of Edinburgh. He has published extensively on modernist and contemporary architecture and housing, and on Scottish historic architecture in general: his books include the award-

Miles Glendinning

winning *Tower Block* (with Stefan Muthesius) and *The Conservation Movement*. His current research is focused on the international history of mass housing.

Michel da Costa Gonçalves is an architect, author and educator; founder of Da Costa Mahindroo Architects (DROO). Educated in France and the UK at the AA where he subsequently taught for 9 years, Michel explores contemporary shared spaces, including several Living Arts projects, synthesising dense and layered urban and cultural conditions into unique

Michel da Costa Gonçalves

design solutions that are in constant dialogue with the city.

Allan Xenius Grige is a Senior Consultant with Theatre Projects and a lecturer in culture and tourism at Copenhagen Business School. His has spent 35+ years in the cultural industries as a performer, tour manager, festival organizer, and CEO of performance venues. As a consultant, he has since 2006 been engaged

Allan Xenius Grige

in the development of venues and festivals in Iceland, the USA, South Korea, China, the Middle East, and across Europe. Alan has contributed an essay on the DR Koncerthuset which appears solely online at www.routledge.com/9781138484382.

David Hamer is a theatre architect working on the design of both new and refurbished performing arts venues. Earlier in his career he worked on the design of opera and theatre productions for many companies including Welsh National Opera, English National Opera and the Royal Shakespeare company.

David Hamer

He currently works for Theatre Projects, where his background in both theatre and architecture gives him valuable insights into how complex theatre spaces are designed around the needs of the users. David has a passion for all stages of the design process from the formation of the client brief through to detailed design and site inspection. Recent buildings he has worked on include the transformation of Greighallen in Bergen and the new Shanghai Conservatory of music.

Elain Harwood is a historian with Historic England specialising in post-war architecture. She completed a PhD on London's South Bank in 2010 after undertaking a thematic study of post-war theatres in England for listing. Her books include Space, Hope and Brutalism (Yale, 2015) and Chamberlin, Powell and Bon (RIBA, 2011). An article 'Theatres in West Germany 1945–70' in Alistair Fair, ed., *Setting the Scene*

Elain Harwood

(Ashgate, 2015) prompted a tour of German theatres, and she was honoured to meet Werner Ruhnau at Gelsenkirchen.

Andy Hayles joined Theatre Projects on the crest of the lottery boom, following a career in touring theatre, lighting and sound. After 8 years at TPC, Andy founded Charcoalblue in 2004 with Jon Stevens, Gavin Green and Jack Tilbury. Andy is a member of the Institute of Theatre Consultants, a member of the Society

Andy Hayles

for the Preservation of Ancient Buildings and served two terms as a Council Member of the ABTT.

Andy's project portfolio includes the Royal Court, the National Theatre, the Young Vic, five theatres for the RSC, Steppenwolf, Chicago Shakespeare Theatre and St Ann's Warehouse in NY.

Roger Hopwood started his career in theatre as a stage technician and Equity Stage Manager with a variety of companies – opera, ballet, variety and light entertainment. He was the commissioning technical director of the Derngate and was part of the team that made this innovative, flexible venue a success. Promoted to General Manager he oversaw the merger of the Royal and Derngate Theatres. He moved to Cardiff as General Manager of St. David's Hall before becoming Arts and Theatres Manager for Cardiff.

Roger Hopwood

Sébastien Jouan is a design-led acoustician with a wealth of experience in the acoustic design of performing arts venues, museums, galleries and music schools. Currently based in Paris, he leads the acoustic team for Theatre Projects working worldwide on performing art centres. He also teaches acoustics to architecture and music students at the Ecoles d'Art Américaines de Fontainebleau. Seb is known for his work in the field of auralisation and was the spokesman for the Arup SoundLab, a 3D sound auralisation suite used by Arup to demonstrate the aural qualities of concert halls. He was also on the board of directors of Cryptic Theatre in Glasgow, a contemporary art house with performances fusing music, sound, art, and multimedia.

Sébastien Jouan

Gaurav Kripalani is currently the Festival Director of the Singapore International Festival of Arts (SIFA) for 2018–2020. Prior to taking on this role, Gaurav was artistic director of Singapore Repertory Theatre (SRT) and produced over 100 plays during his 21-year tenure with the company. Under Gaurav's artistic direction, SRT was the first Singaporean theatre company on Broadway in 1998. This was with *Golden Child*, which went on to earn three Tony Award nominations. SRT has presented work by several renowned international artistes including Ninagawa, Complicité, Peter Brook, Yael Farber and the Royal Shakespeare Company. SRT was also a co-commissioning partner on the Bridge Project – a three-year, Sam Mendes-directed collaboration between the Old Vic in London and BAM in New York.

Gaurav Kripalani

Jörg Kümmel has been a senior member of the Müller-BBM team for over 30 years. His initial studies and qualifications were as an architect before deciding to focus on acoustics and especially the acoustics of performance spaces. He has worked around the world and his projects include the Bolshoi Opera House in Moscow, Mariinsky II in St Petersburg, the Schauspielhaus Hannover and Opéra Bastille in Paris. His projects in China include the Jiang Su Opera House, Nanjing; Hangzhou Opera House; and the Tienjin Grand Theater.

Jörg Kümmel

His concert hall projects include Philharmonia-2 in Moscow; the Concert Hall Megaron Musicis Athens the Thessaloniki Concert Hall both in Greece.

Jörg has held senior management roles in Müller-BBM and has a major reputation in the acoustics field.

Gary McCluskie is a principal at Diamond Schmitt Architects. He has led the design of wide range of award-winning performing arts projects including concert halls - La Maison Symphonique de Montreal, Geffen Hall at Lincoln Center, New York, and First Ontario Centre, St Catharines; theatres for drama and dance - Sidney Harman Hall, Washington D.C., and Dunfield Theatre, Cambridge; opera/

Gary McCluskie

ballet houses - Four Seasons Centre, Toronto and the New Mariinsky Theatre, St. Petersburg, Russia; and community theatres –TCA Lyric Theatre, Toronto and the Burlington Arts Centre.

Shozo Motosugi from 1981–83 had a Scholarship from DAAD, studied at the Freie Universitaet Berlin, Institut fuer Theaterwissenschaft and researched at the Deutsche Oper Berlin and the Schaubühne am Lehniner Platz. Shozo has been a juror for several architectural competitions and designed many cultural facilities in Japan including the New National Theatre, Tokyo; Nara Centennial hall, Matsumoto per-

Shozo Motosugi

forming arts centre. He worked on the Taichung Metropolitan Opera in Taiwan, Suzhou Shishan Art Theater in China in collaboration with various architects.

Raj Patel is an acoustics, audio-visual, multimedia designer. His career merges formal training as a musician and acoustician, with design, technology, and architecture. His skills have been applied to landmark projects around the globe in the real, virtual, and augmented worlds. He is a pioneer in the use of spatial sound and virtual reality for design, art, and performance. His artist collaborations

Raj Patel

have been presented in, amongst others Disney Concert Hall, The Sydney Opera House, Tate Modern, MoMA New York, The Park Avenue Armory, and the British Film Institute.

Nicholas Payne has worked in opera for 50 years since starting at Covent Garden in 1968: including Financial Controller at Welsh National Opera; General Administrator of Leeds-based Opera North; Director of the Royal Opera Covent Garden; and General Director of English National Opera at the London Coliseum. Since 2003 he has been Director of Opera Europa, which he

Nicholas Payne

has established as the leading professional opera association in Europe with a membership of 200 opera companies and festivals from 43 countries.

Robert Shook, FASTC, is a founding partner of Schuler Shook Theatre Planners. He has contributed to the design of scores of performance buildings, including Arts Centre Melbourne (Australia), Pritzker Pavilion (Chicago), Marian Oliver McCaw Hall (Seattle), Moody Performance Hall (Dallas), and Lookingglass Theatre (Chicago). He advocates for close collaboration in the planning

Robert Shook

and design of performing arts buildings, in order to ensure that the facilities fully support the work of the artists.

Simone Solinas graduated in Musicology in 2003. He writes for music organizations and magazines. Since 2001 he has worked at the Teatro Regio Torino, initially in the press office and subsequently as head of editorial and cultural activities, including the management of the website and the historical archive. Over the years, he has edited more than 130 books about

Simone Solinas

operas and ballets, coordinated lectures and conferences with journalists and academics, conceived exhibitions – among them, in 2013, Regio, the factory of dreams, devoted to the 40 years of Carlo Mollino's Teatro Regio.

David Staples is an experienced theatre consultant, having worked in some sixty-seven countries and lectured on every continent except Antarctica. He works with clients to create successful, innovative performing arts buildings and acts as an advisor on the strategic aspects of planning new theatres, concert halls and opera houses.

David Staples

David is a qualified business and management consultant. He is a member and former chairman of the Society of Theatre Consultants, a member of the Association of British Theatre Technicians, and a member and former board member of ISPA – the International Society of Performing Arts. He was also an independent member of the Heathrow Airport Consultative Committee.

He was honoured by the International Society for the Performing Arts with both the Patrick Hayes Award which recognises those who have demonstrated transformative leadership in the performing arts and the International Citation of Merit which is presented for a unique lifetime achievement that has enriched the international performing arts. David was granted Fellowship of the Association of British Theatre Technicians and is a Chartered Fellow of the Chartered Management Institute.

David's projects range from national theatres, concert halls and opera houses to smaller scale venues. They include Esplanade – Theatres on the Bay in Singapore, the Oslo Opera House, the Lowry in Salford, UK and the Portland Performing Arts Center in Oregon, USA.

Lian The, MSc LL.M (1972) is Managing Partner and Senior Consultant/Project Manager at ToornendPartners in Haarlem, The Netherlands. Having obtained a master's degree in Architecture, Urbanism and Building Sciences at the Delft University of Technology, she joined this project management and consultancy company in 1998. Since joining, she

Lian The

has worked on a wide variety of projects for the arts such as museums, art storage buildings and buildings for the performing arts.

Claudia Toni is a distinguished consultant and expert in public arts policy with a long career as manager of cultural institutions. Her credits include positions with the São Paulo Municipal Theater, the Mozarteum Brasileiro, and the Museum of Contemporary Art at the University of São Paulo. As s Executive Director of the Orquestra Sinfônica de São Paulo

Claudia Toni

Ms. Toni implemented a pioneering model of public administration for the Brazilian cultural sector. Claudia is the curator of the Festival SESC de Música de Câmara in São Paulo (2014–2016). She has served on the boards of the Alliance Française, and Instituto de Cultura Contemporânea of São Paulo and the International Society for the Performing Arts. In 2010 she was awarded the Chevalier de l'Ordre du Mérite National of France. Claudia Toni was honored in January 2016 by ISPA with the International Citation of Merit for lifetime achievement in the arts.

David Turnbull is a Director of ATOPIA Innovation, and Design Director of ATOPIA Research/PITCHAfrica, an award winning organisation with a specific focus on the development and construction of building types that address global ecological and social challenges. He is also a Professor of Architecture with 30 years of experience in design education internationally and his academic appointments include the Eero

David Turnbull

Saarinen Visiting Professorship in Architecture at Yale University, and Visiting Professorships at the University of Toronto, Canada and Columbia University's in New York. He was Professor of Architecture at the University of Bath in the UK and visiting Professor of Design & Innovation at the African University of Science & Technology, a Nelson Mandela Institution, in Abuja, Nigeria.

PITCHAfrica's first WATERBANK School was completed in 2012 in Laikipia, Kenya, in collaboration with The Zeitz Foundation, and was named 'The Greenest School on Earth' by the USGBC.

Sir **Graham Vick** is one of the most acclaimed opera directors in the world, known for his experimental and revisionist staging's of traditional and modern operas. He has worked in many of the world's leading opera houses and is currently artistic director of Birmingham Opera Company.

Sir Graham Vick

He has directed Wagner at the Royal Opera House, Chausson in Paris, Verdi at La Scala and Vienna, Mozart at the Salzburg Festival, Monteverdi in Bologna, Schoenberg and Shostakovich at the Metropolitan Opera, Mussorgsky and Prokofiev at the Mariinsky, the Zarzuela Currovargas in Madrid and Rossini at Pesaro. His collaborations with living composers include Luciano Berio's Un re In ascolto in London, Paris and Chicago and Outis at La Scala, Stephen Oliver's Timon Of Athens at English National Opera, Ravi Shankar's Ghanashyam, Jonathan Dove's Life is a Dream and Karlheinz Stockhausen's Wednesday from Light with Birmingham Opera Company, and most recently Georg Friedrich Haas's Morgen und Abend for the Royal Opera House. Recent and future projects include Haas's Morgen und Abend, Britten's Death in Venice and The Queen of Spades in Berlin, Cavalli's Hipermestra for Glyndebourne, Die Tote Stadt at La Scala, Semiramide in Pesaro, Parsifal in Palermo and a new commission by Giorgio Battistelli for Birmingham Opera Company.

He is Director of the Birmingham Opera Company, where his pioneering work has attracted the attention of people and companies worldwide. Although a small operation, Birmingham Opera Company is now seen to be at the forefront of the modernisation of opera and a pioneer in its development as a 21st-century art form. In Birmingham and elsewhere Graham has directed opera in non-traditional spaces – warehouses, factories and other found spaces.

Boštjan Vuga is an architectural practitioner, researcher, educator, and editor. He studied at the Faculty of Architecture in Ljubljana and at the AA School of Architecture in London. In 1996 he founded SADAR+VUGA architectural office along with Jurij Sadar. Boštjan is associate professor for architecture at the Faculty of

Boštjan Vuga

Architecture in Ljubljana. He has taught at the Berlage Institute Rotterdam, the IAAC Barcelona, the Faculty of Architecture Ljubljana, TU Berlin, MSA Muenster, Confluence School of Architecture Lyon, and TU Graz. Currently he is an Architectural Design visiting professor at the Politecnico di Milano. He is the author of numerous articles on contemporary architecture and urban planning. Boštjan Vuga was a co-curator at the Montenegro Pavilion, "Treasures in Disguise" at the 14th Venice Biennale of Architecture "Fundamentals", Venice 2014.

Mark White has had a passion for light and lighting from a very early age. He has worked in many theatres and has had a hand in designing and installing entertainment lighting systems for well over 25 years. He has a keen sense of the history not only of lighting equipment but also of the people who made it and who have used it to make beautiful pictures on stage. He was made a Knight of Illumination in 2009.

Mark White

David Wilmore was educated at Newcastle University where he became involved with the restoration of the Tyne Theatre & Opera House. On Christmas Day 1985 the stage house was gutted by fire and he spent the next two years restoring the theatre a second time. He formed theatresearch in 1986 and has been involved in many theatre restoration

David Wilmore

projects including the Georgian Theatre Royal, Richmond [1788], Theatre Royal Newcastle upon Tyne [1837 & 1901], Theatre Royal, Bristol [1766] and the Gaiety Theatre & Opera House, Isle of Man [1900]. He has a PhD in the development of nineteenth century stage technology and is a past Chairman and Fellow of the Association of British Theatre Technicians.

Karin Winkelsesser, having been a contributor since early in her career, has since 1998 been the Editor of *Bühnentechnische Rundschau* (BTR), the German magazine for stage technology, architecture and scenography. From 1984–2004 she worked as coordinator and translator at the German theatre consulting firm Biste and Gerling, in Berlin. In parallel, Karin was part of the management team of OISTAT from 1992 to 2005, and later an elected member of the Executive Committee. From 2005 to 2008 she served as President of DTHG. The relationship between art and technology has always been an important focus of her work; international exchange and the establishment of a professional network have always played an essential role in her professional life, including regular attendance at international conferences, exhibitions and trade shows.

Karin Winkelsesser

Richard York worked from 1963 in stage and production management roles with coincidental theatre refurbishment. This led to the National Theatre in 1972, bridging a gap between those building it and those who were to operate it. A similar role during the construction of the Barbican Centre led to a long run as Deputy Director. Prior to working as a consultant on cultural projects he was with the City of Birmingham Symphony Orchestra for eleven years which included the procurement of the CBSO Centre, a rehearsal/chamber music hall. The design of theatres and concert halls remains a continuing interest.

Richard York

Photo Credits

The publisher would like to thank the following contributors for their photos:

Photo Research by Sarah Wells

Drawings: David Hamer (see p.564)

Cover photo: Alamy Stock Photo/Hemis

Back cover photos: Philip Vile, David Hamer, Erik Berg/The Norwegian National Opera & Ballet

Index

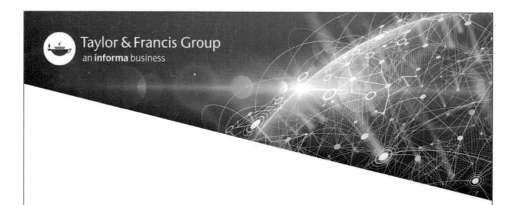